WILDLAND RECREATION

WILDLAND RECREATION

Ecology and Management

SECOND EDITION

William E. Hammitt

Professor of Wildland Recreation
Department of Forest Resources, and Department
* of Parks, Recreation and Tourism Management*
Clemson University.
Clemson, South Carolina

David N. Cole

Research Biologist
Aldo Leopold Wilderness Research Institute
Rocky Mountain Research Station
Forest Service, U.S. Department of Agriculture
Missoula, Montana

JOHN WILEY & SONS, INC.

New York • Chichester • Weinheim • Brisbane • Singapore • Toronto

Library of Congress Cataloging-in-Publication Data:

Hammitt, William E.
    Wildland recreation : ecology and management / William E. Hammitt,
David N. Cole. — 2nd ed.
        p.   cm.
    Includes bibliographical references (p.) and index.
    ISBN 0-471-19461-1 (hardcover : alk. paper)
    1. Wilderness areas—United States—Recreational use—Management.
    2. Wilderness areas—Environmental aspects—United States.
    I. Cole, David N.   II. Title.
    GV191.4.H35   1998
    333.78′0973—dc21   98-14868

Printed in the United States of America.

10   9   8   7   6   5

*To S. Ross Tocher, Professor of Outdoor Recreation
at the University of Michigan from 1965 to 1981,
who knew the field of wildland recreation management*

Contents

Motorboats/Nonmotorized Boats.   Off-Road Vehicles/Stock/Foot Travel. Summary. References.

Preface

Wildland Recreation: Ecology and Management, Second Edition, is concerned with ecological resource problems that arise in wildland areas as a result of recreational use and how these problems can be managed. For our purposes wildland recreation areas are defined as natural areas that are used primarily for dispersed recreation. Everything from wilderness and wildland rivers to primitively developed campgrounds and off-road-vehicle areas are included in our definition of wildland recreation.

The book is intended as a textbook in such disciplines as forest and natural resources recreation, outdoor recreation, park management, geography, and environmental conservation. It should also serve as a useful reference for recreation resource managers already practicing in the field. In addition, it is intended that the ecological treatment of resource impacts will be of interest to ecologists, foresters, wildlife managers, and others who are trained in the biological sciences yet lack training in the area of recreation resources management.

Although the focus of the book is on recreation-caused impacts to wildland resources, we have not ignored the social and economic factors involved in managing these impacts. Public policy has made these areas available for recreational use, and managers must aim to provide public benefits as well as protect the resource base that provides these benefits. The material is presented in six parts. Part I defines wildland recreation and resource impacts, presents an overview of ecological/recreational impacts, and considers the importance of ecological impacts to wildland recreation management. Part II deals with the ecology and impacts occurring to the soil, vegetation, wildlife, and water resources of wildland recreational areas. Spatial and temporal patterns of these impacts are included in Part III, as well as a chapter devoted to how impacts change over time (trends). Part IV discusses the importance of environmental durability, visitor use, and user characteristics in determining the nature and magnitude of recreational impacts. Part V explores strategies and methods for monitoring and managing visitors and site conditions in wildland recreation areas, including impacts occurring in international wildland recreation areas. Finally, Part VI summarizes the book and the importance and challenges of managing ecological impacts.

Portions of the book can be useful without reading the entire text. Parts I and VI provide an overview on recreational impacts. Part V can be useful for managers looking for available management alternatives. Part II is helpful for people wanting a basic understanding of the ecological impacts resulting from recreation use. Part III will be of interest to those wanting information on how impacts change in space and over time.

This book is a second edition of the original text published in 1987. During the decade since the first edition, wildland recreation areas, use, impacts, and management techniques have increased. Although the entire book has been updated and revised, new information is more plentiful in some subject areas than others. For example, this edition contains two new chapters (Chapter 7, "Trends in Wildland Recreation Use and Impacts," and Chapter 14, "International Impact Research And Management"). Other major revisions include new and updated material concerning wildland recreation impacts and ecosystem management, the monitoring of impacts, and strategies/techniques for managing impacts.

Several of our colleagues have contributed to the preparation of this book, for which we are greatly appreciative. We are particularly indebted to Joe Roggenbuck, Richard Strange, and Bruce Hastings for reading portions of the first edition. Jeff Marion and Yu-Fai Leung are acknowledged for contributing Chapter 14 and for the use of their personal libraries on recreation impacts. The U.S. Forest Service is acknowledged for contributing a significant portion of the photographs. The Departments of Parks, Recreation and Tourism Management, and of Forest Resources of Clemson University, Clemson, South Carolina, and the Forest Service Rocky Mountain Research Station, Missoula, Montana, contributed space, sabbatical time, and services during the revision of the manuscript. Final editing and typing of the manuscript were admirably performed by Sheila Ray (first edition) and Karin Emmons (second edition). Most sincerely, Sally and Forest Park Hammitt are thanked for the many hours of loneliness they accepted during the writing and revision of the book.

WILLIAM E. HAMMITT
DAVID N. COLE

Clemson, South Carolina
Missoula, Montana

PART I
Introduction

1 Wildland Recreation and Resource Impacts

Recreational use of wildland areas has increased dramatically in recent decades. Along with this increase in recreational use have come human disturbance and degradation to the natural conditions of wildland areas. Examined in this book are the nature and degree of these disturbances and ways they can be managed. First, we need to define wildland recreation and recreation resource impacts. Then, we must consider the importance of recreational-ecological impacts and the role of the wildland recreation manager in balancing use and preservation of wildland areas.

WHAT IS WILDLAND RECREATION?

Although most types of recreation are fun and nonwork oriented, their goals and benefits are usually diverse. The notions of recreation as constructive, rewarding, and restorative are at least as important as the notion of recreation as fun (Brockman and Merriam 1973). For our purposes recreation is defined as activities that offer a contrast to work-related activities and that offer the possibility of constructive, restorative, and pleasurable benefits. *(definition)*

This broad definition provides room for a tremendous variety of activities. We are restricting ourselves here to recreational activities conducted outdoors in wildland areas that are dependent on the natural resources of these areas (Fig. 1). In *wildland* recreation the importance of the environment or setting for activities is greater than in *developed* recreation situations. Moreover, these wildland settings are largely natural, and management strives to maintain a natural appearance. Facility development is limited both in areal extent and function. Facilities in wildland areas are limited to small sites, if present at all, and are more likely to enhance visitor safety and resource protection than visitor comfort and convenience (Fig. 2). Accessibility is more difficult with wildland recreation. Distances from urban populations are greater. Roads tend to be low standard and less frequently maintained, if present at all. Where absent, trails may or may not be provided. Finally, use tends to be dispersed, creating a social environment with less emphasis on certain types of social interaction. Interaction takes place in smaller groups, with less interparty contact.

FIGURE 1. Recreational activities in wildland areas are greatly dependent on the natural resources of these areas. (*Photo*: National Park Service.)

FIGURE 2. Recreational facilities in wildland areas are limited in both areal extent and function, and are more likely to enhance visitor safety and resource protection than visitor convenience. (*Photo*: W. E. Hammitt.)

Most wildland recreation takes place on public lands such as those managed by the Forest Service, National Park Service, other federal agencies, or state park departments. These lands may or may not be specifically designated for recreational use. For example, trails, campgrounds, and other visitor use areas are designated and specifically managed for visitor enjoyment on National Park Service lands, whereas adjacent and intervening Forest Service land permits recreational use but emphasizes other uses, such as timber production. Similarly, wildland recreation use also occurs on private lands not specifically designated recreation areas. However, most wildland recreation occurs on public lands, and most of the management responsibility falls on public agencies.

This book, then, deals primarily with the recreational use of publicly owned and managed lands. Although many different activities are involved, they are generally dispersed over large areas, resulting in low user density. This dispersal makes management difficult because such a large area is used and disturbed. Moreover, because maintenance of natural or natural-appearing conditions is so important, considerable management of both users and resources is required to avoid excessive resource damage.

WHAT IS RECREATION RESOURCE IMPACT?

Disturbance to natural areas as a result of recreational use has typically been defined as *resource* or *ecological* impact. As pointed out by Lucas (1979), the term *impact* is a neutral term. When combined with *ecological*, it refers to an objective description of the environmental effects of recreational use. Objectively, an impact can be a positive or negative change. In wildland recreation a value judgment has been placed on the term *impact*, denoting an undesirable change in environmental conditions. Of concern to the recreation manager are the type, amount, rate, and duration of undesirable change occurring to the resource base as a result of recreational use. We define undesirable change to the resource base to mean degradation to the soil, vegetation, wildlife, and water resources of a wildland area.

Recreation resource managers are understandably concerned with ecological impacts because many of them have the responsibility of maintaining the quality of recreational resources. This is particularly true for wildland recreational areas, as many are national parks or designated wilderness areas where a major goal is to preserve natural conditions. (When using the term *wilderness*, we mean areas specifically designated as wilderness by Congress; *backcountry* is a more generic term for areas that are not roaded.) To deal effectively with the problem of environmental disturbance in recreation and natural areas, resource managers need to understand recreational impacts in sufficient detail to determine how much and what kind of change is occurring and is acceptable (Cole and Schreiner 1981).

ECOLOGICAL IMPACTS OF WILDLAND RECREATION

All wildland recreation activities disturb the natural environment. Although the specific impacts associated with each activity differ to some extent, they all potentially can affect soil, vegetation, wildlife and water. These effects and their interrelationships are laid out in Fig. 3. Some activities can also affect basic geology and air, as shown in Fig. 3; however, these impacts are less direct and often originate on areas adjacent to wildlands. Presented in this section is an overview of the major resource impacts that will be discussed in more detail in subsequent chapters. In particular, we want to stress the interrelated nature of these different types of impact. One theme that should emerge in this book, particularly when we get to management, is that impacts do not occur in isolation; single activities cause multiple impacts, and each impact tends to exacerbate or compensate for other changes. Management solutions to impact problems must recognize this, or the solution to one problem is likely to be the cause of another.

Impact to soils starts with the destruction of surface organic matter and the compaction of soil or snow. Each of these changes alters basic soil characteristics related to aeration, temperature, moisture, nutrition, and the organisms that live in the soil. These changes, which adversely affect the ability of the soil to support plant life, are most visibly obvious in the barren, compacted soils of campsites (Fig. 4). Compaction, by reducing water infiltration rates, increases runoff and, therefore, erosion. Erosional impacts are most severe on trails and in off-road vehicle areas (Fig. 5).

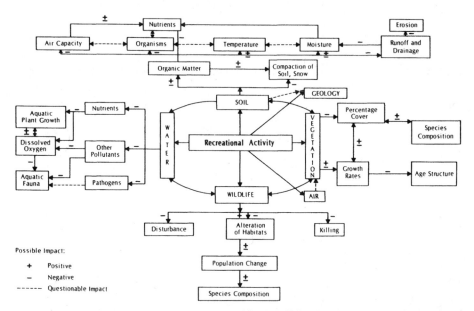

FIGURE 3. Recreational impact interrelationships in wildland areas. (*Source*: "Recreational Impact Interrelationships," by G. Wall and C. Wright in *The Environmental Impact of Outdoor Recreation*, 1977. Reprinted with permission.)

FIGURE 4. Campsites in wildland areas are typically characterized by a heavily impacted zone of compacted soil and the absence of vegetation. (*Photo*: W. E. Hammitt.)

FIGURE 5. Hiking trails on steep slopes and at higher elevations where greater rainfall occurs are easily eroded. (*Photo*: W. E. Hammitt.)

Most of these changes in soil condition inhibit the establishment of new plants and adversely affect the growth of existing vegetation. Moreover, trampling by feet and horse hooves and abrasion by skis and off-road vehicles directly injure and kill existing plants. Plant cover, growth rates, and reproductive capacities are all diminished. For trees, in particular, this alters the age structure of the population. On many campsites, for example, tree populations consist entirely of middle-aged and older trees; reproduction is totally lacking. Even these older trees are often scared by ax marks, lantern burns, and nails (Fig. 6). Understory vegetation varies greatly in its ability to tolerate recreational impact. Since more tolerant species are more likely to survive on recreation sites, changes in species composition shift toward these more tolerant species. An ability to grow close to the ground is one important survival mechanism that partially explains the reduced height of most vegetation on recreation sites.

Although the indirect effects of soil impacts on vegetation are particularly obvious, the same is not true for the indirect effects of vegetation impacts on soils. Loss of vegetation cover exacerbates such impacts as loss of organic matter and increased erosion. It also is related to wildlife impacts, particularly through alteration of habi-

FIGURE 6. Trees on older campsites are often scarred by the burns of gasoline lanterns. This tree has 13 lantern scars. (*Photo*: W. E. Hammitt.)

tats. For large animals the most serious impacts of recreation are direct, either out right killing or unintentional disturbance (harassment). Disturbance can reduce reproduction, as when a disturbed bird leaves her nest, lead to migration to more remote areas, or result in adaptation, as when a bear learns to rely on garbage as a food source. Smaller animals are more affected by habitat alterations. For example, soil impacts, such as loss of organic matter, remove a home and food source for many insects; vegetation impacts, such as a chopped-down tree snag, eliminate homes for cavity-nesting birds. Many of these animals have important effects on soils and vegetation, from their roles as decomposers and grazers and their place in ecosystem nutrient and energy cycles. Altered population structures, spatial distribution and abundance, and even behavior will, consequently, have an influence on soil, vegetation, and water as well.

Water quality is reduced by inputs of nutrients, other pollutants, including increased sedimentation resulting from erosion, and contamination with pathogens. Pathogenic contamination may result from improper disposal of human waste; more commonly, contamination is caused by wild animals that carry disease organisms. Nutrients and pollutants may enter waters as a direct result of recreational use, as when surface films of oil and gasoline pollute lakes with heavy motorboat use. More insidious are the indirect sources such as the reduction in water quality caused by erosion triggered by recreational use. Again, this erosion is promoted by soil and vegetation impact. Water pollution, from many sources, depletes dissolved oxygen and alters aquatic plant and animal growth and survival.

In considering interrelationships among soil, plants, animals, and water, the concept of an *ecosystem* is important. An ecosystem consists of all the organisms in an area, their environment, and the linkages and interactions between them. Ecosystems vary in size from small ecosystems (such as your stomach) to the largest wilderness. According to Franklin (1990, p. 250) human activities can affect several key attributes of ecosystems. First, they can affect the *functional ability* of the ecosystem, the capacity to perform key actions—to fix and cycle energy, conserve and cycle nutrients, and provide suitable habitat for an array of inhabiting species. Second, they can affect the *structure*, or spatial arrangement of the parts, of the ecosystem—whether it is a savanna, meadow, even-aged or uneven-aged forest, or some other type. Third, they can affect the *composition* and *population structure*, that is, the number of species and their relative abundance as well as the densities and age- and size-class distributions of individual species. Finally, human actions can alter the basic *successional patterns*, or trajectories, characteristic of a given site.

RECREATION ECOLOGY

The study of wildland recreation resource impacts and their management has its academic grounding in the field of Recreation Ecology. *Recreation Ecology* deals with the impact of wildland-outdoor recreation on natural or semi-natural environments (Liddle 1991, p. 13). Although this field of study has gained major recognition only since the mid 1960s, its antecedents go back to at least 1759 when Stillingfleet reported differences in the survival of plant species in trampled paths of England (Stillingfleet 1759, as in Liddle 1991). (Cole 1987) suggests that the field as we know it today began about 65 years ago with Meinecke's (1928) work on recreational impacts at California Redwood State Parks. Many of the early, and current, studies in Recreation Ecology have dealt with the effects of trampling on the morphological and physiological characteristics of plants and the ability of various species, plant forms, and environments to resist and recover form trampling damage (Cole 1995; Bayfield 1971; Liddle 1988, 1989). Today, Recreation Ecology deals with the impacts of recreation on all resources (not just vegetation) of wildland areas and with other means of recreational disturbance besides trampling.

Liddle credits Neil Bayfield (1971) as being the first systematic student of Recreation Ecology, based on his many years of work in United Kingdom. Much of the trampling impact research has been concentrated in Europe, examining the effects of trekking and picnicking in the countryside. David Cole, coauthor of this book, has been the leading Recreation Ecology researcher during the last 25 years in the United States. In Australia, Liddle's work on sand dune communities, tropical areas, biological features and strategies of resistance, and impact theory are well recognized (Liddle 1988). His contributions in the area of impact theory are particularly welcomed in an applied field such as Recreation Ecology. Interested readers are encouraged to see Cole (1987) for a more detailed historical development of Recreation Ecology.

THE IMPORTANCE OF ECOLOGICAL IMPACTS

All of the aforementioned impacts occur, but so what? We can go out and measure most of the impacts, determining the *magnitude* of environmental change. It is a very different matter, however, to assess the *importance* or *significance* of these impacts. We might all agree that 95 percent of the spiders on the forest floor of a campsite have been eliminated by recreation use; we are unlikely to agree about how important a change this is. We might not even be able to agree on whether this is a positive or a negative change. In a recreational context, impacts become good or bad, important or insignificant, only when humans make value judgments about them. Those judgments are determined primarily by the type(s) of recreation an area is managed to offer, the objectives of various user groups, and the objectives of resource management.

Different areas offer different types of recreation. This fact has been formalized in the recreational opportunity spectrum, a classification of land based on the types of recreational opportunities they offer. More will be said about this in Chapter 11. The spectrum distinguishes, for example, between the opportunities for primitive recreation of a wilderness area and the ball-playing opportunities of an urban park. Both areas may have experienced, in some places, a conversion from native vegetation to a turf of Kentucky bluegrass. In the wilderness this presents a problem because loss of natural conditions is undesirable in wilderness. The importance of this change is probably related to how large an area is affected and the uniqueness of the vegetation that was lost. In the urban park the conversion is both important and beneficial because it greatly improves the quality of ball playing. As we move along the recreational opportunity spectrum from developed and urban areas to remote and primitive areas, the same impact is likely to become increasingly negative and significant.

Even within the same area people vary in their opinions about impacts. Different recreationists have different ideas. A hiker, confronted with erosion of a hill used by motorcyclists, is more likely to react negatively than the motorcyclists themselves. Conflict, resulting from different perspectives on ecological impact, commonly occurs between motorized and nonmotorized recreationists whether recreation occurs on land, water, or snow. Similar conflicts and differing perspectives occur between hikers and users of horses and pack animals.

It is also interesting to compare the perspectives of the ecologist, recreationist, and manager. The ecologist is most likely to be concerned about impacts that impair the function of ecosystems or destroy unique features. Examples include removal of dead woody debris to burn in fires or elimination of an inconspicuous endangered plant, neither of which is likely to be noticed by many recreationists. Ecologists are also likely to evaluate the importance of a change in terms of how long it takes for recovery to occur. Using this criterion, erosion is extremely serious because it will take centuries to regenerate soils to replace eroded ones.

The spatial scale at which impacts occur is also of interest to ecologists. Today there is particular interest in impacts occurring at large spatial scales, such as landscapes. Some ecologists question the importance of recreation impacts because they tend to be confined to concentrated linkages and nodes. Consequently, impacts may be severe at the scale of the site but negligible at the scale of the landscape. We suggest that there are two reasons recreation impacts should be considered relevant to the ecologist. First, site-scale impacts are not inherently less important than landscape-scale impacts. They are less widespread, but they are often even more intense than landscape impacts. Second, some recreation impacts do have landscape implications. For example, exotic fish and game species have often been introduced to improve fishing and hunting opportunities. Native fish may be displaced or eliminated entirely as a result. This has happened in the Great Smoky Mountains National Park where the introduction of rainbow trout has caused the native brook trout to now be found only in high, isolated, small streams. Other recreation impacts that can have effects at landscape scales include displacement of wildlife through unintentional harassment and extensive livestock grazing (Cole 1990).

Cole and Landres (1996) suggest that the most serious ecological impacts are those that affect large areas, are long lasting and intense, or that affect rare ecosystem attributes. In assessing the importance of any recreation impact, one needs to understand the attribute that is being impacted as well as characteristics of the disturbance itself. The rarity and irreplaceability of the attribute must be considered. One also needs to know whether the disturbance to the ecosystem's function, structure, composition, and dynamics is large or small and whether it is transient or essentially permanent.

Recreationists, as a whole, seem to be more concerned with impacts that decrease the functional use of a site or with "unnatural" objects left by other parties. In

Yosemite National Park, facilities (toilets, tables, etc.) and litter detracted more from enjoyment of backcountry campsites than other impacts (Lee 1975). To an ecologist such impacts are likely to be of little importance because they are easily reversible and do not greatly harm the function of natural ecosystems. Most recreationists do not even recognize ecological impacts (Martin and McCool 1989). Knudson and Curry (1981) asked campers in three Indiana state park campgrounds for their opinions about ground cover conditions. Then they compared these judgments with actual conditions (Table 1). More campers felt conditions were satisfactory or good on the less devegetated sites; however, even at Turkey Run State Park where 99 percent of the sites were more than 75 percent denuded, most campers found conditions satisfactory or better. More than two-thirds of campers saw no tree or shrub damage, despite the fact that virtually every tree was damaged.

Although this lack of recognition and concern for impact characterizes most recreationists, there are exceptions. In wilderness areas there are undoubtedly visitors who are bothered by such impacts. Visitors to four wilderness areas, three in the southeastern United States and another in Montana, found that littering and human damage to campsite trees were among the factors that most affected the quality of their wilderness experiences (Roggenbuck, Williams, and Watson 1993). Shindler and Shelby (1992) compared interest group standards for ecological conditions found at campsites with those of wildland managers. They presented various audience groups with photographic slides of wilderness campsites to measure the acceptability or tolerance for campsite conditions. The authors found that although visitor sensitivity to resource conditions is similar to that of managers at a general level, differences become apparent as one refines the impact level. In fact, small amounts of impact are often considered more acceptable to visitors than no impact at all. For example, small fire rings (less than 16 in. in diameter) were rated more acceptable than no fire rings and small areas of bare ground (less than 156 sq. ft.) were more acceptable than no

TABLE 1. Campsite Ground Cover Conditions and Visitor Opinions

	Versailles		
Cover Conditions	New	Old	Turkey Run
As rated by campers	– – – Percent of Campers – – –		
Very poor	2	3	14
Poor	11	20	29
Satisfactory	53	39	47
Good	30	37	8
Excellent	4	1	2
Actual	– – – Percent of Sites – – –		
≥75 percent bare and disturbed	6	23	99

Source: Knudson and Curry 1981. Reproduced with permission of the Society of American Foresters.

bare ground (Shelby, Vaske, and Harris 1988). However, other studies of visitor perceptions of wilderness impact show little relationship between visitor satisfaction and amount of impact (Lucas 1979). Many visitors do not notice ecological change; of those who do, many do not conceive of change as "damage" or undesirable change. Most visitors do not change their behavior or have less satisfactory experiences even when confronted by impacts that they consider undesirable. For example, even those who dislike the heavy evidence of horse use in the Bob Marshall Wilderness are likely to continue to camp in the same places and travel the same trails and, on the whole, enjoy the experience. In dramatic contrast, site impacts are the foremost concern of managers (Godin and Leonard 1979). Managers are often well aware of such impacts and are charged, as managers, to deal effectively with them.

Maintenance of natural or natural-appearing conditions is important to the wildland manager; so is providing recreational opportunities—and recreation *always* disturbs natural conditions. Impacts that affect visitor enjoyment, particularly those that impair the functionality or desirability of sites, are a particular concern. Legislative mandates and agency guidelines provide additional constraints. Wilderness designation, for example, places some bounds on the types and levels of impact that can be tolerated. Different agencies also have differing perspectives. Even in designated wilderness, presumably subject to the same mandates, each managing agency has a different style. For example, the Fish and Wildlife Service has a particular concern with wildlife. The National Park Service is much more likely to restrict recreational activities to avoid resource impact than the Forest Service (Washburne and Cole 1983). In dealing with recreational impacts, managers must balance the concerns of ecologists, recreationists, other user groups, and the constraints of legislation and agency policies, and tailor all these to the peculiar situation of the areas they manage.

THE MANAGER'S ROLE

While considering the importance of recreational impacts in wildland areas, it is easy for one to develop an antiuser bias toward these areas. Would these wildland recreation areas not be better off if recreational use did not occur in them? This is an unrealistic position to adopt and is certainly not the intent of this book.

Society and public policy have made these areas available for recreational use, and we must accept the propriety of use of wildland resources for recreational purposes. Humans, as recreationists, are to be part of these wildland ecosystems. Because humans are a part of all ecosystems, wildland management is an effort to maintain a natural site environment in which human impact and influence are minimized as much as possible, while still allowing for recreational use. We should *accept* the principle that recreational use can occur in wildlands, and that no matter how small, will produce an impact of some type. Management's role, in general, is not to *halt* change within wildland areas, but to manage for acceptable levels of environmental change.

Acceptability of impact is a function of both the ecological significance of the alteration and human perception. The ecological significance of an alteration, as measured by its magnitude and permanence, may be far different from the degree to which it is sensed as unnatural by the lay person. Ecologically, the most significant human alterations of natural ecosystems are not necessarily the most obvious. What a visitor perceives as natural may have been profoundly and permanently altered. Both managers and users need to broaden their perspectives so they can distinguish between cosmetic and profound ecologic impacts (Franklin 1987).

RECREATIONAL CARRYING CAPACITY

One of the primary tools for meeting the challenge of site and ecosystem impact management is the development of management objectives related to visitor use and acceptable levels of resource impact. This important topic will be introduced in this section and developed in more detail in Chapter 10.

In an attempt to plan for the increases in resource disturbance associated with increasing recreational use, managers and recreation researchers have repeatedly looked to the concept of carrying capacity for solutions. The concept of carrying capacity was borrowed from the disciplines of range and wildlife management. In these fields, carrying capacity refers to the maximum number of animals a given unit of land can support on a sustained basis without destruction of the resource base. In managing recreation areas it was hoped that a maximum number of users could be specified, above which recreation quality could not be sustained. Agency directives, from both the National Park Service and the Forest Service, have actually mandated determination of appropriate use levels or carrying capacities for parks and wilderness areas.

For a number of reasons, determining carrying capacities is neither simple nor particularly useful. First, managing recreation use and associated impacts differs considerably from managing cattle or other animals. In addition to concern with the physical ability of the resource to sustain use, there is an equally important concern with the effect of use on the recreational experience of the user (Graefe, Vaske, and Kuss 1984; Hendee, Stankey, and Lucas 1990; Shelby and Heberlein 1986; and Wagar 1974). Social carrying capacity refers to these visitor experience aspects, and ecological carrying capacity refers to resource aspects. Both are inextricably intertwined. As Frissell and Stankey (1972) note:

> The soil compaction and dying vegetation that accompanies excessive use of a site is of significance not only to the ecologist, but also to the social scientist, for the perception of declining esthetic quality might well be a more important constraint than reduced soil pore space.

More important than the greater complexity of recreational carrying capacity was a misunderstanding of how carrying capacity was used in a field such as range management. Setting carrying capacities for range animals became common practice only when private users were allowed to graze public lands and land managers did not have the time to oversee the operation and monitor changes in conditions. Capacities were conservative, set low so that private users would not damage public lands even in years when forage production was low. Actually, ranges suffered from overgrazing in unproductive years whereas in productive years the limits were wasteful because many more animals could have grazed. On private lands experienced ranchers do not set carrying capacities; they monitor conditions—rainfall or forage condition, for example—and adjust the numbers of animals to achieve their objectives.

In recreation it is possible to select a carrying capacity, but by itself it too will be wasteful. As we will see in subsequent chapters, the relationship between amount of use and amount of impact is not direct. Amount of impact is also affected by the timing, type, and distribution of use, the setting where use occurs, and mitigative actions taken by management. As Washburne (1982) notes:

> There is a separate carrying capacity for horses in meadows in the spring and another in the summer, one for campers who use previously established sites, one for campers who bring stoves rather than build fires, one for noisy and inconsiderate campers who walk through the camps of others . . .

We will explore the importance of many of these variables that affect amount of impact. The point we want to make here is that although carrying capacities *can* be set, they must either be wasteful of legitimate recreational opportunities—set very low to allow for variations in all of the other factors affecting amount of impact—or they must be only a part of a management program. They are not the key to management for which some have been looking. The key to management, in recreation as in range and wildlife management, is specifying management objectives and monitoring conditions.

These key elements of management will be discussed more fully in Chapters 10 and 11. In the following four chapters the ecological effects of recreation are described. The first task for management, once these impacts are understood, is to set objectives for how much impact is too much. In the terminology of Frissell and Stankey (1972) and Stankey, Cole, Lucas, Petersen, and Frissell (1985), managers must set "limits of acceptable change" (Fig. 7). Change in nature is the norm; the natural variation in the rate and character of change is acceptable, except where it poses a safety hazard or, in nonwilderness areas, where it detracts substantially from desired recreation opportunities (i.e., insect infestations). Changes beyond this constitute human-caused change or impact. A certain amount of impact must be considered acceptable even in wilderness. The limit of acceptable change, a management judgment, divides acceptable impact from unacceptable. Management must decide where to draw the line and then hold that line through prescription of management programs (Stankey, McCool, and Stokes 1984).

However, it must be recognized that the decision of where to draw the line is one that cannot be determined *entirely* by ecological criteria. The manager must be prepared to weigh policy, economic, and public use considerations as well when setting limits of acceptable resource change. This is particularly true in wildlands that are not congressionally established wilderness, for they are managed under a broader range of social and economic considerations. Management prescriptions can be based on ecological criteria, but only under the broad umbrella of these other factors.

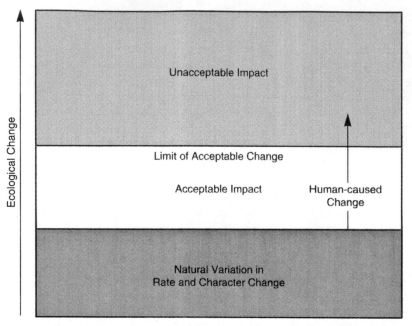

FIGURE 7. Model of acceptable ecological change in wildlands. (*Source*: Adapted from Frissell and Stankey 1972.)

THEMES OF THIS BOOK

This chapter has introduced the topics of wildland recreation and resource impacts. It has defined each topic and its importance to the management of wildland areas. Following this introductory chapter are four major parts to the book: the first dealing with ecological impacts to the four major resource components of wildland areas; the second concerning spatial-temporal distribution and trend changes in impacts; the third describing some key factors that affect resource impacts; and last, a section on the management of recreation resource impacts. Throughout the chapters comprising these topic sections will be a number of recurring themes. These themes form the basis for organizing the material of the book and are summarized as follows to serve as a guide to the reader.

1. The impacts caused by recreation use can be direct or indirect, are interrelated, and are often either synergistic or compensatory. Some are immediately obvious even to untrained eyes. Initials in trees and trampled vegetation are good examples. Others are visible only with microscopes, and some effects have never been identified or studied. Many of these more obscure impacts may be among the more significant. For example, the impact of recreation on soil organisms is very poorly understood, yet it is undoubtedly considerable. Moreover, soil organisms are particularly important to the energy and nutrient cycles of ecosystems, so their disruption

is serious. Some impacts such as disturbance of large wildlife species are almost impossible to identify because there is no way to know what their distribution and behavior were like prior to disturbance, and because of the many other factors that can affect animal behavior.

Many of the more obvious impacts are *direct*; that is, the observed change is a direct result of recreation use. Vegetation loss as a direct result of trampling is an example. Vegetation loss can also reflect poor growth and reproduction in soils that have been compacted by recreation use. This is an *indirect* impact, the result of soil compaction. Indirect impacts illustrate the interrelated nature of many impacts. Many synergistic relationships exist. Loss of organic matter makes a soil more susceptible to erosion, which in turn tends to carry away organic matter. However, sometimes impacts are compensatory. For example, loss of native vegetation cover reduces competition for weedy species, which increases the vegetation cover. Soil moisture levels tend to be reduced because water infiltration rates are reduced, but the soil's capacity to hold water increases at the same time; the result is often little change in available moisture.

2. In addition to understanding what impacts occur—their severity and their interrelationships—it is also important to understand the spatial distribution of impacts and how they change over time. Most impact is highly concentrated. McEwen and Tocher (1976) note, for example, that probably no scenic site in North America is more heavily impacted than that at Athabasca Falls in Jasper National Park, Canada, yet the forest a few yards on either side of the falls is essentially undisturbed. In this book we will be concerned both with areas of concentrated use—primarily camp and picnic sites, but also water-recreation sites, off-road vehicle areas, and scenic sites—and with linear routes, trails, and roads. In all cases undisturbed land is likely to exist a short distance from these places.

There is usually a tendency for these areas and routes to increase in number and size over time. In contrast to these changing spatial patterns, the severity of most impacts tends to increase rapidly with initial use, stabilize, and then remain relatively constant for long periods of time. Thus, trends in various types of impacts will vary over time.

3. Both the nature and severity of impacts vary with type of recreational activity. We will be primarily concerned with impacts associated with picnicking, camping, hiking, skiing, or riding on trails, and recreational boating. Each of these activities is unique in the impacts that result, their spatial distribution, and how they change over time. For example, water pollution is most serious with boating, whereas erosion is most serious on trails and vegetation damage is most serious with camping and picnicking.

4. Although more use tends to cause more impact, the use-impact relationship is seldom direct or linear. Usually, a little use causes most of the impact, and additional use causes less and less additional impact. The nature of this relationship varies widely between different types of impact. Because limits on amount of use are a frequently considered management response to impact, it is very important to understand how each type of impact responds to different levels of use.

5. Even within an activity such as camping, parties vary greatly in their potential to cause impact. This variation between parties is part of the reason that the use-impact relationship is not direct. The method of travel a party uses—foot, horse, or motorized vehicle—has a great effect on amount, type, and spatial distribution of impact. Other important user characteristics are the type of party, its size, and the behavior of individuals within the party. Knowledge and use of low-impact techniques are extremely variable between parties and have much to do with the impact they cause.

6. Another factor affecting impact is the ability of different environments to resist change. For example, different plant species and soil types vary in their ability to resist damage in areas used for recreation. Both *resistance* and *resilience* are important. Resistance is the ability to absorb use without being disturbed (impacted); resilience is the ability to return to an undisturbed state after being disturbed. Resistant sites may or may not be resilient and *vice versa*. Let's compare a bare rock site with a site of lush vegetation. The rock is highly resistant; it would take a stick of dynamite to disturb it, but once dynamited, the scar would be there for a long time. The lush vegetation is not at all resistant, being easily disturbed by a few footprints. However, it would recover in time even if it were greatly disturbed. Resistance varies with the type of activity. The bare rock would never show much evidence of trampling impact, but one campfire would leave a lasting scar. Obviously, it is best to locate recreation sites on resistant and resilient sites and to avoid use of sites that are neither. Approximate management of sites that are resistant but not resilient is very different from management of those that are resilient but not resistant. Resistance and resilience vary seasonally with climatic conditions and the growth stage of plants.

7. In managing impacts, it is important to understand their nature and their spatial and temporal patterns and then decide on limits of acceptable change. Then, armed with knowledge of how impacts relate to amount and type of use and environmental conditions, the manager can manipulate these variables in such a way that impacts are minimized.

8. Another factor to consider in managing recreational impacts is the need to accept wildland recreation as an appropriate use of wildlands. However, recreational use of these areas, because they are easily impacted, is appropriate only if managed. The challenge of the recreation resource manager is to balance the public's desire for wildland recreation and, at the same time, to maintain the natural conditions of wildland areas. We must manage for an acceptable level of recreational use and resource protection.

9. A final theme involves the international occurrence of recreation resource impacts. Wildland recreation impacts are not limited to the temperate environment of the United States, but are common to wildland recreation areas around the world. Whenever recreation occurs in wildland/natural environments around the world, there will be disturbance to natural conditions. The planning and setting aside of international parks, wildernesses, and preserves will not be enough to protect their ecological integrity for future generations if much recreational and ecotourism use occurs in these areas. The human use and resource conditions of international areas require management, in addition to planning and protection.

REFERENCES

Bayfield, N. G. 1971. Some Effects of Walking and Skiing on Vegetation at Cairngorm. In E. Duffey and S. A. Watt, eds. *The Scientific Management of Animal and Plant Communities for Conservation*, Oxford: Blackwell Scientific Publications, pp. 469–485.

Brockman, C. F., and L. C. Merrian. 1973. *Recreational Use of Wildlands*. 3rd. ed. New York: McGraw-Hill.

Cole, D. N. 1987. Research on Soil and Vegetation in Wilderness: A State-of-Knowledge Review. In R. C. Lucas, comp. *Proceedings—National Wilderness Research Conference: Issues, State-of-Knowledge, Future Directions*. USDA Forest Service General Technical Report INT-220, Ogden, UT. pp. 135–177.

Cole, D. N. 1990. Ecological Impacts of Wilderness Recreation and Their Management. In J. C. Hendee, G. H. Stankey, and R. C. Lucas, *Wilderness Management*, 2d. ed. Golden, CO: North American Press. pp. 425–466.

Cole, D. N. 1995. Experimental Trampling of Vegetation, II. Predictors of Resistance and Resilience. *Journal of Applied Ecology* 32:215–224.

Cole, D. N., and P. B. Landres. 1996. Threats to Wilderness Ecosystems: Impacts and Research Needs. *Ecological Applications* 6:168–184.

Cole, D. N., and E. G. S. Schreiner. 1981. Impacts of Backcountry Recreation: Site Management and Rehabilitation—An Annotated Bibliography. USDA Forest Service General Technical Report INT-122.

Franklin, J. F. 1987. Scientific Use of Wilderness. In R. C. Lucas, comp. *Proceedings—National Wilderness Research Conference: Issues, State-of-Knowledge, Future Directions*. USDA Forest Service General Technical Report INT-220, Ogden, UT. pp. 42–46.

Franklin, J. F. 1990. Wilderness Ecosystems. In J. C. Hendee, G. H. Stankey, and R. C. Lucas, *Wilderness Management*, 2d ed. Golden, CO: North American Press, pp. 241–261.

Frissell, S. S., and G. H. Stankey. 1972. Wilderness Environmental Quality: Search for Social and Ecological Harmony. In *Proceedings, Society of American Foresters Annual Meeting*. Hot Springs, AK, pp. 170–183.

Godin, V. B., and R. E. Leonard. 1979. Management Problems in Designated Wilderness Areas. *Journal of Soil and Water Conservation* 34:141–143.

Graefe, A., J. Vaske, and F. Kuss. 1984. Social Carrying Capacity: An Integration and Synthesis of Twenty Years of Research. *Leisure Sciences* 6:395–433.

Hendee, J. C., G. H. Stankey, and R. C. Lucas. 1990. *Wilderness Management*. 2d ed. Golden, CO: North American Press. 546 pp.

Knudson, D. M., and E. B. Curry. 1981. Campers' Perceptions of Site Deterioration and Crowding. *Journal of Forestry* 79:92–94.

Lee, R. G. 1975. The Management of Human Components in the Yosemite National Park Ecosystem. Yosemite National Park, CA: Yosemite Institute. 134 pp.

Liddle, M. J. 1988. Recreation and the Environment: The Ecology of Recreation Impacts. Section 2, Vegetation and Wear (AES Working Paper 1/89), Australian Environmental Studies, Griffith University, Brisbane, Australia.

Liddle, M. J. 1989. Recreation and the Environment: The Ecology of Recreation Impacts. Section 3, Soils and Wear (AES Working Paper 1/89), Australian Environmental Studies, Griffith University, Brisbane, Australia.

Liddle, M. J. 1991. Recreation Ecology: Effects of Trampling on Plants and Corals. *Tree* 6(1):13–17.

Lucas, R. C. 1979. Perceptions of Non-Motorized Recreational Impacts: A Review of Research Findings. In R. Ittner, D. R. Potter, J. Agee, and S. Anschell, eds. *Recreational Impacts on Wildlands*, USDA Forest Service Conference Proceedings, No. R-6-001-1979.

Martin, S. R., and S. F. McCool. 1989. Wilderness Campsite Impacts: Do Managers and Visitors See Them the Same? *Environmental Management* 13(5):623–629.

McEwen, D., and S. R. Tocher. 1976. Zone Management: Key to Controlling Recreational Impact in Developed Campsites. *Journal of Forestry* 74:90–93.

Meinecke, E. P. 1928. The Effect of Excessive Tourist Travel on the California Redwood Parks, California Department of National Resources, Division of Parks. Sacramento, CA

Roggenbuck, J. W., D. R. Williams, and A. E. Watson. 1993. Defining Acceptable Conditions in Wilderness. *Environmental Management* 17 (2):187–197.

Shelby, B., and T. A. Heberlein. 1986. *Carrying Capacity in Recreation Settings*. Corvallis, OR: Oregon State University Press. 164 pp.

Shelby, B., J. J. Vaske, and R. Harris. 1988. User Standards for Ecological Impacts at Wilderness Campsites. *Journal of Leisure Research* 20(3):245–256.

Shindler, B., and B. Shelby. 1992. Regulating Wilderness Use: An Investigation of User Group Support. *Journal of Forestry* 91(2):41–44.

Stankey, G. H., S. F. McCool, and G. L. Stokes. 1984. Limits of Acceptable Change: A New Framework for Managing the Bob Marshall Wilderness Complex. *Western Wildlands* (fall). 5 pp.

Stankey, G. H., D. N. Cole, R. C. Lucas, M. E. Petersen, and S. S. Frissell. 1985. The Limits of Acceptable Change (LAC) System for Wilderness Planning. USDA Forest Service General Technical Report INT-176.

Stillingfleet, B. 1759. *Observations on Grasses in Miscellaneous Tracts Relating to Natural History*. London: Husbandry and Physick.

Wagar, J. A. 1974. Recreational Carrying Capacity Reconsidered. *Journal of Forestry* 72:274–278.

Wall, G., and C. Wright. 1977. The Environmental Impact of Outdoor Recreation. Department of Geology Publication Series 11, University of Waterloo, Waterloo, Ontario. 69 pp.

Washburne, R. F. 1982. Wilderness Recreational Carrying Capacity: Are Numbers Necessary? *Journal of Forestry* 80:726–728.

Washburne, R. F., and D. N. Cole. 1983. Problems and Practices in Wilderness Management: A Survey of Managers. USDA Forest Service Research Paper INT-304. 56 pp.

PART II
Impacts to Resource Components

2 Soil

Along with changes in the characteristics of ground vegetation, soil impacts are the most frequently mentioned of all the effects of outdoor recreation activities. An understanding of ecological impacts presupposes that the reader has had exposure to soil science concepts and terminology. A brief overview of soil characteristics and properties is given and must be understood to appreciate the major impacts of outdoor recreation on soils. Foremost among these characteristics are soil texture, structure, pore space, bulk density, and profile development. For additional information on soils, the following references are suggested: Wilde (1958), Foth (1978), and Brady (1990).

BASIC SOIL ECOLOGY

What Is Soil?

Soil, the basis of all terrestrial life, is commonly misunderstood. Much more than just inert dirt, soil is alive—produced and maintained by interactions between living organisms, rock, air, water, and sunlight (Dasmann 1972). Soils consist of four major components. Minerals and organic matter, both dead and alive, make up the solid portion; the soil solution, water and dissolved substances, and air occupy the pore spaces between solids. Although all of these components are present in all soils, usually so intimately mixed that separation is rather difficult, their relative abundance and distribution vary greatly. These differences affect both the soil's capacity as a medium for supporting life and its response to recreational use.

Soil Texture and Structure

The mineral fraction of soils has been divided into classes based on the size of particles. *Sand* particles are 2.0 to 0.02 mm in diameter, *silt* particles are between 0.02 and 0.002 mm, and *clay* particles are less than 0.002 mm. Particles larger than sand are called coarse fragments. *Texture* describes the proportion of these various particle sizes in a soil. A sandy soil contains a large proportion (at least 70 percent) of the relatively large sand particles; a clay soil contains at least 35 to 40 percent submicroscopic clay particles. Soils with about equal proportions of sand, clay, and silt particles are called loams. Many intermediate classes have also been defined (e.g., silty clay loam).

Sandy soils are *coarse* textured. The relatively large particles do not pack together tightly; consequently, pore spaces are large. Except when soils have recently been wetted, water occupies only small (*capillary*) pores, where it is held by absorption to the soil particles; air occupies the larger pores. Consequently, sandy soils hold more air and less water than soils with smaller pores (Fig. 1). Such soils drain readily and are apt to be excessively dry.

Clay and silt soils are *fine* textured. They hold more water but less air than sand soils. Clay soils can remain waterlogged for long periods of time, providing poor aeration for plant growth. Moreover, despite large quantities of water, much water is held so tightly by the soil particles that it may be unavailable for use by plants. Soils containing equal amounts of sand, silt, and clay such as loam and silt loam soils generally have the best balance of water availability, drainage, and aeration.

Structure refers to how the individual soil particles of different sizes combine into aggregates. Clay particles and organic matter, in particular, promote the aggregation of many individual soil particles into clumps of various shapes and sizes. Thus, a fine textured soil may appear coarse and may function in many ways as a coarse soil, because the fine particles coalesce into large granules with large pores between them (Spurr and Barnes 1980). Soil structure is particularly important in fine-textured soils where aeration can be a problem. Large pores around aggregates provide good water movement and aeration despite relatively small pores around individual particles. Organic matter can improve the structure in soils of various textures. In coarse-textured soils, organic matter can improve the water-holding capacity of the soil because of its capacity to absorb and hold water.

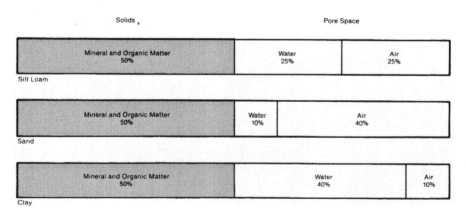

FIGURE 1. Difference in the relative proportion of solid particles, water, and air in representative silt loam, sand, and clay soils.

Favorable soil structure developed under forest conditions may be destroyed by removing the forest vegetation and exposing the soil surface directly to rainfall. The direct impact of rainfall can detach soil particles from aggregates. The detached particles clog spaces between aggregates, forming a crust that is relatively impervious to water. Less water entering the soil means that more is running across the surface, and this increases erosion. The effects of recreational trampling on soil structure can be even more profound. Destruction of leaf litter by trampling eliminates the possibility of its incorporation into the surface soil horizon, decreasing the amount of organic matter that is so important to promoting good soil structure. More will be said about this and the serious effects of soil compaction later.

Pore Space

As was previously mentioned, the pore space is determined largely by the texture and structure of soils. Soils with a large proportion of large particles, such as sands, or with a compacted structure in which particles lie close together have a low *total porosity*. Soils that are medium-textured, high in organic matter, and uncompacted have a high total porosity. Soil pores have been divided into two size classes—*macro* and *micro*. The larger macropores allow the ready movement of air and percolating water, but they retain little water. In contrast, water is retained in micropores, but air and water movement is impeded. Sandy soils have low total porosity, but a large proportion of that porosity consists of macropores. Consequently, the movement of air and water is rapid (Brady 1990).

Despite a large total pore space, movement of air and water in fine-textured soils is relatively slow. Porosity is dominated by micropores, which are often full of water, leaving little pore space for air. In addition, the water occupying the capillary micropores is held tightly to clay particles by tension forces, contributing to the slow movement of water. The significant point here is that the size of individual pore spaces (macro or micro) is more important to the movement of air and water than total pore space.

Bulk Density

Bulk density is a soil weight measurement, defined as the mass (weight) of a unit volume of soil. It is determined primarily by the quantity of pore space within a given volume of soil. Thus, it is closely related to porosity. It is affected by the compactness of the soil and by the soil's composition, particularly its texture, structure, and organic matter content. Soils that are loose and porous will have low weights per unit volume (bulk densities), and those that are compact will have high values. Soils high in fine-textured material and organic matter will have lower bulk densities than soils high in sand and low in organic matter. The bulk densities of clay, clay loam, and silt loam surface soils normally range from 1.00 to as high as 1.60 g/cm^3 whereas sands and sandy loams vary from 1.20 to 1.80 g/cm^3 (Brady 1990). These differences, present under undisturbed conditions, should be kept in mind when using bulk density as a measure of compaction.

Variation in the relationships between soil texture, compaction, and bulk density is illustrated in Fig. 2. The increase in bulk density with compaction is more pronounced in fine-textured soils. Uncompacted, fine-textured soils have low bulk densities because the soil particles can be packed together more tightly than large particles. Consequently, fine-textured soils can be compacted to a greater density than coarse-textured soils.

Moreover, bulk density tends to increase with profile depth. This apparently results from a lower content of organic matter, less aggregation and root penetration, and compaction caused by pressure from the weight of overlying horizons. Compact subsoils may have bulk densities greater than 2.0 g/cm³ (Brady 1990). Bulk density also increases in campsites as one moves from the periphery to the intermediate and the core zones of sites (Stohlgren and Parsons 1986).

Although bulk density is the common measure of compaction in soil sciences, soil penetration resistance is commonly used in recreation field studies. Soil penetration resistance refers to the force necessary to drive a rod of known length into the ground, recorded on an instrument called a penetrometer. Campsite penetrometer readings in wilderness areas have ranged from 70 to 300 percent.

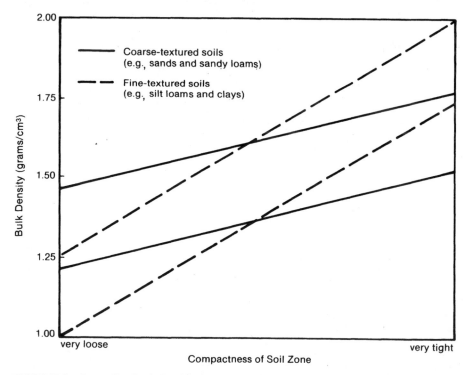

FIGURE 2. Generalized relationship between compactness and the range of bulk densities common in sandy soils and in those of finer texture. (*Source*: Brady 1990.)

The Soil Profile

Soils are not uniform in texture and structure for a given depth. Examination of a vertical section of soil shows the presence of more or less distinct horizontal layers, differing in color, composition, and other properties. Such a section is called a *soil profile*. A typical soil profile will consist of four primary horizontal layers or *horizons* (Fig. 3). These primary horizons, the O, A, B, and C horizons, are subdivided further and may or may not be present in any given soil.

The O, or organic horizon is formed above the mineral soil and often consists of both an O^1 and an O^2 horizon. The O^1 horizon consists of litter—recognizable leaves, twigs, fruits, and dead plants and animals. When this litter decomposes to an unrecognizable state, it is called humus, the primary component of the O^2 horizon. Surface organic horizons are extremely important to healthy soils. They cushion the impact of rainfall and other erosional agents, including recreational use, on

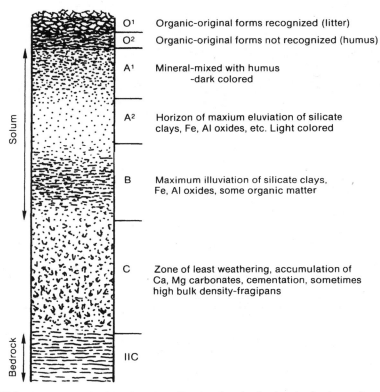

FIGURE 3. A conceptual mineral soil profile showing the four major horizons that may be present. (*Source*: Adapted from Buckman and Brady, 1969. Reprinted with permission of Macmillan Publishing Co., Inc. From *The Nature and Properties of Soils*, 7th Edition, by H. O. Buckman and N. C. Brady. Copyright© 1960, 1969 by Macmillan Publishing Co., Inc.)

underlying mineral horizons. They are important zones of biotic activity and help in the absorption of water. As a source of humus that can move downward into the soil, the organic horizons contribute to the maintenance of healthy soil structure, water relations, and aeration. They are also an important source of nutrients, critical to the maintenance of soil fertility. Unfortunately, the O horizon is often pulverized and removed by recreational utilization of sites receiving concentrated use.

The A horizon is the uppermost layer of mineral soil. It is characterized in moist climates by the leaching of nutrients by downward-moving water and acid solutions. It is subdivided into an upper A^1 horizon, in which organic matter is constantly being added to mineral soil through litter decomposition and mixing by soil organisms, and a lower A^2 horizon, a zone of leaching. Biotic activity is most concentrated in the A^1 horizon.

Below the A is the B horizon, characterized in moist temperature climates by the accumulation of iron and aluminum oxides and minute clay and organic particles, all derived from leaching of the A horizon above. In more arid regions, it is characterized by accumulation of soluble salts such as calcium carbonate. As a result, the B horizon is usually finer-textured and darker-colored than either the A horizon or the original parent material, except in arid regions where accumulated salts are light-colored.

The C horizon is below the zone of accumulation. It has been little affected by biotic activity and consists primarily of disintegrated parent material, similar to that from which the A and B horizons were derived.

IMPACTS ON SOILS

The major impact to soils in wildland recreation areas results from trampling. Trampling and vehicle use cause soil compaction, increased soil density and penetration resistance, changes in soil structure and stability, losses in litter and humus layers, reduced infiltration rates, greater runoff, and increased erosion (Cole and Schreiner 1981; Marion and Cole 1996). In addition to changes in the physical properties of soils, trampling may lead to changes in soil biology and chemistry. Altered macro- and microhabitats in soil and litter result in major changes in the species composition of soil microflora and fauna (Duffey 1975).

The direct weight loads to the ground surface imposed by hikers, backpackers, packstock, and off-road vehicles impose stresses of considerable magnitude on the ground flora and soils of recreational areas (Kuss, Graefe, and Vaske 1990). Data indicate that an adult hiker population made up of an equal number of men and women averaging 150 lb (67.5 kg) in weight with boots and clothing (9.9 lb, 4.5 kg) would exert a ground pressure of 11.7 lb/in.^{2} (0.82 kg/cm^2) of bearing surface when standing at full weight on one foot, as occurs during each step taken (Holmes and Dobson 1976). This translates to roughly 132–180 tons per hiker mile, depending on the stride of the individual. By comparison, Lull (1959) reported that horses may exert pressures as high as 40 lb/in.^{2} (2.77 kg/cm^2).

Manning (1979) provides a useful conceptualization of recreational trampling impact on soils as a seven-step cycle (Fig. 4). Where present, the first step in the cycle is a reduction or removal of the leaf litter and humus layers—the O horizon. Trampling, surface runoff, and, in some places, raking of the site for aesthetic or fire safety reasons contribute to loss of this litter cover. The second step, a reduction in organic matter incorporated into the mineral soil, occurs in some places but not in others. Removal of surface litter cuts off much of the source of organic matter so that in time, as existing soil organic matter decomposes, soil organic matter should decline. Indeed, this does occur in some places. In others, however, some of the pulverized surface organic matter is transported down into the soil by percolating waters, where it accumulates in dark bands (Monti and Mackintosh 1979). In these cases soil organic matter actually increases in response to recreational use.

Regardless of what happens in the first two steps, the third step—compaction—always occurs. Susceptibility to compaction of soil by the pressures of trampling or vehicular travel is increased by loss of organic matter, both at the surface and in the soil, but it will occur in any case. Through compaction, soil particles are forced to pack together more tightly, eliminating much of the interstitial pore space. Soil struc-

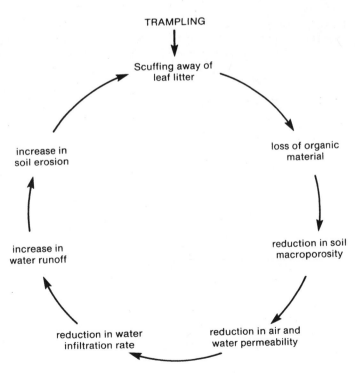

FIGURE 4. Soil impact cycle resulting from human trampling. (*Source*: "Impacts of Recreation on Riparian Soils and Vegetation," by R. E. Manning (1979) in *Water Resources Bulletin* 15(1):30–43. Reprinted with permission of the American Water Resources Association.)

ture is also disrupted as aggregates are broken up and forced together. The result is a reduction in total porosity and macroporosity; the volume of micropores is not greatly affected.

This reduction in macroporosity initiates a chain of events that carries through the sixth step of the cycle, with profound implications for "health" of soils. Because macropores are the primary conduits for the free movement of air and water, their reduction seriously impedes soil aeration and the percolation of water into the soil. Because less water can move through the soil, less can enter the soil, and water infiltration rates are reduced. This can lead to reductions in soil moisture and resulting water stress on plants, although this impact is pronounced only in certain places at certain times. A more universal impact is increased surface runoff, the inevitable result of rainfall on soils with low infiltration rates. This greatly increases the potential for erosion, step seven, particularly if slopes are steep and soils are erosive. Severe erosion truncates soil profiles, and it exacerbates soil impacts by washing away even more surface organic matter, hence the view of the impact process as a never-ending cycle. Let's now take a look at how serious these impacts are in various recreational situations.

Organic Matter

The magnitude of organic matter loss varies with amount of use, the recreational activity involved, and environmental conditions. In desert areas, for example, where organic horizons are very thin and patchy, if present at all, any use of any kind rapidly eliminates organic matter. As the organic matter is so sparse to start with, such losses represent a severe impact. In forested environments, effects vary between deciduous and evergreen forests. Deciduous forests accumulate much more leafy litter in the fall after the main use season. This can promote more rapid overwinter recovery. Litter loss is particularly pronounced and rapid on paths and trails. Trampling is highly concentrated, and the frequency of steep slopes and water channelization contribute to surface erosion of litter from much of the trail surface. On a newly opened nature trail in England, the passage of 8000 people reduced the volume of forest leaf litter by 50 percent in just one week (Burden and Randerson 1972).

Legg and Schneider (1977) found that after two seasons of camping, litter on forested campsites in Michigan was limited to one year's leaf fall, and the humic layer (the O^2 horizon) had been eliminated. The annual leaf fall is rapidly removed within several months after the beginning of each camping season even on light-use sites (Fig. 5). In most cases hardwood litter is more rapidly eliminated during the main use season, but it recovers more rapidly over the winter. Differences in litter cover, between light- and heavy-use sites, were much less pronounced after the fourth year of use (1972) than after the third. In a park in northwest Ontario, Monti and Mackintosh (1979) also reported that most organic litter is lost even with light use.

Loss of litter is less pronounced on campsites in wilderness areas where use is not so great. In the Boundary Waters Canoe Area, Minnesota, litter and humus layers on

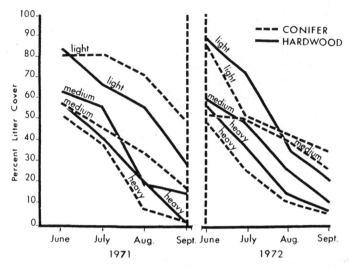

FIGURE 5. Average percent litter cover on established camping units over two visitor use seasons. Note the percent recovery during the off-season, Sept. 1971 to June 1972. (*Source*: Legg and Schneider 1977. Reproduced from *Soil Science Society of American Journal*, Volume 41, pp. 437–441, 1977 by permission of the publisher.)

campsites were reduced in thickness an average of 65 percent below undisturbed control areas (Frissell and Duncan 1965). In the Eagle Cap Wilderness, Oregon, about one-half of the organic horizon has been removed on campsites (Cole and Fichtler 1983). In some places, however, all organic matter has been removed. The mineral soil (A horizon) beneath was exposed over about 30 percent of the Eagle Cap campsites. On the most infrequently used sites little litter was lost. The thickness of organic horizons was reduced only 3 percent on soils used no more than a few times per year. This compares with reductions of 21 percent and 68 percent on sites used about 10 to 20 nights per year and more than 25 nights per year, respectively. Results from 10 years later showed differences between low-use and high-use sites to be even greater (Cole and Hall 1992).

Little litter is likely to remain on trails or campsites that are frequently used, particularly those with roaded access, after they have been used for several years. On lightly used campsites in more remote areas, however, little litter loss may occur if organic horizons are thick. This is very different from the situation in regard to soil compaction where substantial compaction occurs even on very lightly used sites. In places where litter cover is sparse, such as desert areas, even light recreational use can eliminate all litter.

There is some debate about what happens to surface organic matter once it is pulverized. Certainly, most of it is eroded away. However, several researchers report that some of the pulverized organic matter accumulates in the uppermost zone of the A horizon. On Eagle Cap campsites, for example, the organic matter content of the upper 5 cm of mineral soil was 20 percent higher on campsites than on controls. Other researchers report the opposite. Settergren and Cole (1970) found organic matter to be mixed through the surface layers of control sites but absent in campsite soils.

Loss of soil organic matter is serious because it makes the soil more prone to many soil impacts that follow (Marion and Merriam 1985). Susceptibility to reduced rainwater infiltration and nutrient cycling, as well as increased surface erosion, profile truncation, and soil compaction, are all increased when organic matter is removed. Elimination of the surface litter and humus layers greatly reduces the soil's ability to capture rainwater, accumulate and replenish soil organisms and nutrients, and cushion the mineral soil against the impact forces that cause compaction.

Profile Truncation

Destruction of the protective organic horizon leads to an accelerated rate of wind and water erosion, which removes a large proportion of the fine-sized particles on the exposed soil surface. In addition, unprotected mineral soil is readily compacted by human trampling. As a result of the combination of organic matter destruction, wind and sheet erosion, and compaction, the soil profile is reduced in depth, or truncated. Tree roots are commonly exposed and suffer mechanical damage as a result of soil profile truncation (Fig. 6).

FIGURE 6. Tree roots exposed by soil erosion and compaction. (*Photo*: D. N. Cole.)

The profiles of heavily used campsites average 3 in. shallower than those of nearby control sites in the Missouri Ozarks (Settergren and Cole 1970). The profile of one badly abused campsite indicated that as much as 9 in. of surface soil had disappeared following extensive recreational use. In a study of Michigan backcountry campsites, the A^1 horizon was completely eroded from moderately and heavily used sites by the end of four seasons of use. In contrast, the A^1 horizons on control sites were more than 5 cm deep, on average (Legg and Schneider 1977). Therefore, 5 cm had been lost in just four years.

Soil Compaction

Compaction, whether by trampling, vehicular use, or some other source of pressure, is a commonly documented effect of recreational use. The major techniques used to document soil compaction are (Speight 1973):

Penetrometry. Records the force necessary to drive a rod a known length into the ground

Bulk Density. A direct measure of soil density (weight to volume ratio)

Permeability. A measure of how rapidly water permeates the soil

Conductivity. A measure of soil density based on conductivity to electricity or gamma rays

Although these methods measure different characteristics, they all document increased compaction, the forcing of individual soil particles into closer proximity, thereby reducing the area occupied by interstices (Manning 1979). Compaction of soils by recreational use is reflected in increased values for bulk density, penetration resistance, conductivity, and decreased permeability values.

Comparing the degree of compaction found in different areas is difficult because of differences in site conditions and measurement techniques. Bulk density values vary greatly between soil types; certain inherently dense, uncompacted soils (e.g., sands) have even higher bulk densities than soils on highly compacted recreation sites. Examples of reported increases (over control sites) include 0.1 g/cm^3 on Eagle Cap Wilderness campsites (Cole and Fichtler 1983), 0.2 g/cm^3 on campsites in the Delaware Water Gap National Recreation Area (Marion and Cole 1996), 0.4 g/cm^3 on developed camp and picnic sites in Rhode Island (Brown, Kalisz, and Wright 1977), and 0.2 to 0.4 g/cm^3 on paths and trails (Liddle 1975). Dotzenko, Papamichos, and Romine (1967) recorded a bulk density of 1.60 g/cm^3 in a heavily used campground in Rocky Mountain National Park. In off-road vehicle areas, surface bulk densities over 2.00 g/cm^3 have been reported (Wilshire, Nakata, Shipley, and Prestegaard 1978). Weaver and Dale (1978) measured bulk density after experimentally trampling a grassland 1000 times by a hiker, a horse, and a motorcycle. Bulk density increased 0.2 g/cm^3 with hiker use and 0.3 g/cm^3 with horse and motorcycle use.

Soil penetrometer readings also show wide variation in amount of increase. Penetration resistance typically increased 71 percent on campsites in the Bob

Marshall Wilderness, 89 percent in the Rattlesnake, 139 percent in the Mission Mountains, and 220 percent in the Boundary Waters Canoe Area (Cole 1983). In the Bob Marshall the median penetration resistance on sites used by parties with horses was 4.0 kg/cm^2 compared with only 2.6 kg/cm^2 on backpacker-only sites. Higher values and greater increases indicate increasing force needed to penetrate the soil, a reflection of increased compaction. Although soil penetrometer readings are much easier to record than bulk density and more replicate readings can be taken, they vary with differences in water content and other soil characteristics. Consequently, comparison between sites and even over time on the same site should be treated with caution.

In all soils the top layers of the mineral soil are the most compacted; organic horizons are not very susceptible to compaction. Except in areas used by off-road vehicles, compaction on recreation sites is seldom evident more than 5 to 6 in. below the surface (LaPage 1967). Compaction of ORV areas is evident at depths exceeding 3 ft (Wilshire, Nakata, Shipley, and Prestegaard 1978). Unfortunately, it is compaction of the surface soils that is more critical to the alteration of water and air movement, vegetation rooting zones, and the habitat of soil organisms.

The degree of soil compaction is influenced by many soil factors, including organic matter, soil moisture, and soil texture and structure. In general, the soils most prone to compaction are those with a wide range of particle sizes (e.g., loams), those with a low organic content, and those that are frequently wet when trampled. On dry, extremely sandy soils, compaction can even be beneficial. Total porosity remains high because the sand particles simply cannot be pushed together closely; however, some of the macropores are reduced to micropore size, allowing the soil to retain more water, thereby benefiting plant growth.

Degree of compaction varies seasonally. Recovery occurs over the winter season in temperate zones as compaction is lessened by frost action, lack of use, and possibly wind rocking of trees. If all use is curtailed, compaction of recreation sites can be expected to return to normal within about a decade. With continued use any overwinter recovery is short-lived. With the beginning of the next use season, recovery stops and renewed compaction eliminates any overwinter loosening by early summer (Legg and Schneider 1977). Figure 7 illustrates this well.

Evaluation of the significance of compaction per se is difficult. Certainly, the effect of compaction on water and air movement can create serious problems. As the example of the dry, sandy soil illustrates, however, there are cases in which a more dense soil can actually be beneficial. Two direct, plant-related, negative consequences of compaction are the hindrance of plant root elongation and the lack of suitable regeneration sites on compacted soils. Figure 8 illustrates the effects of compaction on the ability of seeding roots to penetrate soil. Serious root impedance occurs at much lower densities on the more fine-textured silt loam soil. On coarser soils, it is difficult to compact soils to a level where pores are too small to penetrate. A poorly developed root system decreases establishment of plants and, for established plants, reduces vigor and growth. Compaction reduces germination through its effect on the smoothness of germination sites. Seeds of different species require a diversity of microhabitats in which to germinate. Germination is usually greater on

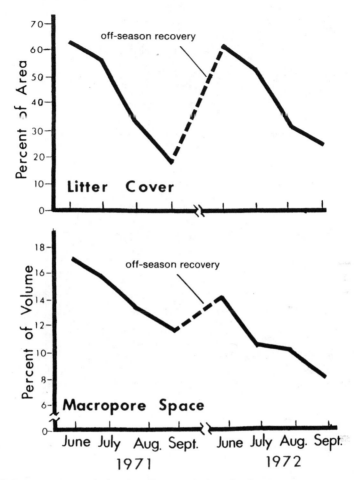

FIGURE 7. Impact recovery during the off-season is short-lived, as impacts resume at the beginning of the new camping season. (*Source*: Legg and Schneider 1977. Reproduced from *Soil Science Society of American Journal*, Volume 41, pp. 437–441, 1977 by permission of the publisher.)

rough surfaces that offer heterogeneous habitats. Compaction typically creates a homogeneous, smooth surface on which germination is inhibited.

Macroporosity and Infiltration Rate

On the central core of developed campsites, Monti and Mackintosh (1979) found that the area of macropore space declined from about 25 percent of soil volume to 2 or 3 percent. Stohlgren and Parsons (1986) found soil compaction and related pore space to increase 2 to 3 times between the periphery and core zones of campsites. These changes are particularly pronounced on fine-textured soils where macropore space is low initially, and susceptibility to compaction is high on account of the smaller soil

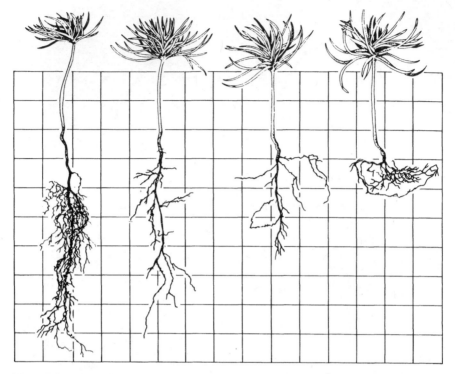

FIGURE 8. Effect of soil bulk density at 1.2, 1.4, 1.6, and 1.8 g/cm³ on Austrian pine seedling growth on sandy loam soil (2 cm grid). (*Source*: Zisa, Halverson, and Stout 1980.)

particles. However, even in sand dune soils, loss of macroporosity can be severe enough to cause anaerobic (low oxygen) conditions (Liddle and Greig-Smith 1975). Smaller soil pore size reduces the mass flow and diffusion of air within the soil and curtails movement of nutrients (Liddle 1975). The movement of O_2 and CO_2 is retarded in the soil, which can lead to respiration and growth problems for vegetation (Legg and Schneider 1977). Root activity decreases as does the ability to absorb water and nutrients. The soil microbiota is adversely affected, and the decomposition of organic matter is slowed.

Legg and Schneider (1977) observed decreases in macropore space on newly opened campsites over a four-year period. In conifer stands macropore space declined from 31.6 percent (control measures) to 17.1 percent after two years to 8.6 percent after four years. The rate at which macroporosity is reduced diminishes with time; macroporosity probably stabilizes at some low level after about five years. Loss of macropores, after both two and four years of use, was greater on heavy-use sites than on moderate- or light-use sites. Even on light use sites, however, four years of use eliminated two-thirds of the macropores.

Reductions in water infiltration rates are probably the most important environmental consequence of compaction. On picnic areas in Connecticut, Lutz (1945) found reductions of 80 percent in sand soils and 95 percent in sandy loam soils. On the sandy loam sites the average length of time for the infiltration of one liter of water was 86 minutes in the picnic area and 4 minutes in the undisturbed area—a twenty-fold difference. On the coarser textured sandy soil, loss of macropores was less severe, and infiltration on the picnic site was four times as fast as on the sandy loam picnic site; one liter infiltrated in 20 minutes.

James, Smith, Mackintosh, Hoffman, and Monti (1979) report a similar twentyfold reduction in infiltration on developed campsites in Ontario. Less severe reductions are characteristic of the less heavily used campsites in wilderness areas. In the Bob Marshall Wilderness, for example, Cole (1983) measured both instantaneous infiltration rates (the time it takes for the first centimeter of water to enter the soil) and saturated rates (the time for the first 5 cm of water). Instantaneous rates for campsites were less than one-third of controls, and saturated rates were one-sixth of controls.

More severe reductions in infiltration have been found in off-road vehicle areas. In one California area, infiltration rates were almost 40 times slower on motorcycle tracks than in adjacent undisturbed areas (Wilshire, Nakata, Shipley, and Prestegaard 1978). Organic matter content and soil texture and structure greatly influence both infiltration rates and the severity of reductions in infiltration rates.

Compaction appears to occur rapidly with light use. Even in wilderness areas low use sites are usually nearly as compacted as high use sites. In the Boundary Waters Canoe Area, increases in bulk density were two-thirds as high on sites used fewer than 12 nights per year as on sites used more than 60 nights per year (Marion and Merriam 1985). In the Eagle Cap, Missions Mountains, and Rattlesnake Wildernesses increases in penetration resistance and infiltration rates were significantly greater on sites used fewer than five nights per year than on sites used many times more (Cole and Fichtler 1983). Macroporosity is also greatly reduced even at low use levels. The relation between compaction-related impacts and amount of use is highly curvilinear—a little use causes most of the impact (Marion and Cole 1996). This is different from the case of litter loss, in which it often takes at least a moderate amount of use before a substantial amount of litter is lost (Cole and Hall 1992).

Soil Moisture

Soil moisture usually decreases as compaction increases, because compaction reduces infiltration and the amount of water available to the soil. However, compaction can also increase the amount of capillary pore space and, consequently, the moisture-holding capacity of soils. This situation is explained by the fact that when the soil is compacted, noncapillary pores too large to hold water against the force of gravity may be reduced to capillary sizes at which they can hold water. Lutz (1945) found the field capacity of trampled sites on sandy loam soils to be 8.9 percent higher than on control sites. Field capacity is the amount of water held in the soil after any water added to the soil has had a chance to drain downward. This increase in field capacity comes at the expense of reduced air capacity and, ironically, a reduced rate of water infiltration.

Settergren and Cole (1970) conducted one of the more detailed studies of soil moisture on a campground in the Missouri Ozarks. Both the field capacity and the permanent wilting point—the moisture left after plants have removed all the water they can—were reduced on campsites. The most significant measure of moisture— that available to plants—was about the same on campsites and controls. At no time was moisture at the 12-in. depth unavailable to plants, although recharge after precipitation and the rate of moisture depletion were both much slower on campsites (Fig. 9). Note the more rapid loss of moisture in dry June and the more rapid increase after late August rains on controls. Although adequate moisture was available at the 12-in. depth, available moisture dropped to zero at the surface in late August. This must be fairly common, given the severe wilting and stag-heading of tree crowns. These seasonal moisture limitations in surface soils are responsible, along with compaction, for creating a poor rooting environment for trees near the surface. A scarcity of shallow roots limits the ability of trees to utilize any surface moisture recharge that occurs in late summer.

The inability of the compacted soil surface to take up water restricts soil moisture recharge, which is particularly important to the survival of herbaceous vegetation during dry months. Many of the annual grasses, sedges, and herbs forming the recreation area ground cover vegetation during the early part of the summer succumb later to severe surface moisture limitations.

The effects of recreational use on soil moisture are complex and variable, being related to factors such as soil compaction, texture, organic content, density of forest cover, and exposure to sun and wind. Soil moisture can also influence rates of compaction and related impacts. Compaction-density penetration resistance relationships

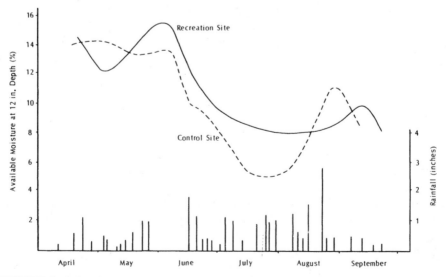

FIGURE 9. Rainfall and moisture availability, Missouri Ozarks, 1973. (*Source*: Settergren and Cole 1970.)

may be reversed when soils contain high moisture levels (Quinn, Morgan, and Smith 1980). Laboratory experiments revealed that soil penetration resistance decreased with increased trampling levels when imposed on a sandy loam at moisture contents near field capacity (45 percent). These findings were confirmed by Whittaker (1978) and Kuss and Jenkins (1985) who reported that under field conditions in Great Smoky Mountains National Park and the White Mountains National Forest (where high soil moisture was combined with fine-textured soils), penetration readings of surface soils declined under hiking pressures of light to moderate intensities. Generally, effects on soil moisture content are probably of less importance than many of the other impacts that have been discussed. They are probably most significant where available moisture declines in soils that were inherently droughty under undisturbed conditions.

Soil Erosion

Erosion is the most permanent, and therefore most serious, of soil impacts. Whereas soil compaction, loss of organic matter, and some other impacts will recover to some degree during periods of nonuse, erosion usually continues, once initiated, whether use continues or not. Gully erosion of trails, in particular, is likely to continue even without use. Most erosion is not caused by trampling or camping. Soil is eroded mostly by wind and water; recreational activities provide the circumstances for erosion and increase its rate of occurrence but are seldom the actual agents of erosion.

Although the most important agent of soil erosion is water, wind is an important erosional force in peat or sandy soils. Wind erosion of sand dunes is the best example of large-scale erosion triggered by recreational activity (Speight 1973). Where recreation destroys the vegetation that stabilizes dunes, the sand is freely moved by wind. Tens of hectares may be eroded at a single site, causing dune erosion to be the most obvious and often quoted impact of recreation in Great Britain. In the United States, wind erosion of dune ecosystems is primarily a problem in the national seashores of the Park Service, lakeshore parks on the Great Lakes, and desert dune areas used by off-road vehicles. Boardwalks to channel visitor use and prohibitions on camping and vehicular traffic are common means of limiting vegetation disturbance and resulting wind erosion.

Water erosion in recreation areas occurs primarily in two forms: sheet and gully. Sheet erosion of campsites, picnic areas, and other fairly level recreation sites occurs when water flows in a sheet across broad expanses of ground, picking up material as it moves. This impact was discussed earlier in this chapter under the heading of "Profile Truncation." Gully erosion, an even more serious problem to recreation management, occurs where water is concentrated in channels. This increases its erosive power. Gully erosion is a common problem on roads, trails, and sometimes on stream banks. Ketchledge and Leonard (1970) have measured trail erosion in the Adirondack Mountains that amounts to an increase in both trail width and depth of 1 in. per year. Surface erosion of up to 2 ft was reported on footpaths near campsites along the Colorado River in Grand Canyon; 1-ft reductions were common (Dolan, Howard, and Gallenson 1974). On a lineal distance basis, trail soil erosion exceeding

1 ft in depth averaged 239 ft per mile, with a cumulative total of 14.6 miles (4.5%) of sampled trails in the Great Smoky Mountains National Park (Marion 1994).

Paths made by horses and trail bikes create conditions that invite accelerated gully erosion. Horse traffic causes significant compaction to the underlying soil layers, thus reducing water infiltration and increasing surface runoff. In addition, the action of a horse hoof tends to dig up and puncture the soil surface. Loose, unconsolidated soil is more prone to erosion than compacted soil and, as a result, the potential for erosion increases on horse trails as compared with hiker trails. A comparison of the erosional impacts of hikers, horses, off-road bicycles and motorcycles showed that the sediment yields from horse trails were greater than those from any other type of use (Seney and Wilson 1991). Four-wheel drive vehicles and trail bikes in the steep and moist southern Appalachian Mountains make trails that erode in places to depths of 6 to 8 ft (Fig. 10). In an off-road vehicle area in California, the annual erosion rate was estimated to be 11,500 tons per km^2. This is 30 times higher than the rate at which the U.S. Bureau of Reclamation considers erosion to be a serious problem (Wilshire, Nakata, Shipley, and Prestegaard 1978). In a study of riverways, Hansen (1975) could not attribute much of the streambank erosion that was occurring to canoe use. Much was natural; some was linked to vehicular access by people fishing, picnicking, or simply watching the floaters.

The extent of erosion on a recreation site is determined by many factors. Slope, drainage, and climate are important (Jubenville and O'Sullivan 1987; Marion 1994).

FIGURE 10. Off-road vehicles have caused excessive erosion on this trail in the Cherokee National Forest, Tennessee. (*Photo*: W. E. Hammitt.)

Erosion is likely to be more serious on steep slopes where water tends to be channelized and in climates with infrequent but intense rainfall. A sparse ground-cover vegetation and lack of an organic horizon also make a site prone to erosion. The most erosive soils are homogeneous-textured soils, particularly those high in silt or fine sands and low in organic matter. Shallow soils may quickly erode down to bedrock.

Other Soil Impacts

Additional impacts, which have been investigated in less detail, include effects on temperature, organisms, and chemistry. Loss of vegetation and surface organic horizons removes an insulating layer, which leads to a greater range of soil temperatures. Temperatures are higher in summer and during the day; they are lower during winter and at night. During winter, soil in trampled areas was observed to be frozen to a depth of 3 to 4 cm whereas under taller vegetation in minimally used areas, the soil temperature remained above freezing (Chappell, Ainsworth, Cameron, and Redfern 1971).

The effect of snowmobiles on soil temperature regimes can be particularly pronounced. Compaction of snow reduces its insulating ability. Wanek (1971) found the duff layer (O horizon) under snowmobile trails to be 11°C cooler than under the undisturbed snow. The A^1 soil horizon under the compacted snow froze approximately one month earlier and thawed an average of 2 to 3 weeks later in the spring. This shortened growing season can be detrimental to the life cycle of flowering plants, particularly those in alpine ecosystems. As Wanek (1974) states:

> The colder temperatures retard the growth and flowering of early spring flowers and reduce their seed productivity and viability. In addition, perennial herbs having large underground storage organs often perish due to intracellular ice crystals producing cytolysis, dehydration, or extracellular ice masses which disrupt tissues. (p. 50)

Changes in soil temperature regimes and decreases in organic matter and air pore space also affect soil organisms. Colder temperatures under snowmobile trails were the presumed cause of a hundredfold reduction in soil bacteria and a two- to tenfold reduction in soil fungi (Wanek 1971). Speight (1973) summarized the influence of trampling on bacteria in woodland soils, whereby bacteria decreased by about one-half. Other studies have shown similar effects on soil fauna and microflora. Ground vegetation communities, before trampling, contain a complex assemblage of animals that feed on dead plants or on fungi, algae, and bryophytes, which grow on decaying material. For example, when areas of a chalk grassland ecosystem were trampled, a serious reduction in arthropods, earthworms, mollusks, and snails occurred (Chappell, Ainsworth, Cameron, and Redfern 1971). Less understood but of particular concern are adverse effects on mycorrhizal fungi (Cole 1990). Mycorrhizal fungi improve nutrient uptake and water absorption in plants and thus often are a limiting factor in revegetating disturbed areas (Reeves, Wagner, Moorman, and Kiel 1979). Reeves reported that 99 percent of the plant cover in undisturbed sites in Colorado sagebrush country contained mycorrhizal fungi, whereas less than 1 percent were found to contain the fungi in severely disturbed areas.

The compaction of soils and loss of pore space can also lead to soils being poorly oxygenated, creating more potential for anaerobic microenvironments and forms of bacteria. Speight (1973) found that nitrifying bacteria, which need an abundance of oxygen, were unable to survive in trampled soils and that anaerobic bacteria were twice as abundant as other forms. Because soil bacteria involved in nitrification (conversion of NH_4 to NO_3) are obligate aerobes, changes in soil structure and aeration, such as occur under heavy soil compaction, adversely affect the availability of nitrate to plants. Between the two processes of denitrification and nitrification, it is possible that nitrogen shortages will occur in soil-impacted environments, such as in campsites and picnic areas. Kuss, Graefe, and Vaske (1990, p. 17) state that "the general conclusion can be drawn that changes in microhabitat caused by a decline in litter and air spaces in the soil are more important than actual physical destruction of individual organisms."

Several changes in soil chemistry have also been recorded on recreation sites. A number of studies have found increases in soil pH on campsites; recreation use somewhat reduces acidity. Results of changes in the concentration of various nutrients have been notably inconsistent. Table 1 shows the relationship between concentrations of nitrogen, phosphorus, and other elements to bulk density, soil moisture, and organic matter in sandy loam soils. Heavily compacted core areas within campsites were compared with intermediate zones and the little disturbed periphery of these areas. Total nitrogen declined by 62 percent from the periphery areas to the heavily impacted zones. Phosphorus showed only a 15 percent decline, whereas K, Mg, and

TABLE 1. Variations in Vegetation Cover and Selected Soil Characteristics as Influenced by Use Levels

Item	Core	Intermediate	Periphery	Percent Change Periphery to Core
Vegetation cover (%)	1.1	15.3	24.8	−96
Soil bulk density (grams/cc)	1.3	0.7	0.5	+171
Macronutrients (ppm)				
N (Total)	28.6	40.4	74.8	−62
NH_4	24.8	36.5	70.6	−10
NO_3	3.8	3.9	4.2	−10
P	47.9	28.1	56.4	−15
K	50.3	65.2	107.2	−53
Mg	7.2	11.4	37.6	−81
Ca	108.8	181.0	967.3	−89
pH	3.7	3.6	3.5	+5
Soil moisture (%)	17.0	39.8	51.6	−67

Source: Stohlgren and Parsons 1986.

Ca declined significantly from periphery to core of the campsites; NO_3 nitrogen was essentially unchanged, suggesting that mineralization of ammonia was inhibited throughout the area by low pH and other unknown factors (Stohlgren and Parsons 1986). All the change were accompanied by a 171 percent increase in bulk density. Cole and Fichtler (1983) found that Mg and Ca concentrations doubled and that Na increased significantly on campsites in the Eagle Cap Wilderness. The authors suggest that the pH and nutrient increases "probably resulted from the scattering of materials, such as campfire ashes, excess food, and soap, as well as from reduced leaching as a result of slower infiltration rates." Chappell, Ainsworth, Cameron, and Redfern (1971) found decreases in nitrate and phosphate, compounds that were unaffected by use in the Eagle Cap. Probably a number of soil impacts, particularly reductions in organic matter, reduced aeration, and impoverishment of soil organism populations act to reduce concentrations of certain soil nutrients; however, this tendency can be compensated for by pollution of the site and reduced leaching. Most of these changes are small, and their significance is not well understood.

Impacts Associated with Campfires

Soil impacts resulting from collecting and burning wood in campfires are quite different from those associated with other activities on campsites and trails. Therefore, they will be discussed separately here. The removal of firewood need not cause the serious problems suggested by some proponents of banning campfires. Nutrient supplies should not be severely depleted in areas where wood is gathered. The majority of soil nutrients supplied by trees are contained in the leaves, needles, and small trees, not the larger branches and small boles of trees that are usually used for firewood (Weetman and Webber 1972). Neither will soil organic matter by substantially reduced. Again, the majority of organic matter added to the system comes from leaves and twigs, tree components seldom collected for firewood. The trampling of leaf and small twig litter is likely to have more of an effect on carbon cycling than the gathering of firewood (Bratton, Strombert, and Harmon 1982).

The most serious effects of firewood gathering result from the collection of large pieces of downed wood, those larger than 3 in. in diameter (Cole and Dalle-Molle 1982). Decaying wood of this size plays an important role in the environment that has only recently been appreciated. Moreover, its role cannot be replaced by any other component of the ecosystem. Decaying wood has an unusually high water-holding capacity, making it important to the water relations of droughty sites in particular. It also accumulates nitrogen, phosphorus, and sometimes calcium and magnesium. Therefore, use of this wood could result in nutrient impoverishment. Decaying wood is the preferred germination site for certain plant species and is a preferred growing medium for microorganisms. Ectomycorrhizal fungi, which develop a symbiotic association with the roots of many plants, improving their ability to extract water and nutrients from infertile soils, are frequently concentrated in decaying wood. Thus, removal of large pieces of wood can be detrimental to soil productivity.

Generally, the area affected by firewood removal is small and locally concentrated. However, this activity can greatly increase the area of disturbance around campsites. In Great Smoky Mountains National Park the area disturbed by firewood gathering was more than nine times the size of the devegetated zone around campsites (Bratton, Hickler, and Graves 1978).

The area disturbed by burning of firewood in campfires is even smaller; however, the effects are considerably more serious. Fenn, Gogue, and Burge (1976) examined the effects on soil of burning 140 lbs of wood, a much larger amount than would be burned at one time in most campfires. Their fires altered organic matter to a depth of 4 in. and destroyed 90 percent of the organic matter in the surface inch of soil. Fires also cause pronounced changes in soil chemistry. Reported fire effects included the loss of nitrogen, sulfur, and phosphorus, increases in pH and many cations, and reductions in the moisture-holding capacity, filtration rates, and mycorrhizal fungi populations of soil. Overall, these changes constitute a sterilization of the soil, likely to render the site less hospitable for the growth of vegetation and likely to require 10 to 15 years to recover, particularly if the site has been used for some time (Cole and Dalle-Molle 1982). Unfortunately, the only other information on campfire effects must be extrapolated from studies of forest and slash fires. In such fires it is common to lose most organic matter, nitrogen, sulfur, and phosphorus and to reduce the soil's moisture-holding capacity and infiltration rate (Tarrant 1956). Because the effects of campfires are so dramatic, many managers try to concentrate them in one place to avoid excessive damage.

SUMMARY

1. Recreational use causes reductions in surface organic horizons and compaction of mineral soil. Compaction leads to loss of macroporosity and reductions in water infiltration rates. This reduces aeration and water movement in the soil, altering the character of soil organism populations and adversely affecting plant vigor and growth. Increased surface runoff often results in accelerated erosion, causing both profile truncation and gully erosion.

2. Where it occurs, erosion is the most serious of these impacts because it is essentially irreversible. Recovery rates vary greatly, particularly with factors like amount of biotic activity, length of the growing season, and the nature of temperatures and moisture fluctuations. Erosional losses are likely to require centuries to recover. Most other impacts should usually recover in a decade and many can be speeded up through human intervention.

3. Compaction-related impacts, particularly reduction in macroporosity and infiltration, occur rapidly with low use. Initial low use causes most of the change, with further use causing less and less additional impact. If surface horizons are thick, loss of litter is less rapid and is pronounced only when use levels are moderate to high. Amount of erosion is related more to site factors than amount of use because the main agents of erosion are water and wind, not trampling.

4. Activities engaged in and type of use affect what impacts occur as well as their severity. Camping and picnicking cause most of these impacts to be severe because use is highly concentrated; however, erosion is less pronounced because use areas are generally flat. On trails, erosion is the most serious problem because of steep slopes and channelization of water. Erosion problems are aggravated when use is by horses or motorized vehicles, because they often loosen the soil rather than compact it. This makes it more easily moved by water, the main agent of erosion.

5. Susceptibility to impact varies between soils and with site factors. Compaction is most pronounced on fine-textured soils, soils with a wide variety of particle sizes, and soils low in organic matter. Erosion is most pronounced in soils with homogenous textures, particularly those high in silt and fine sand and low in organic matter. Erosion is more likely on steep slopes, shallow soils, places with sparse vegetation cover, and places where runoff is concentrated.

REFERENCES

Brady, N. C. 1990. *The Nature and Properties of Soils.* 10th ed. New York: Macmillan. 639 pp.

Bratton, S. P., M. G. Hickler, and J. H. Graves. 1978. Visitor Impact on Backcountry Campsites in the Great Smoky Mountains. *Environmental Management* 2(5):431–442

Bratton, S. P., L. L. Strombert, and M. E. Harmon. 1982. Firewood Gathering Impacts in Backcountry Campsites in Great Smoky Mountains National Park. *Environmental Management* 6(1):63–71.

Brown, J. H., Jr., S. P. Kalisz, and W. R. Wright. 1977. Effects of Recreational Use on Forested Sites. *Environmental Geology* 1:425–431.

Burden, R. F., and P. F. Randerson, 1972. Quantitative Studies of the Effects of Human Trampling on Vegetation as an Aid to the Management of Seminatural Areas. *Journal of Applied Ecology* 9:439–457.

Chappell, H. G., J. F. Ainsworth, R. A. D. Cameron, and M. Redfern. 1971. The Effect of Trampling on a Chalk Grassland Ecosystem. *Journal of Applied Ecology* 8(3):869–882.

Cole, D. N. 1983. Campsite Conditions in the Bob Marshall Wilderness, Montana. USDA Forest Service Research Paper INT-312.

Cole, D. N. 1990. Ecological Impacts of Wilderness Recreation and Their Management. In J. C. Hendee, H. Stankey, and R. C. Lucas, *Wilderness Management*, 2d ed. Golden, CO: North American Press, pp. 425–466.

Cole, D. N., and J. Dalle-Molle, 1982. Managing Campfire Impacts in the Backcountry. USDA Forest Service General Technical Report INT-135. 16 pp.

Cole, D. N., and R. K. Fichtler. 1983. Campsite Impact on Three Western Wilderness Areas. *Environmental Management* 7(3):275–288.

Cole D. N., and T. E. Hall. 1992. Trends in Campsite Condition: Eagle Cap Wilderness, Bob Marshall Wilderness, and Grand Canyon National Park. USDA Forest Research Paper INT-453. 40 pp.

Cole, D. N., and E. G. S. Schreiner. 1981. Impacts of Backcountry Recreation: Site Management and Rehabilitation—An Annotated Bibliography. USDA Forest Service General Technical Report INT-121. 58 pp.

Dasmann, R. F. 1972. *Environmental Conservation*. 3d ed. New York: Wiley. 473 pp.

Dolan, R., A. Howard, and A. Gallenson. 1974. Man's Impact on the Colorado River in the Grand Canyon. *American Scientist* 62:392–401.

Dotzenko, A. D., N. T. Papamichos, and D. S., Romine. 1967. Effects of Recreational Use on Soil and Moisture Conditions in Rocky Mountain National Park. *Journal of Soil and Water Conservation* 22:196–197.

Duffey, E. 1975. The Effects of Human Trampling on the Fauna of Grassland Litter. *Biological Conservation* 7(4):255–274.

Fenn, D. B., G. J. Gogue, and R. E. Burge. 1976. Effects of Campfires on Soil Properties. USDI National Park Service, Ecological Service Bull. No. 5.

Foth, H. D. 1978. *Fundamentals of Soil Science*. 6th ed. New York: Wiley, 436 pp.

Frissell, S. S., Jr., and D. P. Duncan. 1965. Campsite Preference and Deterioration in the Quetico-Superior Canoe Country. *Journal of Forestry* 63:256–260.

Hansen, E. A. 1975. Does Canoeing Increase Streambank Erosion? USDA Forest Service Research Note NC-186.

Holmes, D. O., and H. E. M. Dobson. 1976. Ecological Carrying Capacity Research: Yosemite National Park. Part I. The Effect of Human Trampling and Urine on Subalpine Vegetation—A Survey of Past and Present Backcountry Use and the Ecological Carrying Capacity of Wilderness. U.S. Department of Commerce, National Technical Information Service, Springfield, VA.

James, T. D., D. W. Smith, E. E. Mackintosh, M. K. Hoffman, and P. Monti. 1979. Effects of Camping Recreation on Soil, Jack Pine (*Pinus banksiana*), and Understory Vegetation in a Northwestern Ontario Park, *Forest Science* 25:233–249.

Jubenville, A., and K. O'Sullivan. 1987. Relationship of Vegetation Type and Slope Gradient to Trail Erosion in Interior Alaska. *Journal of Soil and Water Conservation* 42(6):450–452.

Ketchledge, E. H., and R. E. Leonard. 1970. The Impact of Man on the Adirondack High Country. *The Conservationist* 25(2):14–18.

Kuss, F. R., and W. A. Jenkins, 1985. Effects of Footgear Design on Trail Wear. A Summary of Five Years of Research. In *Proceedings of the Southeastern Recreation Research Conference*. USDA Forest Service, Southeast Forest Experiment Station, Asheville, NC, pp. 39–49.

Kuss, F. R., A. R. Graefe, and J. J. Vaske. 1990. Visitor Impact Management: A Review of Research. Washington, DC: National Parks and Conservation Association. 256 pp.

LaPage, W. F. 1967. Some Observations on Campground Trampling and Ground Cover Response: USDA Forest Service Research Paper NE-68.

Legg, M. H., and G. Schneider, 1977. Soil Deterioration on Campsites: Northern Forest Types. *Soil Science Society American Journal* 41:437–441.

Liddle, M. J. 1975. A Selective Review of the Ecological Effects of Human Trampling on Natural Ecosystems. *Biological Conservation* 7:17–34.

Liddle, M. J., and P. Greig-Smith. 1975. A Survey of Tracks and Paths in a Sand Dune Ecosystem. I. Soils. II. Vegetation. *Journal of Applied Ecology* 12:893–930.

Lull, H. W. 1959. Soil Compaction on Forest and Range Lands. USDA Forest Service Miscellaneous Publication 768. Washington, DC.

Lutz, H. J. 1945. Soil Conditions of Picnic Grounds in Public Forest Parks. *Journal of Forestry* 43:121–127.

Manning R. E. 1979. Impacts of Recreation on Riparian Soils and Vegetation. *Water Resources Bulletin* 15(1):30–43.

Marion, J. L. 1994. An Assessment of Trail Conditions in Great Smoky Mountains National Park. USDI National Park Service, Southeast Regions Research/Resources Management Report, Atlanta, GA. 155 pp.

Marion, J. L., and D. N. Cole. 1996. Spatial and Temporal Variation in Soil and Vegetation Impacts on Campsites. *Ecological Applications* 6(2):520–530.

Marion, J. L., and L. C. Merriam. 1985. Recreational Impacts on Well-established Campsites in the Boundary Water Canoe Area Wilderness. University of Minnesota Agricultural Experiment Station Bulletin, AD-SB-2502, St. Paul, MN. 16 pp.

Monti, P., and E. E. Mackintosh. 1979. Effects of Camping on Surface Soil Properties in the Boreal Forest Region of Northwestern Ontario, Canada. *Soil Science Society of American Journal* 43:1024–1029.

Quinn, N. W., R. P. C. Morgan, and L. J. Smith. 1980. Simulation of Soil Erosion Induced by Human Trampling. *Journal of Environmental Management* 10:155–165.

Reeves, F. B., D. Wagner, T. Moorman, and J. Kiel. 1979. The Role of Endomycorrhizae in Vegetation Practices in the Semi-arid West. I. A Comparison of Incidence of Mycorrhizae in Severely Disturbed vs. Natural Environments. *American Journal of Botany* 66:6–13.

Seney, J. P., and J. P. Wilson. 1991. Erosional Impacts of Hikers, Horses, Off-road Bicycles, and Motorcycles on Mountain Trails. Final Research Report to the Wilderness Research Unit, Intermountain Research Station, USDA Forest Service, Missoula, MT. 58 pp.

Settergren, C. D., and D. M. Cole. 1970. Recreation Effects on Soil and Vegetation in the Missouri Ozarks. *Journal of Forestry* 68:231–233.

Speight, M. C. D. 1973. Outdoor Recreation and Its Ecological Effects: A Bibliography and Review. Discussion Paper in Conservation 4, University College, London. 35 pp.

Spurr, S. H., and B. V. Barnes. 1980. *Forest Ecology*. 3d ed. New York: Wiley. 687 pp.

Stohlgren, T. J., and D. J. Parsons. 1986. Vegetation and Soil Recovery in Wilderness Campsites Closed to Visitor Use. *Environmental Management* 10(3):375–380.

Tarrant, R. E. 1956. Effects of Slash Burning on Some Soils of the Douglas-Fir Region. *Soil Science Society American Proceedings* 20:408–411.

Wanek, W. J. 1971. Snowmobile Impacts on Vegetation, Temperatures, and Soil Microbes. In M. Chubb, ed. *Proceedings of the 1971 Snowmobile and Off the Road Vehicle Research Symposium*. Department of Park and Recreation Resources, Technical Report No. 8, Michigan State University, East Lansing, pp. 116–129.

Wanek, W. J. 1974. A Continuing Study of the Ecological Impact of Snowmobiling in Northern Minnesota. Final Research Report for 1973–1974, Center for Environmental Studies, Bemidji State College, Bemidji, MN. 54 pp.

Weaver, T., and D. Dale. 1978. Trampling Effects of Hikers, Motorcycles, and Horses in Meadows and Forests. *Journal of Applied Ecology* 15:451–457.

Weetman, G. F., and B. Webber. 1972. The Influence of Wood Harvesting on the Nutrient Status of Two Spruce Stands. *Canadian Journal of Forest Research* 2:351–369.

Whittaker, P. L. 1978. Comparison of Surface Impact by Hiking and Horseback Riding in the Great Smoky Mountains National Park. USDI National Park Service Management Report 24, Southeast Region, Atlanta. 32 pp.

Wilde, S. A. 1958. *Forest Soils: Their Properties and Relation to Silviculture*. New York: Ronald Press. 537 pp.

Wilshire, H. G., J. K. Nakata, S. Shipley, and K. Prestegaard. 1978. Impacts of Vehicles on Natural Terrain at Seven Sites in the San Francisco Bay Area. *Environmental Geology* 2:295–319.

Zisa, R. P., H. G. Halverson, and B. B. Stout. 1980. Establishment and Early Growth of Conifers on Compact Soils in Urban Areas. USDA Forest Service Research Paper NE-451. 8 pp.

3 Vegetation

Along with water, vegetation is probably the most important resource component affecting visitor selection of recreation sites. Vegetation adds to site desirability by providing shade, screening for campsite privacy, and attractiveness or botanical interest. At the same time, vegetation can be susceptible to damage, particularly from recreational trampling. Consequently, it is often highly altered on recreation sites. Of all changes that occur as a result of recreation, impacts on vegetation are the most readily evident to users (Fig. 1).

VEGETATION IMPACT PARAMETERS

In contrast to the properties of soils investigated, researchers have studied fewer vegetational parameters in their attempt to describe the impacts of recreational use. Moreover, understanding these parameters requires less specialized knowledge about vegetation ecology than is required for soil ecology. Consequently, we will not need to devote as much space to describing vegetational parameters as we did for soils.

Amount of Vegetation

The most common impact parameter studied is vegetation cover, usually defined as the percentage of the ground area covered by the vertical projection of aboveground plant parts. Usually the researcher will place some sample unit over the vegetation, such as a quadrat 1 m on each side, and estimate the percentage of the quadrat area covered by vegetation. For example, Cole (1982) estimated vegetation cover on campsites, using the mean cover of vegetation in fifteen 1 m^2 quadrats systematically dispersed around each site. Other standard techniques for measuring or estimating cover include line intercepts and point intercepts (Marion 1991; Mueller-Dombois and Ellenberg 1974).

Regardless of the technique, the intent is to provide a measure of the amount of vegetation present in the area under study. By comparing such a measure on a recreation site before and after recreational use, the effects of recreation on vegetation can be identified. Where recreational use has already occurred, vegetation impacts can also be identified by comparing vegetation cover on recreation sites with cover on adjacent undisturbed sites (Cole 1995a). The assumption, in this case, is that the undisturbed site

FIGURE 1. Impacts to vegetation in zones above treeline are often severe, long lasting, and readily visible to users for some distance. (*Photo*: W. E. Hammitt.)

(the control) is similar to what the recreation site was like before it was used. Thus, this means of evaluating impact will be accurate only if researchers carefully select controls that are environmentally similar to recreation sites. This requires considerable experience; however, the use of control sites is the preferred procedure for documenting relative ground cover change between used and unused recreation sites.

Although uncommon in the impact literature, other measures of amount of vegetation that have been used are density and biomass. Density is simply a count of the number of individual plants in some unit area (e.g., 10 trees/100 m²). Density can be useful for large, discrete individuals such as trees; it is less useful in working with grasses and plants that grow in clumps where it is difficult to distinguish between individuals. Thus, it has become standard to measure density of trees and sometimes shrubs and cover of the ground level of vegetation. Biomass is a measure of the weight of vegetation in a unit area. It is determined by clipping the vegetation, drying it to remove water, and then weighing it (Sun and Liddle 1991). Although this provides a more objective measure of amount of vegetation than cover does, this method is destructive and quite time-consuming. Therefore, it is seldom used.

Vegetation Composition

In addition to recording amount of all vegetation, it is common also to record cover for individual species, species diversity, and frequency. Plant height and form are sometimes recorded (Sun and Liddle 1991). This information is used to characterize species composition, particularly of the ground level vegetation. The term *species composition* is used to refer to the mix of species that occupies any site. As with total vegetation, recreational impacts on the cover of individual species can be identified. Some researchers have grouped species into classes of particular interest. This allows them to study the effect of recreation on such classes of plants as exotic species and species exhibiting different growth forms. Exotic species are those that are not native to any given area. Such species commonly increase in importance on recreation areas, thriving on disturbed areas where native species have difficulty growing. Growth forms are classes of species grouped on the basis of similarities in their structure, form, and function. Studying how different growth forms respond to recreation use has been helpful in understanding how and why different plants vary in their susceptibility to impact (Cole 1995a).

Tree Condition

A third common parameter of interest is tree condition. In most cases, researchers have documented the percentage, number, or density of trees that have been inflicted with certain types of damage such as root exposure or severe scarring. A few studies have also tried to relate tree growth to recreational use to determine what effect recreation has on growth.

IMPACTS ON VEGETATION

Most vegetation types have a vertical structure that consists of a number of horizontal strata. Although not common to all vegetation types, three important and distinct strata are the ground cover layer, shrubs and saplings, and mature trees. In the following discussion we will explore recreational impacts on each of these three layers.

Ground Cover

Ground cover vegetation is profoundly impacted by visitor use, particularly as a result of trampling. Trampling affects ground cover vegetation both directly and indirectly. Ground cover is directly affected where trampling breaks, bruises, and crushes plants. It is indirectly affected where trampling causes soil compaction and other soil changes which, in turn, lead to changes in vegetation.

The direct effects of trampling are usually detrimental to plants. Although growth of a few species is stimulated by low levels of trampling, most species exhibit reduced abundance, height, vigor, and reproductive capacity on recreation sites. Where trampling is heavy and/or vegetation is fragile, plants are killed outright. Death occurs when plants are ripped out of the ground, have their regenerative tissues destroyed, or, in the case of annuals (plants that live for only one season), lose their ability to reproduce. Less severe trampling damage causes breakage without death; plant stems are knocked back and leaves are torn off. This reduces the area available for photosynthesis. Loss of photosynthesis then leads to reductions in plant vigor and can affect the ability to reproduce. For perennials (plants that live a number of years), repeated loss of photosynthetic area can ultimately cause death of the plant.

Problems resulting from direct impact to aerial plant parts are compounded by the problems of growing and reproducing in compacted soils. Compaction increases the mechanical resistance of the soil to root penetration. As was illustrated in Fig. 8 in Chapter 2, plants growing in soils with high bulk densities have fewer roots that extend only a short distance away from the plant. An important function of these roots is to grow into areas where water and nutrients can be extracted. When water and nutrients are depleted close to the plant, roots must be able to extend farther away from the plant. Compaction makes this more difficult; as a result, plants cannot extract sufficient quantities of water and nutrients from the soil. This problem is compounded by two other consequences of compaction. Loss of macropores in the soil reduces soil aeration, because most oxygen resides in the larger pores in the soil. Oxygen shortages also inhibit root growth, which in turn makes extraction of water and nutrients more difficult. Compaction also reduces water infiltration rates. With less water entering the soil, plant roots will more rapidly exhaust soil moisture adjacent to the plant. This accentuates the need for a large and healthy root system under conditions in which the size and health of root systems are deteriorating. Such indirect effects should cause more serious problems in environments where moisture and/or nutrients are scarce.

Compaction also inhibits the germination, emergence, and establishment of new plants. Seeds lying on a compacted surface crust are prone to dessication and less likely to receive proper incubation and moisture. Studies have shown that germination success is usually greatest on heterogeneous surfaces with a diversity of microsites (Harper, Williams, and Sagar 1965); a smooth, compacted surface does not provide such a diversity of microsites so germination is reduced. Should germination occur, a strong surface crust will make it difficult for the radicle (the incipient primary root) to penetrate the soil to provide stability, water and nutrition. Even if the seedling successfully germinates and emerges from the soil, a number of indirect impacts make premature death likely.

The microclimate of trampled sites is more severe than in untrampled areas. Both vegetation and organic matter serve to moderate temperatures, keeping them from getting too high during the day or too low at night. Trampling, by removing vegetation and organic matter, indirectly subjects seedlings to a greater likelihood of both heat injury and freezing. Another common cause of death is frost heaving, a process in which freezing and thawing of the soil physically lift seedlings out of the soil. Although frost heaving does occur on undisturbed sites, it is most common in bare mineral soil, particularly soils that have been compacted.

The ultimate result of most of these effects of trampling is a reduction in amount of vegetation, usually expressed as a loss of vegetation cover. This type of impact is particularly pronounced on campsites. Even in wilderness areas campsites commonly lose most of their vegetation cover. For example, cover loss on campsites in the Eagle Cap Wilderness, Oregon, average 87 percent (Cole 1982); the average loss on sites in the Boundary Waters Canoe Area Wilderness, Minnesota, was 85 percent

(Frissell and Duncan 1965). Cover loss on developed campsites is sometimes less pronounced because of more active maintenance programs and more durable vegetation. On developed campsites in Rhode Island, for example, Brown, Kalisz, and Wright (1977) found cover loss to be only about 50 percent. Loss of vegetation cover usually exposes underlying organic matter unless this layer has also been worn away and mineral soil or rock is exposed.

Ground cover vegetation can also be destroyed when it is disturbed by off-road vehicles. In the Algodones Dunes area of southern California, areas used by dune buggy and other off-road vehicle enthusiasts had only about 5 percent as many herbaceous plants as undisturbed areas (Luckenbach and Bury 1983).

Many studies have found that the loss of vegetation cover on lightly used sites is nearly as substantial as the loss on heavily used sites. This has been illustrated most frequently on wilderness campsites. For example, in studies in three western wilderness areas, cover loss on sites used only a few nights per year averaged between 55 and 71 percent (Fig. 2). The curve that describes the relationship between vegetation loss and amount of use is not a straight line; it is curvilinear or hyperbolic, to be more precise. Some trampling studies (e.g., Cole 1985b) have found a linear relationship between certain vegetation type covers and the logarithm of amount of use. Cover loss increases rapidly with initial increases in use. Beyond some use threshold the rate of loss decreases as loss approaches 100 percent (Cole 1995b).

The finding that vegetation loss is so severe even on lightly used sites illustrates the susceptibility of ground cover to impact. Although susceptibility varies greatly between vegetation types, a topic that will be discussed in more detail in Chapter 8,

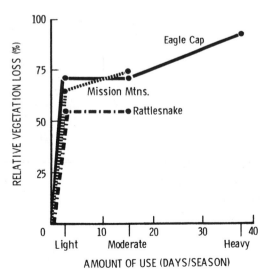

FIGURE 2. Median values of relative vegetation loss plotted in relation to amount of use in the Eagle Cap, Mission Mountain, and Rattlesnake Wildernesses. For the Eagle Cap campsites, the numerical use frequencies are estimates. (*Source*: D. N. Cole.)

the curvilinear relationship between amount of use and vegetation cover is most common. This has important implications for management, implications that will be discussed more fully in Chapters 9 and 12.

Loss of vegetation usually occurs very rapidly once use of campsites begins. LaPage (1967) followed changes on developed campsites in old field grasslands in Pennsylvania over the course of the first three years they were used. After the first year of use, an average of 45 percent cover was lost on the campsites (Fig. 3). Plant cover increased over the winter when no recreational use occurred and then declined over the next use season. However, total cover at the end of the second and third use seasons was actually greater than it had been after the first season of use.

What was happening on these campsites was that the original native occupants of the sites were being replaced by new species that were more resistant to trampling. Although vegetation cover increased from the end of the use season in 1963 to the end of the use season in 1965, the total number of species declined from 29 in 1963 to 23 in 1964 and 17 in 1965. This compares with 37 species found on the sites before use began. Many species were being eliminated by camping, but a few species were increasing in importance. As camping disturbance increased and competition with native species decreased, these trampling-resistant species were able to spread and increase total vegetation cover on the sites. A number of new species actually invaded the site. Four species that were not present before camping began appeared and spread on the sites in subsequent years. However, even with this increase cover remained reduced by about one-third.

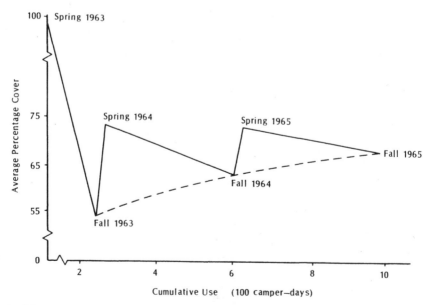

FIGURE 3. Changes in vegetation cover following the initial development and use of a car campground in Pennsylvania. (*Source*: LaPage 1967.)

Beyond loss of cover, this study illustrates several other common vegetation impacts. One is the decline in number of species—a characteristic of plant communities known as species richness. Species richness is one of the components, along with the relative abundance of individual species, of the concept of species diversity. A reduction in species richness almost always occurs where recreational use levels are high. At high-use levels only trampling-resistant species can survive, if any species can. The number of trampling-resistant species is always less than the number of original occupants of the site. However, the highest species richness usually occurs in areas that receive low to moderate levels of use. In such places the original occupants will be reduced in abundance but not eliminated. Less competition with these natives encourages the invasion and spread of trampling-resistant species. Richness is high because both the original occupants and the trampling-resistant invaders occupy the site simultaneously.

Another type of impact reflects the fact that species differ greatly in their resistance to impact. As seen in the Pennsylvania campsite example, some of the original species that occupied the campsites were eliminated much more rapidly than others; indeed, some species actually increased in cover, and other species invaded the site. The most common species before use, cinquefoil, was eliminated entirely after three seasons of use, whereas bluegrass, originally found in only a few places, became the most common species on the campsites. Over time such changes led to development of a plant community with a different species composition than was originally there.

Change in species composition is usually evaluated by reporting differences in the cover of all individual species, either over time or between recreation sites and undisturbed controls. Such lengthy lists of species make it difficult to compare the severity of shifts in species composition in different places. To provide an index of change in species composition, Cole (1978) proposed an index that measured the dissimilarity in composition between two sites. This index, the floristic dissimilarity index, can vary between 0 and 100 percent. A value of 0 means that both sites are identical in terms of both the species there and their relative abundance. Realistically, this value is not possible in nature; even under undisturbed conditions there is considerable variation in species composition, often on the order of 25 percent or so. A value of 100 percent means that the two sites have no species in common.

This index has been used to quantify change in species composition on campsites in a number of recreation areas (Cole 1995b; Marion and Cole 1996). On campsites in the Boundary Waters Canoe Area, the original forest-floor occupants tend to be fragile, and there are a number of trampling-resistant species to invade campsites. Consequently, compositional shifts are pronounced, and the floristic dissimilarity index averaged 88 percent (Marion 1984). On campsites high in the mountains of the Rattlesnake Wilderness, Montana, most of the native dominants are resistant to trampling, and few invader species can grow successfully at such high elevations. The floristic dissimilarity there averaged only 27 percent, little more than one would expect when comparing undisturbed plant communities (Cole and Fichtler 1983).

Whether any individual species will be resistant to trampling or not is largely dependent on its structure or form and characteristics of its life cycle. Of importance are the morphological and physiological characteristics of individual species and plant forms that are tolerant of disturbance (Cole, 1987; Speight 1973). Morphological characteristics that generally make a plant more tolerant include:

1. A procumbent or trailing, rather than erect, growth form
2. A tufted growth form
3. Presence of thorns or prickles
4. Stems that are flexible rather than brittle or rigid, particularly if they are woody
5. Leaves in a basal rosette
6. Small, thick leaves
7. Flexible leaves that can fold under pressure
8. Either very large or very small structure

Physiological characteristics that increase tolerance include:

1. Ability to initiate growth from intercalary as well as apical meristems
2. Ability to initiate seasonal regrowth from buds below the surface
3. Ability to reproduce vegetatively and sexually
4. A rapid growth rate

Although no species will possess all of these characteristics, many highly resistant species will possess a number of them. For example, bluegrass, the species that increased so dramatically on the Pennsylvania campsites, is capable of growing low to the ground (it is capable of erect growth when undisturbed and prostrate growth when disturbed) and has flexible folded leaves, intercalary meristems, buds protected below the ground surface, and the ability to reproduce from rhizomes and initiate rapid growth when injured. For these reasons it is a common lawn grass as well as a common invader of recreation sites. For lists of other species tolerant of impacts, see Cole (1987, 1995a).

Liddle (1991) summarizes many of the 12 characteristics listed earlier into four biological features that promote resistance and recovery from recreation impacts. The first feature is small size; for example, plants not able to grow in rosette, creeping, or other low-growing forms do not survive and rarely appear in trampled flora. The most important characteristics of the second feature, morphology, seem to be the location of the vegetative bud or persistent stem apex of different life forms of plants (Fig. 4). Buds and meristems in contact with the soil surface and cushioned by clusters of folding leaves tend to survive best. In terms of anatomy, two features are important to plant survival. Stems composed of small cells (≤ 0.1 mm) can withstand greater compression without distortion than larger-celled or hollow stems. Second, flexibility of stems and leaves aids survival—lignified tissues, for example, tend to be more rigid and break easily when trampled. The final biological feature concerns survival strategies, which involve the theoretical considerations of morphology and

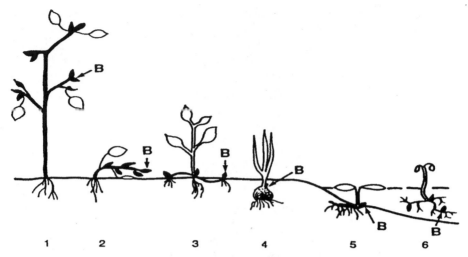

FIGURE 4. The life forms of plants provide a nontaxonomic way of grouping plant species according to their morphology, based on the position of the vegetative buds or persistent stem apex that survives over winter or periods of drought. *(1) Phanerophytes:* woody plants with buds more than 25 cm above soil level. *(2) Chamaephytes:* woody or herbaceous plants with buds above the soil surface but below 25 cm. *(3) Hemicryptophytes:* herbs (very rarely wood plants) with buds at soil level. *(4) Geophytes:* herbs with buds below the soil surface. *(5) Helophytes:* marsh plants. *(6) Hydrophytes:* water plants. *Therophytes*—plants that pass the unfavorable season as seeds—are not shown in the figure. *Cryptophytes* have buds below ground or water level; that is, this group includes geophytes, helophytes and hydrophytes. *Protohemicryptophytes* are hemicryptophytes with leafy stems. B, perennating bud. (*Source:* Liddle 1991.)

anatomy in relation to plant resistance and the physiology of plant recovery from impacts. For example, Bayfield (1979) compared the resistance and recovery response of different species and found there were three groups of species with respect to trampling susceptibility: (1) those most susceptible—with high initial damage and poor recovery, (2) those with moderate susceptibility—moderate to high initial damage and fairly good recovery, and (3) those with low susceptibility—low to moderate damage followed by an increase in cover. More recent studies by Cole (1995a) in mountainous regions and Sun and Liddle (1993) in tropical/subtropical regions have identified species and vegetation types that demonstrate the various combinations of resistance and recovery survival strategies (see Chapter 8).

Many of the most resistant species are exotics, many of which are native to Eurasia. At high elevations in the mountains, exotic species are uncommon. At lower elevations, however, exotics often dominate the vegetation along trails and on campsites. In the Boundary Waters Canoe Area Wilderness, for example, Marion (1984) found at least one exotic species on 62 percent of the campsites he surveyed. One campsite had 12 different exotic species. Three exotic species were among the 10 species found on the largest number of campsites. On campsites in the Bob Marshall

Wilderness, Montana, three of the four most common species on campsites were exotics (Cole 1983).

Generally, researchers have found that graminoids (grasses and grasslike plants such as sedges and rushes) possess more adaptations and survival strategies that allow them to resist impact than other growth forms. For example, in a study of 18 vegetation types, a species of sedge (*Carex nigricans*) was most resistant to trampling, and a wood fern (*Dryopteris campyloptera*) was the least resistant. In the sedge type, substantial cover was lost only after 500 trampling passes. Just 25 passes were required to reduce the fern cover by 33 percent (Cole 1995a). Forbs, herbaceous plants other than graminoids, vary greatly in their resistance. Low-growing, tufted forbs with a basal rosette of small, tough leaves are common survivors on recreation sites. Two common examples, both exotic in the United States, are white clover and common plantain. Forbs that grow in the shade of deep forests are at the other extreme. In trying to gather in as much light as they can, they tend to be tall with large, think leaves. Leaves generally lack tough outer layers so that absorption of light is maximized. They invest more of their energy in producing photosynthetic tissue than in producing tough support systems such as stout stems and branches. These adaptations make them highly susceptible to trampling damage. Low-growing shrubs are intermediate in their resistance to damage. They can usually survive low levels of trampling because of a tendency to have small, tough leaves and woody stems. Their stems are often brittle, however, and so they are usually eliminated at moderate use levels. The loss of shrubs on recreation sites is accentuated by slow rates of regrowth once stems are broken.

Research during the 1990s has concentrated on the vulnerability/durability of vegetation types and species over larger geographical and environmental areas (versus site studies) to better understand patterns of vegetation resistance and recovery toward trampling impacts (Cole 1995a; Sun 1992; Sun and Liddle 1993). Cole reported on the response of 18 vegetation types in five separate mountain regions of the United States, and Sun and Liddle surveyed eight tropical/subtropical areas in Australia. Results of these studies indicated that, in general, (1) plant species in the tropics and temperate areas responded essentially the same to trampling impacts, (2) plant morphological characteristics explained more of the variation in resistance, tolerance, and recovery from trampling than site characteristics, (3) resistance was primarily a function of vegetation stature, erectness, and whether plants were graminoids, forbs, or shrubs; however, even different species of grasses varied in their vulnerability to trampling (Sun and Liddle 1991), (4) recovery or resilience was primarily a function of whether plants had perennating buds located above the ground surface (negatively related), and high growth rate may be an essential feature of species that use a recovery strategy to tolerate trampling, (5) tolerance, the ability of vegetation to withstand a cycle of disturbance and recovery, was correlated more with recovery than resistance, and (6) resistance and recovery of individual species were negatively correlated (Fig. 5). Characteristics that promote the ability initially to resist trampling damage differ from those that enable plants to recover quickly. For example, plants that are resistant to trampling

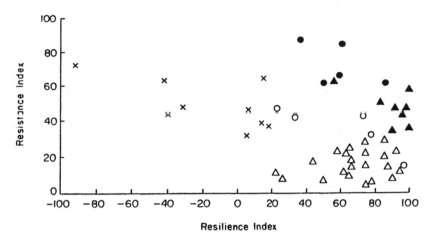

FIGURE 5. Resistance and resilience indices (%) for individual species, classified by morphology as chamaephytes (x), erect graminoids (o), nonerect graminoids (•), erect forbs (▲). Resistance index is mean relative cover after 0–500 passes. Resilience index is mean increase in cover during the year after trampling, as a percentage of the cover loss recorded two weeks after 0–500 passes. Note the inverse relationship between resistance and resilience for most species, but the high resistance/resilience for nonerect graminoids and forbs. (*Source*: Cole 1995a.)

tend to have low growth rates; plants with fast growth rates appear to use a recovery strategy.

Tree seedlings are particularly sensitive and readily killed when trampled. Even in wilderness areas tree seedlings are almost completely eliminated on all but the most lightly used campsites. In the Eagle Cap Wilderness the average number of tree seedlings on a campsite of average size (200 m²) was only 6. The number on a comparably sized undisturbed site was more than 50. This represents an average loss of over 90 percent of all seedlings. Even on the most lightly used sites, those used no more than about five nights per year, about three-fourths of all seedlings had been eliminated (Cole 1982). Similar near-complete losses of tree reproduction have been reported wherever campsite impacts have been studied. Such losses are likely to be even more pronounced on more heavily used, developed sites. For example, in a survey of 137 developed Forest Service camping and picnic sites in California, Magill and Nord (1963) found no seedlings at all on more than one-half of the sites. They also state that, where present, the continued survival of tree seedlings is doubtful.

Loss of ground cover vegetation occurs in campsites wherever trampling occurs. Along trails, ground cover is eliminated on the tread, either during construction or shortly after the start of use. Adjacent to the tread is a trailside zone that receives some trampling pressure and is also affected by habitat changes such as increased light levels caused by brush and tree removal during trail construction. This zone certainly experiences a change in species composition (Boucher, Aviles, Chepote,

Dominguez Gil, and Vilchez 1991; Leung and Marion 1996). Usually, vegetation cover will also be reduced, but sometimes the habitat changes will result in an increase in cover there. Cole (1978) studied loss of cover and change in species composition in the trailside zone in eight different vegetation types in the Eagle Cap Wilderness. Cover loss adjacent to trails was as high as 73 percent in some of the forested types and as low as 12 percent in subalpine meadows. Floristic dissimilarity varied from 37 to 82 percent; the most pronounced shifts occurred in the forested vegetation types.

Where trampling pressure is low, the height of the vegetation can be reduced without incurring a loss of vegetation cover. Vegetation with reduced stature is commonly found at the periphery of campsites and along the edge of trails. This vegetation forms a pronounced zone intermediate between the barren center of the campsite or trail and the undisturbed vegetation beyond. Lightly used trails, particularly those that were user-created, are also characterized by a short but complete vegetation cover. Other changes in plant morphology and physiology where plants are disturbed but not destroyed include a reduction in leaf area, carbohydrate reserves in roots, flower density, and number of seeds per flower (Liddle 1975; Hartley 1976; Sun and Liddle 1993). Liddle (1975) found that 400 passes by a light vehicle reduced the leaflet area of a relatively resistant clover species by 57 percent. When "trampled" by a tractor six times, the average number of flower heads on a species in the pea family decreased from 29 to 1; no seed pods were found on trampled plants. With light foot traffic the number of branches can sometimes increase as a response to frequent damage of terminal buds.

An additional source of impact on ground vegetation, in many Western areas particularly, is grazing and trampling by stock. The trampling effects of stock are generally similar to those caused by humans, except that the potential for causing impact is much more pronounced. Horses weigh much more than humans, and their weight is concentrated on a small bearing surface. This greatly increases the pressure stock exert on both vegetation and soil. Moreover, shod hooves can cause substantial gouging and ripping of the ground. Grazing effects also lead to cover losses and changes in species composition. Changes in composition are accentuated by the fact that stock prefer to eat certain species if they are available. These preferred species, because they are defoliated more frequently, will often decrease and be eliminated more rapidly than other species.

Few data on recreation stock impacts on meadows exist (Cole 1987). Cole (1981) compared the cover and composition of some lightly and heavily grazed mid-elevation meadows in the Eagle Cap Wilderness. The more heavily used meadows had about 30 percent less cover than the lightly used meadows. Graminoids, which are generally more palatable than forbs, comprised only about 35 percent of the cover on the heavily used sites, compared with 80 percent on lightly used sites. The heavily grazed meadows also had more exotic species and more annuals. More detailed and longer-term meadow surveys have been conducted in Sequoia/Kings Canyon National Parks (DeBenedetti and Parsons 1983). More than 40 years of research has documented reduced vegetation cover, erosion, and "weedy" species invasion in meadows, as well as a better understanding of annual fluctuations in the productivity of major plant associations and the response of each association to different levels of grazing. The long-term studies have led to the development of meadow-stock use management and monitoring plans for different representative meadows in the parks.

Shrubs and Saplings

Low lying shrubs suffer from trampling because they are part of the ground cover vegetation. Native blueberries (*Vaccinium*) have been found to be particularly susceptible, as they have poor recovery ability after initial trampling (Cole 1995a). Larger shrubs and saplings are usually large enough to avoid most of the direct effects of trampling. Most impact to this taller vegetation layer is the result of either damage caused by off-road vehicles or the conscious removal of shrub and sapling stems.

Both terrestrial off-road vehicles and snowmobiles can affect shrubs and saplings. Shrub cover was reduced 90 percent in an off-road vehicle area in southern California. Cacti and thorny plants that are usually spared from trampling damage can be run over and killed by vehicles.

Snowmobiles can be particularly damaging to shrubs and saplings. Ground cover plants are likely to be protected by the snow cover, although this is not the case if snow cover is shallow. Mature trees are likely to incur only trunk scars. Shrubs and small saplings, however, are often stiff and brittle during the winter and are readily snapped off when run over by snowmobiles. In some cases, damage to shrub stems causes them to put out sucker shoots. Wanek (1974) found that "most shrubs increase (number of stems and cover) where snowmobiles travel, primarily because of vegetative propagation." He points out that this may not continue indefinitely, because of disease or eventual failure to maintain the large root system of individual plants.

Removal of shrub and tree stems occurs along trails to make it easier for hikers and stock to use a trail. For example, standards on Forest Service trails in wilderness specify removing brush along a corridor 8 ft wide and 10 ft high. In more developed settings, removal of shrubs and saplings is even more pronounced. In terms of biomass removed, trail construction and maintenance are the activities that cause the most impact to shrubs and saplings in wildland recreation areas. The major exception would be in roaded areas where road construction and maintenance remove even more vegetation.

Although not as much biomass is involved, concern with removal of shrubs and saplings usually centers on campsites. Here, loss of stems occurs as a result of the development and expansion of sites as well as the felling of stems for poles and firewood. In the intersite zones of a developed campground in Michigan (intersite zones are the lightly used portions of the campground between high-impact centers of activity—refer to Chapter 6), McEwen and Tocher (1976) found only 76 saplings per acre compared with 338 per acre in adjacent unused portions. Around long-established shelters along the Appalachian Trail in Great Smoky Mountains National Park, saplings less than 3 in. in diameter often cannot be found within 200 ft of shelters; they have been cut down and used for firewood. On campsites in Eagle Cap Wilderness, one-third of the trees had been felled; most of these felled trees were sapling size (Cole 1982).

Perhaps the most serious consequence of this type of impact is its long-term effect on maintenance of forested campsites. Removal of saplings from the immediate

vicinity of campsites is reducing the source of new trees to replace the current overstory when it eventually succumbs to old age. Tree reproduction is almost nil as a
result of trampling. Removal of the few stems that do make it into the sapling size
class forecasts the eventual conversion of forested sites into open vegetation types.
Because campers have been shown to prefer the shading and privacy provided by
both shrubs and trees (Cordell and James 1972), this is a highly undesirable change.

Mature Trees

The major impacts to mature trees on recreation sites result from mechanical damage.
Much is caused consciously, if thoughtlessly, by visitors through a diverse set of acts
that include removing limbs, driving nails into trunks, hacking trees with axes, peel-
ing bark to use as kindling, and felling trees for tent poles or firewood. Other impacts
are caused unconsciously; for example, trees are scarred by lanterns, and roots are
exposed when stock are tied to trees. Finally, considerable impact to trees is caused
by management. Examples include clearing trees along trails and in campsites and
removing hazard trees in danger of falling on people.

   In an intensive survey of tree damage on campsites in the Eagle Cap Wilderness, Cole
(1982) found that more than 90 percent of the mature trees had been scarred, felled, or
had cut or broken branches (Fig. 6). Damage to many of the trees was relatively minor—
lower branches had been broken or nails had been driven into trunks. Twenty-seven percent of these trees, however, bore trunk scars from chopping. Of these scars 22 percent
were larger than 1 ft², and 67 percent were located below breast height, conditions under

FIGURE 6. Tree damage on a campsite in the Eagle Cap Wilderness, Oregon. (*Photo*: D. N. Cole.)

which the probability of decay is particularly high for these spruce and fir species. Another 33 percent of the trees on the campsites had been cut down.

Despite this level of damage to overstory trees, there was little evidence of recreation-related tree mortality or even loss of vigor, except where trees had been felled outright. The fact that more than six decades of recreational use have had little noticeable effect suggests that premature mortality of the overstory may not be a serious problem. Most other studies have also found little evidence of recreation-caused tree mortality. Recreation-caused loss of vigor and death occur most commonly where soils are thin and/or droughty or where trees are thin-barked and particularly susceptible to decay. Mortality of trembling aspen, a widespread thin-barked tree, was studied on 17 developed campgrounds in the Rocky Mountains. The trees were dying at a rate of about 4 percent per year, mostly as a result of canker diseases following mechanical injuries caused by campers (Hinds 1976).

Another place where tree mortality has been a serious problem is the Boundary Waters Canoe Area Wilderness. Merriam and Peterson have followed change over time on a small number of campsites established by the Forest Service in 1967. Just five years after use began, the average percentage of original trees that had died was 15 percent; after 14 years 40 percent of the trees had died (Merriam and Peterson 1983). Aspen and birch dominate a number of these sites; their thin bark and the tendency for campers to peel off bark for kindling make them particularly susceptible to damage. Thin soils and pronounced erosion are also characteristic of these canoe-camping sites. It is not uncommon for almost all of the soil to be removed from surface tree roots. Once this occurs, death may follow.

Exposure of tree roots is a common occurrence on trails, river and lake banks, and campsites. Of 19 campsites with trees in Cole's Eagle Cap survey, 17 had trees with exposed roots. On a typical campsite about one-third of the trees had exposed roots. In the Boundary Waters, 84 percent of the trees on campsites surveyed by Marion (1984) had exposed roots. Once exposed, roots can suffer mechanical damage. Root exposure also makes trees more prone to wind throw.

Because trees are longer-living forms of vegetation, managers and researchers have been interested in the temporal and spatial variation of long-term impacts to trees (see Chapter 7). Long-term studies indicate that spatial impacts (i.e., site expansion) are more important than temporal impacts to trees. Also of concern is the amount of seedling establishment over time on concentrated use sites. In the Delaware Water Gap National Recreational Area, the mean density of trees shorter than 140 cm on campsites (size classes considered indicative of tree reproduction) was only 9 percent of the density of control sites (Marion and Cole 1996, p. 524). In addition, 19 percent of the overstory trees on campsites had been felled and 77 percent of standing trees had been damaged.

In areas that receive large amounts of overnight stock use, tree damage can be especially pronounced. Most of this additional damage reflects the common practice of tying stock to trees. When tied in this way, most animals will paw up the ground, causing erosion and exposure of tree roots. Rope burns on the tree trunks leave scars, and on small trees can girdle and kill the tree. In addition, parties that travel with stock are more likely to carry heavy canvas tents that require felled trees for tent

TABLE 1. Tree Damage on Campsites Used Primarily by Backpackers, Private Horse Parties, or Outfitted Parties[a]

Type of Use	Seedling Loss		Damaged Trees		Felled Trees		Trees with Exposed Roots	
	Median	Range	Median	Range	Median	Range	Median	Range
	Percent		Number of Trees in Disturbed Area					
Backpacker	100	100 a	5	3–29 a	0	0–8 a	1	0–4 a
Horse	100	92–100 a	56	21–180 b	8	0–33 b	25	10–38 b
Outfitter	100	100 a	100	23–500 b	15	3–250 b	37	13–100 b

[a]Any two sets of median and range values followed by the same letter are not significantly different at the 95 percent confidence level, using the randomization test for two independent samples. Seedling loss is relative change.

poles. They are also more likely to carry axes and saws capable of felling trees for firewood. Not every stock party causes these avoidable types of impact, but enough do for tree damage in horse camps to be particularly pronounced.

To illustrate this difference, Cole (1983) compared the number of damaged trees on backpacker, horse, and outfitter campsites in the Bob Marshall Wilderness, Montana (Table 1). Backpacker sites were used only by backpackers; horse sites were used primarily by private horse parties, usually for only a few nights at a time; outfitter camps were sites occupied by outfitted parties for long periods of time, particularly during the fall hunting season. Seedling loss is the same—100 percent—on all three classes of sites; this damage is the inevitable result of trampling and does not vary with type of use. In contrast, there are large differences in damage to mature trees between the three types of sites. This damage is avoidable and related to the type of use occurring on the site.

Likewise, mechanical damage on developed sites can be much more common and serious than that on backcountry sites. Common types of damage on such sites include lantern scars and nails driven into trees to hang objects. In most older national forest and national park campgrounds, mature trees close to tables have numerous scars from gas lanterns. These scars, caused by heating, can weaken trees, particularly if the trees are thin-barked. Once weakening occurs, trees are more prone to breakage and, as hazard trees, must be removed by management. In recent years metal lantern holders have been erected on most sites to avoid this problem. The fact that people tend to stay much longer at developed sites accessible by road and can carry much more equipment provides more opportunity for damage; mature trees bear much of the brunt of this damage.

SUMMARY

1. Trampling affects vegetation both directly and indirectly. These interrelationships are diagrammatically presented in Fig. 7. Breakage and bruising reduce plant vigor and reproductive capacity; severe trampling kills plants directly. Plant vigor

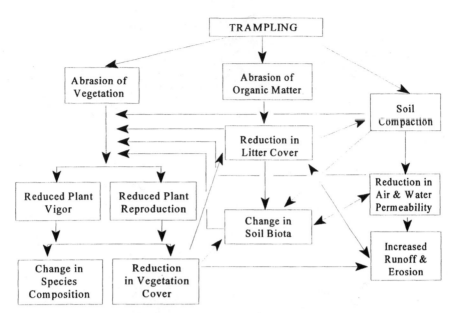

FIGURE 7. A conceptual model of trampling effects, partly based on Liddle (1975) and Manning (1979). Note the numerous reciprocal and cyclic relationships between soil and vegetational impacts.

and reproductive capacity are also reduced as a result of the soil changes described in Chapter 2. Shrubs and saplings are removed to expand the campsite, clear the trail, or collect firewood. Mature trees are mechanically damaged by a variety of actions, conscious and unconscious, taken by both visitors and managers.

2. Of these impacts, the most serious is probably lack of tree regeneration. Even in the many situations where premature mortality is not a problem, the existing overstory will eventually die. On most campsites, however, there is no regeneration to replace these trees when they die. Most seedlings are killed by being trampled, and the ones that do survive are cut down in the sapling stage for firewood or poles. Finding a way to allow trees to grow into the large-sized classes is one of the major challenges to management of campsites.

3. Vegetation impacts occur rapidly during the initial development and use of recreation sites. Most impacts also reach near-maximum levels of impact even on relatively lightly used sites. This reflects the ground cover vegetation's low level of resistance to trampling damage. Damage to mature trees also occurs rapidly with only light use. However, amount of tree damage is strongly influenced by the type of use that occurs on the site. Stock use, for example, tends to cause more damage than use by parties without stock.

4. Susceptibility to damage also varies greatly between different environments. In this chapter we discussed vegetative characteristics that make a plant resistant to trampling impact. We also discussed how damage to mature trees is more pronounced

for thin-barked trees. Damage also is greater where soils are thin and are prone to erosion and/or drought. A more complete discussion of environmental durability will be provided in Chapter 8.

REFERENCES

Bayfield, N. G. 1979. Recovery of Four Montane Heath Communities on Cairngorm, Scotland, from Disturbance by Trampling. *Biological Conservation* 15:165–179.

Boucher, D. H., J. Aviles, R. Chepote, O. E. Dominguez Gil, and B. Vilchez. 1991. Recovery of Trailside Vegetation from Trampling in a Tropical Rain Forest. *Environmental Management* 15(2):257–262.

Brown, J. H., Jr., S. P. Kalisz, and W. R. Wright. 1977. Effects of Recreational Use on Forested Sites. *Environmental Geology* 1:425–431.

Cole, D. N. 1978. Estimating the Susceptibility of Wildland Vegetation to Trailside Alteration. *Journal of Applied Ecology* 15:281–286.

Cole, D. N. 1981. Vegetational Changes Associated with Recreation Use and Fire Suppression in the Eagle Cap Wilderness, Oregon: Some Management Implications. *Biological Conservation* 20:247–270.

Cole, D. N. 1982. Wilderness Campsite Impacts: Effect of Amount of Use. USDA Forest Service Research Paper INT-288.

Cole, D. N. 1983. Campsite Conditions in the Bob Marshall Wilderness, Montana. USDA Forest Service Research Paper INT-312.

Cole, D. N. 1985. Recreational Trampling Effects on Six Habitat Types in Western Montana. USDA Forest Service Research Paper INT-350. 43 pp.

Cole, D. N. 1987. Research on Soil and Vegetation in Wilderness: A State-of-Knowledge Review. In R. C. Lucas, comp. *Proceedings of the National Wilderness Research Conference: Issues, State-of-Knowledge, and Future Directions*. USDA Forest Service Intermountain Research Station, General Technical Report INT-220, pp. 135–177.

Cole, D. N. 1995a. Experimental Trampling of Vegetation. II. Predictors of Resistance and Resilience. *Journal of Applied Ecology* 32:215–224.

Cole, D. N. 1995b. Experimental Trampling of Vegetation. I. Relationship Between Trampling Intensity and Vegetation Response. *Journal of Applied Ecology* 32:203–214.

Cole, D. N., and R. K. Fichtler. 1983. Campsite Impact in Three Western Wilderness Areas. *Environmental Management* 7:275–286.

Cordell, H. K., and G. A. James. 1972. Visitor's Preferences for Certain Physical Characteristics of Developed Campsites. USDA Forest Service Research Paper SE-100.

DeBenedetti, S. H., and D. J. Parsons. 1983. Protecting Mountain Meadows: A Grazing Management Plan. *Parks* 8(3): 11–13.

Frissell, S. S., Jr., and D. P. Duncan. 1965. Campsite Preference and Deterioration in the Quetico-Superior Canoe Country. *Journal of Forestry* 65:256–260.

Harper, J. L., J. T. Williams, and G. R. Sagar. 1965. The Behavior of Seeds in Soil. I. The Heterogeneity of Soil Surfaces and Its Role in Determining the Establishment of Plants from Seed. *Journal of Ecology* 53:273–286.

Hartley, E. A. 1976. Man's Effects on the Stability of Alpine and Subalpine Vegetation in Glacier National Park, Montana. Ph.D. dissertation. Duke University, Durham, NC.

Hinds, T. E. 1976. Aspen Mortality in Rocky Mountain Campgrounds. USDA Forest Service Research Paper RM-164.

LaPage, W. F. 1967. Some Observations on Campground Trampling and Groundcover Response. USDA Forest Service Research Paper NE-68.

Leung, Y., and J. L. Marion. 1996. Trail Degradation as Influenced by Environmental Factors: A State-of-Knowledge Review. *Journal of Soil and Water Conservation* 51(2):130–136.

Liddle, M. J. 1975. A Selective Review of the Ecological Effects of Human Trampling on Natural Ecosystems. *Biological Conservation* 7:17–36.

Liddle, M. J. 1991. Recreation Ecology: Effects of Trampling on Plants and Coral. *Trends in Ecology and Evolution* 6:13–17.

Luckenbach, R. A., and R. B. Bury. 1983. Effects of Off-road Vehicles on the Biota of the Algodones Dunes, Imperial County, California. *Journal of Applied Ecology* 20:265–286.

Magill, A. W., and E. C. Nord. 1963. An Evaluation of Campground Conditions and Needs for Research. USDA Forest Service Research Note PSW-4.

Manning, R. E. 1979. Impacts of Recreation on Riparian Soils and Vegetation. *Water Resources Bulletin* 15:30–43.

Marion, J. L. 1984. Ecological Changes Resulting from Recreational Use: A Study of Backcountry Campsites in the Boundary Waters Canoe Area, Minnesota. Ph.D. dissertation, University of Minnesota, St. Paul.

Marion, J. L. 1991. Developing a Natural Resource Inventory and Monitoring Program for Visitor Impacts on Recreation Sites: A Procedural Manual. USDI National Park Service, National Resource Report NPA/NRVT/NRR-91/06. 59 pp.

Marion, J. L., and D. N. Cole. 1996. Spatial and Temporal Variation in Soil and Vegetation Impacts on Campsites. *Ecological Applications* 6(2):520–530.

McEwen, D., and S. R. Tocher. 1976. Zone Management: Key to Controlling Recreational Impact in Developed Campsites. *Journal of Forestry* 74:90–93.

Merriam, L. C., and R. F. Peterson. 1983. Impact of 15 Years of Use on Some Campsites in the Boundary Waters Canoe Area. Minnesota Forest Research Note 282, University of Minnesota, St. Paul.

Mueller-Dombois, D., and H. Ellenberg. 1974. *Aims and Methods of Vegetation Ecology.* New York: Wiley.

Speight, M. C. D. 1973. Outdoor Recreation and Its Ecological Effects: A Bibliography and Review. Discussion Paper in Conservation 4, University College, London. 35 pp.

Sun, D. 1992. Trampling Resistance, Recovery, and Growth Rate of Eight Plant Species. *Agriculture, Ecosystems, and Environment* 38:265–273.

Sun, D., and M. J. Liddle. 1991. Field Occurrence, Recovery, and Simulated Trampling Resistance and Recovery of Two Grasses. *Biological Conservation* 57:187–203.

Sun, D., and M. J. Liddle. 1993. A Survey of Trampling Effects on Vegetation and Soil in Eight Tropical and Subtropical Sites. *Environmental Management* 17(4):497–510.

Wanek, W. J. 1974. A Continuing Study of the Ecological Impact of Snowmobiling in Northern Minnesota. Final Research Report for 1973–1974. Center for Environmental Studies, Bemidji State College, Bemidji, MN. 54 pp.

4 Wildlife

The effects of wildland recreation on wildlife have received little systematic attention, resulting in a knowledge base that is disparate and seldom definitive. This is because wildlife species are not stationary, as are plants, and the effects of impacts are not immediately obvious, direct, or easily measured. Nevertheless, numerous impacts to wildlife as a result of recreation have been documented, and in some cases well researched (Ream 1980; Boyle and Samson 1985; Knight and Gutzwiller 1995). Boyle and Samson, for example, reviewed 166 articles that contained original data on the effects of nonconsumptive outdoor recreation on wildlife. These studies show that human disturbances result in changes in wildlife physiology, behavior, reproduction, population levels, and species composition and diversity. Studies also show that there are at least six factors of recreational disturbances that influence wildlife responses: type of recreational activity, recreationists' behavior, impact predictability, impact frequency and magnitude, timing, and location (Knight and Cole 1995). In many cases the major source of wildlife impacts is the recreationist who innocently produces stressful situations for wildlife, primarily through unintentional harassment of wild animals. However, some wildlife are attracted to recreationists and alter their behavior in response to the presence of humans. Panhandler black bears and chipmunks in campgrounds that seek out human foods are typical examples. This chapter reviews the major types of ecological disturbances caused by recreationists-wildlife interactions and the major impacts on some species of animals where management problems are most evident.

RECREATION INFLUENCES ON WILDLIFE RESPONSES

There are many recreation-related factors that influence the responses of wildlife when disturbed. It is important to have an introduction to and understanding of these major factors before advancing to specific types of recreation-wildlife impacts and the animals affected.

As mentioned earlier, Knight and Cole (1995) recognize six factors of recreational disturbances that influence wildlife responses. The first of these is *type of activity*. There are many types of recreational activities, each differing in activity style, equipment used, habitat occupied, and animal interactions (see Chapter 4 in Knight and Gutzwiller 1995 for a discussion of individual activities). Motorized types of activities—with their speed, area covered, and noise—certainly have different influences on wildlife response than nonmotorized activities. Noise associated with aircraft, boats, and all-terrain vehicles is a factor of great concern in managing wildlife impacts (Bowles 1995).

The *behavior of recreationists* when carrying out recreational activities and interacting with wildlife can have a profound influence on wildlife responses. A person's rapid movement directly toward wildlife frightens them, whereas movement away from or at an oblique angle to them, and at a slower speed, has less influence. *Predictability* of events and of recreationists' behavior is also an important factor affecting wildlife response. "When animals perceive a disturbance as frequent enough to be expected and nonthreatening, they show little overt response" (Knight and Cole 1995, p. 72). On the other hand, animals react quite differently when they perceive disturbance as predictable and threatening. Birds are particularly sensitive in this respect.

The *frequency and magnitude* of disturbance influences the reactions of wildlife. A number of studies have shown that the nesting behavior and reproductive success of birds are negatively influenced when nesting areas are frequently visited. However, thresholds of disturbance frequencies above which critical levels of impacts to wildlife may occur are poorly understood. For example, number of hunters afield, hours of hunting per unit area, hiker intensity on trails, and road traffic loads are known to influence animal movement, feeding habits, and habitat occupation, but few threshold levels have been identified for these factors.

Timing and *location* factors involve the season of year and the space in which wildlife are disturbed. The breeding season for animals is a critical time, when recreation disturbance may be most detrimental. Wildlife may respond during the breeding season by abandoning nests or young, which can lead to total reproduction failure. Recreational activity can also alter parental attentiveness, thus increasing the risk of the young being preyed upon, disrupting feeding patterns, or exposing the young to adverse environmental stress. As indicated in the case studies in Knight and Gutzwiller's book (1995), bird studies dominate research in this area. Recreational disturbance outside the breeding season can also be quite influential, particularly in ways that potentially reduce energy acquisition (i.e., foraging) or increase energy expenditure (i.e., fleeing). Closely related to breeding season disturbances are nest and den location impacts. Disturbance that occurs in feeding and watering locations is also an important factor influencing animal response. Moreover, research has shown that many animals perceive activities that occur above them to be a greater threat to their safety and ability to escape than activities below. Bighorn sheep, peregrine falcons, and some other wildlife are particularly sensitive when approached from above.

In addition to the aforementioned six factors that influence wildlife response to disturbance, there are also certain characteristics of wildlife that shape their responses to disturbance. Just as the type of recreational activity can be important, so is the *type of animal* important. "Animals with different life-history traits and evolutionary strategies (e.g., longevity, parental care, reproductive effort) vary in their reactions to recreational disturbance" (Knight and Cole 1995, p. 74). Species with specialized food and shelter requirements and other limiting factors are more vulnerable to disturbance than are species with more generalized requirements. *Group size* also influences disturbance response. In general, animals in groups respond to approaching threats at greater distances and are less sensitive to disturbances than solitary individuals. The *age* and *sex* composition of groups also influences their response. Females with young are more likely to flee when disturbed than groups without young. For example, Singer and Beattie (1986) found that cow and calf groups of caribou in Alaska were more likely to react than all cow groups, and bull groups were least likely to flee.

HUMAN-WILDLIFE INTERACTIONS

The response of wildlife to recreational disturbance is complex, being neither uniform nor consistent. Different species of wildlife have different tolerances for interactions with humans. Although some species may be completely displaced from an area of concentrated recreational use, other species have actually increased in abundance. In general, species less tolerant of recreational disturbance will be replaced by those better adapted to the new environmental conditions (Kuss, Graefe, and Vaske 1984).

Even within a species, tolerance levels for interactions will vary by time of year, breeding season, animal age, habitat type, and individual animal experience with recreationists. Recreationists may produce critical situations at certain times and places but have no effect on the same species or individuals under other conditions. Seasonal and spatial effects appear to be strongly tied to habitat requirements and utilization (Anderson 1995). For example, if a species is already under physiological stress from limited food and other environmental factors, interactions with humans may be especially serious.

The relationship between amount of recreational use and wildlife impacts is not well understood. Very few studies have systematically examined the effects of varying numbers of visitors on wildlife. Even fewer wildlife studies have determined an accurate population count of organisms prior to the introduction of recreation. There is also a lack of studies that have systematically controlled for environmental and population dynamic influences during recreation use and impact studies. Thus, it has been difficult to document a uniform relationship between amount of recreational use and wildlife impacts. In fact, there may be no *uniform* relationship. Previous research indicates the complexity of the relationship by stating that the number of visitors cannot be considered in isolation from species requirements and habits, population dynamics, setting attributes, and type of recreational use. Various aspects of use intensity are also involved, including frequency and regularity of use and number of people at one time (Speight 1973; Knight and Gutzwiller 1995). There is evidence that the effects of human-wildlife interactions depend more on the frequency of human presence than on the amount of total recreational use or on the number of people present at any one time.

Although human-wildlife interactions are too complex to classify, an attempt to generalize about the form of impacts may be useful. The influence of wildland recreation on wildlife occurs in the forms of *direct* and *indirect* impacts. Direct impacts include the effects on animals caused by primary disturbances and interactions with humans. Indirect impacts are the secondary results of disturbances to habitat and other environmental parameters as a result of recreational use of natural environments. Although indirect impacts of human-wildlife interactions are secondary in nature, they are far more prevalent in affecting most wildlife (Speight 1973; Cole and Landres 1995). Cole and Landres (1995, p. 193) state that "indirect impacts differ from direct impacts in two ways: (1) indirect impacts are inevitable, occurring wherever and whenever recreational use occurs; and (2) they generally occur over long periods of time, with effects that are long-lasting and that may take place only after a time lag." According to Kuss, Graefe, and Vaske (1984), "Larger game species tend to be affected more by direct contact with people while smaller forms of wildlife appear to be more susceptible to indirect impact on habitat."

Recreational impacts on wildlife may also be classified as *selective* versus *nonselective*. Selective impacts are associated with recreational activities that focus on certain wildlife species. For example, nature study and collecting as well as hunting and fishing are often restricted to a limited number of species and, in some cases, unique or rare species. Nonselective impacts result from coincidental interactions by visitors of whatever wildlife they confront. Hiking, camping, and picnicking are activities that typically lead to nonselective impacts.

As with any attempt to generalize or classify complex phenomena, obvious overlap and interrelatedness exist among parameters. Hunting has been studied more than any other human-wildlife interaction and demonstrates well the difficulty of classifying impacts. Although hunting would at first appear to be a form of direct, selective impact, it also results in indirect and nonselective forms of disturbance. Habitat manipulation for certain game species can have detrimental effects on nongame species. Introduction of exotic species for hunting purposes also has indirect impacts on native species. Regulated hunting of animals is considered to be very selective, resulting in the management of specific wildlife populations on a sustained basis. However, even here the impacts are not as selective as one might wish. Speight (1973) reports a study in which 30 percent of wildfowlers could not distinguish game species from rare, protected species. Salo (in Wall and Wright 1977) found that wounding rates in hunting appear to range between 24 and 30 percent. The point is best summarized, although exaggerated, by a chief naturalist at Yellowstone National Park who stated, "In order to get 5000 elk shot by hunters, it would be necessary to accept that in addition 196 moose, 17 men, and an undetermined number of bears, coyotes, bighorn sheep, antelope, bison, mule deer, and horses would be shot by mistake" (Fraser and Eichhorn 1969).

Obviously, the many parameters related to human-wildlife interactions are complex. Nevertheless, understanding these parameters is essential if recreational impacts on wildlife are to be managed.

RECREATION-WILDLIFE IMPACTS

The intrusion of humans into wildlife habitats during recreational activities can cause various types and levels of change in both animals and their habitat. These changes are not entirely detrimental to animals; although many animals are repelled by the presence of humans, others are attracted. Neither are all the changes a direct result of contact with humans; some are indirect. Figure 1 presents a conceptual framework of the major impacts associated with recreational activity in wildlife areas. Alternative frameworks are offered by Pomerantz, Decker, Goff, and Purdy (1988); Kuss, Graefe, and Vaske (1990); and Knight and Cole (1995).

When recreational activity occurs in wildlife habitats, two forms of interaction can occur. The recreationists may interact with the animals directly or indirectly through altering the habitat. Direct interaction with wildlife results in two major types of impact: various levels of disturbance and harassment and the actual killing of animals. These two impacts, along with habitat modification, can lead to three responses by wildlife. First, the normal behavior of animals may be altered to various degrees, all the way from habituation to slight modifications to migration from impacted sites. Second, animals may be displaced completely to a new habitat or, in the case of sport hunting, displaced from the population. Third, all three impacts can cause a reduction in the reproductive level of many species. Ultimately, these impacts result in a change in the species composition and structure of wildlife populations. The major impacts presented in Fig. 1 will now be briefly discussed.

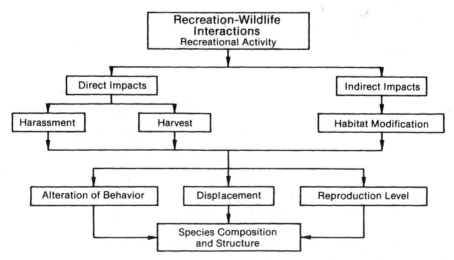

FIGURE 1. Major impacts of recreation-wildlife interactions. (*Source*: Adapted from Wall and Wright 1977.)

Animal Disturbance and Harassment

O'Shea (1995) cites the following Endangered Species Act definition of wildlife harassment: "An intentional or negligent act or omission which creates the likelihood of injury to wildlife by annoying it to such an extent as to significantly disrupt normal behavior patterns which include, but are not limited to, feeding or sheltering." Although intentional harassment of wildlife does occur, the major impact is caused by recreationists who unknowingly and innocently produce stressful situations for wildlife (Fig. 2). The effects of photographers and bird-watchers who seek out the nesting areas of secluded species, backcountry campers who camp within critical watering and feeding habitats of large mammals, and off-road vehicle users who seek a closer look are but a few examples of unintentional forms of wildlife harassment. Of course, the chasing of winter-stressed wildlife by snowmobiles and certain forms of hunting are some extremes of intentional harassment. Harassment is such a common phenomenon in human-wildlife interactions that it has led some authors to state that there is no such thing as "nonconsumptive" use of activities concerning wildlife (Weeden 1976; Wilkes 1977). Wilkes rejects completely the concept that certain passive outdoor recreational activities are nonconsumptive and points out several impacts on wildlife by naturalists, photographers, and hikers. Wilkes even suggests the need for a skills test to be associated with the licensing of wildland recreationists because of the damage caused to wildlife resources by uninformed, unskilled people.

FIGURE 2. Recreationists unknowingly and innocently often produce stressful situations for wildlife. (*Photo*: Bruce C. Hastings.)

Many factors influence the effects or severity of harassment on animals. "Well-fed, healthy animals with ample refuges from disturbance can withstand more harassment than wildlife already under stress from severe weather, malnutrition, parasite loads, birth or nesting, or inadequate security areas" (Ream 1979, p. 153). Geist (1972, 1975) emphasizes the importance of physiological and psychological stresses to various wildlife, particularly bighorn sheep, and how stresses can compound the impacts of harassment. Although some species seem to habituate to the presence of humans, others are very stress-prone in regard to humans. The location of human-wildlife interactions is also a critical factor. The presence of people at key locations such as wolf dens, desert bighorn waterholes, snowfields used by caribou to escape heat and insects, ungulate migration routes, and salt licks may present major impacts (Ream 1979). Locational harassment impacts can be managed simply by protecting key areas from roads and trails, by locating campsites in appropriate areas, and by seasonally closing critical breeding habitats. Ream (1980, p. 7) suggests, "The primary targets of management should be critical times of the year and key locations of wildlife species vulnerable to harassment. Time and effort spent in alleviating harassment in other situations are wasted if habitat loss and wildlife mortality continue to occur at critical times and places."

The mere presence of people has been shown to be sufficient to cause harassment to some species whatever the recreational activity or number of people involved. Shore-nesting birds during the breeding season seem particularly susceptible to the presence of humans. The presence of even a few people inhibited the little tern (*Sterna albifrons*) in Great Britain from returning to its nest (Norman and Saunders, in Speight 1973). A survey of the breeding status of the species revealed a number of instances of breeding failure, apparently related to fishermen and sunbathers on the nesting beaches. Similar results have been reported for the ringed plover (*Charadrius hiaticula*). The red deer (*Cervis elephas*) of Europe and the bighorn sheep (*Ovis canadensis*) of the United States have also been observed to be sensitive to the presence of people. The situation may be more aggravated if people are wearing bright-colored clothing (Speight 1973).

The documentation of animal movement and behavior, including that related to human-caused disturbances, has been greatly aided by radio telemetry studies. Telemetry has commonly been used to determine location and movement of radioed animals. It is now possible to distinguish feeding, resting or rumination, and walking activity in elk (Ward, Cupal, Lea, Oakley, and Weeks 1973). Johnson and Pelton (1979) have used telemetry to study the denning behavior of the black bear in Great Smoky Mountains National Park. Black bears have been shown to enter winter dens 31 days earlier in areas with high levels of outdoor recreation; moreover, the bears were more likely to abandon dens when disturbed (Goodrich and Berger, in Knight and Cole 1995). Heart-rate telemetry is also used to determine the reaction of big game to disturbance by vehicles, recreationists, livestock, and other wildlife (Ward 1977). Future use of telemetry will allow scientists to measure alarm or harassment through increased heart rate of running animals as well as in animals in which the flight reaction is inhibited. It can also be used to estimate energy expenditures and time required to recover from exertion, and to facilitate testing of methods to mitigate fear and stress (Ream 1979).

Harvest

Although harassment may produce a considerable amount of stress on wildlife and may even lead to the death of individual animals, such stress is second to that produced by recreational hunting, fishing, and trapping. Entire populations of wildlife in heavily hunted and fished areas are influenced by these recreational activities (Small, Holzwart, and Rusch 1991). In addition, certain types of hunting with dogs and particular types of trapping may lead to additional stress beyond that caused by the normal processes of harvesting wildlife. Martinka (1979) stated that many wild animals display the ability to differentiate various human activities and react more intensively to those perceived as threats to their life, based on past experience. Comparative studies of hunted versus nonhunted animals show that hunted wildlife are especially sensitive to humans during hunting seasons and tend to retreat from most forms of recreational activity at these times (Wood 1993).

Knight and Cole (1995) review additional responses of wildlife to hunting. The reproduction behavior of elk in Colorado appears to have been influenced by heavy hunting pressure. The conception dates of female elk showed a bimodal distribution, coinciding with hunting season dates. Other studies show that hunted animals often feed at night, returning to diurnal feeding only after hunting ceases. The spatial and temporal patterns of waterfowl are particularly sensitive to hunting. Hunted geese were six times more prevalent in a field on a day when shooting had not occurred during the previous afternoon.

History has documented the elimination or near elimination of many game species, including the passenger pigeon, beaver, bison, and other big game species. However, it was market and subsistence hunting in the context of reduced and fragmented habitat rather than recreational hunting that primarily led to the removal of these species. Recreational hunting, fishing, and trapping may eliminate a species on a local basis, but it is unlikely that these activities alone could directly result in the extinction of wildlife species.

Recreational activities directly associated with the harvesting of animals can lead to three major changes in the size of wildlife populations that, in turn, affect the quality of these recreational activities. These changes are (1) near elimination of a game species on a local level, (2) reduction beyond a viable breeding population, and (3) reduction beyond a viable hunting or fishing population. In the first instance, heavy hunting and fishing pressures on local populations of wildlife can locally extirpate certain species. The strong tradition of raccoon hunting and year-round training of raccoon dogs in the southern Appalachian Mountains of East Tennessee has caused the near extirpation of this animal in several counties. Similarly, the traditional hunting of black bear in the southern Appalachians has eliminated the species from many local areas. Second, harvesting of wildlife may not extirpate a population, but it may reduce the number or sex ratio of individuals to such low numbers that the population can no longer breed successfully. Again, habitat loss is typically involved with harvest when this occurs. Finally, a population may have sufficient numbers to maintain a viable breeding unit but lack an adequate surplus to provide a rewarding harvest yield to the majority of hunters and fishermen. Of course, wildlife management agencies have the ability to regulate and manage all three of these situations.

Habitat Modification

For every animal species affected directly by wildland recreational activities, many more must be affected indirectly by modification of habitat (Cole and Landres 1995). Habitat change can affect the behavior, distribution, survivorship, and reproductive ability of individual wildlife. Impacts also occur at the population, community, and ecosystem levels over long time periods. Habitat modification is the primary impact of humans on insect, amphibian, reptile, bird, and small mammal populations. Soil organisms have been shown to decrease by up to a hundredfold in compacted soils and under snowmobile trails. Mice, voles, and shrews depend on the insulating properties of snow, which are lost when snow is compacted by snowmobiling and other winter recreational activities (Stace-Smith 1975). Tunnels and burrows of certain species are collapsed by off-road vehicles, particularly on beach dunes and desert lands (Bury, Wendling, and McCool 1976). Over a 10-year study of off-road vehicle impacts at Dove Springs within the California Desert, Berry (1973) documented loss of the desert tortoise, a protected and threatened species, and a reduction in both the density and diversity of small mammals and lizard populations. Not only do the tires of dune buggies cause physical damage to animals through the collapse of animal burrows, but they also eliminate their means of escape from extreme desert temperatures and desiccation.

In campgrounds, removal of shrubs and hazardous trees eliminates sources of food and shelter for birds and small mammals (Webb 1968). Blakesley and Reese (1988) report that seven bird species were associated with campgrounds while a different seven species were common to non-campgrounds. In improving or creating aquatic recreational sites, the removal of large quantities of shallow-water vegetation is responsible for loss of spawning grounds for freshwater fish. Sedimentation, pollution, and eutrophication of lakes by recreational homes and activities that modify the habitat of many species are common in many recreational areas.

Although recreational activities cause primarily a negative impact on wildlife habitat, there are several examples of habitat gain as a result of wildland recreation. Speight (1973) summarized these, including (1) the increased availability of nesting sites for mallards and wood ducks and over-wintering sites for species that use open water lakes and reservoirs developed for recreation, (2) increased food source as a result of organic litter left around campsites and picnic areas and the planned food plots of wildlife management agencies, (3) habitat changes and population localization of bear and wild boar as a result of campground rubbish dumpsites, and (4) creation of habitat for ecotone species as a result of trail, campsite, and pond development.

From his review of the literature, Speight (1973, p. 19) summarized the effects of recreation on habitat modification as follows:

> Increasing intensities of recreation use would seem to exert their most profound effects on microhabitats, by causing a progressive simplification of vegetation, ground surface, and soil structure. Invertebrate species particularly associated with soil or ground flora are in consequence perhaps more likely to be affected by trampling than vertebrates. In any event, the evidence suggests that a net decrease in animal species-diversity can be expected when an area is exposed to outdoor recreation, in parallel with any decrease in plant species-diversity that occurs, but offset to some extent by an influx of scavenging species. Species associated with ephemeral habitats such as bare ground might be expected to maintain their numbers or even increase in abundance at the expense of species associated with more stable ecosystem conditions like woodland.

Alteration of Behavior

The behavior of wild animals is often drastically altered by the frequent presence of humans. The behavioral changes can range from complete disappearance to slight modifications in habitat and daily use patterns to the habituation and taming of animals.

Habituation of wildlife in recreation areas is most often associated with food availability. Garbage dumps and litter at campsites have attracted bears, deer, birds, rodents, and insects, altering the natural feeding habits of these animals (Fig. 3). Skunks,

FIGURE 3. The natural feeding habits of animals are commonly altered by the availability of human food sources. (*Photo*: Jane Tate.)

chipmunks, and mice have become so dependent on human food sources at back-country shelters and front country campsites that they are a nuisance in many U.S. national parks. The number of birds in Yosemite National Park, California was actually increased by the presence of campgrounds (Foin, Garton, Bowen, Everingham, Schultz, and Holton 1977). However, most of the increase was attributed to an abundance of a few species, especially Brewer's blackbird (*Euphagas cyanocephalus*) and the mountain chickadee (*Parus gambeli*). Clark's nutcracker (*Nucifraga columbiana*) and various species of jays have demonstrated a similar attraction to campsites and trails. At the same time, most other species decline in campgrounds.

Several other species have been shown to alter their behavior in response to recreational activities. Eagles and waterfowl have been documented as not returning to feeding sites until several hours after human disturbance (Anthony, Steidl, and McGarigal 1995), and large mammals have had their movement and feeding patterns modified by park traffic and roads. Singer, Otto, Tipton, and Hable (1981) found that average daily movement was greater for disturbed wild boars in Great Smoky Mountains National Park than for those with no disturbance. In another study Singer (1978) documented five possible responses of mountain goats to disturbances associated with highway crossings in Glacier National Park: (1) unsuccessful crossing attempts, (2) separation of nannies from kids, (3) alterations of crossing routes, (4) apparent alteration of crossing times, and (5) alteration of normal behavior and posture of goats. In Yellowstone National Park, when cross-country skiers approached within 400 m, elk moved an average of 1765 m to steep slopes nearer trees and often into another drainage area (Cassirer et al., in Knight and Cole 1995).

Species Displacement and Reproduction Level

Species displacement results in an animal being removed from a familiar environment and placed in a new habitat. Often, the replacement environment is of poorer quality or has more competing elements than the original area. Because of these factors, displacement is a more drastic change for wildlife than recreational harassment and habitat modification. The latter two impacts do not require that the animal move from a familiar environment. This may be a particular advantage in breeding success, inasmuch as familiar habitat and territory play a key role in wildlife reproduction. Although reproduction levels of wildlife are affected by most recreation-caused impacts, species displacement is likely to have the most drastic effects.

Species of wildlife that are secretive and sensitive to the presence of humans may become permanently displaced from recreational areas. Bighorn sheep and mountain goats have been forced into smaller areas and poorer, more remote ranges because of human encroachment. In Colorado bighorn sheep were forced into higher elevation ranges during lambing season, thus encountering weather conditions that caused an 80 percent incidence of pneumonia and a resultant decline in population (Woodward, Gutierrez, and Rutherford 1974). Batcheler (1968) found that red deer, when hunted and harassed in areas of good habitat, were displaced to poor habitat and did not return to the good habitat even after prolonged cessation of hunting and harassment.

In addition, deer displaced to the poorer habitat became nocturnal and experienced reduced reproductive rates and lower fat deposition.

Hunting and fishing have led to species reduction and displacement. Species eliminated locally by hunting and shooting tend to be predators at the end of food chains. Elimination or displacement of predators has an indirect effect on the population levels of other food chain members. In addition, the management of fish and game animals has resulted in some displacement impacts. In Great Smoky Mountains National Park, rainbow trout (*Salmo gairdnerii*), introduced in the early 1900s by loggers, have now out-competed the native brook trout (*Salvelinus fontinalis*) in many of the streams. Several other introductions of exotic species for recreational purposes have displaced original species, including native flora as well as native animals.

Hobby collecting of rare butterflies is the most important single factor contributing to the decline of two species of butterflies in Great Britain (Speight 1973). The British race of the large copper butterfly is extinct in Great Britain because of over-collecting. Certain plants like ginseng, orchids, and wild ramps have been displaced locally in many parts of the southern Appalachian Mountains because of hobby collecting and selling of the items.

Species Composition and Structure

The end result of the previously discussed impact parameters is an alteration of species composition and structure among wildlife populations (Anderson 1995). Gains, losses, and modification occur in both habitat and types of species. In general, the consequence of recreational activities in an area results in an overall decrease in species diversity in all trophic groups in all parts of the ecosystem (Speight 1973, p. 19). This follows a general decrease in structural differentiation of the ecosystem (i.e., loss of a proportion of the habitats present without their replacement by new habitats) and increase in the degree of resource sterilization (i.e., human simplification of site conditions). Certain populations of organisms increase as a consequence of recreational activities but usually at the expense of species diversity and richness.

IMPACTS ON WILDLIFE SPECIES

Large Mammals

Large mammals are mobile and difficult to study. However, three large animals that have received considerable attention are bears, bighorn sheep, and deer. Each represents a different type of major impact and set of management implications. For additional case studies concerning bald eagles, waterfowl, hawks, beach-area nesting birds, manatees, and rattlesnakes, see Knight and Gutzwiller (1995).

Black Bears.   The black bear (*Ursus americanus*), because of its size, potential danger, and historical attraction to recreational sites, has been studied more than most other animals. The major impact problem with the bear is the alteration of its natural behavior, more specifically, its habituation to human food sources. Black bears have learned to associate people and their camping equipment with food. This process is accelerated by the willingness of many recreationists to offer them handouts (Fig. 4). In Great Smoky Mountains National Park, 5 to 10 percent of these bears, euphemistically known as panhandlers, forsake their shy and secretive nature and soon begin to beg along roadsides, raid picnic tables, tear open coolers and backpacks, and break into vehicles and tents (Tate and Pelton 1983). Although panhandling behavior is not restricted to bears only, the size and strength of these animals make such encounters with people potentially dangerous. Singer and Bratton (1976) reported 107 incidents of human injury and 715 of property damage in Great Smoky Mountains National Park, Tennessee, in 1964 through 1976. Park records listed property damage at 83 incidents in 1977 and 189 in 1978, with injuries totaling 8 and 16 for those years, respectively (Tate and Pelton 1983).

Similar injury and property damage impacts have been recorded in Yosemite National Park, California (Table 1). Interactions between bears and humans have occurred in Yosemite since the 1920s, leading to alterations in natural behavior, foraging habits, distribution, and population levels (Keay and VanWagtendonk 1983). Bears in marginal natural habitats appear more dependent on visitor foods than bears in prime natural habitat. Keay and Van Wagtendonk also found a positive linear relationship between numbers of visitors and bear incidents, suggesting that visitor density reflects a level of food availability that attracts bears. After a certain level of

FIGURE 4. Panhandler bears in Great Smoky Mountains National Park visit backcountry shelters for food handouts. (*Photo*: Bruce C. Hastings.)

TABLE 1. Visitor Use, Reported Bear Incidents, and Property Damage Estimates for the Backcountry, Yosemite National Park, 1976–1979

Year	Visitors	Visitor Nights	Bear Incidents	Dollar Damage
1976	71,066	186,526	165	4,758
1977	74,537	194,243	371	9,397
1978	70,909	172,472	277	9,398
1979	66,053	181,775	225	8,553
Mean	70,641	183,754	260	8,027

Source: Keay and Van Wagtendonk 1983. Copyright © by International Association for Bear Research and Management.

bear-human interaction and/or food availability is reached, bears might more likely be drawn into a camp area and cause more incidents than in sparsely used zones. As a result of the high incidence of bear-human interactions in Yosemite, an intensive management program was initiated in 1975. The program included public information and education, removal of artificial food sources, enforcement of regulations, control of problem bears, and research and monitoring. From 1975 to 1979, this program resulted in decreases of bear incidents and property damage from 879 to 161 incidents, and from more than $100,000 to $13,000 in damages.

Habituating behaviors of black bears at a garbage dump was documented in Jasper National Park, Canada. At the park garbage dump bears exploited the resource by forming social aggregations, tolerating other bears at shorter distances when at the dump than when away (Herrero 1983). Social interactions between bears were characterized by tolerance, avoidance, and spacing. The dump was visited by 7500 to 10,000 park visitors during a 1968 study, and "despite hundreds of close approaches, including 57 situations in which people threw rocks or chased bears, a bear never struck, bit, or touched a person." Herrero observed that the average litter (2.67 offspring) was higher for bears that regularly visited the dump, suggesting that the food source contributed to reproductive success.

National parks that once contained open garbage dumps, and in some cases actually fed bears at the dump sites for public viewing, have now eliminated the dumps, forcing bears into natural feeding areas. Bear-proof trash cans in frontcountry campgrounds and the hanging of food out of the reach of bears in backcountry campgrounds have also decreased the incidence of bear-camper interactions. Although these management actions return bears to a dependence on natural food sources, there is evidence that in some instances the practice has decreased the reproductive success, health, and number of bears in certain populations.

The issue of roads and their effects on bear behavior has been addressed by a number of authors (i.e., Workshop on Bears and Roads, 10th International IBA Conference, Fairbanks, AK, 1995). Results range from bears being attracted to roads (i.e., roads used as travel corridors, particularly in habitat protected from hunting) to roads being avoided (areas of heavy human use and hunting). Particular attention is now being directed toward identifying the characteristics (physical and biological) of corridors and strategic road crossing sites (Brody and Pelton 1989). Most of the previous work documented some impacts of roads on individual animals. How this translates to measurable population impacts is more speculative. However, Brandenburg (1996) reported on a small population of black bears that were nearly extirpated because of extensive road kills.

Bighorn Sheep.   Bighorn sheep represent a different type of impact conflict. Human encroachment on bighorn habitat has contributed to displacement and a decline in sheep populations (Dunaway 1970). In the Sierra Nevada Mountains of California where recreational use is heavy, backcountry hiking disrupts the local migration and movement routes of bighorns. In areas heavily used by campers, hunters, or off-road vehicles, use of high-value habitat by bighorns can be excluded completely. Light (1971) found that bighorns tolerate only limited human disturbance before being driven from home ranges. Ewes with young were less tolerant of human approaches than individual ewes and rams.

Most observational studies have stressed the intolerance of bighorns to human encroachment, resulting in strict management policies on recreational use in some areas. However, the need for such policies is not exactly clear. Wehausen, Hicks, Garber, and Elder (1977) report that when zoological areas were established in the Sierra Nevadas to protect bighorns from assumed adverse effects of human disturbance, the results suggested that human disturbance was not as significant a factor as supposed. An eight-year study of sheep in Death Valley National Monument, Nevada, showed that only "unchecked human encroachment appears to actually threaten bighorns." Deliberate attempts of humans to conduct themselves within limits acceptable to bighorn sheep led to tolerance of human presence. Even though the limits and specific effects of human encroachment on bighorns are not completely understood, most resource managers are recommending that prompt conservation action should be taken, with the alternative in mind that management policy can be altered if the actions are proven unnecessary.

The monitoring of wildlife-road corridor interactions are a major concern in many recreation areas. This is particularly true in a wilderness-type park like Denali National Park in Alaska, where access to the park is by one major road. Between 1973 and 1983, there was a 50 percent increase in daily vehicular traffic on the main park road. This elevated volume correlated with a 72 percent decrease in moose sightings per trip and a 32 percent decrease in grizzly bear sightings (Singer and Beattie 1986). In the case of Dall sheep, Murie (1944) believed that the road enhanced predation on sheep by wolves because it provided easy access to winter range and escape cover, and blind corners provided opportunities for wolves to approach sheep without detection. More recent studies have shown that heavy bus and car traffic have blocked Dall sheep from moving across the road corridor and, in some instances, caused them to engage in running retreats from road activity (Dalle-Molle and Van Horn 1991). Current monitoring shows that the number of Dall sheep groups seen per trip on the Denali road has declined from 4.6 in 1977 to 3.4 in 1982, 2.21 in 1995, and 2.32 in 1996.

White-Tailed Deer.   In a survey of professional resource managers, the majority of respondents "felt that white-tailed deer were the most harassed species in their areas" (Huff, Savage, Urich, and Watlov 1972). Harassment and additional stress during winter months when deer are attempting to conserve metabolic energy are a major concern with winter recreational activities. Deer are naturally adapted to energy-conserving behaviors and mechanisms during snow seasons when range size is restricted. Energy conservation of up to 1000 Kcal/day for a 60 kg deer can result from reduced activity levels such as seeking level land, reducing snow depth, and walking slowly (Moen 1976). Winter harassment by hunting, snowmobiling, or skiing, whether intentional or not, is detrimental to the energy-conserving adaptations of deer. Moen, Whittemore, and Buxton (1981) reported that heart rate among captive deer in controlled tests increased an average of 2.5 times above normal rates when snowmobiles moved tangentially to the deer and 2.9 times above normal rates when circling the deer.

Research on the displacement of deer by snowmobile traffic has been mixed in its findings. During a test of 10 radio-collared deer in Wisconsin, results indicated that the deer did not significantly increase or decrease the size of their home ranges during three weekends of snowmobiling. Noise from the snowmobiles seemed to have little effect; snowmobiles had to be within sight of the deer before the animals would move away. Although animals were displaced from the snowmobile trails, the displacement was very temporary. The deer returned to areas along trails within hours after snowmobiling ceased. The research also revealed that deer will change the location of home ranges markedly even if snowmobiles are not present (Bollinger, Rongstad, Soom, and Eckstein 1973).

Studies by Dorrance, Savage, and Huff (1975) in Minnesota indicate that deer in snowmobile use areas may become habituated to snowmobile traffic. Home range size, movement, and distance from radio-collared deer to the nearest trail increased with snowmobile activity at a wildlife management area where public snowmobiling was held constant, but remained unchanged at a state park where numbers of snowmobiles per day averaged 10 on weekdays and 195 on weekends. However, the number of deer seen immediately adjacent to trails decreased with snowmobile use in the state park (Fig. 5). The deer did return to areas along trails within hours after snowmobiling ceased. Dorrance Savage, and Huff (1975) hypothesized that the subtle movements away from trails by deer result in little impact to deer, except during severe winters on poor ranges. In sensitive areas where some deer change their home ranges to entirely different locations, the authors believe that these effects could cause changes in the animal's energy budget that could be detrimental, especially during severe winters.

Deer are capable of habituating to the presence of people and vehicles. Deer often remain close to men working with chain saws and heavy equipment and are often attracted to established snowmobile trails that make walking easier in deep snow and browse more available. Research has also indicated that deer in areas open to

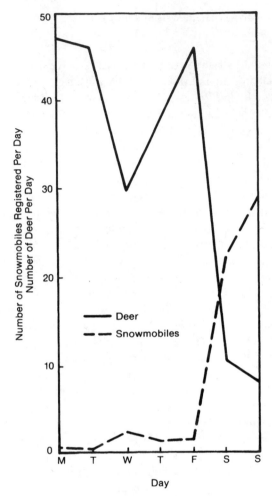

FIGURE 5. Mean number of deer observed per day, according to day of week, along a 10-km snowmobile trail in St. Croix State Park, Minnesota, 1973. (*Source:* Dorrance, M. J., P. J. Savage, and D. E. Huff, in *Journal of Wildlife Management*, Volume 39, Number 3, pp. 563–569. Copyright © 1975 by the Wildlife Society. Reprinted with permission.)

snowmobile use react initially to the machines, but further snowmobile traffic has little effect on their movement.

Other Ungulates.   Although Nordic skiers cannot travel as far and as fast as snowmobiles, they can have similar adverse impacts on wildlife during the stressful winter months. Ferguson and Keith (1982) studied the influence of Nordic skiing on the distribution of moose and elk in a park in central Alberta. They found that elk and moose both tended to move away from ski trails. Significantly, movement away from trails was caused by the first skier encountered; the passage of additional skiers did not result in additional disturbance. Although there is little information on adverse consequences of such movements on reproduction and survival, we do know that this increases the necessary caloric intake of these animals. Where food is limited, this could adversely affect the animals.

Medium-Sized Animals

Habituation to recreation-related food sources similar to that of black bears occurs among many medium-sized animals. Raccoons and skunks are common elements of many frontcountry campgrounds, particularly at night. Skunks in Great Smoky Mountain National Park have become so numerous and habituated to humans that they are common visitors during daylight hours, usually meandering through campsites. Local populations in these recreation areas increase rapidly, leading to population densities at which wildlife disease epidemics can be a serious problem.

Foxes and wolves show more avoidance toward recreationists. This is more true of wolves than red fox, as the latter has been shown to increase activity on and near snowmobile and snowshoe trails. This behavior may be a result of easier walking on the compacted snow or of the presence of cottontail rabbits, snowshoe hares, and other prey of fox that commonly use compacted snow trails. Wolves have been extensively studied in Isle Royale National Park, Michigan, because movement of the wolves is confined to the island and visitor use is heavy. Peterson (1977) found that wolf use of Isle Royale trails declines after visitors arrive in the spring. Selection of den and rendezvous sites indicates pronounced avoidance of humans. Management suggestions include limiting visitation, enlarging backcountry campsites rather than establishing new campgrounds, disallowing further trail development, and the assessment of discouraging winter visitor use.

The impacts of snowmobiles on medium-sized animals is inconclusive. Snowshoe hares were observed to avoid snowmobile trails, but red foxes were more active near and in such trails (Neumann and Merriam 1972). Schmid (1971) also observed that red foxes and deer were commonly seen following snowmobile trails. Apparently, the animals penetrate the snow less in the tracks of snowmobiles and find it easier to travel in the tracks. Penetrometer readings and measurements of animal penetration in snow off trails indicate an increase of about 85 percent (Neumann and Merriam 1972).

The indirect impact on predator species such as foxes, wolves, coyotes, bobcats, owls, hawks, and eagles by lowering the population of small animals in snowmobile use areas is a concern that has not been investigated. Snowmobile activity can have a detrimental effect on the numbers of small mammals surviving under compacted snow cover.

Easier and accelerated harvesting of animals because of increasing access to remote areas by snowmobiles is a concern of resource managers. The overharvesting of beaver and other furbearers has been suggested but not conclusively documented (Malaher 1967; Usher 1972). There is also little evidence that the snowmobile is likely to lead to significantly increased hunting pressure on big game. This is not to say that the incidence of illegal hunting and harassment by snowmobiles is not a concern, but rather that the overharvesting of animals as a result of snowmobiles has little support.

The popularity of river recreation has presented new levels of impact on many water-based species. Floating on white-water and backcountry rivers has increased rapidly in the United States, increasing the incidence of human interaction with waterfowl, eagles, osprey, and similar species. On canoeing rivers and lakes where overnight camping is common, the impact on loon populations is a concern. Increasing use of loon nesting islands for camping by canoeists appears to be the primary cause of decrease in loon productivity in the Boundary Waters Canoe Area, Minnesota. Osprey in Minnesota were also observed to build nests farther from lake and river shores, presumably because of increased watercraft activity.

Small Animals

Because the niche and microhabits of small animals are small, the habitat of these species is susceptible to destruction during the improvement and alteration of recreation sites. Clearing of both terrestrial and aquatic vegetation eliminates herbs, shrubs, and trees, which serve as sources of food and shelter for birds and small mammals. At the same time, human food sources attract rodents and certain species of small mammals and birds. Surveys of the riparian zone of the Colorado River showed abnormally high and unhealthy populations of rock squirrels, resulting from feeding by hikers. Lizard populations, which utilize driftwood for shelter and foraging, were reduced through the reduction of driftwood, used for campfires.

The effects of campgrounds on rodents are alteration of the feeding behavior and an increase in the population density of opportunistic feeders such as wood rats and deer mice. Backcountry overnight shelters along the 2000-mi long Appalachian Trail receive heavy visitation at night by mice, requiring proper storage of backpacker food. The same is true for food storage during daylight hours because of chipmunks and ground squirrels. Similar results have been found for campgrounds in Canyonlands, Arches, and Yosemite National Parks.

The influence of recreation on birds has already been discussed to some extent. The major impacts to songbirds and small nongame species are related to modification of the structure of vegetation and harassment during nesting. However, the presence of vegetation changes, of humans, and of food debris in campgrounds leads to an increase in numbers among some bird species. Brewer's blackbird, the brown headed cowbird, and robins were significantly more abundant in campgrounds of Yosemite National Park, but Oregon juncos were less abundant than in surrounding areas (Garton, Hall, and Foin 1977).

Harassment during wildlife viewing and photographing is also becoming a major issue. Bird-watching is one of the most popular forms of nonconsumptive, wildlife recreation. However, balancing wildlife viewing with wildlife impacts is a growing concern. Of five different recreationist-user groups at a wildlife refuge in Florida, photographers were the most disruptive, as they were most likely to stop, leave their vehicles, and approach wildlife (Klein 1993).

The most dramatic impact on small animals is caused by off-road vehicles, particularly snowmobiles. The compaction of snow by snowmobiles causes a reduction or destruction of the subnivean space, resulting in a mechanical barrier to the movement of small animals. The tunnels of these animals are collapsed and the feeding area greatly reduced. The compaction also reduces the insulating qualities of the snow, causing stress and death to small mammals through reduced temperatures (Schmid 1971). Schmid (1972) further documents the effects by stating:

> Experimental manipulation of a snowfield has shown that the winter mortality of small mammals is markedly increased under snowmobile compaction. We recovered none of 21 marked animals from the experimental plot, whereas 8 to 18 marked specimens were captured at least once on an adjacent control plot. (p. 37).

Fish

Fish are not commonly thought of as wildlife by the general public, yet the recreating public can be an impacting agent on this specific form of wildlife. Lakes and streams concentrate recreational activities both from a water-based and shore-based perspective, leading to concentrated levels of impact on aquatic organisms (Fig. 6). Unfortunately, recreational impacts on fish populations are not well documented. Anglers have been shown to decrease the presence and feeding of bald eagles and ravens.

Direct impacts in the form of displacement occur through removal by fishing and introduction of exotic game species. Wilderness camping at popular alpine lake areas have "fished out" some lakes and reduced populations to numbers where the native populations are hardly viable. Accelerated harvesting as a result of Off-Road Vehicle (ORV) and snowmobile access to remote lakes has been documented, with one report

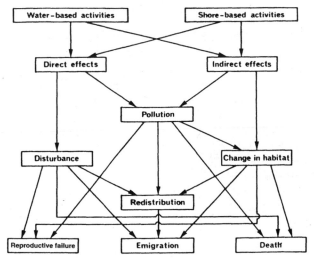

FIGURE 6. Impacts of water-based and shore-based recreation activities on wildlife. (*Source*: Liddle and Scorgie 1980.)

indicating 556 lbs of fish being harvested from a remote lake on a single winter day. "This would have been an entire season's catch if snowmobile access had not been possible" (Cooney and Preston, in Bury, Wendling, and McCool 1976). The introduction of rainbow trout to the streams of Great Smoky Mountains National Park by loggers before the area was designated a park has led to the displacement of the native brook trout from many of the streams. Fishing for the native brookies is no longer permitted in the park.

Most recreational impacts to fish result from indirect impacts to water quality and ecosystems. Eutrophication, pollution, and mechanical disturbance to aquatic vegetation as a result of wave action from boats all have the potential to disturb fish to varying degrees. Boating also contributes to increased turbidity, human-waste disposal, and the deposit of gasoline/oil mixtures on water surfaces. Concentrations of gasoline/oil mixtures have led to unacceptable levels of depleted oxygen supply for certain fish species and the off-flavoring of the flesh in fish.

SUMMARY

1. Different species of wildlife have different tolerances for interactions with humans. Even within a species, tolerance level for interactions will vary by time of year, breeding season, animal age, habitat type, and individual animal experience with recreationists.

2. Recreational impacts on wildlife may be *direct* or *indirect*. Direct impacts include the effects on animals by primary disturbances and interactions with humans. Indirect impacts are the secondary results of disturbance to habitat and other environmental parameters by recreationists. Larger game species are more affected by direct impacts and smaller species are more affected by indirect impacts of habitat modification.

3. The major impact to wildlife by recreationists is unintentional harassment, caused by individuals who unknowingly and innocently produce stressful situations for wildlife. Physiological and psychological stresses, particularly during winter, can greatly compound the severity of harassment impacts. The location and time of human-wildlife interactions are key elements in managing harassment impacts. Wildlife species vulnerable to harassment can be protected by protecting critical areas from roads and trails, by locating campsites in appropriate areas, and by seasonally closing critical breeding habitats.

4. The frequent presence of humans in wildland areas can alter the normal behavior of animals drastically. Slight modifications in habitat use and daily use patterns and the habituation and taming of animals are the most common behavioral changes. The availability of human food has led to altering the natural feeding habits of many animals in recreation areas.

5. In general, the consequence of recreational activities in an area results in an overall decrease in species diversity. A change in species composition and structure among wildlife populations is the ultimate result of human-wildlife interactions.

REFERENCES

Anderson, S. H. 1995. Recreation Disturbance and Wildlife Populations. In R. L. Knight and K. J. Gutzwiller, eds. *Wildlife and Recreationists.* Washington, DC: Island Press, pp. 157–168.

Anthony, R. G., R. J. Steidl, and K. McGarigal. 1995. Recreation and Bald Eagles in the Pacific Northwest. In R. L. Knight and K. J. Gutzwiller, eds. *Wildlife and Recreationists.* Washington, DC: Island Press, pp. 223–242.

Batcheler, C. L. 1968. Compensatory Responses of Artificially Controlled Mammal Populations. In *New Zealand Ecological Society Proceedings* 15:25–30.

Berry, J., ed. 1973. Preliminary Studies on the Effects of Off-road Vehicles on the Northwestern Mojave Desert: A Collection of Papers. Privately printed, Ridgecrest, CA. 100 pp.

Blakesley, J. A., and K. P. Reese. 1988. Avian Use of Campgrounds and Noncampground Sites in Riparian Zones. *Journal of Wildlife Management* 52:399–402.

Bollinger, J. G., O. J. Rongstad, A. Soom, and R. G. Eckstein. 1973. Snowmobile Noise Effects on Wildlife, 1972–1973 Report. Engineering Experiment Station, University of Wisconsin, Madison, WI. 85 pp.

Bowles, A. E. 1995. Responses of Wildlife to Noise. In R. L. Knight and K. J. Gutzwiller, eds. *Wildlife and Recreationists.* Washington, DC: Island Press, pp. 109–156.

Boyle, S. A., and F. B. Samson. 1985. Effects of Nonconsumptive Recreation on Wildlife: A Review. *Wildlife Society Bulletin* 13:110–116.

Brandenburg, D. M. 1996. Effects of Roads on Behavior and Survival of Black Bears in Coastal North Carolina. Master's thesis. University of Tennessee, Knoxville. 131 pp.

Brody, A. J., and M. R. Pelton. 1989. Effects of Roads on Black Bear Movements in Western North Carolina. *Wildlife Society Bulletin* 17:5–10.

Bury, R. L., R. C. Wendling, and S. F. McCool. 1976. Off-road Recreation Vehicles—A Research Summary, 1969–1975. Texas Agricultural Experiment Station, College Station, TX. Texas A & M University System. 84 pp.

Cole, D. N., and P. B. Landres. 1995. Indirect Effects of Recreationists on Wildlife. In R. L. Knight and K. J. Gutzwiller, eds. *Wildlife and Recreationists.* Washington, DC: Island Press, pp. 183–202.

Dalle-Molle, J., and J. Van Horn. 1991. Observation of Vehicle Traffic Interfering with Migration of Dall Sheep. *Ovis dalli dalli* in Denali National Park, Alaska. *Canadian Field Naturalist* 105:409–411.

Dorrance, M. J., P. J. Savage, and D. E. Huff. 1975. Effects of Snowmobiles on White-Tailed Deer. *Journal of Wildlife Management* 39:563–569.

Dunaway, D. J. 1970. Status of Bighorn Sheep Populations and Habitat Studies on the Inyo National Forest. *Transactions of Desert Bighorn Council* 14:127–146.

Ferguson, M. S. D., and L. B. Keith. 1982. Influence of Nordic Skiing on Distribution of Moose and Elk in Elk Island National Park, Alberta. *Canadian Field Naturalist* 96:69–78.

Foin, T. C., E. O. Garton, C. W. Bowen, J. M. Everingham, R. O. Schultz, and B. Holton, Jr. 1977. Quantitative Studies of Visitor Impacts on Environments of Yosemite National Park, California, and Their Implications for Park Management Policy. *Journal of Environmental Management* 5:1–22.

Fraser, D. F., and N. D. Eichhorn. 1969. Man and Nature in the National Parks: A Reflection on Policy. Conservation Foundation. Washington, DC.

Garton, E. O., B. Hall, and T. C. Foin, Jr. 1977. The Impact of a Campground on the Bird Community of a Lodgepole Pine Forest. In T. C. Foin, Jr., ed. *Visitor Impacts on National Parks: The Yosemite Ecological Impact Study.* University of California, Davis: Institute for Ecology. Publication No. 10. 99 pp.

Geist, V. 1972. On the Management of Large Mammals on National Parks. *Park News* 8(4):7–14, 8(5):16–24.

Geist, V. 1975. Mountain Sheep and Man in the Northern Wilds. Ithaca, NY: Cornell University Press. 248 pp.

Herrero, S. 1983. Social Behavior of Black Bears at a Garbage Dump in Jasper National Park. In E. C. Meslow, ed. *Bears—Their Biology and Management.* International Conference for Bear Research and Management 5:54–70.

Huff, D. E., P. J. Savage, D. L. Urich, and R. L. Watlov. 1972. Wildlife-Snowmobile Interaction Project—Preliminary Report. University of Minnesota and Minnesota Department of Natural Resources. 34 pp.

Johnson, K. G., and M. R. Pelton. 1979. Denning Behavior of Black Bears in the Great Smoky Mountains National Park. *Proceedings Annual Conference Southeastern Association of Fish and Wildlife Agencies* 33:239–249.

Keay, J. A., and J. W. VanWagtendonk. 1983. Effect of Yosemite Backcountry Use Levels on Incidents with Black Bears. In E. C. Meslow, ed. *Bears—Their Biology and Management.* International Conference for Bear Research and Management 5:307–311.

Klein, M. L. 1993. Waterbird Behavioral Responses to Human Disturbances. *Wildlife Society Bulletin* 21:31–39.

Knight, R. L., and D. N. Cole. 1995. Factors That Influence Wildlife Responses to Recreationists. In R. L. Knight and K. J. Gutzwiller, eds. *Wildlife and Recreationists.* Washington, DC: Island Press, pp. 71–80.

Knight, R. L., and K. J. Gutzwiller, eds. 1995. *Wildlife and Recreationists.* Washington, DC: Island Press. 372 pp.

Kuss, F. R., A. R. Graefe, and J. J. Vaske. 1984. Recreation Impacts and Carrying Capacity: A Review and Synthesis of Ecological and Social Research. Draft Review Report, University of Maryland, College Park, MD. 180 pp.

Kuss, F. R., A. R. Graefe, and J. J. Vaske. 1990. *Visitor Impact Management: A Review of Research.* Vol. 1. Washington, DC: National Parks and Conservation Association. 256 pp.

Liddle, M. J., and H. R. A. Scorgie. 1980. The Effects of Recreation on Freshwater Plants and Animals: A Review. *Biological Conservation* 17(2):183–206.

Light, J. T. R. 1971. An Ecological View of Bighorn Habitat on Mount San Antonio. *Transactions of the North American Wild Sheep Conference* 1:150–157.

Malaher, G. W. 1967. Improper Use of Snow Vehicles for Hunting. In Transactions, 32nd North American Wildlife and Natural Resources Conference. Wildlife Management Institute, Washington, DC. pp. 429–433.

Martinka, C. J. 1979. Measuring Effects of Human Presence on Wintering Wildlife in National Parks. In *Proceedings of the Second Conference on Scientific Research in the National Parks.* USDI National Park Service. San Francisco, CA. 6:199–211.

Moen, A. N. 1976. Energy Conservation by White-Tailed Deer in the Winter. *Ecology* 57(1):192–198.

Moen, A. N., S. Whittemore, and B. Buxton. 1981. Snowmobile Effects on Heart Rates of Captive White-Tailed Deer. Unpublished Paper. Department of Zoology. Auburn University, Auburn, AL. 18 pp.

Murie, A. 1944. *The Wolves of Mount McKinley.* Washington, DC: U.S. Government Printing Office. 235 pp.

Neumann, P. W., and H. G. Merriam. 1972. Ecological Effects of Snowmobiles. *Canadian Field Naturalist* 86:207–212.

O'Shea, T. J. 1995. Waterborne Recreation and the Florida Manatee. In R. L. Knight and K. J. Gutzwiller, eds. *Wildlife and Recreationists.* Washington, DC: Island Press, pp. 297–312.

Peterson, R. O. 1977. Management Implication of Wolf-Moose Research, Isle Royale National Park, Michigan. Report to the USDI National Park Service. Washington, DC. 14 pp.

Pomerantz, G. A., D. J. Decker, G. R. Goff, and K. G. Purdy. 1988. Assessing Impact of Recreation on Wildlife: A Classification Scheme. *Wildlife Society Bulletin* 16:58–62.

Ream, C. H. 1979. Human-Wildlife Conflicts in Backcountry: Possible Solutions. In R. Ittner, D. R. Potter, and J. K. Agee, eds. *Recreational Impacts on Wildlands.* USDA Forest Service Pacific Northwest Region, Seattle, WA, pp. 153–163.

Ream, C. H. 1980. Impacts of Backcountry Recreationists on Wildlife: An Annotated Bibliography. USDA Forest Service General Technical Report INT-81. 62 pp.

Schmid, W. D. 1971. Modification of the Subnivean Microclimate by Snowmobiles. In *Proceedings of Snow and Ice Symposium.* Cooperative Wildlife Research Unit, Iowa State University, Ames, IA, pp. 251–257.

Schmid, W. D. 1972. Snowmobile Activity, Subnivean Microclimate, and Winter Mortality of Small Mammals. *Bulletin of Ecological Society of America* 53(2):37.

Singer, F. J. 1978. Behavior of Mountain Goats in Relation to U.S. Highway 2, Glacier National Park, Montana. *Journal of Wildlife Management* 42(3):591–597.

Singer, F. J., and J. B. Beattie. 1986. The Controlled Traffic System and Associated Wildlife Responses in Denali National Park. *Arctic* 39:195–203

Singer, F. J., and S. P. Bratton. 1976. Black Bear Management in Great Smoky Mountains National Park. Uplands Field Research Laboratory Management Report No. 13. USDI National Park Service, Great Smoky Mountains National Park, Gatlinburg, TN. 34 pp.

Singer, F. J., D. K. Otto, A. R. Tipton, and C. P. Hable. 1981. Home Ranges, Movements, and Habitat Use of European Wild Boar in Tennessee. *Journal of Wildlife Management* 45(2):343–353.

Small, R. J., J. C. Holzwart, and D. H. Rusch. 1991. Predation and Hunting Mortality of Ruffed Grouse in Central Wisconsin. *Journal of Wildlife Management* 55:512–520.

Speight, M. C. D. 1973. Outdoor Recreation and Its Ecological Effects: A Bibliography and Review. Discussion Paper in Conservation 4, University College, London, 35 pp.

Stace-Smith, R. 1975. The Misuse of Snowmobiles Against Wildlife in Canada. *Nature Canada* 4:3–8.

Tate, J., and M. R. Pelton. 1983. Human-Bear Interactions in Great Smoky Mountains National Park. In E. C. Meslow, ed. *Bears—Their Biology and Management.* International Conference for Bear Research and Management 5:312–321.

Usher, R. J. 1972. Use of Snowmobiles for Trapping on Banks Island. *Arctic* 25:170–181.

Wall, G., and C. Wright. 1977. *The Environmental Impact of Outdoor Recreation.* Department of Geography Publication Series No. 11. University of Ontario, Waterloo. 69 pp.

Ward, A. L., 1977. The Effects of Highway Operation Practices and Facilities on Elk, Mule Deer, and Pronghorn Antelope. Project No. 942-41-42-13-0088-33 F2-6-2580. Annual Report of the Federal Highway Administration, Office of Research and Development. Washington, DC. 53 pp.

Ward, A. L., J. J. Cupal, A. L. Lea, C. A. Oakley, and R. W. Weeks. 1973. Elk Behavior in Relation to Cattle Grazing, Forest Recreation, and Traffic. *Transactions of the 38th North American Wildlife and Natural Resources Conference* 38:327–337.

Webb, W. L. 1968. Public Use of Forest Wildlife: Quantity and Quality Considerations. *Journal of Forestry* 66:106–110.

Weeden, R. 1976. Nonconsumptive Users: A Myth. *Alaskan Conservation Review* 27(9):3–15.

Wehausen, J. D., L. L. Hicks, D. P. Garber, and J. Elder. 1977. Bighorn Sheep Management in the Sierra Nevada. *Transactions of the Desert Bighorn Council* 21:30–32.

Wilkes, B. 1977. The Myth of the Nonconsumptive User. *Canadian Field Naturalist* 91(4):343–349.

Wood, A. K. 1993. Parallels Between Old-Growth Forests and Wildlife Population Management. *Wildlife Society Bulletin* 21:91–95.

Woodward, T. N., R. J. Gutierrez, and W. H. Rutherford. 1974. Bighorn Ram Production, Survival, and Mortality in Southcentral Colorado. *Journal of Wildlife Management* 38(4):771–774.

Workshop on Bears and Roads. 1995. 10th International IBA Conference, Fairbanks, AK.

5 Water

Among the various impacts of wildland recreation, its influence on aquatic ecosystems is seldom mentioned or understood, yet water quality is a major concern in recreation areas. It serves as both a medium for water-based activities, including body contact sports, and a drinking source for users. Thus, water-related impacts are somewhat unique, different from soil, vegetation, and wildlife impacts in that water quality is more directly related to human health.

Although water quality is sanctioned by law in highly developed recreation areas and has been researched fairly extensively at cottage-based lakes, far less is known about water-related impacts in remote wildland areas. Because of the lack of developed sanitation facilities in these areas, drinking water and human waste disposal are concerns. The problem is compounded by the concentration of backcountry users at alpine lakes and streams. This chapter reviews some of the major physical, chemical, and bacteriological problems of water sources in wildland recreation areas. Lake and river impacts related to high residential development (cottages) will not be considered. For additional review of the effects of recreation on water resources, see Kuss, Graefe, and Vaske 1990.

BASIC WATER ECOLOGY

Aquatic ecosystems, like terrestrial ecosystems, have many parameters that interact to determine water quality. Some of these impact parameters are *direct*, occurring on or in the water. Other impacts to water systems are *indirect*, characterized by inputs that originate from actions that occur on shore or in the watershed (Liddle and Scorgie 1980). Major impact parameters influencing water quality are (1) nutrients, (2) suspended solids, (3) amount of dissolved oxygen, (4) temperature and flow, (5) pH, (6) fecal bacteria and pathogens, (7) dissolved solids, and (8) transparency (Kuss, Graefe, and Vaske 1990). Recreation-related impact research has focused on (1) nutrient enrichment of the water, (2) suspended solids (turbidity), (3) reduced dissolved oxygen, and (4) bacterial contamination in the form of fecal waste. Water temperature and flow, as well as seasonal and site factors, influence the importance of each of the variables.

Water Temperature and Flow

Water impacts reach unacceptable levels commonly under the conditions of warm temperatures and low flow rate. Dissolved oxygen often reaches its lowest levels during warm summer evenings when water flow also is low. Warm temperatures tend to increase the growth of aquatic plants and bacteria, problems of warm water systems. Temperature also affects animal life. Recreational activities can indirectly increase the temperature of lakes and streams, affecting the species composition of fish populations. Some fish can tolerate temperatures as high as about 30°C, whereas trout can survive an absolute maximum of 25°C to 26°C for only a short period of time. As a rule of thumb, trout waters should never exceed 20°C. Removal of stream bank foliage may increase the temperature of trout streams above acceptable levels. In lakes, depletion of oxygen at lower depths (the hypolimnion) forces trout to move to upper layers with sufficient oxygen but higher temperatures, which may be fatal.

Water flow is related to dilution capacities, influencing the concentration of pollutants in water sources at any particular time. Restricted bays and inlets to lakes, as well as slow-flowing springs and streams, often contain the highest bacterial counts and lowest oxygen supplies. In water systems that show a rapid flushing rate or a high flow rate, the danger of poor water quality appears to be minimized. Precipitation patterns and the dilution capacity of a water system can greatly influence the degree of recreation-caused impacts. However, the influence of storms is mixed. The rapid flushing rate of storms can help in removing suspended and dissolved nutrients from streams, but at the same time storms are a major agent at flushing nutrients and soil from disturbed watersheds into lakes and streams. Nutrient influx and coliform bacteria are sometimes most prevalent just following a storm.

Nutrients

Nutrients in lakes are directly related to the aging of these water systems, a process known as eutrophication. The addition of nutrients, primarily nitrogen and phosphorus, stimulates the net productivity of water bodies. A lake normally undergoes natural succession from a young, nutrient-deficient, unproductive lake with high oxygen levels (oligotrophic) to increased nutrient levels, higher production, greater deposits of organic matter, and low oxygen levels (eutrophic). Eutrophication can be accelerated by recreational activities and actions that increase the rate at which nutrients are added to lakes. The additional nutrients increase the rate and amount of plant growth and, if excessive, lead to undesirable weed growth, algal blooms, or the replacement of sport fish by less attractive species. The excessive vegetation also leads to a depletion of the dissolved oxygen supply during decay of the organic plant materials.

For most recreational use, high water quality means low productivity so that lakes are clear, cool, and deep—suitable for swimming, boating, and good habitats for sport fish (Wall and Wright 1977). In alpine lakes even minute changes in nutrients can cause increases in algae populations. Heavy shoreline use of such lakes and streams accelerates soil erosion, leading to an influx of nitrates into these water bodies. Lake edge and stream bank erosion not only accelerate the rate of nutrient influx, but they influence water clarity, an important indicator of water quality for recreation purposes. Water clarity is conditioned by many factors, including productivity levels of the water as influenced by phytoplankton densities, turbidity, and water color.

Phosphorus, in the form of phosphate, tends to be the limiting factor in aquatic plant growth. It has a strong affinity for soil particles and tends to be tied up in the bottom sediments of lakes. However, swimming, wading, boating, and other activities that stir the bottom sediments of streams and shallow lakes may release concentrations of phosphate and other nutrients. Phosphates contained in motor boat oil and in detergents find their way into aquatic systems, although not as much as in the past. Detergents, for example, now contain fewer phosphates than in the past.

The response of lakes to nutrients and their vulnerability to accelerated eutrophication are based on many site factors. Size of watershed or drainage basin, shoreline configuration, mean depth, elevational position, and present trophic status are important (Sargent and Zayer 1976). Shallow lakes with numerous bays and inlets at low elevations with warm temperatures will show the most impact to recreational activities. The type of soils and geology surrounding the lake, as well as type and extent of forest or vegetation cover, will also have an influence on rate of eutrophication.

Dissolved Oxygen

Dissolved oxygen is necessary in respiration of most aquatic organisms. When the depletion of oxygen by respiring organisms occurs at a faster rate than it is being diffused in from the atmosphere or produced by photosynthetic organisms, a deficit in oxygen level may develop. If plant growth and decomposition are excessive, the dissolved oxygen supply of the bottom layer of lakes (hypolimnion) will be depleted by the decay of organic matter. With the increased decay of organic matter, bacterial respiration is high. The depletion is most pronounced in warm lakes because oxygen solubility varies inversely with temperature.

The depletion of oxygen in aquatic ecosystems has several impacts on aquatic animals and plants. The minimal requirements of species vary and often limit the spatial distribution of certain forms in aquatic communities (Reid 1961). Cold-water fish such as trout need a minimum of 6 to 7 parts per million (ppm) of dissolved oxygen; warm-water fish such as bass need a minimum of 5 ppm. Fish kills resulting from oxygen depletion have occurred in lakes, ponds, and streams (Hynes 1970). Many species of aquatic insects are typically replaced by less oxygen-demanding species as an oxygen deficit develops, causing further changes in aquatic populations positioned higher on the food chain. Availability of oxygen affects plants in primarily two ways: species composition and nutrient uptake. Some submerged species of aquatic plants are sensitive to low levels of dissolved oxygen and are replaced by more tolerant species. In terms of nutrient levels, phosphate increases under anoxic conditions and becomes more readily available for plant production in the surface layers of lakes. Thus, nutrient level, plant production and decomposition, and dissolved oxygen supply are all intricately related. In relation to recreational use, the impact can be summarized as follows: with recreational use, production in lakes can be quickly altered from acceptable rates to excessive growth rates with associated changes in oxygen supply and species composition of aquatic organisms (Vander Wal and Stedwill, 1975).

Pathogens and Other Pollutants

The major concern with recreational aquatic impacts involves the presence of pathogens and pollutants that directly influence human health. Pathogens are disease-causing organisms that are transmitted by the feces of human and other warm-blooded animals. The major source is raw or inadequately treated sewage, a particular concern in remote recreational areas. Pathogens at unacceptable levels are a serious health hazard, making water sources unfit for body contact and drinking.

Human feces contain more than 100 viruses, bacteria, and protozoa that cause disease or death to infected humans (Cowgill 1971). The common indicator bacteria such as total coliforms, fecal coliforms (FC), and fecal streptococci (FS) are widespread in fecally contaminated environments and originate from diverse sources, including the intestinal tract of humans, other mammals, birds, and reptiles (Kabler and Clarke 1960; Kuss, Graefe and Vaske 1990). The presence of coliforms in a stream or lake usually indicates recent fecal pollution and the possible presence of enteric pathogens. Coliform bacteria themselves are nonpathogenic but are used as indicators because they are more easily measured than the pathogens with which they are associated.

The relationship of fecal coliform (associated with humans) to fecal streptococcus (associated with other animals) density (FC/FS ratio) is used to provide information as to sources of pollution.

> Based on per capita contributions of indicator bacteria from man and domestic livestock, FC/FS ratios greater than about 4:1 are usually indicative of man's body wastes. Ratios less than about 0.7:1 suggest contamination originated from livestock, wildlife, storm water runoff, and other nonhuman sources (Gary 1982, p. 5).

As will be documented later in this chapter, animal sources of coliform appear to be more prevalent in wilderness areas than are human sources.

Human wastes are also a source of nutrients. Feces of humans may contain as much as 1.5 g of phosphorus and 10.4 g of nitrogen per person per day (Liddle and Scorgie, in Kuss, Graefe, and Vaske 1990). In sterile, remote environments human and animal feces located around heavily used lakes can be two of the most common sources of bacterial influx to these aquatic systems (Merriam, Smith, Miller, Huang, Tappeiner, Goeckerman, Bloemendal, and Costello 1973).

Other major sources of pollutants in wildland aquatic areas fall into the categories of oil products, solid wastes, and sediments. All three of these water quality impacts are greatly associated with motor boating. Muratori (1968) suggests that 500 million liters of unburned outboard fuel are discharged every year into the navigable waters of the United States. Litter, in the form of bottles and cans, finds its way to the bottom of lakes and streams. Finally, turbidity of streams and lakes, which is due to boat propeller action and aquatic activities, can influence light penetration through water and reduce photosynthesis.

IMPACTS ON WATER QUALITY

Nutrient Influx

Nutrients, primarily nitrogen and phosphorus, enter wildland water systems mostly as a result of shoreline and campsite erosion. However, seasonal data to indicate that wildland recreation activities are a major impact on nutrient balance in lakes and streams are generally lacking (Gosz 1982). Studies in campgrounds usually fail to show increased nutrient levels in associated waters (Brickler and Utter 1975; Gary 1982; Segall and Oakley 1975). In some cases moderately eutrophic conditions are found in streams in campgrounds, but analyses upstream indicate that the nutrients are primarily from natural sources. Potter, Gosz, and Carlson (1984) list natural sources to include precipitation, run off, bottom sediments, decomposing plankton, transient waterfowl, falling tree leaves, bedrock type and natural soils.

Gary (1982) surveyed over a three-month period the nutrient balance of a Colorado stream as water entered and left a small commercial campground. Levels of NO_3-N did not exhibit any definite seasonal trend, and concentrations at three study sites were not significantly different. Other chemical and physical properties remained unchanged and were not significantly increased by campground use. Similar results have been obtained for campgrounds that are equipped with modern sanitation facilities (Gosz 1982).

In mountainous backcountry areas where lakes are normally oligotrophic and are popular recreation areas, the impact of nutrient influx is a particular concern. Algae populations in oligotrophic lakes respond to only small changes in nutrients. Shoreline and campsite erosion and water contamination by campers are potential sources of nutrients in these systems. Silverman and Erman (1979) studied two lake basins, one receiving high visitor use and the other low use, in Kings Canyon National Park, California, for differences in water quality. Visitor use was found not to affect the condition of the lakes; however, there were extreme differences between the basins because of natural sources. The basin lakes receiving low use had about 60 times more nitrates than the high-use lakes early in the summer. Phosphate concentration was similar for all lakes. Background levels and natural sources of nutrients are a major problem when relating recreational use to nutrient influx. In many cases natural sources contribute the largest quantities of nutrients, making comparative studies difficult to interpret (Barton 1969). Baseline studies of conditions before and after recreation occurs in an area are needed, rather than studies that compare areas of high and low visitor use. However, this procedure may not be the complete solution. Stuart, Bissonnette, Goodrich, and Walter (1971) found that a closed watershed, when opened for "limited recreation and logging," actually decreased in bacterial contamination.

Phosphate appears to be more of a nutrient input in wildland areas than nitrogen. Water quality studies carried out at nine campground sites and controls in the Boundary Waters Canoe Area, Minnesota, indicated that recreational use increased phosphate concentration and coliform bacteria in the lake water near campsites. Flushing of the bare, campsite impact zones and of fire pits is a common occurrence with each rainstorm and contributes to the nutrient input of the lakes (Fig. 1). Even though phosphate and coliform levels increased at the BWCA campsites, other water quality parameters, including temperature, dissolved oxygen, pH, specific conductance, nitrate concentration, and nitrogen were not affected by recreational use.

Dickman and Dorais (1977) found that human trampling of the shoreline and steep-sided basin of a semiwilderness lake in Canada led to an exceptionally high phosphorus loading of the lake. Over a 20-year period (1956–1976) recreational use of the small lake increased tenfold, significantly reducing plant cover in the lake basin and increasing erosion on its steep slopes. The trampling and resulting erosion caused a phosphorus loading of 854 mg/m^2 of lake surface, placing Pinks Lake among the most eutrophic lakes of North America (Dickman and Dorais 1977). However, the lake receives no municipal, agricultural or rural effluent discharge because of its location in a semiwilderness, forested watershed. A significant portion of the dissolved phosphorus is entering the eutrophic zone of the lake from apatite-rich rock, which has eroded following the destruction of ground cover as a result of human trampling. The causal link between human trampling and the high phosphate concentrations was further corroborated by leachate tests of the eroded apatite rock material near the edge of the lake. The tests independently supported the hypothesis that apatite-derived, dissolved phosphorus was the principal factor responsible for the high concentrations of phosphorus in the spring.

FIGURE 1. Rainstorms flush nutrients and pollutants from campsites and fire pits directly into the nearby lake, Boundary Waters Canoe Area, Minnesota. (*Photo*: W. E. Hammitt.)

Coliform Bacteria and Other Pathogens

The major controversy over recreational use of water is based on a sanitation concern. Many studies suggest that recreational activity is a significant source of bacterial contamination. Likewise, many studies fail to show significant water quality degradation because of wildland recreation. Many results are site specific, and in a number of cases, conflict with each other. Thus, there is a divergence of opinion on the question of recreational impact on bacterial water quality levels (Aukerman and Springer 1975; Gosz 1982; Kuss, Graefe, and Vaske 1990; Wall and Wright 1977).

Studies conducted in wildland areas show that while sewage-flow rates may be the most significant source of bacterial contamination in developed recreational areas, this is not the case with wildland recreation. Campgrounds and other use areas in wildlands often have little or no water directly associated with sewage disposal (pit, vault privies, or no facility), as well as lower production (i.e., fewer individuals, as well as per capita production of sewage wastes in terms of laundry, dish water, etc.). The primary source of bacterial contamination in wildlands is from surface soil, a result of both background levels of microorganisms and those associated with human and domestic animal waste products (Gosz 1982). Regardless of the presence or absence of humans, natural bacterial densities in soils are high enough so that precipitation can be expected to increase the bacterial counts in nearby streams and lakes. No natural water source could consistently meet potable water standards, because of the normal influx of bacteria (Potter, Gosz, and Carlson 1984; Silverman and Erman 1979).

One of the first backcountry studies to indicate that recreational use affects coliform bacteria was the work of King and Mace (1974) in the Boundary Waters Canoe Area, Minnesota. They found that coliform bacteria populations of water at canoe campsites were significantly higher than at control points (Table 1). The average coliform levels at the campsites were above the maximum (2.2 organisms/100 ml) considered safe for drinking water. The difference between campsites and controls was larger for the high- and medium-use campsites, suggesting a relationship between use level and coliform bacteria density. High bacterial counts were found only adjacent

TABLE 1. Coliform Populations for the Various Use Classes of Campsites: University of Minnesota, BWCA Campsite Study, 1970

Location	(Number of Coliform/100 ml) Use Categories		
	High[a]	Medium	Low
Campsite	4.61	6.63	5.83
Control	0.28	1.95	4.68
Difference	4.33	4.68	1.15

Source: Merriam, Smith, Miller, Huang, Tappeiner, Goeckermann, Bloemendal, and Costello 1973.

[a] High-use sites had over 1100 visitor days total use, medium-use sites had over 500 visitor days total use, and low-use sites had under 300 visitor days total use.

to the campsites, indicating that the effect on the lakes is generally small. Effluent from the pit toilet on each campsite was determined as the probable source of the bacteria (Fig. 2). Because the soils are shallow, effluents reach bedrock quickly and drain into lake basins. Shoreline activities at the campsites such as swimming, washing dishes, cleaning fish, and boat launching are other probable causes (King and Mace 1974). Such activities stir bottom sediments, shown to be a microbial habitat where the organisms from the fecal matter of warm-blooded animals can persist and concentrate (Van Donsel and Geldreich 1971).

In the heavily used backcountry areas of the White Mountains of the northeastern United States, coliform levels have been a problem near shelters and huts. In untreated water supplies at shelters or major trails, the presence of fecal and total bacteria was found to vary seasonally for most lakes, springs and streams. Highest counts occurred in late July, with some counts in excess of recommended public health standards. However, by late August most waters sampled were nearly clear of bacteria.

At developed campgrounds in wildland recreation areas, Varness, Pacha, and Lapen (1978) and Johnson and Middlebrooks (1975) reported significant increases of coliform bacteria associated with recreational use. Varness, Pacha, and Lapen (1978) found higher bacteria densities downstream from heavily used camping areas without sanitary facilities, and Johnson and Middlebrooks (1975) found that sharp increases in fecal coliform counts coincided with peak recreational use at areas having toilets. The peak use levels of bacteria dropped sharply at the end of the recreation season.

Where water quality problems have been identified with recreational activities, most appear where use is concentrated and density dependent. Bacterial pollution resulting

FIGURE 2. Pit toilets, if located on shallow soils and near water, can be a source of coliform bacteria and associated pathogens. (*Photo:* W. E. Hammitt.)

from recreation use appears to be more closely related to the total number of people visiting an area during a given seasonal period than to total length of stay. "These impacts relate to: 1) effects that are highly density dependent, such as peak season, holiday, or weekend use versus weekday use; 2) location of sites that concentrate use; 3) the number of sites within the watershed; 4) the frequency with which the sites are used; and 5) the condition of available facilities" (Kuss, Graefe, and Vaske 1990, p. 124).

Other investigations in both remote backcountry areas and at developed facilities in wildland recreation areas support the argument that recreational use has *no* significant adverse impact on the bacterial quality of water. Aukerman and Springer (1975) found no significant increases in coliform bacteria at heavily used developed campgrounds or at remote backcountry campsites in Colorado. In fact, they found an inverse relationship between cases of bacterial density increases and levels of campground utilization. The study is significant in that it involved three types of camping (i.e., campgrounds off paved roads, campgrounds off unpaved roads, and roadless backpacking sites), a number of campgrounds, and a heavily used recreational area. The authors concluded that "although campers are contributing to the bacterial pollution of the Cache la Poudre River watershed, the amount contributed at each campground is insignificant in terms of established water quality standards."

Similar results showing insignificant levels of coliform bacteria have been reported for alpine lakes in Kings Canyon National Park, California (Silverman and Erman, 1979), for water sources in Great Smoky Mountains National Park (Silsbee, Plastas, and Plastas 1976), and for developed campgrounds in Colorado (Gary 1982) and Wyoming (Skinner, Adams, Richard, and Beetle 1974). In Kings Canyon National Park only 10 percent of the water samples had positive total or fecal coliform, and at most two per sample. Fecal streptococci levels were somewhat higher than coliform (52 percent positive samples and a maximum count of eight colonies per sample), indicating wildlife as the source. Skinner, Adams, Richard and Beetle (1974), studying a natural watershed open only to hikers and wildlife, found yearly means for fecal coliform in 1970, 1971, and 1972, to be 1.2, 0.6, and 0.2 organisms/100 ml, respectively. The fecal streptococci bacteria counts for the same years were 22, 2, and 3/100 ml.

An important issue concerning recreational areas that contain hazardous levels of bacteria is the source of the contamination. Many studies that have identified the source report the contamination to be from nonhumans. Livestock is responsible in some cases (Marnell, Foster, and Chilman 1978; Silsbee, Plastas, and Plastas 1976), and in many instances wildlife contaminate the water (Potter, Gosz and Carlson 1980; Silsbee, Plastas, and Plastas 1976). In the Great Smoky Mountains National Park, European wild boars that root and wallow in springs and other water drinking sources are a major source of fecal streptococci bacteria. Bacteria in the feces of wildlife are as much a health hazard as those of humans. Therefore, reducing or managing the number of recreation users to an area may not necessarily reduce the bacterial levels to within safety limits. Moreover, drinking and cooking water may need to be boiled even in areas receiving little or no recreational use.

There are some instances that suggest that in remote wildland areas light recreational use will improve the bacteriological quality of water sources because wildlife will avoid the areas (Stuart, Bissonnette, Goodrich, and Walter 1971; Walter, Bissonnette, and

Stuart 1971). Walter and Bottman (1967) compared a closed watershed and one open to recreational use. They found that bacterial counts (fecal coliforms and fecal streptococci) were higher for the closed watershed than for the open watershed, which in 1970 had been opened for "limited recreation and logging." Bacterial contamination decreased in the streams after the watershed had been made available for human use. The authors concluded that human activities had resulted in a reduced wildlife population, which had contributed substantially to the previous bacterial pollution.

Little is currently known about the accumulation of bacterial organisms and nutrients in the bottom sediments of wildland water sources. Most studies of bacterial contamination examine only the surface waters when, in fact, the bottom sediments may contain the larger concentrations of organisms and nutrients. Brickler and Tunnicliff (1980) found fecal coliform densities in bottom sediments to be significantly higher than in surface water of rivers and tributaries in Arizona. Surface water FC densities ranged from 2.1 to 8.0/ml in the Colorado River, whereas densities in bottom sediment reached 48,000/ml. Forty-three percent of the sediment samples exceeded 500/ml, and 34 percent of them exceeded 1000/ml. Bacterial levels in bottom sediments are of considerable importance since several recreational activities such as swimming and boating cause suspension of bottom sediments and direct contact of the microorganisms with recreationists. As more bottom sediment analyses are conducted, they may modify considerably our thinking about the status of water quality as represented by analyses of surface water alone (Gosz 1982).

Backcountry Camping and Drinking Sources

The previous discussion on coliform bacteria dealt with levels found in lakes and streams, with no specific attention devoted strictly to drinking sources in backcountry camping areas. Because water is not chemically treated in these areas and is often taken from springs or very small tributaries, bacterial contamination is a concern. Giardiasis, hepatitis, and other diseases are a constant potential threat in these situations (Fig. 3).

Giardiasis, an intestinal disease caused by the protozoan pathogen *Giardia lamblia*, has been reported with increasing incidence by recreationists utilizing sources of water that drain forested and mountain areas. In recent years, cysts of *Giardia* have been reported in surface waters of Rocky Mountain, Olympic, Sequoia, and Yosemite National Parks as well as several national forests and wilderness areas (Monzingo, Kunkle, Stevens, and Wilson 1986; Cole 1990). As stated by Cole, it is not clear whether incident of *Giardia* is increasing because contamination is spreading or whether the disease is being more frequently and accurately diagnosed. Nevertheless, giardiasis infections have caused almost 50 percent of the reported waterborne disease outbreaks in the country since 1971 (Martin, Kunkle, and Brown 1986).

The disease is transmitted through fecal contamination of food and water or through direct fecal-oral contact. Beaver, muskrat, rodent, elk, domestic cattle, and dogs have been linked as major vectors of waterborne giardiasis. Symptoms of the disease include diarrhea, abdominal cramps, flatulence, greasy and foul-smelling stools, abdominal bloating, fatigue, weight loss, anorexia, and nausea (Monzingo and Stevens 1986).

FIGURE 3. Bacterial contamination is a constant concern with drinking sources in the back-country. (*Photo*: W. E. Hammitt.)

It has been established that where large numbers of outdoor recreationists concentrate, as many as one in ten animals may be carriers of *Giardia* cysts (Monzingo, Kunkle, Stevens, and Wilson 1986). For example, examination of several watersheds in Rocky Mountain National Park has led to the conclusion that the risk of ingesting viable *Giardia* cysts from contaminated water is high in areas where beaver are active, moderate in high human-use areas or where marginal beaver habitat occurs, and low in areas of limited human use and poor beaver habitat. Kuss, Graefe, and Vaske (1990, p.114) recommend that "because of the rising incidence of the disease and the number of vectors, however, all surface water should be suspect and sterilized by boiling."

Silsbee, Plastas, and Plastas (1976) surveyed the fecal coliform and streptococci concentrations in four types of water sources in Great Smoky Mountains National Park: flowing springs, seepage springs, spring-fed streams, and tributary-fed streams. A flowing spring is a spring that flows from a localized source and can be sampled directly as it comes from the ground. A seepage spring seeps from the ground over a wide area and after it has flowed over the ground surface for some distance, drinking water can be obtained from it. Spring-fed or primary streams are fed mainly by a spring or by seepage. A tributary-fed or secondary stream is one fed by various tributaries.

Flowing springs tended to be the best drinking water sources, giving consistently low coliform counts (Table 2). Seepage springs were highly variable, giving both low and high counts. Small spring-fed streams also tended to be variable and gave high counts at times. Larger tributary-fed streams generally gave consistent levels of contamination although somewhat higher than flowing springs. These results indicate that following springs are the best drinking sources, followed by secondary streams. However, even in the secondary streams the coliform levels average in the danger zone.

Sources of bacteria in the four drinking sources were primarily wildlife. Most of the FC/FS ratios indicated animal sources of contamination. Data collected from above and below campsites and outhouses showed that they did not have a major effect on the bacteriological quality of the water in the areas tested. The backcountry staff of Great Smoky Mountains National Park strongly recommend that campers boil all drinking water used in the backcountry.

Solid Waste and Foreign Materials

Solid waste in the form of litter tends to accumulate at the bottom of streams and lakes. The amount of solid waste carried into backcountry areas is potentially greater for watercraft activities than for backpacking since the materials are more easily transported. During the summer of 1969, solid waste left behind by recreational users of the Boundary Waters Canoe Area, Minnesota, totaled an estimated 360,000 lbs of bottles, cans, and other nonburnable refuse (King and Mace 1974). This averages to about 3 lbs per recreation user. Barton (1969) estimates that the solid waste figure of 360,000 lbs is equivalent to 1 ton of phosphates and 13 tons of nitrogen. In addition, decomposition of the material provides an abundant supply of trace elements as well as some major ions (Barton 1969). Since the 1970s the Boundary Water Canoe Area and other areas have prohibited bottles and cans on the backcountry lakes (Fig. 4).

TABLE 2. Comparison of Different Types of Backcountry Water Sources and Fecal Coliform Densities

Source Type	Range of Fecal Coliform Counts (Percent)					Number of Samples
	0	1–10	11–30	31–100	>100	
Primary stream	32	20	20	24	4	21
Secondary stream	15	77	7	1	0	72
Flowing spring	72	28	0	0	0	32
Seepage spring	33	40	15	8	4	21
All streams	20	62	10	7	1	93
All springs	57	32	5	4	2	53

Source: Silsbee, Plastas, and Plastas 1976.

FIGURE 4. Some heavily used water resource areas prohibit the use of bottles and cans in the backcountry. (*Photo*: D. W. Lime.)

Much concern has been expressed over the potential harm of oil and gasoline from outboard motors in aquatic ecosystems. Because outboard motors are two-stroke engines, the engine lubricant oil is mixed directly with the gasoline. The exhaust discharged into water by outboard engines contains oil and gasoline residues. Muratori (1968) and Stewart and Howard (1968) report that "as much as 4 gal of gasoline mixture out of every 10 may be discharged into the water from outboard motors." Modern motors should usually discharge between 10 to 20 percent of their fuels into the water. Besides the gasoline and oil being discharged into the water, the use of leaded gasolines has the potential of ejecting tetraethal leads into the water, which accumulate in bottom muds and may affect aquatic organisms (Barton 1969). English, Surber, and McDermott (1963) reported that outboard motor exhaust-water contains an average of 105 g/gal of nonvolatile oil, 57 g/gal of volatile oil, 0.53 g/gal of lead, and 0.60 g/gal of phenols.

The primary ecological effect of outboard motors is the deposition of oil on aquatic organisms. Oil in water attaches to the surface of unicellular plankton and other plants to interfere with air-gas exchange. Oil films also inhibit the growth of many forms of algae, disturbing the food chain of fish and other aquatic organisms. In addition to coating the surface of floating plants to interfere with gas exchange, oil can lead to oxygen depletion. One gram of oil in water requires 3.3 g of oxygen for complete oxidation (Barton 1969). Oil extracts can also stimulate bacterial growth, which is significant in that these organisms are competitors with algae for oxygen and nutrients found in water.

Phosphates and other chemicals contained in fuel-oil mixtures can also affect aquatic organisms, although little conclusive data exist (Jackivicz and Kuzminski 1973; Liddle and Scorgie 1980). Tainting of fish flesh occurs at a fuel-usage level of 8 gal of outboard motor fuel per million gal of lake water per season (English, Surber, and McDermott 1963). Oil also has an adverse effect on fish growth and longevity. However, in experimental ponds, Lagler, Hazzard, Hazan, and Tomkins (1950) found no effects on population of fish or plants that could be attributed to outboard motor exhaust.

Suspended Matter and Turbidity

Suspended matter may be the single most common factor influencing alterations in water quality in recreation areas. Anderson, Hoover, and Reinhart (1976) estimate that 80 percent of the deterioration in water quality is due to suspended solids. While in suspension, such solids cause waters to be turbid; reduced light penetration may restrict the photosynthetic activity of plants and the vision of animals. These finely divided materials at high concentrations are known to interfere with the feeding of filter feeder organisms and are abrasive to sensitive structures such as the gills of fish (Warren 1971). Reproduction of fish, particularly trout, and fish food are affected as these materials settle out. Perhaps most important for recreation purposes, increased loads of suspended solids greatly reduce the clarity of water and the public's desire to enter it.

Turbidity, related to recreation, can originate in water bodies from primarily three zones: bottom sediments, shorelines and adjacent banks, and the surrounding watershed. The disturbance of stream and lake sediments by boats and swimmers has been reported. Liddle and Scorgie (1980) report numerous aquatic plants that are uprooted by the wash and turbulence resulting from outboard motor propellers in shallow waters. Narrow channels are particularly sensitive because of the repeated use of such areas. Boats propelled by oars and/or paddles impart relatively little impact to stream bottoms, except in shallow stream riffles where canoes commonly scrape periphyton from rocks. Although boating may increase turbidity in selected high use areas, there seems to be little quantitative evidence that it is a major impact factor (Hansen 1975; Lagler, Hazzard, Hazan, and Tomkins 1950; Liddle and Scorgie 1980). For example, Lagler and colleagues found no recordable increase in turbidity because of outboard motors in their experimental ponds, even though there was considerable movement of the bottom sediments. There was some redistribution of benthic invertebrates, but no damage was recorded.

Swimming, wading, and fishing contribute to turbidity but only when concentrated in space and time. Gary (1982) recorded dramatic increases in suspended solids from waders near a small commercial campground on a few days when use was high. As soon as recreationists left the sampled area, suspended solid levels fell to almost predisturbance levels. Waders and swimmers in Great Smoky Mountains National Park also have an influence near campgrounds and heavy use segments of streams.

Streambank erosion and resulting suspended sediments are largely a result of trampling. Many wildland recreation activities concentrate at one time or another near the edges of water bodies. People walking in and out of water and up and down streambanks can quickly destroy the vegetation that protects shoreline soils from erosion (Fig. 5). Marginal vegetation and soils may also be damaged by those walking parallel to the water's edge but not directly engaged in water activities. Larson and Hammitt (1981) found that onlookers were a dominant source contributing to streambank impacts near family campgrounds. The crossing of streams by ORVs and horses also disturbs streambanks and bottom sediments, but again the impacts are usually quite isolated (Fig. 6).

Turbidity impacts from watershed disturbances are associated primarily with certain multiple-use land management practices (e.g., logging) and some recreation-caused erosion. Off-road vehicle and hiking trails in the southern Appalachian Mountains of the United States erode quickly where 80 to 90 in. of annual rainfall may be present. However, gravel roads, logging trails, and cutting practices in multiple-use recreational areas are probably a bigger contributor of watershed impacts than recreational use trails.

FIGURE 5. Swimmers and innertube floaters are causing streambank erosion at the put-in and take-out locations in Great Smoky Mountains National Park. (*Photo*: W. E. Hammitt.)

FIGURE 6. Off-road vehicles can greatly disturb streambanks and bottom sediments when crossing streams (*Photo*: W. E. Hammitt.)

SUMMARY

1. Water quality is a major concern, but not a frequent impact, in wildland recreation areas. It serves as a medium for body contact sports and as a drinking source for users. Thus, water-related impacts are unique in that they are more directly related to human health than soil, vegetation, and wildlife impacts.

2. Nutrient level, aquatic plant production and decomposition, and dissolved oxygen supply in aquatic ecosystems are all intricately related. With recreational use, plant production in warm lakes and streams can be quickly altered from acceptable rates to excessive growth rates with associated changes in oxygen supply and species composition of aquatic organisms.

3. Although coliform bacteria and quality of drinking water are obvious concerns in wildland recreation areas, there is conflicting research evidence that backcountry recreation drastically impacts water quality. More studies have failed than have shown significant increases in coliform counts as a result of recreational use. In several situations wildlife have been the dominant source of bacteria contamination in drinking water sources.

4. Suspended matter and turbidity may be the single most important water quality factor in the eyes of recreationists. Increased loads of suspended solids greatly reduce the clarity of water and the public's desire to use it.

REFERENCES

Anderson, H. W., M. D. Hoover, and K. G. Reinhart. 1976. Forests and Water: Effects of Forest Management on Floods, Sedimentation, and Water Supply. USDA Forest Service General Technical Report PSW-18.

Aukerman, R., and W. T. Springer. 1975. Effects of Recreation on Water Quality in Wildlands. Final Report, Eisenhower Consortium Grant EC-105. 67 pp.

Barton, M. A. 1969. Water Pollution in Remote Recreational Areas. *Journal of Soil and Water Conservation* 24:132–134.

Brickler, S. K., and B. Tunnicliff. 1980. Water Quality Analyses of the Colorado River Corridor of Grand Canyon. College of Agriculture Paper 350, University of Arizona, Tucson, AZ. 134 pp.

Brickler, S. K., and J. G. Utter. 1975. Impact of Recreation Use and Development on Water Quality in Arizona: An Overview. In J. D. Mertes, ed. *Man, Leisure and Wildlands: A Complex Interaction*. Eisenhower Consortium Bull. 1, pp. 195–201.

Cole, D. N. 1990. Ecological Impacts of Wilderness Recreation and Their Management. In J. C. Hendee, G. H. Stankey, and R. C. Lucas, eds. *Wilderness Management*. Golden, CO: North American Press, pp. 425–466.

Cowgill, P. 1971. Too Many People on the Colorado River. *The Environmental Journal* 45:10–14.

Dickman, M., and M. Dorais. 1977. The Impact of Human Trampling on Phosphorus Loading to a Small Lake in Gatineau Park, Quebec, Canada. *Journal of Environmental Management* 5:335–344.

English, J. N., E. W. Surber, and G. N. McDermott. 1963. Pollutional Effects of Outboard Motor Exhaust—Field Studies. *Journal of the Water Pollution Control Federation* 35:1121–1132.

Gary, H. L. 1982. Stream Water Quality in a Small Commercial Campground in Colorado. *Journal of Environmental Health* 45(1):5–12.

Gosz, J. R. 1982. Non-Point Source Pollution of Water by Recreation: Research Assessment and Research Needs. Eisenhower Consortium Bull. 13. 14 pp.

Hansen, E. A. 1975. Does Canoeing Increase Streambank Erosion? USDA Forest Service Research Note NC-186.

Hynes, H. B. N. 1970. *The Ecology of Running Waters*. Toronto: University of Toronto Press, 555 pp.

Jackivicz, T. P., and L. N. Kuzminski. 1973 A Review of Outboard Motor Effects on the Aquatic Environment. *Journal of Water Pollution Control Federation* 45:1759–1770.

Johnson, B. A., and E. J. Middlebrooks. 1975. Water Quality as an Approach to Managing Recreational Use and Development on a Mountain Watershed South Fork of the Ogden River-Ogden Valley Area, PRWA21-1. College of Engineering, Utah State University, Ogden, UT. 84 pp.

Kabler, P. W., and H. F. Clarke. 1960. Coliform Group and Fecal Coliform Group Organisms as Indicators of Pollution in Drinking Waters. *Journal of American Water Works Association* 52:1577–1579.

King, J. C., and A. C. Mace, Jr. 1974. Effects of Recreation on Water Quality. *Journal of Water Pollution Control Federation* 46(11):2453–2459.

Kuss, F. R., A. R. Graefe, and J. J. Vaske. 1990. *Visitor Impact Management: A Review of Research*. Vol. 1. Washington, DC: National Parks and Conservation Association. 256 pp.

Lagler, K. F., A. S. Hazzard, W. E. Hazan, and W. A. Tomkins. 1950. Outboard Motors in Relation to Fish Behavior, Fish Production and Angling Success. *Transactions North American Wildlife Conference* 15:280–303.

Larson, G. L., and W. E. Hammitt. 1981. Management Concerns for Swimming, Tubing, and Wading in the Great Smoky Mountains National Park. *Environmental Management* 5(4):353–362.

Liddle, M. J., and H. R. A. Scorgie. 1980. The Effects of Recreation on Freshwater Plants and Animals: A Review. *Biological Conservation* 17:183–206.

Marnell, L., D. Foster, and K. Chilman. 1978. River Recreation Research Conducted at Ozark Scenic Riverways 1970–1977: A Summary of Research Projects and Findings. USDI National Park Service, Van Buren, MO. 139 pp.

Martin, K. L., S. H. Kunkle, and G. W. Brown. 1986. *Giardia* and Other Pathogens in Western Watersheds. USDI National Park Service and Colorado State University Water Resources Division. Report No. 86-1. Fort Collins, CO.

Merriam, L. C., Jr., C. K. Smith, D. E. Miller, C. T. Huang, J. C. Tappeiner II, K. Goeckerman, J. A. Bloemendal, and T. M. Costello. 1973. Newly Developed Campsites in the Boundary Waters Canoe Area: A Study of Five Years' Use. University of Minnesota Agricultural Experiment Station Bull. No. 511.

Monzingo, D. L., and D. R. Stevens. 1986. *Giardia* Contamination of Surface Waters: A Survey of Three Selected Backcountry Streams in Rocky Mountain National Park. USDI National Park Service and Colorado State University. Water Resources Division. Report No. 86-2. Fort Collins, CO.

Monzingo, D. L., S. H. Kunkle, D. R. Stevens, and J. T. Wilson. 1986. *Giardia* in Backcountry Watersheds and Wildlife of Rocky Mountain National Park. Paper presented at the American Water Resources Association International Conference on Water and Human Health. Atlanta, GA.

Muratori, A. 1968. How Outboards Contribute to Water Pollution. *Conservationist* 22:6–8.

Potter, L. D., J. R. Gosz, and C. A. Carlson. 1984. Forest Recreational Use, Water, and Aquatic Life: An Assessment of Research Results for Land-Use Managers in the Southern Rockies and High Plains. Eisenhower Consortium Bulletin No. 6, USDA Forest Service, Rocky Mountain Forest and Range Experiment Station.

Reid, G. K. 1961. *Ecology of Inland Waters and Estuaries*. New York: Reinhold. 375 pp.

Sargent, F. O., and F. Zayer. 1976. Land Use Patterns, Eutrophication, and Pollution in Selected Lakes. Technical Report, USDI Office of Water Research and Technology. 47 pp.

Segall, B. A., and S. M. Oakley. 1975. Development of a System for Monitoring the Physical and Chemical Characteristics of Forest Lakes, Final Report, Eisenhower Consortium Grant EC-90. 77 pp.

Silsbee, D., L. A. Plastas, and H. J. Plastas. 1976. A Survey of Backcountry Water Quality in Great Smoky Mountains National Park. Management Report No. 10. Uplands Field Research Laboratory, Gatlinburg, TN. 66 pp.

Silverman, G., and D. C. Erman. 1979. Alpine Lakes in Kings Canyon National Park, California: Baseline Conditions and Possible Effects of Visitor Use. *Journal of Environmental Management* 8:73–87.

Skinner, Q. D., J. C.. Adams, P. A. Richard, and A. A. Beetle. 1974. Effect of Summer Use of a Mountain Watershed on Bacterial Water Quality. *Journal of Environmental Quality* 3:329–335.

Stewart, R. H., and H. W. Howard. 1968. Water Pollution by Outboard Motors. *The Conservationist* 22(6):6–8, 31.

Stuart, D. G., G. K. Bissonnette, T. D. Goodrich, and W. G. Walter. 1971. Effects of Multiple Use on Water Quality of High Mountain Watersheds. Bacteriological Investigations of Mountain Streams. *Applied Microbiology* 22:1048–1054.

Vander Wal, J., and R. J. Stedwill. 1975. A Lake Ranking Program Conducted on Forty-three Lakes in the Thunder Bay Area. ("Cited by") Wall, G., and C. Wright. 1977. The Environmental Impact of Outdoor Recreation. Dept. of Geography Publication Series, No. 11. University of Waterloo, Waterloo, Ontario.

Van Donsel, D. J., and E. E. Geldreich. 1971. Relationship of Salmonella to Fecal Coliform in Bottom Sediment. *Water Research* 5:1075–1087.

Varness, K. J., R. E. Pacha, and R. F. Lapen. 1978. Effects of Dispersed Recreational Activities on the Microbiological Quality of Forest Surface Water. *Applied and Environmental Microbiology* 36:95–104.

Wall, G., and C. Wright. 1977. The Environmental Impact of Outdoor Recreation. Dept. of Geography Publication Series, No. 11, University of Waterloo, Waterloo, Ontario.

Walter, W. G., and R. P. Bottman. 1967. Microbiological and Chemical Studies of an Opened and Closed Watershed. *Journal of Environmental Health* 30:157–163.

Walter, W. G., G. K. Bissonnette, and G. W. Stuart. 1971. A Microbiological and Chemical Investigation of Effects of Multiple Use on Water Quality of High Mountain Watersheds. Montana University Joint Water Resources Research Center, Report 17. 130 pp.

Warren, C. E. 1971. *Biology and Water Pollution Control*. Philadelphia: Saunders.

PART III
Impact Patterns and Trends

6 Impact Patterns

Chapters 2 through 5 described impacts of wildland recreation on soil, vegetation, wildlife, and water resources. These impacts often exhibit predictable patterns both in space and over time. Recreationists consistently tend to use the same places. Visitors to developed campgrounds concentrate on shaded sites near comfort stations and water sources, whereas backcountry campers congregate around spectacular lakes with good fishing and near streams. Such places tend to be more highly impacted than less popular places. Consistent use distributions result in characteristic patterns of impact on individual sites such as trails and campsites. Impacts on both trails and campsites generally decrease as one moves from the center to the edge of the site. However, total area of campsites and width of trails commonly increase over years of use. Much of this chapter will explore the nature of spatial patterns of impact on trails and campsites.

Recreation sites and impacts are not static; they change over time. Temporal impact patterns are the second subject of this chapter. Impact to soil and ground cover vegetation generally occurs rapidly, with the rate of deterioration tending to taper off over time. However, rates of change differ with type of impact and between environments. For example, in forested areas, soil compaction and vegetation loss occur rapidly and loss of organic horizons occurs more slowly. In deserts, loss of organic horizons may occur more rapidly than soil compaction. Some impacts also continue to increase over time, such as campsite area expansion, number of campsites, and trail erosion. Recovery rates vary greatly from place to place, although they are always slower than rates of deterioration.

SPATIAL PATTERNS OF IMPACT

One of the most distinctive characteristics of recreation use is its highly concentrated nature. Most use is restricted to a small number of travel routes and destination areas. Manning (1979) calls this the "node and linkage" pattern of recreation use and impact. Nodes of impact occur at destination areas; linkages develop along the routes between nodes. The table and firepit location at a campsite, the edge of the cliff at a scenic overlook, and the riverbank at a boat put-in are examples of nodes where use is concentrated. Examples of linkages include hiking and equestrian trails, canoe portages, and the access trails between individual sites, the comfort station, and water sources in a developed campground. Concentration of use means that pronounced impacts, although locally severe, occur in only a small proportion of any recreation area. Wagar (1975) estimated that one European park, by restricting use to developed trails, has confined the direct impacts of use to only 0.1 percent of the park's 42,000 acres. In the Eagle Cap Wilderness, where users are free to travel where they will, Cole (1981) estimated that no more than about 0.5 percent of two popular drainage basins had been substantially disturbed by use of campsites or trails. Even around two very popular subalpine lakes, in the same wilderness, the proportion of the area that had been substantially disturbed was less than 2 percent (Cole 1982). In properly designed, developed campgrounds where camping pads are highly disturbed, much of the total campground may remain relatively undisturbed.

Many factors contribute to this concentration of use. Certain locations attract people over and over again. Waterfalls, lakes, and scenic viewpoints are all good examples. People also tend to be attracted to edges. Rivers, lakes, and cliff edges attract people as does the boundary between meadow and forest. Use also concentrates for reasons of safety and ease of use. Many people are more comfortable and feel safer camping or walking in places that obviously have been used before. It is also easier to walk on existing trails and to camp on sites that have already been cleared of brush and rocks. All of these factors, and others, often cause wildland users to develop an emotional bond with certain recreation sites. These users become attached to these favorite places, returning to them for repeat visits (Williams, Patterson, Ruggenbuck, and Watson 1992).

The tendency for use to be concentrated within certain parts of a recreation area can be either good or bad. Situations where this is advantageous or not will be discussed in Chapter 13, along with techniques managers can use to encourage either use concentration or its counterpart—use dispersal.

Use is also concentrated within individual sites. Typically, campers in developed sites spend more than three-quarters of their in-camp time close to the table, tent pad, and fire grill. In undeveloped sites, backpackers spend most of their in-camp time around the tent and fire areas. In fact, the installation of fire grates in backcountry is recommended as a means to concentrate users and reduce total area of disturbance (Marion 1995). These areas are the most severely impacted. The "core" campsite area is surrounded by a less intensively used area where wood may be gathered and people may walk to and from water or toilet facilities. Beyond this area is a zone that is rarely penetrated by the recreationist. On developed campsites McEwen and Tocher (1976) have called these three distinct areas the impact, intersite, and buffer zones, respectively (Fig. 1). They argue that these zones are a consistent and important feature of campsites. These zones should be recognized, their distinctive types and levels of impact should be understood, and management should be tailored to maintenance and enhancement of these zones. Because the concept of impact zones has such important implications for managing ecological impacts on campgrounds and other high-density recreation sites, McEwen and Tocher's summary of impacts and management implications for each zone is described in the following subsections.

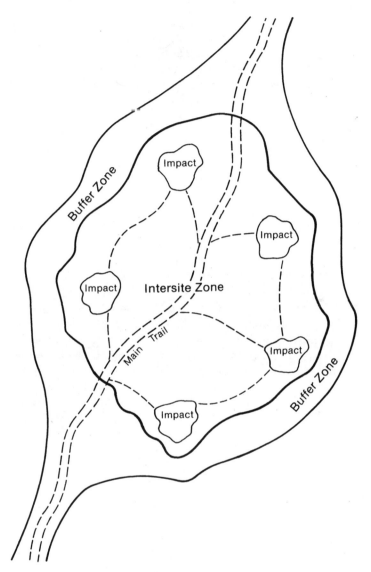

FIGURE 1. Impact, intersite, and buffer zones for a cluster of campsites in a backcountry recreation area. (*Source:* D. N. Cole.)

Impact Zone

Deterioration of soil and ground cover vegetation is severe, so impact zones quickly degenerate into hard, barren pads. Trampling pulverizes and scuffs away litter cover, eliminates herbaceous and small woody stems, and compacts soil. Soil compaction and loss of litter cover cause water infiltration rates to be severely reduced. This increases the severity of erosion. These changes occur within the first couple years of use, even with only moderate levels of visitor use. Moreover, recovery of impact zones will require long periods of time. They are likely to never recover as long as use continues. High impact zones must be accepted, although problems can be minimized through site design to keep impact zones small and hardening of surfaces with gravel, sand, or wood chips (see Chapter 13). Encouraging continued, concentrated use of these impact zones is important. Therefore, it is critical to keep these areas attractive and clean. If they become trashy, dirty, dusty, or muddy, they are likely to be abandoned, and new areas will be impacted. Key objectives for management of impact zones are to keep them as small and as attractive as possible.

Intersite Zone

Vegetation and litter are lost and soil is compacted, but these impacts are pronounced only on informal trail systems. Elsewhere, the health and vigor of soil and vegetation are not seriously reduced. Species composition of vegetation and wildlife is likely to be altered, but this will not be evident to most visitors. Of particular importance, the capacity of vegetation to regenerate is not severely compromised. Intersite zones will be the nurseries for future generations of trees, and they provide screening between individual sites. Without them, one campsite tends to blend into the next. The greatest concern with intersite zones is that they will be eliminated through expansion of impact zones. This can be avoided by creating intersite zones during the initial site design phase and by maintaining impact zones so that they do not expand. Some planting of trees, shrubs, and placing of logs and rocks may be necessary both to minimize use of intersite zones and to provide protected regeneration sites, particularly for tree seedlings. Establishment and hardening of an "official" system of informal trails between impact zones, other sites, and conveniences such as water supplies and toilets are often necessary to avoid excessive trail proliferation.

Buffer Zone

Few impacts occur in the buffer zone other than those resulting from some firewood removal, a few hiking trails, and roadways. In most primitive campgrounds the buffer zone is simply a transition zone between the developed site and the surrounding natural community. As with intersite zones, buffer zones should be delineated and protected. Avoiding encroachment from expanding intersite zones is the major concern; no active management of vegetation or soil is needed because the zone is natural.

Although these three zones have been described for campgrounds where they are most useful, the concept can also be applied to other high-use sites. Trails exhibit parallel zones, from the highly impacted trail tread through a less altered trailside zone to the undisturbed adjacent area. On most trails the tread is barren and compacted. Because it is often trenched below the local ground surface, the trail tread channels water and is subject to accelerated erosion. Where erosion is severe, roots and rocks are exposed and the trail can become difficult to use. Hikers and stock may leave the tread to walk on easier ground, enlarging the area of impact. As with the impact zone on campsites, the trail tread is an inevitable—usually purposely constructed—zone of extreme impact. Management must strive to keep the tread functional so users stay in the tread and avoid widening the impacted zone. The goals are usually to avoid erosion by diverting running water off the tread and to provide a comfortable walking surface. This may require some type of paving or bridging, particularly in wet or boggy areas. Regular monitoring and maintenance is often more essential for trails than for campsites.

The adjacent trailside zone is similar to the intersite zone. It is not natural, but the impacts that have occurred are not evident to most users. Vegetation often grows along the trailside, although its composition is usually very different from that of undisturbed environments (Cole 1981, 1991). Plants are usually low-growing, and many of the species growing here are exotic weeds inadvertently brought into the area. Soil compaction and erosion may occur, but it is less pronounced than on the tread. Perhaps the major source of impact is the initial construction of the trail. During construction, vegetation clearing opens up the trailside environment, increasing light intensities and changing moisture relationships. Moisture levels frequently increase along trails for several reasons. Fewer trees intercept less precipitation; fewer plants lose less water through evapotranspiration; and the compacted trail sheds water along its sides.

Trail construction also creates new habitats alongside trails. Rock faces are frequently either created or eliminated where trails are blasted out of rock outcrops. Flat, soil-covered surfaces are often created where trails cross steep boulder slopes on which soil and vegetation were minimal. Trails also interrupt drainages, leading to the development of boggy areas or to the drainage of areas that formerly were wet. Management of trailside zones should attempt to minimize disturbance by avoiding excessive alteration during trail construction. Thereafter, as with management of intersite zones on campsites, the most important thing is to avoid lateral expansion of the impacted tread into the trailside zones. One of the best ways to do this is to keep trailside zones rough and natural. This will tend to keep hikers and stock on the tread. The greater the contrast between the trail tread and the trailside zone, in terms of ease of walking, the easier it will be to avoid expansion of the highly disturbed tread.

Impact patterns are less evident where use is more diffuse than it is on campsites and trails. This applies to cross-country travel by motorized or nonmotorized means and certain scenic areas, picnic areas, or places where stock are allowed to roam and graze. Even in such situations, however, there is usually a gradient from high impact zones to the natural community. Where concentrated use around nodes, edges, and facilities leads to pronounced impact, management will need to control use distribution in such a way that impact zones do not expand and proliferate over time. Recognition of these zones and spatial patterns is an important first step in devising management strategies for controlling impact. We will discuss this further in Chapter 13 on site management.

Spatial patterns are most pronounced and important in describing and managing impacts on vegetation and soil, components of the ecosystem that are stationary. Patterns are less distinctive when we consider animals and water, components that move around. Smaller animals are affected primarily by habitat alteration; as with vegetation and soil, such impact is highly concentrated. Larger animals, however, may be affected over very large areas. A grizzly bear or bald eagle population may be affected over its entire range, even though recreational use is highly localized and concentrated. This is especially true where recreational use is concentrated on an animal's preferred habitat or on critical feeding or breeding grounds. For many animals that live on or in the water, for example, it may be irrelevant that recreational use and impact are minimal a few yards from the water; if all of their habitat is subject to disturbance by recreational use, then they are likely to be highly disturbed. Bird populations, disturbed at their nesting sites, may show evidence of this disturbance in their wintering grounds, even if no recreational use occurs there. Impacts on water can also be felt far from the point where pollution occurs. Dilution of pollutants by water tends to reduce the severity of impact, but it increases the area affected. Because wildlife- and water-related impacts can spread far beyond the places where disturbance originates, management of these impacts provides challenges that vegetation and soil impacts do not.

TEMPORAL PATTERNS OF IMPACT

The rate at which impact occurs varies with type of impact. As mentioned before, herbaceous vegetation loss generally occurs more rapidly than loss of soil organic horizons. Rates are also dependent on use levels. Impact occurs most rapidly where use levels are heavy. Generally, however, impacts on vegetation and soil occur rapidly wherever use levels are even moderate (Fig. 2). A number of studies also show that the relationship between site impacts and the age of a site is asymptotic rather than linear (Fig. 3). That is, impacts increase rapidly during the first few years after a site is used

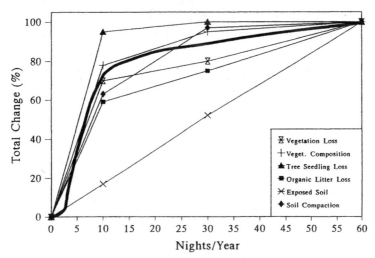

Total Change represents the difference between indicator measures taken on undisturbed control plots and on campsites with 60 or more nights of visitation annually. Thus, approximately 70% of the vegetation loss that occurs on campsites receiving 60+ nights/year has already occurred after only 10 nights/year.

FIGURE 2. Change in campsite impact parameters under low to moderate levels of annual visitation, Boundary Waters Canoe Area Wilderness. (*Source:* Leung and Marion 1995.)

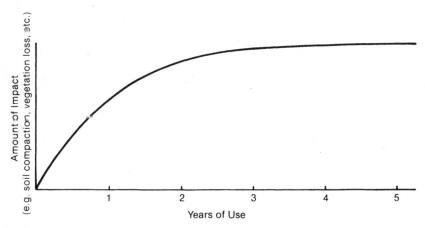

FIGURE 3. Most impact on recreation sites occurs within the first few years after the site is opened. (*Source:* D. N. Cole.)

and then increase more slowly, if at all, thereafter (Cole and Marion 1986). In describing developed campsites, Hart (1982) distinguishes between a short break-in period, when the campsite is developed and initially used by campers—the period when most of the impact occurs—and a dynamic equilibrium period when changes are minimal. During the equilibrium period additional impacts caused by use tend to be offset by maintenance activities and natural rejuvenation processes. On forested campsites the final change is death of the overstory. This death may or may not be hastened by recreational use. When it occurs, the forested site will usually be replaced by an open campsite because there is usually no tree regeneration to replace the overstory.

The impacts resulting from development and initial use of campsites have been studied in wilderness by Merriam, Smith, Miller, Huang, Tappeiner, Goeckermann, Bloemendal, and Costello (1973) and in a developed campground by LaPage (1967). After two years of use, soil penetration resistance (compaction) on campsites in the Boundary Waters Canoe Area Wilderness reached near-maximum levels that were not substantially surpassed in the following years. Follow-up studies by Merriam and students at 7 and 14 years after original site development showed that bare soil area and site expansion were the major impacts to increase over time (Marion 1984; Merriam and Peterson 1983). On car campgrounds in Pennsylvania, vegetation loss was most severe after the first year of use; vegetation cover actually increased in the following years, as trampling-tolerant non-native species replaced the original native occupants of the site.

Other impacts on campsites do not occur so rapidly with initial use and may continue to deteriorate with time. The most important of these types of impact are site expansion, damage to trees, and loss of organic matter (Cole and Marion 1986; Cole and Hall 1992). Site expansion occurs whenever a party either needs more space or prefers to use an unused portion of the site. Thus it is most likely to occur where sites are used by large parties or where impact zones are unattractive or undesirable (e.g., muddy or not flat). Over 5 years, 10 newly developed campsites in the Boundary Waters Canoe Area increased more than 50 percent in size, and the size of another 4 more than doubled. Figure 4 shows an example of how one of these Boundary Waters campsites doubled in size in just two years. Note the expansion to contiguous areas the first year, followed by development of a satellite site the second year. Some of the most serious problems with site expansion occur on campsites used by outfitters. Outfitted parties often consist of numerous unaffiliated groups of people, each seeking some privacy from the other groups. In their seeking out private places to set up tents, a large area is affected.

Satellite campsites often develop into new campsites, or they may expand and become incorporated into the original campsite, increasing the total disturbed area. Studies of longer-term changes in campsite impacts also indicate that a major increase occurs in the number of newly created campsites. Cole (1993) examined proliferation and campsite conditions in three wilderness areas over 12- to 16-year periods. A dramatic increase in the number of campsites in all three areas was the primary impact occurring during the trend study. This is not to imply that some campsites do not improve, as newly created sites may defer use pressures on original campsites (Fig. 5). However, the "site-pioneering" behavior of campers over longer periods of time and the proliferation of campsites are of major concern to wildland recreation managers. In fact, the systemwide or ecological unit proliferation of campsites and

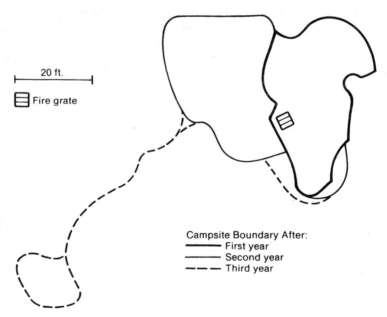

FIGURE 4. Campsites tend to expand in size over time. Development of satellite sites is a common pattern of site expansion. (*Source:* Adapted from Merriam, Smith, Miller, Huang, Tappeiner, Goeckermann, Bloemendal, and Costello. "Newly Developed Campsites in the BWCA: Study of Five Years Use," in University of Minnesota Agricultural Experimental Station Bulletin, 1973. Used with permission of the publisher.)

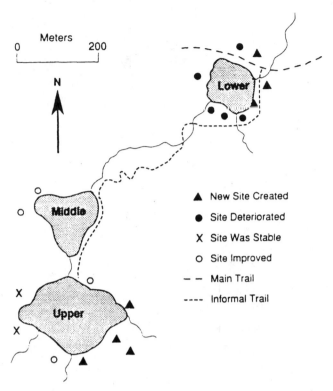

FIGURE 5. Proliferation and change in campsite condition over a 16-year period (1972–1988), Jerome Rock Lakes, Lee Metcalf Wilderness, MT. (*Source:* Cole 1993.)

their associated impacts appear more important than individual site deterioration over time. More will be said about this topic in Chapter 7, in which longer-term trends are the focus.

Damage to trees is cumulative and, therefore, increases over time. Exposure of tree roots, physical damage to tree trunks, and sapling removal are long-term processes that may affect the vigor and growth rate of trees. Once a tree is felled or severely scarred, it will remain that way until it rots. Because old damage is slow to disappear, any new damage represents an increase in impact over time. Even though tree damage is one of those impacts that does increase over time, most tree damage occurs in the impact zone shortly after a site is opened.

Loss of organic matter over time is somewhat different. Loss of organic matter caused by scuffing and erosion of litter can be offset by the yearly leaf fall of hardwoods or the more continuous needle fall of conifers. However, loss of litter exceeds yearly litter fall on all but the most lightly used campsites. Consequently, a net loss occurs, and litter depth and cover decline over time (Cole and Marion 1986). On forested sites, the decline is not as rapid as vegetation loss, so near-maximum levels of litter loss occur at a more advanced age than vegetation loss. On Boundary Waters Canoe Area campsites mineral

FIGURE 6. Trail widening in the form of multiple braided trails is a common impact pattern. (*Photo:* R. C. Lucas.)

soil was not exposed until sometime between the second and fifth years of use, and it was still increasing 14 years after the campsites were first developed.

On trails the rate at which impact occurs may be even more rapid. Initial impacts associated with trail development include intentional felling of trees, removal of brush and ground vegetation, surface flattening, soil compaction, and drainage alteration. Once these changes have been initiated, those associated with trail use are usually of less importance. Two impacts that can become more pronounced with time are trail widening and erosion (Cole 1991; Marion 1984). Trail widening is analogous to campsite expansion. It occurs where the trail tread is difficult to walk on, particularly where it is muddy or rocky. Widening can be continuous, or it can occur as a series of braided trails (Fig. 6).

Although trampling can cause erosion of some trails, its principal effect is to make the trail surface more susceptible to erosion, by churning up the soil, reducing infiltration rates, removing vegetation, and channeling water. The primary agent of erosion is running water from intercepted streams, snowmelt, springs, and even intense precipitation. Once water is channeled down a trail, erosion will occur and will probably increase in severity over time. Such erosion is likely to continue, with or without use, until water bars or some other drainage control device is installed to divert water off the trail.

Temporal patterns of impact on wildlife and water are less well understood. For wildlife they vary greatly between species and even within species. Some animals such as white-tailed deer can become habituated to disturbance. This creates a pattern of change over time that is analogous to vegetation loss on campsites. Initial impact is serious, but disturbance decreases over time as the animal develops a tolerance for disturbance. Many animals can develop a tolerance for predictable disturbances, but are adversely affected by unpredictable types of disturbance.

Other animals can tolerate infrequent disturbance but become bothered by frequent disturbance. This pattern is the opposite of changes in vegetation and soil. In this case there is an initial resistance to impact, but once disturbance becomes frequent, a severe reaction takes place. Disturbance of certain types of nesting birds provides a good example. Parents may put up with the first few groups of visitors that come close to their nests. At some point, however, their tolerance of these intrusions will be exceeded, and they will abandon their nest.

Impacts on water also vary between the two extremes of rapid response to initial disturbance and initial resistance followed by a severe response. Fecal contamination at any place or time may be serious one day and gone the next, provided the input is not continuous. On the other hand, some pollutants accumulate over time. Initially, they may not present problems because they are diluted by water, but over time they may reach levels that present problems. For example, recreational use around alpine lakes in Kings Canyon National Park caused trace elements to accumulate to levels that eventually led to changes in biota. These changes have not been reversed by more than a decade of reduced use levels (Taylor and Erman 1979).

RECOVERY RATES OF IMPACTS

Recovery rates are more variable than deterioration rates because they are more dependent on environmental factors. For example, 1000 people walking single file across wildflower fields on a mountain top and in a valley bottom would, in both cases, kill all plants in their path in one day; however, recovery of the mountain top vegetation might take many times longer than recovery of the valley bottom vegetation because the growing season on the mountaintop is much shorter and soils are poorer.

Recovery rates for soils may be less variable than rates for vegetation. Although compaction levels are not consistent between studies, several studies report that compaction levels can return to normal after 6 to 18 years (Cole and Hall 1992; Hatchell and Ralston 1971; Parsons and DeBenedetti 1979; Stohlgren and Parsons 1986). Recovery of organic matter levels may take longer. In Kings Canyon National Park, Parsons and DeBenedetti (1979) found that the depth of organic horizons and accumulation of woody fuels on campsites closed for 15 years had not returned to normal. Recovery from erosion will take even longer. Once it occurs, recovery will require centuries.

Recovery of vegetation on trails subjected to experimental trampling illustrates the variability of recovery rates. Some trails in the southern Appalachians were almost completely revegetated just one year after trampling (Studlar 1983). In contrast, the vegetation cover of dry alpine meadows in Glacier National Park had recovered only 24 percent after six years (Hartley 1976). Rates can even be highly variable in different environments within the same general area. For example, five years after being experimentally trampled by horses, vegetation cover of a grassland was 100 percent of normal; cover in a nearby forest was only 26 percent of normal (Weaver, Dale, and Hartley 1979).

More recent trampling experiments have concentrated on spatial and temporal recovery rates among species within zones of campsites, and in tropical environments. Sun (1992) and Sun and Liddle (1991) found that the trampling resistance and recovery rates among eight species varied greatly. Plant resistance was not significantly correlated with recovery or growth rate, whereas recovery rate was positively correlated with growth rate. High resistance and high recovery appear to be two exclusive characteristics of plant species. Plants that are resistant to trampling tend to have low growth rates; plants with fast growth rates appear to use a recovery strategy (Sun 1992). In addition to species differences in recovery, research has shown that the spatial zones within a campsite or trail recover at different rates (Stohlgren and Parsons 1986; Taylor, Reader, and Larson 1993). The stratification of use zones in campsite impacts can be an important step in assessing recovery. For example, closure of campsites for three years resulted in bulk density of soils in the core (impact) zone of campsites to recover more slowly each year than the intermediate (intersite) and periphery (buffer) zones. Mean foliar cover also recovered much more slowly in the core areas than in intermediate areas. Taylor, Reader, and Larson (1993) looked at zones of trail impacts while examining the question, "To what degree is vegetation response to trampling consistent among different temporal (short- vs. long-term) and spatial (path vs. wider corridors) scales of trampling?" They found that as trampling frequently increased, community composition changed progressively at both 4 m and 1 m distances from the trail centerline. Species richness was less affected by trampling and decreased only within 1 m of the trail centerline at the highest level of trampling (25,000 passes per season for 18 years).

Trampling, and even nontrampling, studies indicate that recovery rates of impact always require more time than resistance rates, and that plentiful rainfall and longer growth seasons increase the rate of recovery (Marion and Cole 1996). For example, recovery rates tend to be faster in the southern Appalachians than in the drier mountains of the western United States. Studies in tropical rain forests also indicate a more rapid recovery rate than reported for temperate forest. Study of a trail in Costa Rica, abandoned for 32 months, showed that recovery was significant and that herbs and seedlings were more abundant along the recovering trail than in undisturbed forest (Boucher, Aviles, Chepote, Dominquez Gil, and Vilchez 1991). These authors conclude that the rapid rate of recovery suggests that trail closure for a few years may be sufficient to allow vegetation recovery in tropical rain forests. The speed of recovery also lends support to the hypothesis that highly productive forests, although sensitive to trampling impact, will also have high levels of resilience (Kuss 1986; Cole and Marion 1988).

Management practices, of course, can have a significant influence on the rate at which impacts recover. The elimination of some closely spaced designated campsites and the installation of anchored fire grates reduced the total area of campsite disturbances by 50 percent over a five-year period (Marion 1995; Marion and Cole 1996). Fire grate installation provided a focal point within campsites that increased the concentration of activities, allowing peripheral areas to recover. Campsite impacts not only recovered; they decreased rapidly once disturbance was terminated. The fertile environment of the Delaware Water Gap National Recreation Area was a factor in rapid recovery (Marion and Cole 1996). This study also indicated that although the

management actions increased the intensity of use on and within individual campsites, there was no resultant increase in the intensity of impact on individual campsites. This is probably due to the fact that the established sites were already stabilized
in terms of use-intensity-related impacts, and that the fire grates focused use patterns.
Over the five-year period, campsites, in general, decreased in areal extent (Fig. 7).

SUMMARY

1. Recreational resource impacts do not occur randomly in space, but exhibit
concentrated and predictable spatial patterns. Most impacts, like use patterns, are
restricted to a small number of travel routes and destination areas.

2. In campsites, three distinct areas or zones of impact occur: (1) the impact, (2)
intersite, and (3) buffer zones. Each zone of impact has distinct types and levels of
impact and management implications.

3. Most impacts on vegetation and soil show an asymptotic rather than linear
relationship over time. Vegetation disturbance and soil compaction increase rapidly

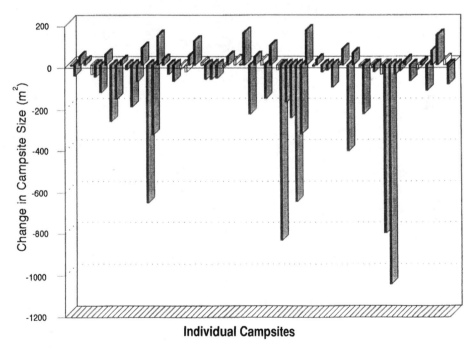

FIGURE 7. Change in campsite size from 1986 to 1991 after initiation of management
actions, Delaware Water Gap Recreation Area, PA. Campsites with positive bar values
increased in size, negative values decreased in size, and those bars not shaded did not change
enough to meet the 20 percent estimated measurement error. (*Source:* Marion 1995.)

during the first couple of years after a site is used, but increase more slowly thereafter. However, some impacts, such as site expansion, continue to increase over time.

4. The rate at which impacts occur (resistance) and recover (resilience) vary over space and time and are influenced by many use, environmental, and management conditions. However, recovery rates are almost always slower than impact rates. Rates of recovery are quite slow on heavily used, established sites. Longer-term trend studies indicate that proliferation of new campsites is more important than increases in impacts of established sites. Thus, changes in areawide or systemwide impacts over time may be a greater management concern than established site impacts.

REFERENCES

Boucher, D. H., J. Aviles, R. Chepote, O. E. Dominquez Gil, and B. Vilchez. 1991. Recovery of Trailside Vegetation from Trampling in a Tropical Rain Forest. *Environmental Management* 15(2):257–262.

Cole, D. N. 1981. Vegetational Changes Associated with Recreational Use and Fire Suppression in the Eagle Cap Wilderness, Oregon: Some Management Implications. *Biological Conservation* 20:247–270.

Cole, D. N. 1982. Controlling the Spread of Campsites at Popular Wilderness Destinations. *Journal of Soil and Water Conservation* 37:291–295.

Cole, D. N. 1991. Changes on Trails in the Selway-Bitterroot Wilderness, Montana, 1978–89. USDA Forest Service Research Paper INT-450. 5 pp.

Cole, D. N. 1993. Campsites in Three Western Wildernesses: Proliferation and Changes in Condition over 12 to 16 Years. USDA Forest Service Research Paper INT-463. 15 pp.

Cole, D. N., and T. E. Hall. 1992. Trends in Campsite Condition: Eagle Cap Wilderness, Bob Marshall Wilderness, and Grand Canyon National Park. USDA Forest Service Research Paper INT-453. 40 pp.

Cole, D. N., and J. L. Marion. 1986. Wilderness Campsite Impacts: Changes over Time. In R. C. Lucas, comp. *Proceedings—National Wilderness Research Conference: Current Research.* USDA Forest Service General Technical Report INT-212, Ogden, UT, pp. 144–151.

Cole, D. N., and J. L. Marion. 1988. Recreation Impacts in Some Riparian Forests of the Eastern United States. *Environmental Management* 12(1):99–107.

Hart, J. B., Jr. 1982. Ecological Effects of Recreation Use on Campsites. In D. W. Countryman and D. M. Sofranko, eds. *Guiding Land Use Decisions: Planning and Management for Forests and Recreation.* Baltimore, MD: Johns Hopkins Press, pp. 150–182.

Hartley, E. A. 1976. Man's Effects on the Stability of Alpine and Subalpine Vegetation in Glacier National Park, Montana. Ph.D. dissertation, Duke University, Durham, NC.

Hatchell, G. E., and C. W. Ralston. 1971. National Recovery of Surface Soils Disturbed in Logging. *Tree Planters Notes* 22(2):5–9.

Kuss, F. R. 1986. A Review of Major Factors Influencing Plant Responses to Recreation Impacts. *Environmental Management* 10:637–650.

LaPage, W. F. 1967. Some Observations on Campground Trampling and Groundcover Response. USDA Forest Service Research Paper NE-68. 11 pp.

Leung, Y. F., and J. L. Marion. 1995. A Survey of Campsite Conditions in Eleven Wilderness

Areas of the Jefferson National Forest. USDI National Biological Service Report, Virginia Tech Cooperative Park Studies Unit, Virginia Tech University, Blacksburg, VA. 79 pp.

Manning, R. E. 1979. Impacts of Recreation on Riparian Soils and Vegetation. *Water Resources Bulletin* 15:30–43.

Marion, J. L. 1984, Ecological Changes Resulting from Recreational Use: A Study of Backcountry Campsites in the Boundary Water Canoe Area Wilderness, Minnesota. Ph.D. dissertation, University of Minnesota, St. Paul.

Marion, J. L. 1995. Environmental Auditing Capabilities and Management Utility of Recreation Impact Monitoring Programs. *Environmental Management* 19(5)763–771.

Marion, J. L., and D. N. Cole. 1996. Spatial and Temporal Variation in Soil and Vegetation Impacts on Campsites. *Ecological Applications* 6(2):520–530.

McEwen, D., and S. R. Tocher, 1976. Zone Management: Key to Controlling Recreational Impact in Developed Campsites. *Journal of Forestry* 74:90–93.

Merriam, L. C., and R. F. Peterson. 1983. Impacts of 15 Years of Use on Some Campsites in the Boundary Waters Canoe Area. Research Note 282, Agricultural Experiment Station, University of Minnesota, St. Paul. 3 pp.

Merriam, L. C., Jr., C. K. Smith, D. E. Miller, C. T. Huang, J. C. Tappeiner II, K. Goeckermann, J. A. Bloemendal, and T. M. Costello. 1973. Newly Developed Campsites in the Boundary Waters Canoe Area—A Study of Five Years' Use, Agricultural Experiment Station Bull. 511, University of Minnesota, St. Paul. 27 pp.

Parsons, D. J., and S. H. DeBenedetti. 1979. Wilderness Protection in the High Sierra: Effects of a Fifteen Year Closure. In R. M. Linn, ed. *Proceedings of Conference on Scientific Research in the National Parks,* pp. 1313–1318. USDI National Park Service Transactions and Proceedings Ser. 5. Washington, DC: U.S. Government Printing Office.

Stohlgren, T. J., and D. J. Parsons. 1986. Vegetation and Soil Recovery in Wilderness Campsites Closed to Visitor Use. *Environmental Management* 10(3):375–380.

Studlar, S. M. 1983. Recovery of Trampled Bryophyte Communities near Mountain Lake, Virginia. *Bulletin of the Torrey Botanical Club* 110:1–11.

Sun, D. 1992. Trampling Resistance, Recovery, and Growth Rate of Eight Plant Species. *Agriculture, Ecosystems, and Environment* 38:265–273.

Sun, D., and M. J. Liddle. 1991. Field Occurrence, Recovery and Simulated Trampling Resistance and Recovery of Two Grasses. *Biological Conservation* 57:187–203.

Taylor, T. P., and D. C. Erman. 1979. The Response of Benthic Plants to Past Levels of Human Use in High Mountain Lakes in Kings Canyon National Park, California. *Journal of Environmental Management* 9:271–278.

Taylor, K. C., R. J. Reader, and D. W. Larson. 1993. Scale-Dependent Inconsistencies in the Effects of Trampling on a Forest Understory Community. *Environmental Management* 17(2):239–248.

Wagar, J. A. 1975. Recreation Insights from Europe. *Journal of Forestry* 73:353–357.

Weaver, T., D. Dale, and E. Hartley. 1979. The Relationship of Trail Conditions to Use, Vegetation, User, Slope, Season, and Time. In R. Ittner, D. R. Potter, J. K. Agee, and S. Anschell, eds. *Proceedings, Recreational Impacts on Wildlands.* pp. 94–100. USDA Forest Service, Pacific Northwest Region, R-6-001-1979, Portland, OR.

Williams, D. R., M. E. Patterson, J. W. Roggenbuck, and A. E. Watson. 1992. Beyond the Commodity Metaphor: Examining Emotional and Symbolic Attachment to Place. *Leisure Sciences* 14:29–46.

7 Trends in Wildland Recreation Use and Impacts

The severity of ecological impact problems in wildland areas stems from an ever-increasing participation in wildland types of recreation. Studies conducted over long periods of time, documenting escalating trends in ecological impacts, are nonexistent; however, recent trend data from studies conducted during the late 1980s and 1990s are available. Trend data on nationwide participation in outdoor recreation are much more readily available inasmuch as general use surveys have been conducted since the 1960s.

This chapter reviews the early recreational use of wildland areas, continues with the more current and projected trends in outdoor recreation participation, and concludes with an overview of trends concerning wildland recreation use, users, and impacts. Examination of these general trends in recreation use, and impact trends in some specific wildland areas, provides an indication of the changing relationships, over time, of recreational use and impacts.

EARLY OUTDOOR RECREATION USE

The ecological impacts resulting from recreational use are particularly critical in wilderness and backcountry areas because management objectives for such areas stress maintaining high levels of natural integrity. Early use of wilderness areas increased at a rate faster than most other wildlands. For example, annual growth rates in the use of parks and recreation facilities often exceeded 10 percent from the early postwar period through the mid-1960s. Recreational visits to U.S. Forest Service wilderness increased fourteenfold between 1946 and 1970 (Stankey 1973). Forest Service wilderness areas in California showed an average 16 percent annual increase in use for the 1970 to 1975 period (Hendee, Stankey, and Lucas 1990). Although rates of increase slowed down during the late 1970s and early 1980s, use is still increasing. In fact, the rate of wilderness use started increasing again in the late 1980s and has continued into the 1990s (Cole 1996). Moreover, the land base on which use occurs is decreasing. Designated wilderness acreage is growing, but nondesignated backcountry is shrinking drastically as areas are designated wilderness or becoming roaded.

Among wildland recreation activities on national forests, increases in winter sports have been very rapid (Table 1). Use nearly tripled between 1966 and 1979. Although

TABLE 1. National Forest Recreation Use by Activity
(Thousands of Visitor Days)

Activity	1966		1979	
	Use	Percent of Total	Use	Percent of Total
Camping	39,564.5	26.2	54,780.3	24.9
Recreational travel (mechanical)	31,301.1	20.7	49,536.5	22.5
Fishing	14,709.1	9.7	16,776.0	7.6
Hunting	13,118.6	8.7	15,327.9	6.7
Recreational residence use	7,960.5	5.3	6,651.6	3.0
Picnicking	7,887.5	5.2	8,874.2	4.0
Winter sports	5,219.6	3.5	14,485.0	6.6
Hiking and mountain climbing	4,277.8	2.8	11,176.9	5.1
Organizational camp use	4,287.2	2.8	4,086.8	1.8
Boating	4,006.5	2.6	7,072.1	3.2
Viewing scenes and sports entertainment	3,926.8	2.6	8.321.1	3.8
Resort use	4,003.5	2.6	4,308.9	1.9
Swimming and scuba diving	3,076.9	2.0	4,632.3	2.1
Horseback riding	2,065.9	1.4	3,166.4	1.4
Visitors information services	2,058.8	1.4	4,121.8	1.9
Gathering forest products	1,241.7	.8	3,916.1	1.8
Nature study	796.4	.5	1,210.9	.5
Waterskiing and other water sports	641.0	.4	888.0	.4
Games and team sports	585.5	.4	832.8	.4
Total	150,728.9	99.6	220,165.6	99.6

Source: U.S. Forest Service.

much of this growth represents increased use of developed downhill ski areas, participation in cross-country skiing and snowmobiling also increased dramatically. Hiking and mountain climbing also increased nearly threefold over this period. Similar increases have occurred on lands outside the national forests. A public survey conducted in 1965 for the Bureau of Outdoor Recreation showed that 9.9 million Americans hiked or backpacked. This number had increased to 28.1 million Americans when the survey was repeated in 1977.

Backcountry camping figures for the National Park Service have been kept on a nationwide basis only since 1972. However, individual parks have trend data over a longer period of time. For Great Smoky Mountains National Park, backcountry overnight use was about 105,000 user nights in 1975, a 53 percent increase over 1972 use levels and a 250 percent increase over 1963 use (Bratton, Hickler, and Graves 1978). Between 1967 and 1972, backcountry camping in Yosemite National Park increased 184 percent, from 78,000 to 221,000 user nights. Overnight use in the Shenandoah National Park backcountry quadrupled between 1967 and 1974; total backcountry use of Rocky Mountain National Park increased more than seven times between 1966 and 1976 (Hendee, Stankey, and Lucas 1990).

River recreation has also rapidly expanded. The history of whitewater floating on the Colorado River through the Grand Canyon is a classic example. Prior to 1960 fewer than 650 people had *ever* floated the river; 10 years later 10,000 people were floating the river *every* year. Between 1966 and 1972 the number of people floating the river increased sixteenfold, from 1,067 to 16,432 (Table 2). Since then it has continued to increase, but at a rate controlled by the number of permits issued. Leatherberry, Lime, and Thompson (1980) report that ownership of kayaks and canoes has increased much faster than ownership of other types of watercraft. Between 1973 and 1976 there was a 68 percent increase in number of canoes and a 107 percent increase in number of kayaks. This accelerating trend in river use has led public resource agencies to restrict use on many rivers. The number of rivers with use restrictions increased from 8 in 1972 to 38 in 1977 (McCool, Lime, and Anderson 1977). On some rivers the number of persons applying for a limited number of permits has been as much as 20 times the number of permits handed out. The waiting list to float through the Grand Canyon is so long that new applicants may have to wait more than 10 years for a chance to float the river. Ecological impacts on river resources can be particularly severe because use is concentrated along a narrow linear corridor.

Off-road vehicle use has also increased dramatically in recent decades. In the 1960 nationwide survey on outdoor recreation, so few people used off-road vehicles that they were not included in the survey; by 1982, 11 percent of people 12 years old and older used wheeled off-road vehicles, and 3 percent used snowmobiles (USDI National Park Service 1984). On national forest lands off-road vehicle use doubled during the 1970s to a 1979 use level of 5.3 million visitor days for wheeled vehicles and 3.3 million visitor days for snowmobiles (Feuchter, 1980). Most vehicular recreation takes place on roads; almost 50 million visitor days of recreational driving took place on national forest roads in 1979. This is fortunate because the impacts of recreational vehicles, when used off roads, are unusually severe.

The most common activity causing ecological impact in wildland recreation areas is camping, whether by people in cars and recreational vehicles or by backcountry users. According to a 1979 survey, camping ranked third, behind swimming and bicycling, among outdoor recreation activities. Cole and LaPage (1980) report that a national survey conducted in 1960 showed 3 to 4 million active camping households in the United States. This figure had grown to 12.4 million households by 1971 and to 17.5 million households by 1978. Camping grew at an average annual rate of 20 percent in the 1960s, 8 percent in the early 1970s, and less than 5 percent in the late 1970s. Much of the early interest in recreational impacts in the United States grew out of this rapid increase in camping during the 1960s.

TABLE 2. Travel on the Colorado River Through the Grand Canyon of Arizona

Year	Number of People
1867	1[a]
1869–1940	41
1941	4
1942	8
1943	0
1944	0
1945	0
1946	0
1947	4
1948	6
1949	12
1950	7
1951	29
1952	19
1953	31
1954	21
1955	70
1956	55
1957	135
1958	80
1959	120
1960	205
1961	255
1962	372
1963–1964	44[b]
1965	547
1966	1,067
1967	2,099
1968	3,609
1969	6,019
1970	9,935
1971	10,385
1972	16,432
1973	15,219
1974	14,253[c]

Source: U.S. Forest Service.

[a]Some contend that James White, a trapper fleeing Indians, floated through the Grand Canyon on a makeshift log raft two years before the famous expedition of John Wesley Powell.

[b]Travel on the Colorado River in those years was curtailed by the completion of Glen Canyon Dam upstream and the resultant disruption of flow.

[c]The downturn in visitation was the result of the institution by management of a quota system. The numbers applying for the available permits continued to rise sharply.

CURRENT AND PROJECTED OUTDOOR RECREATION TRENDS

Several National Recreation Surveys (NRSs) have been conducted since the initial Outdoor Recreation Resources Review Commission survey of 1960. The studies since then, conducted in 1965, 1970, 1972, 1977, 1982–1983, 1987, and 1994–1995, allow for examining some current, and even projected, trends in recreation participation. Although the outdoor recreation surveys of the last 35 years are not strictly comparable, they do point to some general trends for specific activities related to wildland recreational use and resource impacts.

Comparisons of data from the 1960 and 1982 NRSs indicate that *day hiking* grew significantly in popularity between 1960 and 1982, with 14 percent of the NRS respondents participating in 1982. Data from the 1987 survey indicate that 10 days annually is the median participation per person and about 20 percent of participants go hiking more than 15 days annually. *Camping,* including backpacking, almost doubled in rate of participation between 1960 and 1982 (Cordell, Bergstrom, Hartmann, and English 1990). The 1987 survey showed that 20 percent of the recreating public camped at developed sites, with a median of 9 days annually. Another 11 percent camped in primitive campgrounds, with a median of 8 days annually. *Backpacking* involves about 5 percent of the recreating public, with a median of 7 days of annual use.

Survey data from several sources were used by Flather and Cordell (1995) to update outdoor recreation participation for the decade 1982 through 1992 (Table 3). Bicycling, day hiking, swimming, motorboating, and off-road vehicle driving continue to be popular activities. These five activities, along with developed-site camping, also have the highest frequency of participation (days of use).

More current data from the 1994–1995 survey, when compared with the 1982–1983 results (Table 4), indicate that hiking and backpacking are the second and third fastest-growing outdoor activities among persons 16 years or older (Cordell, Lewis, and McDonald 1995). Downhill skiing and primitive camping, two other wildland recreation activities, ranked fourth and fifth in growth rate during the 12-year comparison period. The activities of hiking, backpacking, and primitive camping are all closely associated with trail and campsite resources, and the fast growth of these activities is likely to have direct impacts on the quality of these resources.

Trends in wildlife-dependent activities have been mixed over the last three decades (Flather and Cordell 1995). Fishing continues to be the most popular wildlife activity, with nearly 25 percent of U.S. inhabitants participating in 1985. In contrast to the increase in number of anglers, the number of hunters has remained essentially unchanged since 1975. The stability in the total number of hunters, however, is misleading. Small game and migratory bird hunters have declined substantially since 1972, whereas the number of hunters pursuing big game species has increased during every five-year Fish and Wildlife Service survey period since 1955 (Flather and Cordell 1995, p. 5). It is speculated that big game hunting will have more impact on wildland recreation resources, since it is often associated with horse or off-road use and overnight camping. Growing faster in popularity relative to traditional wildlife and fishing pursuits are nonconsumptive wildlife-related activities (Duffus and

TABLE 3. Participation Trends for Outdoor Recreational Activities Not Dependent on Wildlife, 1982–1992

Activities	Millions of Persons ≥ 12 Years Old Participating			Millions of Persons Participating ≥ 10 Days in 1992
	1982–1983	1985–1987	1992	
Land based				
Bicycling	60	72	86	60.3
Camping in developed campgrounds	32	40	48	13.2
Day hiking	26	32	50	13.4
Nature study/ photography	22	24/26	—[a]	—[a]
Driving motorized vehicles off-road	21	24	38	16.2
Camping in primitive campgrounds	19	22	25	6.7
Horseback riding	17	20	19	6.7
Backpacking	9	10	8	3.6
Water-based				
Swimming in lakes, streams, ocean	60	70	90	41.4
Motorboating	36	42	65	24.6
Waterskiing	17	20	21	7.6
Canoeing/kayaking	15	18	19	3.2
Snow- and/or Ice-based				
Downhill skiing	11	14	21	3.6
Snowmobiling	6	8	8	1.7
Cross-country skiing	6	8	8	2.9

Sources: 1982–1983 National Recreation Survey, USDI National Park Service; 1985–1987 Public Area Recreation Visitors Survey, USDA Forest Service; and the 1992 Pilot of the National Survey on Recreation and the Environment (unweighted data), USDA Forest Service.
[a]Participation in nature study/photography not estimated in 1992.

Dearden 1990). The number of people who actually traveled more than 1.6 km from their residences to observe, photograph, or feed wildlife increased from 22.9 to 37.5 million from 1980 to 1990.

Projections of future demand for outdoor recreation were developed from the 1987 survey data. Projections of the public's maximum preferred future demand for land, water, and snow and ice activities were estimated for each decade to the year 2040 (Table 5). Among individual activities, those projected to exhibit the most rapid rates of demand growth by the American public include downhill skiing, cross-country skiing, pool swimming, backpacking, visiting prehistoric sites, running and jogging, rafting, and day hiking. Based on projected future demand for activities that commonly occur in wildland areas and wilderness, demand increases seem evident. For

TABLE 4. Ten Fastest-Growing Outdoor Activities Among Persons 16 Years or Older in the United States 1982–1995

Activity	Number 16 Years + 1982–1983 (Millions)	Number 16 Years + 1994–1995 (Millions)	Percentage Growth
Bird-watching	21.2	54.1	155.2
Hiking	24.7	47.7	93.0
Backpacking	8.8	15.2	72.7
Downhill skiing	10.6	16.8	58.5
Primitive camping	17.7	28.0	58.2
Walking	93.6	133.6	42.7
Motorboating	33.6	46.9	39.9
Sightseeing	81.3	113.4	39.5
Developed camping	30.0	41.5	38.3
Swimming in natural waters	56.5	78.1	38.2

Source: Cordell, Lewis, and McDonald 1995.

example, backpacking is projected to grow 155 percent by the year 2040, wildlife observation and photography 74 percent, day hiking 193 percent, and general outdoor photography 105 percent (Cordell, Bergstrom, Hartmann, and English 1990).

RECENT TRENDS IN WILDLAND USE

Recent trend studies by wilderness researchers allow for assessing specific trends in wildland recreation use, users, and impacts over the last 10 to 15 years. As reported in the previous section on early recreation use, wilderness and wildland recreation use increased very rapidly during the 1960s and 1970s after establishment of the 1964 National Wilderness Preservation System. However, by the late 1980s, Lucas and several co-workers (Lucas 1989; Lucas and McCool 1988; Lucas and Stankey 1989; Roggenbuck and Watson 1988) reported a different trend. Although recreation use of the entire National Wilderness Preservation System was still increasing, they concluded that "use of individual wilderness has stabilized or is declining" (Roggenbuck and Watson 1988, p. 354) because "much of the apparent growth is accounted for by the rapid expansion in the number of wilderness units" (Lucas 1989, p. 54).

Three lines of reasoning, based on visitor-use data available through 1986, were used to arrive at this conclusion:

1. Annual growth rates in total use of all designated wilderness decreased from double-digit increases prior to the mid-1960s to a 1 percent increase in the early 1980s (Lucas and Stankey 1989).
2. Wilderness use declined on a per-acre basis between 1975 and 1986 (Roggenbuck and Watson 1988).

TABLE 5. Maximum Preferred Demand for Recreational Trips Away from Home and Indices of Future Demand Growth to 2040

Resource Category and Activity	Trips in 1987 (Millions)	Future Number of Trips as Percentage of 1987 Demand				
		2000	2010	2020	2030	2040
Land						
Wildlife observation and photography	69.5	116	131	146	162	174
Camping in primitive campgrounds	38.1	114	127	140	154	164
Backpacking	26.0	134	164	196	230	255
Nature study	70.8	105	113	120	131	138
Horseback riding	63.2	123	141	160	177	190
Day hiking	91.2	131	161	198	244	293
Photography	42.0	123	143	165	188	205
Visiting prehistoric sites	16.7	133	160	192	233	278
Collecting berries	19.0	113	126	143	166	192
Collecting firewood	30.3	112	124	138	157	178
Walking for pleasure	266.5	116	131	146	164	177
Running/jogging	83.7	133	163	197	234	262
Bicycle riding	114.6	125	148	173	202	222
Driving vehicles or motorcycles off-road	80.2	105	111	118	125	130
Visiting museums or info. centers	9.7	118	136	153	174	188
Attending special events	73.7	114	127	141	157	168
Visiting historic sites	73.1	122	143	169	203	241
Driving for pleasure	421.6	115	128	142	157	167
Family gatherings	74.4	119	135	152	170	182
Sightseeing	292.7	118	136	156	183	212
Picnicking	262.0	108	117	126	136	144
Camping in developed campgrounds	60.6	120	137	155	173	186
Water						
Canoeing/kayaking	39.8	113	126	140	157	169
Stream/lake/ocean swimming	238.8	105	110	117	124	129
Rafting/tubing	8.9	111	136	164	215	255
Rowing/paddling/other boating	61.8	112	124	136	150	159
Motorboating	219.5	106	111	117	123	127
Water skiing	107.5	111	121	131	141	148
Pool swimming	221.0	137	169	205	242	269
Snow and Ice						
Cross-country skiing	9.7	147	177	199	212	195
Downhill skiing	64.3	153	197	247	298	333

Source: Cordell, Bergstrom, Hartmann, and English 1990. *1985–87 Public Area Recreation Visitor Survey.*

3. Use decreased during the early 1980s, both in the original Forest Service wilderness (the core system of areas established in 1964 by the Wilderness Act) and in National Park Service backcountry. Most of these areas experienced their peak year of use prior to 1980 (Lucas and Stankey 1989).

A decade (1986–1996) of use data has accumulated since the 1980s, when it appeared that wildland recreation use was stabilizing and decreasing. Cole (1996) has analyzed the last 10 years of use data, as well as use during the period of 1965–1996. His conclusions indicate that wildland recreation use of the National Wilderness Preservation System has steadily increased during the period 1965–1996. People are recreating in designated wilderness more than ever. Recreational use of the National Wilderness Preservation System increased almost sixfold between 1965 and 1994, when recreation use approached 17 million recreation visitor-days. Most of this use occurs in wilderness managed by the Forest Service and the National Park Service (Fig. 1). The average annual increase in use over this period was 6.3 percent, and growth was remarkably constant.

Over the same period that the National Wilderness Preservation System experienced a sixfold increase in recreation use, it experienced an eightfold increase in acreage. During the 1960s and 1970s, visitor use increased more rapidly than acreage. Use intensity, measured as use per acre of the entire system, increased from 0.32 recreation visitor-days per acre in 1965 to 0.40 visitor-days per acre in 1979 (Fig. 2). After 1979, use per acre declined to 0.16 recreation visitor-days per acre in 1989 and to 0.18 recreation visitor-days in 1994.

These data show a decline in recreation use per acre of the entire National Wilderness Preservation System since 1979; however, visitor use has not necessarily

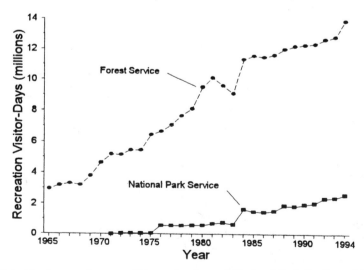

FIGURE 1. Total recreation use of Forest Service and National Park Service wildernesses. (*Source:* Cole 1996.)

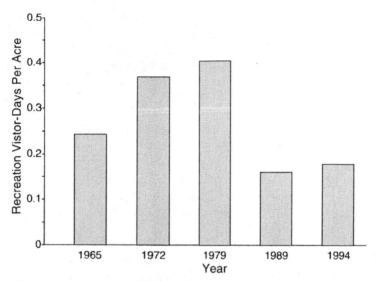

FIGURE 2. Use intensity (recreation visitor days per acre) of the National Wilderness Preservation System. (*Source:* Cole 1996.)

declined in any of these wildernesses. In 1980, 56 million acres of wilderness were designated in Alaska, doubling the size of the National Wilderness Preservation System overnight. But, recreational use of these lands is minimal (0.02 recreation visitor-days per acre in 1994). Excluding Alaska, the 1994 recreational use intensity was as high as it has ever been—about 0.40 recreation visitor-days per acre (Fig. 3).

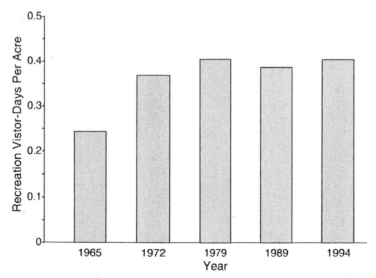

FIGURE 3. Use intensity of the National Wilderness Preservation System, excluding Alaska. (*Source:* Cole 1996.)

Although the size of the National Wilderness Preservation System has greatly increased since 1964 (from 54 areas and 9 million acres to 630 areas and 103 million acres today), many wildernesses are also used more heavily than ever. At least one-half of all designated wildernesses experienced their highest levels of use during the 1990s. Moreover, use increased during the 1990s in virtually every wilderness, even those that experienced high levels of visitation in the late 1970s or 1980s. The only group of areas for which a substantial majority experienced peak use prior to the 1990s was the "core" group of original Forest Service areas. Recent growth is particularly pronounced in National Park Service units, where double-digit growth rates are comparable to those of several decades ago.

These use trend conclusions drawn from recent data are different from reports in the late 1980s that suggested that wilderness use was stable or declining. One reason for this change is that use trends reversed in the wildernesses and parks that were analyzed in earlier studies. Now we can see that the period of declining use, for those wildernesses and parks that experienced declining use, ended in the late 1980s just as the reports were being written, suggesting that wilderness use was declining. Use of these areas began increasing again almost as soon as the apparent decline was identified. With the benefit of an additional 10 years of data, it now appears that the decline was limited to a brief period and to a subset of wildernesses. The prominent trend has been one of increasing use. In some areas, increases have been slow and steady; in other areas, particularly in many national parks, periods of explosive growth have been separated by a period of pronounced decline (Cole 1996).

The continued increase in use of wildland areas for recreation has many management implications. The demand for wildland recreation experiences will likely continue to grow. Consequently, avoidance of management problems associated with increased future use (crowding and associated resource damage) continues to be a valid reason for designating additional wilderness and managing it within a limit of acceptable change framework. Part IV of this book will deal in more detail with the management implications of increased use and the resulting resource impacts.

RECENT TRENDS IN WILDLAND USERS

Although estimates of the amount of recreational use occurring in wildland areas are commonly determined on an annual basis by management agencies, data concerning user characteristics are not. The characteristics of users, their use patterns, and behavioral preferences are usually obtained on a case-study and, often, one-time basis. Thus, it is difficult to find trend data on wildland recreation users because of the lack of repeat and longitudinal studies of area users. Visitor surveys that replicate earlier studies of wildland recreation users are necessary before trend analyses can be conducted.

To better understand trends among wilderness visitors, Cole, Watson, and Roggenbuck (1995) replicated three earlier visitor use surveys in the Boundary Waters Canoe Area Wilderness, Minnesota, in the Shining Rock Wilderness, North Carolina, and in the Desolation Wilderness, California. The years 1969 and 1991 were compared in the Boundary Waters, 1978 and 1990 in Shining Rock, and 1972 and 1990 in Desolation. Prior to these three visitor trend studies there had been only one detailed visitor trend study—that of visitors to the Bob Marshall Wilderness Complex, Montana, in 1970 and 1982 (Lucas 1985). Results of the three studies were compared with the earlier study of the Bob Marshall visitors. These case studies provide examples from four different regions of the United States with substantial wilderness acreage and include one canoe wilderness and one wilderness with substantial stock use. However, the examples do not vary much in use intensity. Although the Bob Marshall Wilderness Complex is relatively lightly used, the three other wildernesses are heavily used.

The earlier Bob Marshall trend study found few differences in characteristics of visitors. The most pronounced differences were as follows: more hikers relative to horse and mule users in 1982, smaller party sizes, shorter lengths of stay, less use of outfitters, more summer use relative to fall use, a wider distribution of use across trailheads, some shift in activities from more consumptive to more contemplative, and less dependence on wood fires in 1982. The data also showed an increase among 1982 visitors in the proportion of women, education levels, professional and technical occupations, and a decrease in amount of previous experience in the Bob Marshall Wilderness Complex. Visitors in 1982 were more concerned about crowding, conflict, and poor trails and were less able to find their desired level of campsite solitude. They were more likely than 1970 visitors to feel that soil and vegetation impacts were a problem and less likely to feel that litter was a problem.

These findings have been cited in an attempt to generalize about overall trends in wilderness use. For example, Roggenbuck and Lucas (1987) suggest that there may be a trend toward fewer wilderness impacts per party, and Roggenbuck and Watson (1988) suggest that groups are getting smaller and stays are getting shorter. However, these changes may be unique to the Bob Marshall Wilderness Complex, which is an unusual area in a number of ways: it is one of the largest wilderness complexes outside Alaska and is unusual in the amount of horse, outfitter, and hunting use it receives.

Another long-term visitor study in a wilderness-like (wildland) area was conducted in the backcountry of the Great Smoky Mountains National Park in 1973 and 1983 (Burde and Curran 1986). As in the Bob Marshall study, recent visitors were older, more likely to be female, and visited in smaller parties. In contrast to those in the Bob Marshall study, recent visitors to the Great Smoky Mountains National Park had more experience with wilderness, were more likely to be family groups, and had no change in length of stay.

The recent trend analysis by Cole, Watson, and Roggenbuck (1995) of visitors to three wilderness areas allows for a synthesis and summary of trend differences among these three areas and the Bob Marshall and Great Smoky areas. An attempt was made to identify trends that might be widespread across the National Wilderness Preservation System. Realizing the limitations of generalizing about overall wilderness trends from a small number of case studies, the authors categorized the trends into five classes, based on strength and consistency of trends across the five study areas (Table 6).

TABLE 6. Strength and Consistency of Trends Across Five Wildernesses for 63 Variables

---

Strong Consistent Trends

Older visitors; higher educational attainment; more females; more visitors who have been to other wildernesses; better ratings for litter conditions.

Weak Consistent Trends

Increased income; fewer first-time wilderness visitors; visitors were older when they first visited wilderness; more solo visitors; smaller groups; fewer organized groups; shorter overnight stays; more day use; less fishing; more mountain climbing; use more concentrated in summer; higher total encounter rates; less support for low-standard trails and leaving a few trees blown down across the trail; more support for high-standard trails, bridges over creeks, bridges over rivers, natural lightning fires, packing unburnable garbage out of the wilderness, prohibiting wood fires where dead wood is scarce, and limiting the size of visitor groups.

Variables That Did Not Change

Population of current residence; days spent in wilderness in the past year; proportion of visitors who hike, photograph, and swim; off-trail travel; number of campsite encounters; ability to find preferred level of campsite solitude; ratings of "wear and tear;" support for outhouses, cement fireplaces, interpretive signs, a natural fishery, and restricting use if area is overused.

Weak Inconsistent Changes

Number of wilderness visits in the past year; typical frequency of wilderness visits; proportion of groups with family members; proportion of hiking groups; distance traveled; number of different campsites used; concentration of use on weekends; concentration of use at certain trailheads; overall trip quality ratings; visitor opinions about the number of other people they encountered; preferred campsite encounter rates; visitor support for trailless areas, fire rings, assigning campsites, and administrative use of chain saws.

Strong Inconsistent Changes

Proportion of visitors who are students and members of conservation organizations; first-time visitors to the specific wilderness; number of previous visits to the specific wilderness; proportion of visitors who hunt and study nature; number of encounters with large groups; relationship between satisfaction estimates and hypothetical encounter rates.

Source: Cole, Watson, and Roggenbuck 1995.

Conclusions Drawn from Trend Synthesis

As can be seen from the categories in Table 6, there was considerable variation in user trends across the five wilderness areas. For example, only 5 of the 63 variables assessed exhibited strong and consistent trends. Rather than a detailed discussion of trends, a summary of conclusions drawn from the synthesis of trend differences is offered.

All Wildernesses Are Not Alike. The lack of substantial consistent change in trend variables across the five wildernesses suggests that every area can be unique and that it is dangerous to generalize about trends across the entire wilderness system. Study results for one wilderness at one point in time may be site specific and of limited value beyond that wilderness.

Visitors Have Changed More Than Their Visits. The characteristics of wilderness visitors changed more than the types of trips they took, their use patterns during trips, and their evaluation of conditions they encountered. Today's visitors are generally older, more highly educated, more likely female, and more likely to be day users than in the past. The increase in day users, particularly in some wildernesses, indicates that solo visitors are more common, groups are smaller, and stays are shorter. However, trend data for all wilderness areas seem to indicate that there has been little substantial change in group size (two to four people) and length of stay (one to three nights) over the last 20 years.

Perceptions of Impact Conditions Basically Unchanged. Although evidence for the study areas indicates that current visitors consistently feel that litter is a less severe problem, there is little similar evidence regarding interparty contacts and impact potential of groups. Virtually everyone supports the "pack out your garbage" policy, and it seems to work. However, there is no clear evidence that today's wilderness visitors are any more or less tolerant of encounters with others than their predecessors. But, again, this finding varies with the specific area studied. Current Shining Rock visitors felt that "too many people" was less a problem than their predecessors did, despite encountering more people. Reported satisfaction also decreased more slowly, with increasing numbers of encounters, in 1990 than in 1978. All these results suggest an increased tolerance for frequent interparty encounters. At Desolation, the tolerance of day users was higher than that of overnight visitors; moreover, the tolerance of day users increased over time, but the tolerance of overnight visitors was unchanged. These differences between day and overnight visitors suggest that the increased tolerance of Shining Rock visitors may simply reflect an increase in day use in that area. Finally, the tolerance of Boundary Waters visitors decreased over time. Current visitors are more likely to consider the area crowded, despite no significant change in number of encounters. Moreover, reported satisfaction declined much more rapidly with increasing numbers of encounters in 1991 than in 1969.

Users of Desolation, Boundary Waters, and Shining Rock were not optimistic that a shift toward the use of low-impact behaviors was occurring. Use concentration remains high in these wildernesses, and trip and group characteristics remain largely unchanged. However, evidence of more people using stoves, packing out litter, and using some other basic low-impact practices is a promising trend.

Inconsistent and Declining Attitudes. Many wilderness areas are currently involved with management of natural fires and natural fisheries (no stocking and leaving barren lakes alone) in natural wilderness ecosystems. Early studies showed that visitors considered both practices undesirable. The follow-up studies in two of the wildernesses

(Bob Marshall and Desolation) showed that visitors still reject the idea of natural fisheries; however, attitudes in support of natural fires have increased dramatically. This suggests that visitors will support the goal of preserving natural conditions in wilderness ecosystems, but perhaps only when this does not disrupt their preferred activities. Current attitudes also tend to support high-standard trails and bridges over creeks more than the purist attitudes found in the earlier studies. For example, there were significant increases in concern about poor trail maintenance, poor trail marking, and inadequate information about trail locations in the Shining Rock area. Increased day use in Shining Rock may have led to a reduction in self-reliance and more interest in easy access and travel within the wilderness.

Some Management Cautions.   The vast majority of today's visitors to the five study areas were very satisfied with their trips, just as in the past. However, because so few of the trend variables changed consistently across the five wildernesses, it is difficult to attribute the satisfaction level to specific trends. It is also very dangerous to extrapolate results from one wilderness to another. It may be possible, however, to identify groups of wildernesses for which trends are likely to be relatively similar. For example, many heavily day-used wildernesses close to large urban areas with universities may change in similar ways.

The finding that day-users are often quite different from overnight users and that day use is increasing, at least in some areas, is of importance. Day users have seldom been studied; they are seldom monitored; and their use is frequently uncontrolled. Managers of wildernesses with substantial amounts of day use would be wise to pay more attention to these users and their impacts.

The observation that people who come to wildernesses have changed, without a pronounced shift in the kinds of trips that visitors take or in their preferences for the conditions they encounter, must also be interpreted with caution. This finding can be partially explained as changes in the sociodemographic characteristics of visitors who keep coming to wildernesses. For example, visitors in 1972 who kept returning to Desolation would be older in 1990 and less likely to be students. Alternatively, this finding might suggest that wilderness visit characteristics and visitor attitudes and management preferences can remain stable despite pronounced shifts in the kinds of people who visit wildernesses (such as more women).

RECENT TRENDS IN WILDLAND IMPACTS

Wildland recreation impacts, unlike wildland recreation use, are seldom estimated on an annual basis and therefore do not lend themselves as well to trend analyses. Only within the last 10 to 15 years have empirically based impact studies been replicated so that impact changes over time could be examined. These studies have concentrated on trail and campsite impact trends within wilderness and other wildland areas.

Although a number of studies of trail and campsite impacts have been conducted (Cole 1987), most studies have assessed conditions at only one point in time. They provide a "snapshot" of conditions, but little perspective on how conditions are changing over time. Although it is true that many wildland recreation management areas commonly monitor impact conditions on a periodic basis, these data are seldom subjected to trend analysis or published. We can assume from the amount of trail and campsite maintenance and reconstruction done every year that deterioration is occurring; however, we have little quantitative information about trends in impact condition in wildland areas (Cole 1991).

Trail Impact Trends

Four studies of change over time on trail systems have been conducted in wildland areas (Cole 1991). Studies by Bayfield (1985, 1986) and by Lance, Baugh, and Love (1989) have been conducted in wild areas in Scotland. Data on changes in trail width are available for periods of as much as 12 years. These investigators found that many trails increased in width, but some trails were relatively stable. Generally, newly developed trails and those experiencing increased use were most subject to change. In Rocky Mountain National Park, Colorado, Summer (1980, 1986) also found considerable variation in response between trails over 7 years; four of nine trail segments widened substantially, whereas the others were generally stable. Two of five segments deepened substantially. Summer (1980) found that new trails were particularly prone to deterioration and that extent of deterioration was often related to terrain characteristics.

Fish, Brothers, and Lewis (1981) and Tinsley and Fish (1985) studied trail erosion in Guadalupe Mountains National Park, Texas. Over a 3.5-year period, little net erosion occurred. Some trail segments experienced erosion, and others experienced deposition. The net effect was not significantly different from what was occurring off-trail. A similar result was reported by Cole (1983) in a study of 2 years of change on a trail in the Selway-Bitterroot Wilderness, Montana.

Cole (1991) extended his initial 2-year Selway-Bitterroot Wilderness study to cover an 11-year period, 1978–1989. Over the 11-year period, changes in trail depth were not significant. Individual trail locations were prone to change, but the trail system as a whole was relatively stable. There was virtually no net erosion or deposition. Total trail width, a measure of the width of the zone disturbed by trampling, did increase. However, bare trail width (a measure of the zone devoid of vegetation) did not change significantly. These results suggest greater change at the periphery of the trail corridor—increasing total width—than in the central portion of the trail zone.

The finding that trail width varied more than depth, with amount of use, is not surprising. Trampling is the primary agent of trail widening, whereas the primary agent of deepening is running water. Consequently, the critical factors that influence depth are more likely to be related to environment (for example, soil characteristics or slope steepness) rather than use.

Campsite Impact Trends

Wilderness managers cite campsite deterioration as a problem more than any of the other potential problems in wilderness (Washburne and Cole 1983). Camping in natural and wildland areas commonly causes locally severe impacts, particularly on the vegetation and soils at destination sites. Many campsites have lost virtually all ground cover vegetation and tree reproduction; organic soil horizons have been lost, and exposed mineral soil has been severely compacted. Although there is information on campsite conditions in wildland areas, few data are available on the changes in campsite conditions over time. However, change on established campsites over time is only one of the pieces of information needed to evaluate change in campsite condition. Campsite impact is a function of both the number of campsites and the condition of these sites. If the number of campsites increases greatly over time, campsite impact problems will increase dramatically even if the conditions of the original sites are relatively stable or unchanged. Thus, a review of trends in campsite impacts must include both change over time of existing campsite conditions and the proliferation of new impacted areas over time.

Established Campsite Impacts. The results of studies on impact changes of established campsites over periods of 5 to 11 years present a complex picture (Cole and Hall 1992; Merriam and Peterson 1983). Some campsites improve, other deteriorate, and other remain relatively stable. Even on the same campsite, some impacts may increase while others diminish. The types of impact that tend most frequently to increase over time are campsite expansion (size of area), exposure of mineral soil, and cumulative damage to trees. In contrast, study results indicate that impacts to ground cover vegetation tend to decline or stabilize. However, the overall trend for four wilderness areas studied to date is one of slight deterioration on established campsites (Cole and Hall 1992; Merriam and Peterson 1983).

Researchers have also compared changes on high-use and low-use sites, and on sites that were no longer being camped on. Over time, with few exceptions, high-use sites either deteriorated or were stable. The findings for low-use sites were more variable. Certain low-use sites deteriorated as much as the high-use sites, but others improved substantially (Cole and Hall 1992). Concerning sites no longer used, more highly impacted sites tended to recover more slowly than lightly impacted sites, depending on previous impact level and on environmental recovery characteristics.

Cole and Hall (1992) draw two conclusions from their work on campsite impact trends—that established sites tend to deteriorate slowly and that closed sites recover at variable rates. This information can be added to previous research on impact changes to suggest the following typical campsite "life history" (Fig. 4).

As a campsite first develops, deterioration is rapid, often reaching near-maximum levels of impact after a few years of use. This "development" phase is followed by a more stable phase during which deterioration continues but at a much slower rate. Campsite expansion, tree damage, and mineral soil exposure are the impacts that most frequently continue to increase during this phase. If a site is effectively closed to use, recovery will occur. The rate of recovery is variable, but always slower than the rate of deterioration. Recovery will occur more rapidly where growing conditions are more favorable and on sites that were not severely impacted.

The authors further conclude that the results of trend studies give little reason to be either optimistic or pessimistic about the future condition of established campsites. There is a lack of evidence to suggest that established campsites are much worse than they were a decade ago. Many wilderness campsites have been severely impacted for

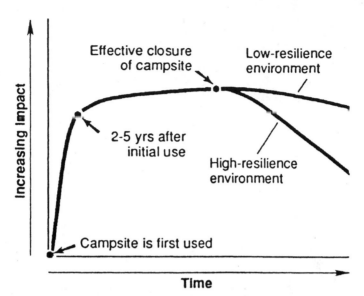

FIGURE 4. The "life history" of a typical campsite. (*Source:* Cole and Hall 1992.)

decades. Continued use of these sites may cause further deterioration, but at rates that are low when compared with the impact that has already occurred. However, there is also little likelihood that management can do much to improve the condition of these sites without drastic restrictions on use.

New Campsite Impacts. The establishment and proliferation of new campsites is a major concern of wildland recreation managers, particularly over extended time periods. Cole (1993) reports on changes in the number and condition of campsites over a 12- to 16-year period in portions of three wildernesses. The number of campsites increased 53 percent in the Selway-Bitterroot, 84 percent in the Lee Metcalf, and 123 percent in the Eagle Cap. The study showed that campsite impact increased substantially, not because existing campsites had deteriorated, but primarily because new campsites were developed. For example, in the Bear Creek drainage of the Selway-Bitterroot Wilderness, 16 new campsites were created and 13 sites remained stable, while only 5 sites deteriorated during a 12-year period (Fig. 5).

Based on the research of established campsite impacts and of newly established sites, Cole concluded that if these study areas are typical of other wilderness areas—and there is little reason to suspect they are not—campsite impacts may have increased substantially in other wildland areas over the past 10 to 15 years. The primary reason impact has increased is the creation of new campsites, even though the condition of some established sites has deteriorated.

The magnitude of the trend increase in number of new campsites suggests that an increase in site-pioneering behavior (i.e., campers creating new campsites) has occurred. In the Spanish Peaks Wilderness, for example, the number of new campsites

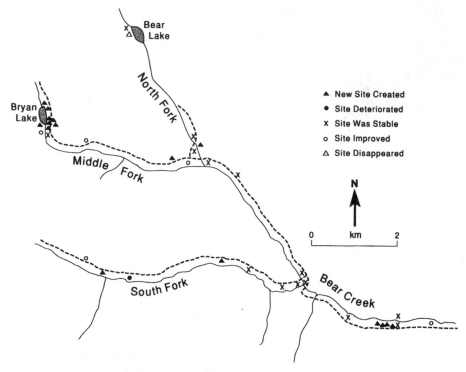

FIGURE 5. Changes in campsite condition in the Bear Creek drainage, Selway-Bitterroot Wilderness, MT, between 1977 and 1989. During the 12-year period, 16 new campsites were created, 13 sites were stable, 5 sites improved, 1 site deteriorated, and 1 site disappeared. (*Source:* Cole 1993.)

created between 1972 and 1988, a period of relatively stable use, almost equals the number created during the many decades of increasing use that preceded 1972. Site densities at some low-use lakes currently exceed the densities that existed at high-use lakes in the mid-1970s, even though use levels are thought to have been stable since the mid-1970s. These changes are too dramatic to simply reflect the passage of time. They suggest that campers today are much more likely to pioneer a new campsite than they were 15 to 20 years ago.

The interpretation suggests that campsite proliferation over the past 10 to 15 years is primarily a result of (1) an increase in site-pioneering behavior, in many cases with the encouragement of management, and (2) passive management programs that do little to attempt to decrease the number of campsites. These problems tend to be more severe in more heavily used places. But as campsite density increases, fewer potential campsites have never been used. Consequently, the risk of proliferation may be relatively low at very heavily used places because they have few suitable sites that have never been used. The places most at risk today are the regularly used destination areas with numerous potential campsites that have never been used.

SUMMARY

1. This chapter has reviewed trends in wildland recreation use and impacts over the last 20- to 40-year period, depending on the length of time for which data were available. The major changes over time indicate that overall wildland and wilderness use is increasing. However, individual wildernesses vary greatly, with use decreasing in specific areas.

2. Although amount of use is changing, the use patterns of visitors are fairly stable. Increases in day use and number of females using wilderness are the major visitor changes.

3. Impacts to wildland resources have also increased over time. Perhaps the most relevant change for managers is the proliferation of new campsites in wildland areas. Managers should be concerned about this type of impact and should develop strategies to reduce it. As more long-term and repeat study data become available to document trends in use and impacts, wildland managers will have to improve management of these changes.

REFERENCES

Bayfield, N. G. 1985. The Effects of Extended Use on Mountain Footpaths in Britain. In *The Ecological Impacts of Outdoor Recreation on Mountain Areas in Europe and North America.* Recreation Ecology Research Group Report No. 9. Wye, UK: Wye College, pp. 100–111.

Bayfield, N. G. 1986. Penetration of the Cairngorm Mountains, Scotland, by Vehicle Tracks and Footpaths: Impacts and Recovery. In R. C. Lucas, comp. *Proceedings—National Wilderness Research Conference: Current Research.* USDA Forest Service General Technical Report INT-212, Ogden, UT, pp. 121–127.

Bratton, S. P., M. G. Hickler, and J. H. Graves. 1978. Visitor Impact on Backcountry Campsites in the Great Smoky Mountains. *Environmental Management* 2:431–442.

Burde, J. H., and K. A. Curran. 1986. User Perception of Backcountry Management Policies at Great Smoky Mountains National Park. In D. L. Kulhavy and R. N. Conner, eds. *Wilderness and Natural Areas in the Eastern United States: A Management Challenge.* Nacogdoches, TX: Center for Applied Studies, School of Forestry, Stephen F. Austin State University, pp. 223–228.

Cole, D. N. 1983. Assessing and Monitoring Backcountry Trail Conditions. USDA Forest Service Research Paper INT-303. 10 pp.

Cole, D. N. 1987. Research on Soil and Vegetation in Wilderness: A State-of-Knowledge Review. In R. C. Lucas, comp. *Proceedings—National Wilderness Research Conference: Issues, State-of-Knowledge, and Future Directions.* USDA Forest Service General Technical Report INT-220, Ogden, UT, pp. 135–177.

Cole, D. N. 1991. Changes on Trails in the Selway-Bitterroot Wilderness, Montana, 1978–89. USDA Forest Service Research Paper INT-450. 5 pp.

Cole, D. N. 1993. Campsites in Three Western Wildernesses: Proliferation and Changes in Condition over 12 to 16 Years. USDA Forest Service Research Paper INT-463. 15 pp.

Cole, D. N. 1996. Wilderness Recreation Use Trends, 1965 Through 1994. USDA Forest Service Research Paper INT-RP-448. 10 pp.

Cole, D. N., and T. E. Hall. 1992. Trends in Campsite Condition: Eagle Cap Wilderness, Bob Marshall Wilderness, and Grand Canyon National Park. USDA Forest Service Research Paper INT-453. 40 pp.

Cole, D. N., A. E. Watson, and J. W. Roggenbuck. 1995. Trends in Wilderness Visitors and Visits: Boundary Waters Canoe Area, Shining Rock, and Desolation Wildernesses. USDA Forest Service Research Paper INT-RP-483. 38 pp.

Cole, G. L., and W. F. LaPage. 1980. Camping and RV Travel Trends. In W. F. LaPage, ed. *Proceedings 1980 National Outdoor Recreation Trends Symposium.* USDA Forest Service General Technical Report NE-57, pp. 165–178.

Cordell, H. K., J. C. Bergstrom, L. A. Hartmann, and D. B. K. English. 1990. An Analysis of the Outdoor Recreation and Wilderness Situation in the United States: 1989–2040. USDA Forest Service General Technical Report RM-189.

Cordell, H. K., B. Lewis, and B. L. McDonald. 1995. Long-term Outdoor Recreation Participation Trends. In J. L. Thompson, D. W. Lime, B. Gartner, W. M. Sames, comps. *Proceedings of the Fourth International Outdoor Recreation and Tourism Trends Symposium and the 1995 National Recreation Resources Planning Conference.* St. Paul: College of Natural Resources and Minnesota Extension Service, University of Minnesota, pp. 35–38.

Duffus, D. A., and P. Dearden. 1990. Non-consumptive Wildlife-Oriented Recreation: A Conceptual Framework. *Biological Conservation* 53:213–231.

Fish, E. B., G. L. Brothers, and R. B. Lewis. 1981. Erosional Impacts of Trails in Guadalupe Mountains National Park, Texas. *Landscape Planning* 8:387–398.

Feuchter, R. 1980. Off-road Vehicle Use: The U.S. Forest Service Perspective. In R. N. L. Andrews, and P. F. Nowak, eds. *Off-road Vehicle Use: A Management Challenge.* Washington, DC: Office of Environmental Quality, pp. 148–155.

Flather, C. H., and H. K. Cordell. 1995. Outdoor Recreation: Historical and Anticipated Trends. In R. L. Knight and K. J. Gutzwiller, eds. *Wildlife and Recreationists,* Washington, DC: Island Press, pp. 3–16.

Hendee, J. C., G. H. Stankey, and R. C. Lucas. 1990. *Wilderness Management.* 2d ed. Golden, CO: North American Press. 546 pp.

Lance, A. N., I. D. Baugh, and J. A. Love. 1989. Continued Footpath Widening in the Cairngorm Mountains, Scotland. *Biological Conservation* 49:201–214.

Leatherberry, E. C., D. W. Lime, and J. L. Thompson. 1980. Trends in River Recreation. In W. F. LaPage, ed. *Proceedings 1980 Outdoor Recreation Trends Symposium.* USDA Forest Service General Technical Report NE-57, pp. 147–164.

Lucas, R. C. 1985. Visitor Characteristics, Attitudes, and Use Patterns in the Bob Marshall Wilderness Complex, 1970–82. USDA Forest Service Research Paper INT-345. 32 pp.

Lucas, R. C. 1989. A Look at Wilderness Use and Users in Transition. *Natural Resources Journal* 29:41–55.

Lucas, R. C., and S. F. McCool. 1988. Trends in Wilderness Recreational Use: Causes and Implications. *Western Wildlands* 14(3):15–20.

Lucas, R. C., and G. H. Stankey. 1989. Shifting Trends in Wilderness Recreational Use. In A. E. Watson, comp. *Outdoor Recreation Benchmark 1988: Proceedings of the National*

Outdoor Recreation Forum. USDA Forest Service General Technical Report SE-52, pp. 357–367.

McCool, S. F., D. W. Lime, and D. H. Anderson. 1977. Simulation Modeling as a Tool for Managing River Recreation. In *Proceedings: River Recreation Management and Research.* USDA Forest Service General Technical Report NC-28, pp. 304–311.

Merriam, L. C., and R. F. Peterson. 1983. Impacts of 15 Years of Use on Some Campsites in the Boundary Waters Canoe Area. Agricultural Experiment Station Research Note 282, University of Minnesota: St. Paul. 3 pp.

Roggenbuck, J. W., and R. C. Lucas. 1987. Wilderness Use and User Characteristics: A State-of-Knowledge Review. In R. C. Lucas, comp. *Proceedings—National Wilderness Research Conference: Issues, State-of-Knowledge, and Future Directions.* USDA Forest Service General Technical Report INT-220, Ogden, UT, pp. 204–245.

Roggenbuck, J. W., and A. E. Watson. 1988. Wilderness Recreation Use: The Current Situation. In A. E. Watson, comp. *Outdoor Recreation Benchmark 1988: Proceedings of the National Outdoor Recreation Forum.* USDA Forest Service General Technical Report SE-52, pp. 346–356.

Stankey, G. H. 1973. Visitor Perception of Wilderness Recreation Carrying Capacity. USDA Forest Service Research Paper INT-142. 61 pp.

Summer, R. M. 1980. Impact of Horse Traffic on Trails in Rocky Mountain National Park. *Journal of Soil and Water Conservation* 35:85–87.

Summer, R. M. 1986. Geomorphic Impacts of Horse Traffic on Montana Landforms. *Journal of Soil and Water Conservation* 41:125–128.

Tinsley, B. E., and E. B. Fish. 1985. Evaluation of Trail Erosion in Guadalupe Mountains National Park, Texas. *Landscape Planning* 12:29–47.

USDI National Park Service. 1984. The 1982–1983 Nationwide Survey: Summary of Selected Findings. National Park Service, Washington, DC.

Washburne, R. F., and D. N. Cole. 1983. Problems and Practices in Wilderness Management: A Survey of Managers. USDA Forest Service Research Paper INT-304. 56 pp.

PART IV
Factors Affecting Impacts

8 Environmental Durability

Now that we have developed an understanding of recreational impacts on soil, vegetation, wildlife, and water and the patterns these impacts exhibit in space and over time, we will examine some factors that influence impact patterns. This is critical because it is through manipulation of these factors that managers can control recreational impacts. Many factors affect amount of impact and impact patterns on the land. Certain of these factors relate to environmental characteristics of the sites where recreational use is occurring. Both inherent site conditions and site durability during the season when use occurs can be important. These topics will be the focus of this chapter. Use characteristics, of course, are also highly influential. The importance of various characteristics of use will be the topic of Chapter 9.

Of all the topics in this book, environmental durability is probably the most difficult topic to do justice to in just one chapter; it is an extremely complex subject and one for which there is much suggestive information but few definitive answers. One characteristic may make a site durable while another makes it vulnerable. For example, a meadow may be resistant to vegetation loss, while its soils are highly vulnerable to erosion. There is also an important distinction between the properties of *resistance* and *resilience*. Resistance is the site's ability to tolerate recreational use without changing or being disturbed. It might be quantified in terms of the amount of use a site can absorb before some level of impact is reached. Resilience is the ability to recover from any changes that do occur. It might be quantified in terms of the number of years it takes for a site to recover from some level of impact to its predisturbance condition. Some sites are resistant but not resilient. They can tolerate a substantial amount of use; however, once impact occurs, it lasts for a long time. Many desert and alpine sites provide good examples. Other sites, such as many riparian areas, are resilient but not resistant. They are rapidly impacted, but recovery is also rapid. On sites designated for long-term recreation use, such as developed campgrounds, resilience may be much less important than resistance. Because these sites will be used in perpetuity, recovery is not an issue. In areas of highly dispersed use, however, resilience is at least as important as resistance because management objectives in such places stress the avoidance of permanently impacted sites. Sun and Liddle (1991) compared the trampling response of a resistant grass species to that of a resilient grass. The resistant grass maintained more biomass when trampling occurred throughout the growing season. The resilient grass did better when the trampled plants remained untrampled for a relatively long time. Both resistance and resilience must be considered, and their relative importance varies with management objectives.

Much more is known about the durability of vegetation and soil than about that of wildlife and water. Consequently, most of this chapter will deal with effects on vegetation and soil. Separate sections on wildlife and water are provided near the end of the chapter. It is convenient to group the environmental characteristics that influence vegetation and soil impact into vegetation characteristics, soil characteristics, and topographic characteristics. At a higher level of generalization, it is also possible to describe the importance of ecosystem-level characteristics. Durability is further affected by broad differences in regional climates, but regional climates will not be discussed because they cannot be influenced by management.

VEGETATIONAL RESISTANCE

Much of a site's durability can be assessed by examining vegetation characteristics. Influential characteristics include the resistance of individual species, species composition of the vegetation, total amount of vegetation cover, and vegetation structure (physiognomy). Characteristics that make individual species resistant were described in Chapter 3.

Attempts to generalize about the relative durability of various groups of plants provide useful guidelines for assessing the durability of different environments. Places where resistant plants are abundant will obviously be more resistant to vegetation loss than places where most plants are fragile. As mentioned earlier, mature trees and graminoids (grasslike plants) are generally resistant; mosses are neither highly resistant nor highly sensitive; and lichens and tree seedlings are highly sensitive. Shrubs are moderately resistant, but their resilience is usually low once they are seriously damaged. Forbs vary from moderately resistant to highly sensitive, but resilience is usually greater than for shrubs. The likely response of forbs, for which variation in resistance between species is high, can be predicted using the list of resistant characteristics in Chapter 3. Erect forbs, growing in moist areas in the forest, are particularly sensitive. Prostrate, low-growing forbs are more resistant.

Despite these general trends, there are numerous exceptions. Even the response of two individual plants within the same species can be variable. Ecotypic differences—genetic differences between individuals that result from adaptations to different environments—can result in pronounced variations in resistance. High elevation ecotypes are often shorter and more matted than their low elevation counterparts; consequently, they are likely to be more resistant (Kuss and Graefe 1985). Other species exhibit important phenotypic differences—differences in form and structure that are not genetically based. Bluegrass, for example, can abandon the erect form it exhibits in undisturbed environments and adopt a prostrate growth form in trampled areas. This increases its ability to tolerate trampling (Burden and Randerson 1972). In Australia, Sun (Sun 1990; Sun and Liddle 1993) showed that trampling resistance of a grass increased with plant age and number of tillers.

The relative resistance of plants also differs between seasons. Many forbs are particularly fragile early in the season when they are growing rapidly; shrubs are often more fragile late in the season, when their dry branches and stems are particularly brittle. The resistance of a species even depends on the other species with which it is associated. Holmes and Dobson (1976), working in subalpine meadows in Yosemite National Park, California, found that survival rates for the same species were generally about three times greater in communities of several species than when it grew in pure stands. Cole (1988) found that sensitive species could tolerate more trampling when growing interspersed with more resistant species. Generally, resistance increases where there are several vegetation layers. Tall layers of plants absorb impact, protecting lower layers. Lower layers provide a cushioning effect that somewhat reduces impact to taller layers.

Many analyses of the relative resistance of entire species assemblages have been made. Commonly a researcher will experimentally trample several different vegetation types and compare responses to see which types decrease in cover most rapidly. Although many studies have examined the initial resistance of vegetation, only a few have followed recovery to evaluate resilience.

The graph in Fig. 1 provides some data from an experimental trampling study undertaken in western Montana (Cole 1985). Two vegetation types are compared. Type 1 is a forest with an understory dominated by lush, erect forbs, species adapted to growth in heavy shade (Fig. 2). Type 2 is a forest with an understory dominated by shrubs that spread along the ground only a few inches off the surface. In each type

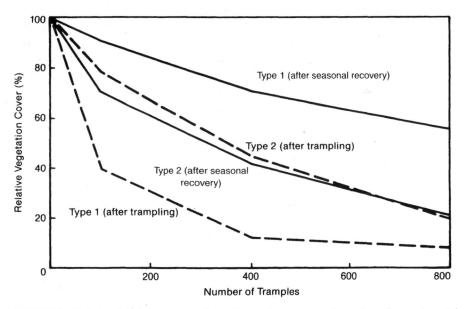

FIGURE 1. Relationship between surviving vegetation cover and number of experimental tramples for two vegetation types in western Montana. Type 1 is a forest with a ground cover dominated by lush forbs. Type 2 is a forest dominated by low-lying shrubs. One set of measurements, relevant to evaluating resistance, shows cover after trampling. Another set of measurements, relevant to evaluating resilience, shows cover after an over-winter recovery period. (*Source:* D. N. Cole, 1985.)

FIGURE 2. This vegetation type, with an understory dominated by lush forbs, has low resistance and high resilience. (*Photo:* J. L. Marion.)

people walked a given number of times back and forth across the vegetation; each one-way pass was a "trample." The low resistance of the forbs in type 1 is reflected in the "after trampling" graph in which more than one-half of the cover is lost after fewer than 100 tramples. The low shrubs in type 2 are much more resistant; about 300 tramples are required before one-half of the cover is lost. This conforms to our expectations based on the relative resistance of these two growth forms. Although not presented in the graph, a grassland retained over one-half of its cover after 1600 tramples (Cole 1985), illustrating the much greater resistance of graminoids (Fig. 3). At the highest level of trampling reported—800 tramples—the difference in cover between types 1 and 2 is diminishing. Eventually all cover will be lost on even the most resistant vegetation type. The importance of differences in resistance between vegetation types is greatest at low to moderate use intensities. This fact has important management implications. There is little value to worrying about encouraging use of resistant vegetation when use levels are high. Where use levels are low, however, selection of durable sites can be quite effective in minimizing impact.

The two other lines on the graph show vegetation cover on each type in early summer, about nine months after trampling stopped. These data provide some idea about the ability of these vegetation types to recover from trampling. Type 1 recovered well; places that had been trampled 800 times recovered from less than 10 percent cover (after trampling) to more than 50 percent cover over the winter. Although most of the aboveground cover of forbs was destroyed by trampling, the

FIGURE 3. Grasslands tend to be particularly resistant to damage from trampling. (*Photo:* M. E. Petersen.)

forbs were able to reproduce or initiate new growth from buds. Recovery was also improved by the abundant moisture in this vegetation type. After a second season of trampling, however, the amount of over-winter recovery in type 1 was greatly reduced. This suggests that resilience declines with successive years of disturbance (Cole 1987).

The high resilience of type 1 is in marked contrast to the low resilience of type 2. Cover in type 2 actually decreased slightly over the winter. Delayed trampling damage is common in shrubs, particularly ericaceous heaths and huckleberries (Bayfield 1979; Cole 1995b). Stems and branches of the shrubs apparently were damaged during trampling but continued to provide cover until winter when they fell off. Very little regrowth or reproduction occurred over winter to offset this loss of cover.

Cole (1995a, 1995b) has conducted the most extensive experimental trampling study to date. He studied 18 different vegetation types, distributed over wide elevational ranges in five separate mountain regions in the United States—in Washington, Montana, Colorado, New Hampshire and North Carolina. He found tremendous variation in response to trampling—at least a 30-fold difference in resistance. In an alpine sedge meadow in Washington, it took 600 "tramples" to eliminate 50 percent of the vegetation cover. It took just 20 tramples in a spruce-fir forest with a fern-dominated understory, in Great Smoky Mountains National Park, to eliminate 50 percent of the vegetation cover. In many places, particularly subalpine ecosystems—where the diversity of vegetation types with different growth forms is unusually high—vegetation types that differ in resistance by a factor of 10 or more grow interspersed with each other. This suggests that there is great potential to reduce impact by channeling use through more resistant vegetation types.

As noted earlier, many researchers have suggested that vegetation resistance to trampling is largely a function of the growth form of constituent species. Cole (1995b) was able to verify this hypothesis empirically. In the 18 vegetation types he studied, resistance to trampling was positively related to the abundance of graminoids (particularly tufted grasses and sedges) and shrubs; it was negatively related to mean vegetation height and the abundance of erect plants (particularly forbs). Sixty-eight percent of the variation in resistance of individual species could be predicted simply by noting whether they were shrubs, forbs, or grasslike plants. Graminoids were resistant, forbs were sensitive, and shrubs were intermediate in response (Fig. 4). There are exceptions to this generalization, of course. Nevertheless, the simplicity of this finding suggests that it may be reasonable to teach recreationists to recognize resistant and sensitive vegetation types.

Resilience was also strongly affected by growth form. In the 18 vegetation types, resilience to trampling was positively related to the abundance of forbs and negatively related to the abundance of shrubs. Plants with regenerating buds located above the ground surface—all shrubs and a few other plants—recover very slowly once disturbed. The buds themselves are often destroyed by trampling, and woody plant tissues typically grow more slowly than herbaceous tissues. Resilience also declined with elevation, although the effect of elevation was minor as compared with the effect of growth form. It has been suggested that—as compared with resistance—resilience

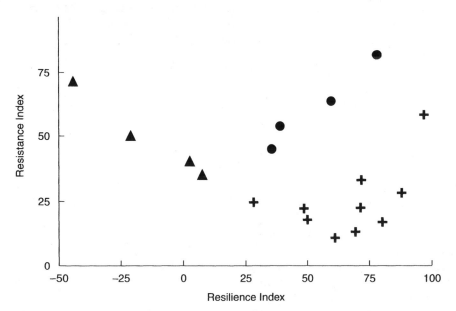

FIGURE 4. Resistance and resilience of 18 vegetation types with understory vegetation dominated by shrubs (▲), graminoids (●), or forbs (+). (*Source:* Adapted from data presented in Cole 1995b.)

should be more strongly influenced by a number of environmental variables such as soil fertility, length of the growing season, sunlight levels, and moisture levels (Cole 1988). The importance of these factors will be discussed later in more detail.

The effect of amount of vegetation cover on durability is complex. Both sparsely and densely vegetated plant communities can be highly resistant; both can also be fragile. Cole (1995b) found a positive relationship—in the 18 vegetation types he studied—between resistance to trampling and total vegetation cover. It may be that plants growing in a dense turf are less susceptible to being uprooted by the gouging actions of feet. Perhaps the most important effect of vegetation cover is its ability to inhibit erosion. Vegetation acts to hold soil in place and reduce the erosive force of running water. Vegetation types that can retain a dense vegetation cover, despite being subjected to trampling, will resist damage from erosion more effectively than other types. Types with abundant graminoids and/or exotic, trampling-resistant species are particularly likely to retain a dense cover, as are highly resilient vegetation types.

The most significant aspect of vegetation structure is the effect of tree canopy closure on vegetation loss. As we have noted before, plants that grow in heavy shade tend to be more fragile than those that inhabit more open communities. This is well illustrated in Table 1, which shows vegetation cover and loss on campsites in the Boundary Waters Canoe Area in relation to canopy cover. Mean cover is the mean vegetation cover on campsites. Absolute difference is an estimate of the vegetation loss that has occurred as a result of campsite use. It is obtained by calculating the difference in cover between campsites and neighboring undisturbed control sites. Both measures show much greater impact where tree cover exceeds 25 percent. Impact increases with each increase in tree cover; very little cover (only 3.5 percent) survives on the most shaded sites. In his trampling study, Cole (1995b) found that tree canopy cover was the variable that explained most of the variation in resistance to trampling. The effect of canopy cover is primarily indirect, however. Canopy cover influences plant growth form because certain growth forms grow better than others under closed canopies; growth form, in turn, determines resistance to trampling.

TABLE 1. Relationship Between Tree Canopy Cover and Vegetation Cover on Campsites in the Boundary Waters Canoe Area, Minnesota

Tree Cover (%)	Vegetation Cover (%)	
	Mean[a]	Absolute Difference[b]
0–25	52.4	−43.6
26–50	25.8	−60.7
51–75	14.9	−70.3
76–100	3.5	−77.1

Source: Marion 1984.

[a]Means are for surviving vegetation cover on campsites.

[b]Absolute difference is the difference in cover between campsites and undisturbed control sites—an estimate of vegetation loss.

SOIL CHARACTERISTICS

Soil characteristics that have a pronounced effect on durability include soil texture, stoniness, organic matter, moisture, fertility, and depth. The soil textures with the fewest limitations for campsites and trails are medium-textured soils—sandy loams, fine sandy loams, and loams. Such soils usually have good drainage, are not highly erodible, and have a high potential for plant growth. Their major drawback is that their wide range of particle sizes makes them particularly susceptible to compaction. Coarse soils generally resist water and wind erosion because large particles are not easily moved by wind or water. However, structural instability makes coarse soils vulnerable to trail widening, and their low water-holding capacity and cation exchange capacity (ability to hold cations that may be important nutrients) make them relatively impoverished environments for plant growth. Such drawbacks are likely to be more serious for trails than for campsites. In remote backcountry situations where use is low and dispersed, sandy soils may be particularly resistant sites for camping.

Coarse soils are clearly a better alternative than fine-textured soils. Silts and fine sands are highly erodible because soil particles are both readily detached and moved, the two requisites for erosion to occur. Moreover, silt is particularly prone to the formation of needle ice and to frost heaving, processes that increase erosion and make revegetation of bare areas difficult. Silt soils also become dusty when dry, making them undesirable trail locations. The permeability is greatly reduced when clay soil is compacted. This promotes increased runoff and erosion. Although clay particles resist detachment, they are readily moved by running water. Clays have a limited ability to support loads because they deform readily when wet. They also tend to be sticky when wet, and they dry slowly (Leeson 1979). All of these characteristics make clay soils particularly poor locations for recreational facilities.

The effect of stones and rocks on soil durability is variable. Leeson (1979) suggests, based on studies of trails in the Canadian Rockies, that it is advantageous for stones and rocks to comprise up to 25 percent of a soil's volume. Small amounts of stone in the soil reduce susceptibility to compaction (Stewart and Cameron 1992). Stones also increase the resistance of soil particles to being picked up by moving water. Above 25 percent, however, stones and rocks make footing difficult and construction and maintenance costly. Once stones are loose on the trail, they increase the turbulence of running water (increasing erosion) and erode the trail themselves when tumbled down the trail by water. Summer (1980) suggests not categorically removing all stones from trails because this sets up a never-ending cycle of deterioration. Removal of rocks leads to exposure and erosion of underlying fine particles, which, once they are removed, exposes more rocks at the surface.

Many of the most serious trail problems occur where soils are stone-free and homogeneous in texture. Such soils, which frequently occur in mountain meadows, are highly vulnerable to erosion (Bryan 1977). Deep and narrow seasonally muddy trails force hikers and stock out of the rutted, muddy trails. New ruts develop alongside the old ones, quickly scarring scenic meadows with numerous parallel ruts (Fig. 5).

FIGURE 5. Multiple trails are developing in this meadow. The main tread is deep, muddy, and wet, making it difficult to use. Hikers prefer to leave the tread, creating new parallel trails. (*Photo:* R. F. Washburne.)

The advantages and disadvantages of organic matter are also complex, varying with amount and type of organic matter and with associated soil characteristics. Organic soils, those in which organic content exceeds 20 to 30 percent, are the soils least capable of supporting recreation use. They tend to occur where drainage is or has been poor; they are particularly common at high elevations and latitudes where decomposition of organic matter is slow. Such soils have little ability to support heavy loads, particularly when they are wet. Recreational use of areas with organic soils rapidly creates wide, muddy quagmires. However, a thick organic horizon on top of mineral soil tends to shield the mineral soil from compaction and inhibits runoff and erosion. Incorporated into the mineral soil, organic matter promotes good structural development, which enhances drainage, inhibits compaction, helps resist dispersion and detachment of particles, and promotes plant growth because of its tendency to increase water-holding capacity and nutrient availability.

Soil moisture, as with most soil parameters, is most advantageous in moderate quantities, where it is sufficient to promote plant growth and recovery but not so abundant that it causes the problems common to poorly drained, wet soils. Soils with excessive moisture cannot bear loads without becoming muddy and greatly compacted. Wet soils are more susceptible to truncation because of their increased stickiness and adhesion to footwear of hikers (Stewart and Cameron 1992). Moisture problems are most serious in fine-textured soils and are most likely to cause problems on trails. Such problems are particularly severe where stock use is heavy because of the great pressure stock exert on the soil. The majority of trail problems, other than erosion on steep slopes, result from locating trails in areas that are poorly drained or that have high water tables (Cole 1991).

Limited data suggest that the vegetation on moderately fertile soils is more resistant to impact than that on either highly fertile soils or infertile soils (Harrison 1981; Kuss 1986). There are insufficient data, however, to evaluate whether or not these results are generally applicable. Certainly the resilience of more fertile sites should be greater than that of sites poor in nutrients.

Finally, deep soils are often better suited to recreational use than shallow soils. This primarily reflects the high erodibility of very shallow soils and the vulnerability of vegetation established in pockets of thin soil. Another concern relates to the difficulty of disposing of human waste in environments where soils are shallow. On the other hand, some of the most resistant sites for low-use, dispersed backcountry camping are on bedrock, where the impacts of recreation use are likely to be minimal.

Table 2 summarizes, in very general terms, how soil properties influence site durability. As the preceding discussion suggests, there are exceptions to most of these generalizations. Still, they do provide some useful guidelines for locating facilities such as trails and campsites. The most serious and widespread problems occur where trails are located on soils with homogeneous textures (the usual problem is creation of a system of deeply incised, braided trails in meadows) or where any facility is located on wet mineral or organic soils (the usual problem is creation of a wide and muddy quagmire).

Soil maps can be a helpful means of incorporating knowledge about soil durability into recreation impact management. For example, Bailey and Pilgrim (1983) mapped the soils of the White Mountains in New Hampshire. Then they developed a table listing the suitability of these different soil types for different recreation uses. The soils most suitable for dispersed camping and trails were typic Haplorthods developed on friable till, at elevations below about 2500 feet and on slopes of less than 15 percent. This analysis provides only a very coarse perspective on facility location, however. Field observations and concern for a broader array of soil criteria are needed for more precise locational decisions.

TABLE 2. Relationships Between Soil Characteristics and Susceptibility to Impact

Soil Property	Level of Susceptibility		
	Low	Moderate	High
Texture	Medium	Coarse	Homogeneous; fine
Stoniness	Moderate	High	Low
Organic context	Moderate	Low	High
Soil moisture	Moderate	Low	High
Fertility	Moderate	High	Low
Soil depth	None	Deep	Shallow

TOPOGRAPHIC CHARACTERISTICS

Durability is often related to slope steepness and position, topography, elevation, and aspect. Slope steepness and position are most important in influencing impacts on trails and roads or in places where cross-country travel occurs regularly. Generally, erosion potential increases with slope. For example, Coleman (1981) studied the prevalence of erosion problems on trail segments of variable slope. On trails with a slope no greater than 9 degrees, erosion problems were nonexistent; between 9 and 18 degrees erosion problems occurred, but most segments were not eroding; above 18 degrees most trails were eroding (Fig. 6). She also found that both trail width and depth increased as the slope of the trail increased. The increase in trail depth with slope reflects greater erosion caused by the increased velocity of water running down steeper trails. In Alaska, Jubenville and O'Sullivan (1987) found a positive relationship between slope gradient and trail erosion; however, gradient explained only 34 percent of the variance, suggesting that other determinants of erosion are important. The increase in width may result from either people walking on the sides of deeply eroded, steep trails to get better footing or the tendency for people to spread out

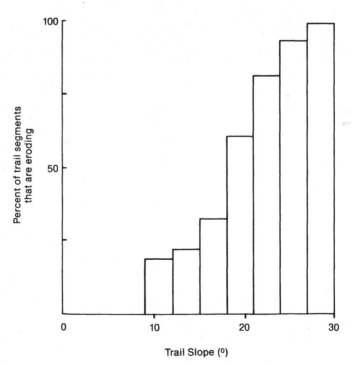

FIGURE 6. The frequency of erosion problems tends to increase as trail slope increases. Data are from footpaths in the Lake District of England. (*Source:* Adapted from Coleman, R. "Footpath Erosion in the English Lake District," in *Applied Geography.* Copyright © 1981. Used with permission of the publisher.)

laterally when negotiating a steep slope. In Great Smoky Mountains National Park, Marion (1994) also found that trails with steep slopes were substantially wider than those that were less steep.

Where steep slopes cannot be avoided, problems can frequently be averted by putting in water drainage devices such as drainage dips and water bars (see Chapter 13). Problems also occur on trail segments where there is no slope at all. Trail segments without any slope drain poorly. Poor drainage leads to the development of muddy quagmires that expand in width as hikers and stock try to skirt the mud. Campsites with poor drainage are undesirable when wet. Campers who do use such areas often end up excavating trenches around their tents when rainfall is intense. Such impact can be avoided by locating sites where there is some slope and drainage.

Trails and roads located high on slopes have smaller watersheds from which they collect water than those located close to the base of slopes. This smaller watershed reduces erosion potential. However, trails on upper slopes are often unusually wide (Leung and Marion 1996). Locations close to the base of slopes can also have problems with excessive moisture because springs may be intercepted by roads or trails cut into the slope (Cole 1983; Marion 1994). Midslope positions are usually the best choice.

A more significant variable than slope position is the alignment of a trail in relation to the prevailing slope. Trails that directly ascend the fall line are susceptible to degradation regardless of slope angle. Flat sideslopes offer little hindrance to trail widening, and trail drainage can be a problem. Trails that more closely follow contours are less problematic. Drainage is better and hikers are more likely to stay on the constructed trail. The importance of trail alignment increases as trail slope increases (Leung and Marion 1996).

Variable results are available concerning the effect of elevation on site durability. In the Great Smoky Mountains National park, Bratton, Hickler, and Graves (1979) report that both trail and campsite deterioration increase with elevation. This has been confirmed by more recent trail surveys in the Smoky Mountains (Marion 1994). Higher rainfall and thinner soils occur at the higher elevations, contributing to more pronounced erosion and other soil impacts. Deterioration problems are also reported to be more severe at high elevations in the northeastern United States (Fay, Rice, and Berg 1977). In the Sierra Nevada in California, campsite alteration was greater at both high and low elevations than at moderate elevations (Dykema 1971). As noted earlier, Cole (1995b) found that vegetation resistance declined with increasing elevation, but the effect was miniscule in comparison to the effect of plant growth form.

The complexity of factors influencing environmental tolerance makes it unlikely for a variable like elevation to relate strongly to durability. Perhaps the most important effect of increasing elevation is a decrease in length of the growing season. This, along with locally variable factors such as frequent high winds and needle ice, often make resilience low at high elevations. Depending on the growth forms present, high elevation vegetation can be either resistant or fragile; however, because of the short growing season it will always recover slowly from any damage that occurs. In desert regions, higher elevations receive more precipitation, which is likely to increase resilience. If the increase in resilience because of higher moisture levels compensates for the decreases in resilience related to a shorter growing season, then even resilience will increase with elevation.

Within a local area it may be possible to identify a relationship between the incidence of impact problems and elevation. This is what Bratton and her colleagues (1979) did for trails and campsites in the Great Smoky Mountains. However, such relationships are unlikely to be broadly applicable. Moreover, the effect of elevation on resistance may be different from its effect on resilience. Effects are also likely to differ between vegetation, soil, wildlife, and water and between types of facilities and activities. Guidelines relating elevation to durability, although useful, should be used cautiously.

The same is true for aspect. North-facing aspects may be more durable in one place and more fragile in another. One of the most common aspect-related problems occurs high in the mountains, where late snowmelt on north-facing aspects keeps soils water-saturated. Trails through water-saturated soils become wide, muddy quagmires. They are also eroded by meltwater, channeled down the entrenched trail. Under droughty, low elevation conditions, however, north-facing aspects may be particularly resilient because of higher moisture levels that promote plant growth. In Iowa, Dawson, Hinz, and Gordon (1974) found that trails on north-facing slopes were less compacted and had lost less ground cover than trails on floodplains or south-facing slopes. As with elevation, such generalizations can be useful within localized areas, but they have little general utility.

ECOSYSTEM CHARACTERISTICS

Some researchers have proposed that vegetation durability increases with increases in an ecosystem's primary productivity (Liddle 1975) and is greater in more advanced successional stages (Goldsmith 1974). Primary productivity refers to the quantity of organic matter produced by plants through photosynthesis. It is dependent on many factors, from broad climatic characteristics such as temperature and rainfall, to soil characteristics such as nutrient availability. Liddle believed that productivity summarized, in one measure, potential for regrowth as well as the general ability of the environment to support growth. Resilience probably is strongly related to productivity. For example, campsites in productive riparian forests in the eastern United States recovered substantially in just six years (Marion and Cole 1996). Trails in Costa Rican rain forest recovered dramatically in 32 months (Boucher, Aviles, Chepote, Gil, and Vilchez 1991). Resistance is not strongly related to productivity, however. For example, desert shrubs are resistant, despite their not being highly productive. A moisture rich, temperate forest is productive, but the vegetation is quickly eliminated by trampling. As we have seen before, resilience is related to general environmental factors, but vegetation resistance is dependent primarily on the growth forms of constituent species.

Communities and ecosystems change with time. Succession is the relatively orderly change from young, simple ecosystems to more diverse and specialized older ecosystems. The more advanced stages of succession may be more resilient because their higher productivity, diversity, and higher degree of specialization promote more rapid recovery following damage. However, resistance is not so clearly related to successional stage. Some early successional stages such as grassy fields and dry meadows are much more resistant than the later forested stage of succession. Trails in mature forest in the Great Smoky Mountains were more substantially impacted then trails in early successional forest (Bratton, Hickler, and Graves 1979). Again, growth form probably has more influence on vegetation resistance than successional stage, and individual soil characteristics such as texture have more influence on soil resistance.

There is no doubt that environmental factors profoundly influence amount of impact. The problem is that so many of the relationships between environment and impact are highly site specific. Relationships that apply in one place may not apply in another. In this chapter we have described some of the factors that are likely to influence durability. Ultimately, each area will have to develop its own guidelines for where to develop facilities. A good example is provided in Table 3. These guidelines specify likely problems in different vegetation types in the mountains of New England. They were developed over the years by observing where certain problems generally occur. They are useful in New England, although they may not apply elsewhere.

WILDLIFE IMPACTS

Much was said about the vulnerability of different wildlife species in Chapter 4. For a given species, susceptibility also varies among different environments. Unfortunately, very little work has been done on this subject. Therefore, all we will be able to do here is present some relatively simple principles. Vulnerability to disturbance is usually greatest at certain key locations, particularly breeding areas, feeding areas, and watering holes. Disturbance of nesting birds has caused adults to fly off, leaving eggs and hatchlings open to predation (Burger 1995). Severe or prolonged disturbance can lead to nest abandonment. Prolonged disturbance of animals in prime feeding and water areas can force them to use poor habitat. In one study deer displaced to poor habitat had lower reproductive rates and less body fat. Moreover, they did not return to the better habitat even after disturbance had stopped (Batcheler 1968). Such disturbances can be particularly damaging to wildlife populations during periods of harsh weather or during unproductive years. Generally, sensitive environments are those key locations where the consequences of disturbance, flight, or displacement are particularly detrimental. Exactly which environments these are will vary between species, but certain habitats such as riparian areas are almost always critical for many species.

Wildlife are often more adversely affected when approached from above. Hikers approaching bighorn sheep from upslope caused stronger reactions than those approaching from downslope, presumably because sheep perceive less ability to escape when upslope escape options are eliminated (Geist, Stemp, and Johnston 1985).

TABLE 3. Vegetation Type and Plant Tolerance to Dispersed Recreation Impacts in New England Mountains

Vegetation	Conditions to Which Vegetation Is Intolerant
Alpine plants	Trampling easily destroys these fragile plants. Due to the short growing season and other harsh conditions, alpine plants are very slow to regenerate
Subalpine bog plants; sphagnum moss, sedges, dwarfed heath shrubs	Roots of bog plants are easily crushed by foot traffic, though some species are adapted to colonizing disturbed denuded soils.
Krummholz	These trees are very slow growing. Clearing for tent sites rapidly destroys the krummholz and exposes them to wind damage.
Spruce-fir forests	Susceptible to windthrow where large openings have been cut. Compaction of soil around roots reduces tree vigor by reducing water and air infiltration and increasing their susceptibility to disease. Basal wounds make trees susceptible to fungal infections.
Mixed beech, sugar maple, birch forest	Can sustain a moderate amount of soil compaction and bark wounding.
Red maple trees	Can sustain a moderate amount of soil compaction and bark wounding.
Pure yellow or paper birch stands	Trees subject to bark peeling and cutting for firewood. This becomes visually unesthetic and also reduces the vigor of the trees by increasing their susceptibility to disease. Openings cut in stands cause trees near opening edges to be subject to wind damage and dieback.
Pines, oaks, rhododendrons	Moderately durable vegetation.
Alders, willows	Moderately durable vegetation, though sites are generally unattractive to camping due to moist conditions.

Source: Adapted from Leonard, Spencer, and Plumley, 1981. Copyright © 1981 by Appalachian Mountain Club, used with permission of publisher.

WATER IMPACTS

As in the case of wildlife impacts, there is little research on the susceptibility of different aquatic environments to recreation-related water impacts. Obviously, recreational activities undertaken in or near water have more potential for causing water pollution than those occurring far from water. On-land recreational activities are also more likely to adversely alter water quality where soils are highly erodible. For example, building roads and trails through areas of highly erosive material can greatly increase water turbidity, a change with negative effects on aquatic flora and fauna.

Water bodies themselves also differ in their ability to tolerate impact. Those that are frequently flushed out by large quantities of water or that have chemical properties that can buffer pollutants are less vulnerable to impacts than those without these properties. Lakes at high elevations commonly have low temperatures, few nutrients, and low levels of productivity. They often are in pristine areas where baseline disturbance levels are low. Recreational use on or around such lakes can cause pronounced deviations in biological, chemical, and physical properties from those found under baseline conditions. Lakes and streams at lower elevations tend to be more productive and less vulnerable to alteration than alpine lakes.

SEASON OF USE

The durability of an environment varies substantially between seasons. Vegetation and soil, for example, are protected from impact, to a great extent, when there is a thick blanket of winter snow. They may be particularly vulnerable in spring, however, when soils are saturated with snowmelt or spring rains. Young, tender herbaceous plants are particularly susceptible to trampling in the spring, causing early season loss of photosynthetic tissues, which means that plants must go an entire season without adding to their food reserves.

Season of use can be influential in determining the vulnerability of certain wildlife species and of water quality. Recreational activities have traditionally been considered particularly disturbing to animals during the breeding season. However, recent research indicates that disturbance during other seasons can be equally detrimental (Hobbs 1989; Skagen, Knight, and Orians 1991). The consequences of disturbance during different seasons are variable. During breeding season, disturbance affects productivity. During other seasons it affects fitness and survival. Animals are particularly vulnerable to disturbance during times of the year when they are weak. A number of animals, including deer, adapt to severe winter conditions by decreasing their level of activity and, thereby, conserving their energy. If encounters with recreationists cause them to flee, this strategy is undermined. Increased activity requires more food; if sufficient food is not available, it can lead to reduced vigor and reproductive capacity or even death. Hobbs (1989) suggests that the effect of disturbance on food intake is more detrimental than its effect on energy expenditure. Harassment of wildlife species during winter months, when they are under physiological stress, is one of the most serious impact problems associated with snow recreation on skis or snowmobiles. Although winter is the season when the vulnerability of soil and vegetation is generally lowest, it may be the season when wildlife vulnerability is highest (Fig. 7).

Water quality is most likely to be adversely affected if recreation use occurs during the season when soils are saturated with water from snowmelt. Vehicular travel on roads during this period can cause serious erosion, because vehicles churn up the soil to the point where it can be easily moved by running water. Serious erosion of roads increases

FIGURE 7. Wildlife disturbance can be particularly detrimental during winter when movement requires large amounts of energy and animals have little energy to spare. (*Photo:* R. C. Lucas.)

road maintenance costs; it also increases siltation of streams. This can have numerous adverse impacts, particularly on fish such as trout, that are sensitive to stream turbidity.

Vulnerability also varies greatly between seasons where there is erosion of trails and trampling damage to meadows used by recreational packstock. In both cases, problems are most severe during the spring when snowmelt and spring rains keep soils saturated. The trail erosion problems are similar to the road erosion problems caused by motorized use. Wet soils are easily broken up, making them sensitive to movement where snowmelt is channeled down the trail. Trail use, particularly by stock, should be discouraged during snowmelt. Drainage devices, to divert water off the tread, are also important if severe erosion is to be avoided.

Meadow soil and vegetation can be rapidly disturbed when trampled during spring when soils are wet. Wet soils are more prone to compaction and more readily churned. This breaks up the meadow sod into a honeycombed topography, leading to both an increase in erosion and a lowering of the water table. In Sequoia and Kings Canyon National Parks, meadows dried out as water tables dropped, and this permitted trees to invade and replace meadows (DeBenedetti and Parsons 1979).

Vegetational tolerance varies between seasons, but differences are usually not very pronounced. Resistance of plants to trampling damage is often low during early spring when many herbs are succulent and during late season when plant parts are dry and brittle. However, resilience may be reduced more dramatically by trampling early in the season when perennial plants are still utilizing carbohydrate reserves for growth and before annual plants have had a chance to produce viable seeds. Strand

(1979) showed that the vegetation damage inflicted by horse trampling was greater and lasted longer in a wet meadow than in a dry meadow.

In the mountains, spring is usually the most vulnerable season; soil moisture levels are high and many wildlife species are breeding, as well as recovering from the stresses of winter. Winter is a season of low vulnerability, except for impact to certain wildlife species. The summer season of maximum recreation use is generally intermediate in terms of susceptibility to impact. These general guidelines break down, however, when applied to coastal areas, deserts, areas that do not receive snowfall, and areas that receive intense summer rainfall. In such places the seasons of highest vulnerability are most often those when soils are frequently water saturated and when the consequences of wildlife disturbance are particularly severe.

SUMMARY

1. The list of properties that either enhance or detract from site durability is long. Only a few of the important ones have been discussed in the preceding sections. Understanding differences in site durability is critical to any impact management program, because locating facilities appropriately and encouraging use of durable sites are important means of limiting impact. Patterns of differential tolerance are highly site specific, however. Specific guidelines on site durability will have to be developed for each individual recreation area (although much information can be borrowed from other areas in similar environments).

2. Field judgments by experienced people, capable of incorporating a wide array of influential factors, are the best means to judge durability. Alternatively, it is possible to develop guidelines that can be used by less experienced evaluators. For example, Garland (1990) developed an index of trail erosion susceptibility for a proposed wilderness area in the Natal Drakensberg, South Africa. The index was based on (1) the amount of rain falling on the wettest day of the year, (2) rock type, and (3) slope. The index has possible scores between 3 and 13. Trails built on sites with index values of 3 are likely to require little maintenance. Trails built on sites with ratings of 4 to 6 are likely to experience little erosion, but a few places may require frequent maintenance. Where sites have ratings greater than 6, maintenance is likely to be frequently necessary and erosion risk is high. In Shenandoah National Park, Williams and Marion (1995) developed an index of the desirability of alternative campsite locations to help managers attempting to identify locations for designated campsites. This index combines both social and environmental durability criteria. It includes (1) location in relation to trails and other campsites, (2) slope, (3) vegetation composition and cover, (4) forest canopy, (5) aspect, and (6) campsite expansion potential—the surface roughness and vegetation density of adjacent areas.

3. Another technique that is useful in deciding where to build facilities or encourage use is to map locations that are particularly sensitive. A series of overlays of sensitive areas and attractions can identify both desirable and undesirable locations. Figure 8 shows maps of some of the factors to be considered when locating campsites

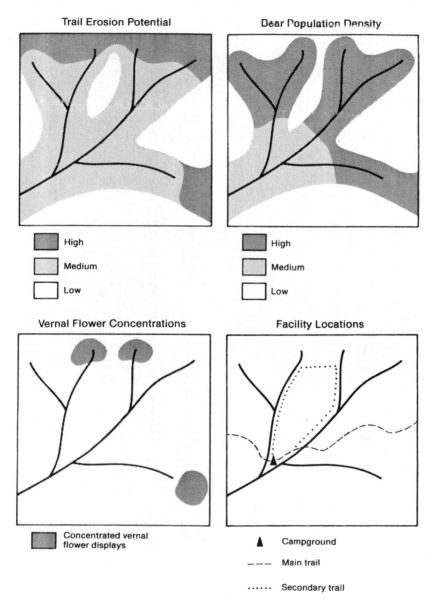

FIGURE 8. Maps of environmental factors that influence the placement of trails and campsites in Great Smoky Mountains National Park. (*Source:* Modified from Bratton 1977.)

in Great Smoky Mountains National Park. The campground was located away from places with high bear densities and flower concentrations, but close to water. The main trail stayed in areas with low erosion potential, except where it descended to the campground. Secondary trails were built up to the areas of flower concentrations but attempted to avoid areas where erosion potential was high.

REFERENCES

Bailey, G. D., and S. A. L. Pilgrim. 1983. Soils of the White Mountains of New Hampshire and Their Suitability for Recreational Development. *Mountain Research and Development* 3:53–60.

Batcheler, C. L. 1968. Compensatory Responses of Artificially Controlled Mammal Populations. *New Zealand Ecological Society Proceedings* 15:25–30.

Bayfield, N. G. 1979. Recovery of Four Montane Heath Communities on Cairngorm, Scotland, from Disturbance by Trampling. *Biological Conservation* 15:165–179.

Boucher, D. H., J. Aviles, R. Chepote, O. E. D. Gil, and B. Vilchez. 1991. Recovery of Trailside Vegetation from Trampling in a Tropical Rain Forest. *Environmental Management* 15:257–262.

Bratton, S. P. 1977. Visitor Management. Unpublished report. Uplands Field Research Laboratory, Great Smoky Mountains National Park, Gatlinburg, TN. 22 pp.

Bratton, S. P., M. G. Hickler, and J. H. Graves. 1979. Trail Erosion Patterns in Great Smoky Mountains National Park. *Environmental Management* 3:431–445.

Bryan, R. B. 1977. The Influence of Soil Properties on Degradation of Mountain Hiking Trails at Grovelsjon. *Geografiska Annaler* 59A: 49–65.

Burden, R. F., and P. F. Randerson. 1972. Quantitative Studies of the Effects of Human Trampling on Vegetation as an Aid to the Management of Semi-Natural Areas. *Journal of Applied Ecology* 9:439–457.

Burger, J. 1995. Beach Recreation and Nesting Birds. In R. L. Knight and K. J. Gutzwiller, eds. *Wildlife and Recreationists*. Washington, DC: Island Press, pp. 281–295.

Cole, D. N. 1983. Assessing and Monitoring Backcountry Trail Conditions. USDA Forest Service Research Paper INT-303. 10 pp.

Cole, D. N. 1985. Recreational Trampling Effects on Six Habitat Types in Western Montana. USDA Forest Service Research Paper INT-350. 43 pp.

Cole, D. N. 1987. Effects of Three Seasons of Experimental Trampling on Five Montane Forest Communities and a Grassland in Western Montana, USA. *Biological Conservation* 40:219–244.

Cole, D. N. 1988. Disturbance and Recovery of Trampled Montane Grassland and Forests in Montana. USDA Forest Service Research Paper INT-389. 37 pp.

Cole, D. N. 1991. Changes on Trails in the Selway-Bitterroot Wilderness, Montana, 1978–89. USDA Forest Service Research Paper INT-450. 5 pp.

Cole, D. N. 1995a. Experimental Trampling of Vegetation. I. Relationship Between Trampling Intensity and Vegetation Response. *Journal of Applied Ecology* 32:203–214.

Cole, D. N. 1995b. Experimental Trampling of Vegetation. II. Predictors of Resistance and Resilience. *Journal of Applied Ecology* 32:215–224.

Coleman, R. 1981. Footpath Erosion in the English Lake District. *Applied Geography* 1:121–131.

Dawson, J. O., P. N. Hinz, and J. C. Gordon. 1974. Hiking Trail Impact on Iowa Stream Valley Forest Preserves. *Iowa State Journal of Research* 48:329–337.

DeBenedetti, S. H., and D. J. Parsons. 1979. Mountain Meadow Management and Research in Sequoia and Kings Canyon National Parks: A Review and Update. In R. M. Linn, ed. *Proceedings of Conference on Scientific Research in the National Parks,* pp. 1305–1311.

USDI National Park Service Transactions and Proceedings Ser. 5; Washington, DC: U.S. Government Printing Office.

Dykema, J. A. 1971. Ecological Impact of Camping upon the Southern Sierra Nevada. Ph.D. dissertation. University of California, Los Angeles. 156 pp.

Fay, S. C., S. K. Rice, and S. P. Berg. 1977. Guidelines for Design and Location of Overnight Backcountry Facilities. Unpublished report. USDA Forest Service, Northeast Forest Experiment Station, Broomall, PA. 33 pp.

Garland, G. G. 1990. Technique for Assessing Erosion Risk from Mountain Footpaths. *Environmental Management* 14:793–798.

Geist, V., R. E. Stemp, and R. H. Johnson. 1985. Heart-Rate Telemetry of Bighorn Sheep as a Means to Investigate Disturbances. In N. G. Bayfield and G. C. Barrow, eds. *The Ecological Impacts of Outdoor Recreation on Mountain Areas in Europe and North America*, pp. 92–99. R. E. R. G. Report No. 9. Recreation Ecology Research Group, Wye, England.

Goldsmith, F. B. 1974. Ecological Effects of Visitors in the Countryside. In A. Warren and F. B. Goldsmith, eds. *Conservation Practice*. London: Wiley, pp. 217–232.

Harrison, C. 1981. Recovery of Lowland Grassland and Heathland in Southern England from Disturbance by Seasonal Trampling. *Biological Conservation* 19:119–130.

Hobbs, N. T. 1989. Linking Energy Balance to Survival in Mule Deer: Development and Testing of a Simulation Model. Wildlife Monograph 101. 39 pp.

Holmes, D. O., and H. E. M. Dobson. 1976. Ecological Carrying Capacity Research in Yosemite National Park. Part I. The Effects of Human Trampling and Urine on Subalpine Vegetation, a Survey of Past and Present Backcountry Use, and the Ecological Carrying Capacity of Wilderness. U.S. Dept. of Commerce, National Technical Information Center PB-270-955. 247 pp.

Jubenville, A., and K. O'Sullivan. 1987. Relationship of Vegetation Type and Slope Gradient to Trail Erosion in Interior Alaska. *Journal of Soil and Water Conservation* 42:450–452.

Kuss, F. R. 1986. A Review of Major Factors Influencing Plant Responses to Recreation Impacts. *Environmental Management* 10:637–650.

Kuss, F. R., and A. R. Graefe. 1985. Effects of Recreation Trampling on Natural Area Vegetation. *Journal of Leisure Research* 17:165–183.

Leeson, B. F. 1979. Research on Wildland Recreation Impact in the Canadian Rockies. In R. Ittner, D. R. Potter, J. K. Agee, and S. Anschell, eds. *Proceedings, Recreational Impact on Wildlands*, pp. 64–65. USDA Forest Service, Pacific Northwest Region, R-6-001-1979, Portland, OR.

Leonard, R. E., E. L. Spencer, and H. J. Plumley. 1981. *Backcountry Facilities: Design and Maintenance*. Boston: Appalachian Mountain Club. 214 pp.

Leung, Y., and J. L. Marion. 1996. Trail Degradation as Influenced by Environmental Factors: A State-of-the-Knowledge Review. *Journal of Soil and Water Conservation* 51:130–136.

Liddle, M. J. 1975. A Theoretical Relationship Between the Primary Productivity of Vegetation and Its Ability to Tolerate Trampling. *Biological Conservation* 8:251–255.

Marion, J. L. 1984. Ecological Changes Resulting from Recreational Use: A Study of Backcountry Campsites in the Boundary Waters Canoe Area, Minnesota. Ph.D. dissertation. University of Minnesota, St. Paul. 279 pp.

Marion, J. L. 1994. An Assessment of Trail Conditions in Great Smoky Mountains National Park. Final report. USDI National Park Service, Great Smoky Mountains National Park, Gatlinburg, TN. 155 pp.

Marion, J. L., and D. N. Cole. 1996. Spatial and Temporal Variation in Soil and Vegetation Impacts on Campsites. *Ecological Applications* 6:520–530.

Skagen, S. K., R. L. Knight, and G. H. Orians. 1991. Human Disturbance of an Avian Scavenging Guild. *Ecological Applications* 1:215–225.

Stewart, D. P. C., and K. C. Cameron. 1992. Effect of Trampling on the Soils of the St. James Walkway, New Zealand. *Soil Use and Management* 8:30–36.

Strand, S. 1979. The Impact of Pack Stock on Wilderness Meadows in Sequoia-Kings Canyon National Park. In J. T. Stanley Jr., H. T. Harvey, and R. J. Hartesveldt, eds. *A Report on the Wilderness Impact Study*. San Francisco: Sierra Club Outing Committee, pp. 77–87.

Summer, R. M. 1980. Impact of Horse Traffic on Trails in Rocky Mountain National Park. *Journal of Soil and Water Conservation* 35:85–97.

Sun, D. 1990. Effect of Plant Age on Tolerance of Two Grasses to Simulated Trampling. *Australian Journal of Ecology* 16:183–188.

Sun, D., and M. J. Liddle. 1991. Field Occurrence, Recovery, and Simulated Trampling Resistance and Recovery of Two Grasses. *Biological Conservation* 57:187–203.

Sun, D., and M. J. Liddle. 1993. The Morphological Responses of Some Australian Tussock Grasses and the Importance of Tiller Number in Their Resistance to Trampling. *Biological Conservation* 65:43–49.

Williams, P. B., and J. L. Marion. 1995. Assessing Campsite Conditions for Limits of Acceptable Change Management in Shenandoah National Park. USDI National Park Service Technical Report NPS/MARSHEN/NRTR-95/071. 138 pp.

9 Visitor Use

Many characteristics of visitor use influence the degree, type, and distribution of ecological impacts in wildland recreation areas. The amount of use an area receives obviously has some effect on impact patterns in the area. This fact spurred the interest in the concept of carrying capacity that was discussed in Chapter 1. Beyond the amount of use an area receives, impacts are strongly influenced by other use characteristics—who the users are, where they go, and what they do. In wilderness, for example, Hendee, Stankey, and Lucas (1990) suggest ranking various groups in the following order of decreasing environmental impact:

1. Large parties of horse users
2. Small parties of horse users
3. Large parties of overnight campers
4. Small parties of overnight campers using wood fires
5. Large parties of day hikers
6. Small parties of overnight campers using camp stoves and not building wood fires
7. Small parties of day hikers

From this it is clear that the potential to cause impact varies with party size (large vs. small), type of user (overnight campers vs. day hikers), behavior (using wood fires vs. camp stoves), and mode of travel (horse users vs. hikers). The potential to cause impact also varies with where users go—use distribution—and various characteristics that can influence behavior, specifically knowledge of low-impact camping techniques, motivations, experience level, social groups and structure, and place bonding. For example, impacts such as human litter, harassment of wildlife, and pollution of water sources are inappropriate or illegal behaviors that have a serious impact on recreational resources and experiences. In most situations a variety of visitor use and behavioral variables must be examined to accurately determine the consequences of recreational use on wildland park resources. In this chapter we will discuss these user characteristics.

AMOUNT OF USE

Conventional wisdom has often held that amount of use is the most important factor influencing amount of impact. Such thinking has been supported by describing the cause of impact with terms like "overuse" and proposing that solutions can be found

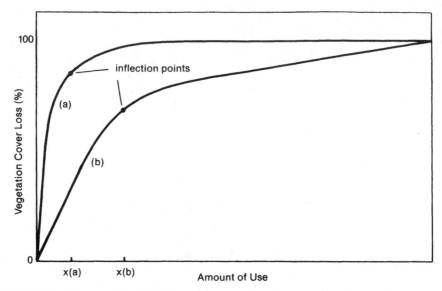

FIGURE 1. The general relationship between amount of use and loss of vegetation cover for (a) a fragile vegetation type and (b) a more resistant type. (*Source:* D. N. Cole.)

by prescribing a "carrying capacity." Research shows such thinking to be oversimplified at best and erroneous at worst. The importance of amount of use varies between environments, between activities, with impact parameter, and with the range of use levels being examined. In addition, effects differ depending on whether concern is with rate, intensity, or areal extent of change.

Research on the relationship between use and impact began in the early 1960s with Frissell and Duncan's (1965) cross-sectional analysis of Boundary Waters Canoe Area campsites and Wagar's (1964) experimental trampling study. Both studies examined the effect of various use levels on amount of vegetation cover. Frissell and Duncan found that the most lightly used campsites (with use estimated at 0 to 30 nights/year) had lost 80 percent of their inferred original cover and heavily used sites (60 to 90 nights/year) had lost 87 percent. Impact increases as use increases, but lightly used sites are almost as highly impacted as heavily used sites. This asymptotic curvilinear relationship between amount of use and loss of ground cover vegetation has been seriously contradicted only by one of six similar studies in wilderness, five on developed campsites, and about 30 experimental trampling studies (Fig. 1).

The asymptotic curvilinear relationship between amount of use and vegetation loss demonstrated by so many studies suggests a number of generalizations. First, at very low use levels, differences in amount of use are related to rapid changes in ground cover vegetation. Second, at higher use levels vegetation loss continues to gradually increase (toward a maximum possible limit of complete cover loss) as use increases, but differences in cover loss are seldom substantial, even when use levels of several orders of magnitude are compared. These two generalizations describe the curvilinear relationship between use and intensity of vegetation impact. Third, degree of curvilinearity increases as fragility increases. In fragile environments cover loss increases rapidly with increases in use at the very lowest use levels, and the inflection point, above which even substantial increases in use cause only minor increases in cover loss, comes at a low use level. In resistant environments cover loss increases more slowly with increasing use at the lowest use levels; the inflection point also comes at a higher use level. In Fig. 1 differences in amount of use are likely to have a substantial effect on vegetation cover if at least one of the use levels is well below X(a) or X(b). Most studies have examined only sites with use levels beyond those that correspond to the inflection points on the curve; consequently, cover differences are not substantial.

The relevance of the relationship demonstrated in Fig. 1, particularly the location of the inflection points of the curves, is substantial to wildland recreation management. Attempting to minimize cover loss by keeping use levels low will be effective only where use levels can be kept substantially below the use thresholds that correspond to the inflection points. In several fragile subalpine forest vegetation types, even use levels of no more than five nights/year exceeded threshold levels (Cole and Fichtler 1983). However, use thresholds are likely to be much higher on resistant vegetation types. For example, on developed campgrounds in the Atlantic Coastal Flatwoods region of South Carolina, Dunn, Lockaby, and Johnson (1980) found no significant loss of vegetation cover except on heavy use sites. As in most other studies, lack of adequate use measures makes it impossible to establish use thresholds for these South Carolina campsites. More research, employing better use estimates, and controlled experiments could enable us to establish use thresholds for important environments across the country (Marion and Cole 1996).

Trampling studies are one means of correlating visitor use to impacts under field experiment conditions. When trampling experiments were applied to six different vegetation types for three successive summers in the northern Rocky Mountains, use thresholds varied for each of the six vegetation types (Cole 1987). Thresholds were lower for vegetation cover loss than for species loss or increase in soil penetration resistance. However, there are some limitations in translating or equating experimental passes as an estimate of use. For example, how do you compare trampling number of passes to number of visitors, considering the fact that use of a site involves more impacts than those resulting from trampling passes? Through a series of observation studies of camping behavior and some use assumptions, Cole (1985) has estimated that 75 to 150 passes per year simulates the amount of trampling that occurs in the central part of a campsite during one night of use by a typical party of three backpackers. Validity checks of actual campsite use measures with experimental trampling passes have shown vegetation impacts to be quite similar.

Other research also suggests a strong relationship between amount of use and the *rate* of vegetation loss. For example, in an experimental trampling study on alpine meadows in Mt. Rainier National Park, vegetation cover was reduced to 50 percent of control values in three weeks when trampled at 75 passes/week. At 18 passes/week, it took eight weeks of trampling for cover to be reduced to 50 percent of controls (Singer 1971). The areal extent of vegetation loss is also strongly related to amount of use (Bratton, Hickler, and Graves 1978; Cole 1982). The finding that most levels of increased use have little effect on amount of vegetation loss but a pronounced effect on area of loss suggests the value of concentrating and channeling use on a small proportion of any area (Cole 1981; Cole and Hall 1992).

Many other impact parameters have been examined on campsites receiving different amounts of use. Those, like vegetation cover, for which a highly curvilinear relationship exists (Fig. 2), include bulk density, penetration resistance, macropore space, infiltration rate, changes in soil chemistry, loss of tree seedlings, and tree damage (Cole and Hall 1992; Cole and Fichtler 1983; Dunn, Lockaby, and Johnson 1980; Legg and Schneider 1977; Marion 1984; Young and Gilmore 1976). Loss of organic horizons, exposure of mineral soil, severe root exposure, and site enlargement are all changes related to use in a less curvilinear manner (Cole and Fichtler 1983; Coombs 1976; Marion 1984; Young 1978); there is more inherent resistance to these types of change, and use thresholds are higher. Changes in these parameters are easier to limit through manipulation of use intensities on campsites.

On trails, vegetation cover, bulk density, penetration resistance, and trail width relationships are highly curvilinear as they are on campsites (Crawford and Liddle 1977;

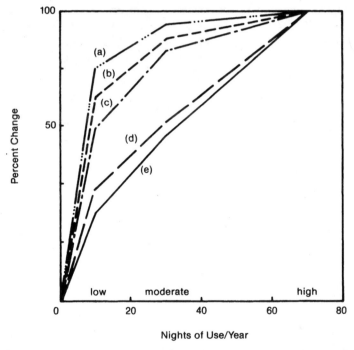

FIGURE 2. Relationship between amount of use and amount of impact in the Boundary Waters Canoe Area. (*Source:* Marion 1984). Numeric use levels are estimated from ordinal classes of low (0–12 nights/year), moderate (20–40 nights/year), and high (> 60 nights/year). Impact parameters are (*a*) tree damage, (*b*) loss of vegetation cover (*c*) increase in soil penetration resistance, (*d*) increase in exposed roots, mineral soil and rock, and (*e*) campsite area. Percent change is expressed as a percentage of the change on high-use sites.

Dale and Weaver 1974). Trail depth and the frequency of impact problems such as muddiness are generally not related to amount of use (Dale and Weaver 1974; Helgath 1975; Leung and Marion 1996). Such situations relate more to location and design features, although they obviously must be triggered by some use or construction.

In sum, these results suggest that there is little value, in terms of reduced impact, in limiting use of constructed trails. On campsites, limiting use is likely to be effective only if use levels can be kept very low. This is possible in some wildernesses but not in popular destination areas. In popular areas, channeling and concentrating use will have to be practiced to counteract the tendency for increased use to enlarge the areal extent of impact. Because the tipping point for each of these opposing strategies—dispersing use to keep levels low or concentrating use to minimize areal extent—varies greatly among environments, use thresholds need to be identified for major ecosystem types.

USE DISTRIBUTION

Visitors of wildland recreation areas often concentrate use in a few popular places, campsites, and trails. Such use behavior results in some zones of recreational areas being overused while other zones are seldom used. Because distribution of use is related to the distribution of resource impacts, use distribution is a major management concern for recreation resource managers. For example, if visitors are concentrating use on impact-resistant trails and campsites, management will want to encourage existing patterns of use. Also, use occurring on already heavily impacted sites does less damage than on new sites. However, in fragile areas or low use areas, management may want to disperse users from areas of concentrated use.

Numerous studies have documented the concentrated use patterns of wildland recreationists. In one of the most heavily used wildland areas, the Boundary Waters Canoe Area of Minnesota, nearly 70 percent of the user groups entered through only seven of the area's 70 entry points in 1974. Two entry points near population centers accounted for one-third of all user groups. Impacts are concentrated not only on these few entry points but also on the few portages and campsites near these entry points. In the Mission Mountains in Montana, more than 90 percent of user groups entered at only two of the area's 19 trailheads (Lucas, Shreuder, and James 1971). When one considers that backcountry trips average only three to four days, there is little chance for these heavy concentrations of trailhead users to disperse. Visitor solitude and resource impacts are both concerns with these patterns of concentrated use.

Over longer periods of time, campers commonly shift use from some existing sites to newly located sites that they "pioneer" (Cole 1993). Certain trails and lake routes within areas also show an uneven distribution of use. The Appalachian Trail within Great Smoky Mountains National Park (Tennessee-North Carolina) comprises only 12 percent of the park's trail system yet receives 45 percent of the overnight use. In the Spanish Peaks Primitive Area (Montana) 10 percent of the trail system accounted for 50 percent of the trail miles hiked in 1970, and a third of the trail system accounted for three-fourths of trail use. Many other wildland recreation areas show similar patterns of concentrated trail use, particularly areas receiving large percentages of horse and day use. Both activities tend to concentrate use on main trails. As day use of wild-lands has increased in popularity, so has the concentration of impacts near trailheads and sightseeing destinations.

Although less concentrated than trails, campsites and scenic sites also show an uneven pattern of use. In the Desolation Wilderness (California) 50 percent of all use occurred on only 16 percent of the most popular campsites. Preferred sites for camp-ing and hiking are often lake and stream edges, scenic overviews, and well-known physiographic attractions (i.e., peaks, gorges) of an area. Brown and Schomaker (1974) showed the most preferred and used campsites in the Spanish Peaks Primitive Area to have the following characteristics in common:

1. Proximity to both water and fishing opportunities
2. Scenic and lake views
3. Location within 700 ft of a trail
4. Availability of at least 500 ft^2 of level land
5. Availability of firewood within 300 ft

They found that about one-half of the campsites were within 50 ft of the shoreline of a lake or stream, almost two-thirds were within 100 ft, and 85 percent were within 200 ft. The shorelines of lakes and streams are considered to be particularly sensitive to ecological impacts, although research by Cole (1982) suggests that lakeshore sites may have impacts little different from sites set back from lakeshores. In trampling experiments conducted in Waterton Lakes National Park (Canada), Nagy and Scotter (1974) found less vegetation change in a subalpine lakeshore meadow community than in the coniferous forests around the lake.

TYPE OF USER GROUP

Obviously, not all types of user groups produce the same type or amount of impacts. Certain types of users, because of length of stay, the activities they engage in, and the demands they place on wildland resources, cause more impacts than do other groups of users. Overnight campers produce more and different types of impacts than day hik-ers. Campers use wildland resources for a longer period of time, use a larger propor-tion of the resource (i.e., campsites), and use a greater diversity of the available resources (i.e., firewood, water). Because they stay overnight, they concentrate use on campsites, meaning that these nodes receive a proportionately larger amount of impact per person than do trails. Spatial patterns of impacts of overnight campers tend to be more nodal, whereas those of day hikers are, for the most part, linkage-oriented.

In addition to length of stay, the type of activity the user group is engaged in influ-ences environmental impacts. For example, canoe parties in the Boundary Waters Canoe Area and hunting parties in many of the Western wildland areas tend to be more destination-oriented and spend more time in camp than backpacking parties (Fig. 3). They also tend to carry more equipment and nonburnable materials, which

FIGURE 3. Destination-oriented use parties that spend several nights in the same camp (e.g., hunters) often manipulate the site, such as by building campsite furniture. (*Photo:* D. N. Cole.)

serve as potential sources of litter, than hikers do into the backcountry. Many of these activities cause specific environmental impacts that are in addition to those impacts directly related to backcountry camping. Campers fishing at alpine lakes often deposit fish entrails at the lake's edge and cause more trampling impacts to the riparian zone of lakes than do nonfishing campers.

PARTY SIZE

Large parties of users are thought to cause greater impacts to certain aspects of the biophysical resource than smaller parties. Large parties are typically defined in wilderness areas as groups larger than 8 to 10 members. Although large parties tend to make up a small proportion of all parties visiting wildland recreation areas, they can contribute a disproportionate amount of certain environmental impacts. Expansion of campsite boundaries is a particular impact attributed to large groups. Large parties often expand campsites by clearing areas to facilitate additional tents, other equipment, eating space, and space for tying horses and storing canoes. Most backcountry campsites, like developed campsites, are designed for a capacity of one tent party per site. However, recreation parties often consist of more than one tenting subgroup. When multiple tenting parties want to camp together on a site, it is only natural that they expand the existing site or develop satellite sites adjacent to the boundaries of the existing site to facilitate their spatial needs.

Larger parties of users are also often associated with horseback, canoe, and vehicular modes of travel (Fig. 4). Both horses and vehicles, particularly when overnight use is involved, require additional space at campsite locations and lead to impacts beyond the specific campsite boundaries.

In addition to needing greater space, larger groups commonly exhibit behavioral use patterns that can lead to greater impacts. In the Boundary Waters Canoe Area large canoeing parties were characteristically found to stay longer, move camp more often, and penetrate farther into the backcountry than small parties (Lime 1972). This high mobility of larger groups suggests that they utilize more campsites and portages than small parties do and consequently have the potential for damaging more places. As pointed out by Lime (1972, p. 4):

> Because more than half of the large parties kept moving, their impact on individual campsites was dispersed rather than concentrated. Staying in one location might be less damaging than using many sites, because the disturbance is increased by making and breaking camp several times.

However, extended length of stay can often lead to greater amounts of impact to a given area.

Large parties are also capable of increasing the rate at which impacts occur. They concentrate a heavy amount of use in a short period of time on a site. Two nights of camping by a party of 30 individuals on a previously unused site in New York resulted in a 10 to 15 percent decrease in ground cover (Bogucki, Malanchuk, and

FIGURE 4. Larger parties of users are often associated with horseback, canoe, and vehicular modes of travel. (*Photo:* R. C. Lucas.)

Schenck 1975). The results of this study and others suggest that even short-term use by large parties may severely alter the ground cover vegetation of fragile environments. Large parties are a particular problem in more pristine areas.

Large parties probably have no more resource impact on trails than many small parties as long as they remain on the trail tread. In the case of wildlife impacts, large parties may have less impact than several small parties if the frequency of disturbance is important, as is the situation with bird life.

USER BEHAVIOR

In any setting the actions of individuals may be considered appropriate, inappropriate, or even illegal, depending on the normative behavior and conditions accepted for the situation and setting. In addition, these actions are determined by many behavioral factors. The motivating force behind one's actions, the group context within which an action is carried out, and one's education and past experience with a particular action all have an influence on whether the action will be conducted in an appropriate or inappropriate manner. In the case of resource impacts, all these factors affect the on-site behavior of recreationists, which in turn influences the appropriateness of their actions and the level of impacts that they can cause to wildland resources. Understanding the factors that determine user behavior and their relationship to resource impacts allows management to modify the inappropriate actions of users and thus reduce resource impacts. Next, we will discuss these behavioral factors and their relationship to impacts.

Minimum Impact Knowledge

Many of the techniques involved in conducting wildland recreational activities can be performed in a number of ways that lead to differing levels of impact. As a result, most agencies involved with the management of wildland resources have informational programs aimed at educating users about how to reduce resource impacts (Fig. 5). An example is the Leave No Trace (LNT) program, an effort that unites four federal agencies—The National Park Service, U.S. Forest Service, Bureau of Land Management, and U.S. Fish and Wildlife Service—and outdoor retailers, manufacturers, user groups, educators, and individuals who have a responsibility to maintain and protect wildlands (Marion and Brame 1996, p. 24). The program emphasizes the education and skills necessary to reduce visitor impacts, along with promoting the outdoor ethics and judgment necessary to guide the selection and application of low-impact skills. Often, visitors are simply unaware of certain skills and techniques that result in minimum levels of resource disturbance. By educating visitors about wildland resources and their proper use, managers hope to create a minimum impact ethic that will eventually lead to a permanent behavioral change in visitors. Minimum impact camping techniques are a prerequisite if impacts are to be limited in wilderness areas where policy prohibits major site development practices (Cole 1990).

Certain impacts can be greatly reduced or nearly eliminated through the practice of minimum impact techniques, but other impacts are essentially inevitable if use

FIGURE 5. Minimum impact information, such as the proper use of lanterns in campgrounds, is a useful management tool. (*Photo:* W. E. Hammitt.)

occurs to any degree. The replacement of campfires with light-weight stoves, the nontrenching of tents, the packing out of all garbage, the proper disposal of human waste, and campsite landscaping on leaving a site can produce a backcountry camp-site with the appearance of having been used minimally (Hampton and Cole 1995). Simply requiring camp stoves and educating users of proper firewood practices should eliminate some obvious campsite impacts. In the Eagle Cap Wilderness, Oregon, researchers observed that 95 percent of the overstory trees in campsites had been damaged by people collecting firewood and causing physical impacts to tree trunks (Cole and Benedict 1983). Particularly disturbing was the fact that more than one-third of the trees had been cut down. Requiring the use of camp stoves, along with a minimum impact education program, could modify inappropriate behavior of this nature among future users. On the other hand, trampling impacts on campsites and trails are inherent changes that occur if people recreate in natural areas.

Knowledge of minimum-impact techniques and education programs in achieving low impact are key components in managing wildland recreation impacts and have been quite successful in reducing certain types of impacts. The early Pack It In, Pack It Out program has been quite successful at reducing the amount of litter left in wildland recreation areas. However, it cannot be expected to eliminate backcountry litter The Leave No Trace program, with its many publications, videos, and other materials aimed at specific activities (e.g., horseback riding and climbing) and specific areas (e.g., the LNT brochure for Great Smoky Mountains National Park) are having an influence on how recreation visitors select sites and use them. Even books, like *Soft Paths: How to Enjoy the Wilderness Without Harming It* (Hampton and Cole 1995), are available to educate users, organized groups, and managers on reducing resource impacts in wildland recreation areas.

Experience Level

Experienced visitors, in terms of amount of on-site experience, have been found to be more sensitive to social impacts and to take more precautions to avoid situations of social conflict (Heberlein and Dunwiddie 1979; Vaske, Donnelly, and Heberlein 1980). The same should hold true for ecological impacts. While observing actual campsite selection behavior of wilderness users, Heberlein and Dunwiddie found that experienced visitors distinguished themselves from novices by selecting camp-sites that were (1) farther from other visitors, (2) farther from the nearest campsite, whether it was occupied or not, and (3) in an area with few other sites. It is usually the more experienced visitor who is displaced from crowded or heavily impacted areas. In a study of visitor perception of river environmental impacts, Hammitt and McDonald (1983) found that the more experienced users were, the more perceptive they were of river impacts and the more willing they were to support management controls aimed at correcting the problems. More experienced users often have an ear-lier "frame of reference" and set of norms of what an area "used to be like" and use this frame of reference when evaluating current impacts.

Because experienced visitors are more aware and sensitive to social impacts, it fol-lows that they are also likely to be more sensitive about causing ecological impacts to recreational resources. Certain forms of visitor behavior, such as littering, trench-ing around tents, hanging lanterns on trees, or camping in fragile meadows, may not be considered inappropriate behavior by novice campers, yet experienced campers are likely to recognize the potential impacts caused by each of these actions.

User Motivation

The *reasons* that recreationists engage in certain activities or that they are motivated to visit certain recreational environments can influence the impacts they contribute to a recreational area. For example, the individual who is motivated to visit an area for solitude and a passive form of recreation is likely to produce fewer impacts than the individual who is motivated to visit by a desire to affiliate with others in a motorized form of recreation. Similarly, the person *attracted* to wildland areas to experience and observe nature is likely to produce fewer impacts than the individual who visits wild-land areas as simply a means to *escape* the home and work environment. However, caution is necessary when speculating on the influence of user motivations on resources impacts, for little research has been conducted in this area, and visitor behavior is a complex phenomenon, seldom determined by one variable.

Considerable research has been conducted on user motivations from a psychological and visitor management perspective in outdoor recreation (Driver, 1976; Knopf 1983, 1987; Manning 1986; McDonald and Hammitt 1983; Schreyer and Roggenbuck 1978). This research has demonstrated that (1) visitors engage in different activities for different reasons and in different ways, (2) visitors participate in the same activities for different reasons, and (3) they utilize recreational environments in different ways to achieve the experiences they desire. The information generated from these and similar studies has been quite useful in planning recreational areas and in managing visitors for the different recreational opportunities and experiences desired (Brown, Driver, and McConnell 1978; Driver and Brown 1978). However, all of the motivational studies have involved the experience outcomes desired by visitors, with little emphasis devoted to the influence of user motivations on the impacts to resource settings. Clark and Stankey (1979) have come as close as anyone in applying user motivations and resource settings to impacts through an application of the "recreation opportunity spectrum" concept. Others have suggested that many vandalism-associated impacts are related to the moods and motivational forces underlying individual behavior while on site. For example, the need for excitement may lead to the chopping of trees, whereas the need for skill development and achievement may lead to the building of furniture within backcountry campsites.

Application of user motivation in managing site impacts can be illustrated through use of campground data reported by Hendee and Campbell (1969). They found that many of the campers of developed campgrounds desired to camp with two or more other families or their extended family (e.g., grandparents) on the same campsite. Seven out of 10 campers preferring developed sites thought all campgrounds should have several units so two families can camp together. For these campers the desire to affiliate with another family is a major motive for their camping, and they require a double-sized site if resource impacts are to be restricted to the designed campsite and to a minimum. This same phenomenon applies to multiunit backcountry groups that are motivated to share their backcountry experience with others on the same site.

Social Group and Structure

Almost all activities that occur in wildland recreation areas occur in the context of a group. Even in wilderness use where solitude is particularly important, we find that less than 3 to 4 percent participate alone. Most individuals participate as members of a family, friendship, mixed family and friendship, or organized group. The group in which one participates and the structure of members within the group are determinants of outdoor recreation behavior and can influence the amount and type of impacts occurring to the resource base.

As an example, two backcountry camping parties made up of eight members each, one consisting of two families and the other of early aged teenagers, would function as two distinctly different groups. Peer pressure and sanctions toward certain behaviors in the two groups of users would likely be different. Disposal of human waste, size of fires, and activities beyond the boundaries of the campsite impact zone are more likely to be a problem among the teenagers. Vandalism, which can greatly impact wildland resources, is particularly prominent among groups of preteens and young teenagers (Clark, Hendee, and Campbell 1971). Unsupervised children are the headache of many campground managers, with many inappropriate actions of children leading to resource impacts.

In a study of inner-tube floaters of National Park Service and U.S. Forest Service rivers, we observed that organized groups of users (e.g., church, clubs) utilized the river resource in a gregarious fashion, necessitating more area use of resources than the resource base was physically capable of or designed to accommodate (Hammitt and McDonald 1981; McDonald and Hammitt 1981). Because organized and friendship groups often utilize resources differently from family groups, areas sensitive to impacts may have to be designed for these user groups or restricted from their use.

Place Bonding

Wildland recreation places, whether wilderness areas, campsites, or favorite fishing holes, matter to people, and an emotional bond commonly develops between visitors and these places during recreation engagements. This developmental process is commonly referred to as place bonding, place attachment, sense of place, or other such terms. People often develop an emotional bond, a sense of belonging, and even a dependence on a wildland recreation area, to the extent that it becomes "their place," "a favorite place," or the "only place" for wildland recreation pursuits. Through an emotional bonding process that occurs over repeated exposures to certain places and associated transactional place-people interactions, these places can take on identities of their own.

The place-bonding behavior that commonly develops between recreationists and wildland places can have both negative and positive effects on wildland impacts. When the strength and character of the place bond is very strong, visitors become deeply attached to their favorite place. They will consider no other place to fish or camp, and become "rooted" in that specific place. Many individuals are known to have specific campsites, trails, or fishing sites that they use again and again. Such repeated use, particularly if other visitors have an emotional bond with the same specific place, can result in serious site and place impacts. Worst of all, it is commonly difficult to shift or distribute use from such places because of the strong emotional bonds that exist between place and user. On the other hand, one could speculate that those visitors who are strongly bonded to a place—specific place on which they are dependent for their particular activity—would take better care of the place and cause fewer impacts.

The relationship between place bonding and wildland recreation resource impacts has been little researched. It is likely to be quite complex, for the phenomenon of place bonding itself is known to be quite complex, according to Stokols and Shumaker (1981). Adapting the thinking of these authors to wildland recreation, we know that emotional bonding with a recreation place does not refer only to the perceptual prominence of physical environments, but rather to the functional, motivational, and evaluative significance of place. Perception, and not just physical presence (e.g., a recreation setting visit), is certainly relevant in discussing emotional bonding with recreation settings. The *strength* and *character* of emotional bonds developed with wildland recreation places are associated with a set of collectively held images that evolve as a result of direct or indirect interaction with a particular place.

Hammitt and Stewart (1996) have proposed a taxonomy of recreation place bonding, in which many of the dimensions of emotional bonding with place are classified (Fig. 6). The taxonomy is based on a proposed graduated intensity of emotional bonding and character of the bonding relationship. The emotional bond between an individual and a particular place may vary in intensity from an immediate sense of familiarity to a long-lasting and deeply rooted attachment (Tuan 1974). Place bonding also contains an element of character or specificity, whereby the functionality, necessity, and dependence on a recreation place may vary from a less focused mode to a very focused, specialized emotional dependence on a particular place. It is proposed (Fig. 6) that both the intensity and the character of place-bonding relationships ascend the taxonomy of the emotional bonding pyramid, moving from familiarity to rootedness. However, a hierarchical order of ascending from lower to the next higher level within the pyramid is not necessarily implied.

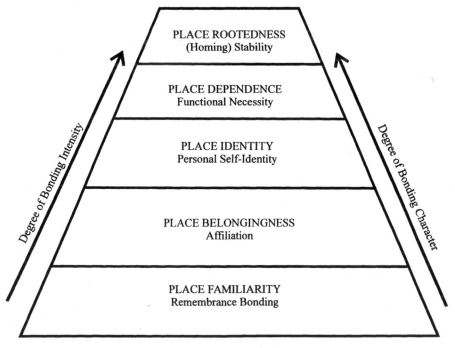

FIGURE 6. A taxonomy of dimensions of emotional bonding with recreation places.

As a demonstration of how the proposed taxonomy can enhance the classification and differentiation of levels of emotional bonding with recreation places, two of the levels will be briefly described. *Place familiarity* is proposed as the most elementary of the types of emotional bonding, both in terms of bond intensity and character. It implies both a sense of knowing and recognition of a place that results from acquaintances and remembrances associated with a recreation place. And because places visited during wildland recreation engagements involve an element of free choice and self-selection, the acquaintances, memories, and lasting images are usually part of fond and affectionate experiences that promote emotional bonding with these places. During the familiarity process, environmental spaces are emotionally identified, boundaries are developed to define them as places, and a human-place "structural coupling" begins (Roberts 1996). It is possible for wildland recreation visitors to have a feeling of familiarity with a place, yet in no way feel a strong identity with or dependence on that specific place. However, certain familiar places can come to mind when a person is selecting a place for recreation. Thus, repeat visits and resource impacts are likely to be associated with the place familiarity phenomenon.

At the other extreme of the pyramid is *place rootedness*. Tuan (1980, p. 4) characterizes place rootedness as a very strong and focused emotional bond that "in its essence means being completely at home—that is, unreflectively secure and comfortable in a particular locality." It is the only place, a one-of-a-kind place, for people who have formed this bond.

Wildland recreationists sometimes speak about a certain deer hunting or fishing locality in the same sense that Tuan speaks about a native place of habitation. A deer hunting camp in Northern Michigan may be the only place an extended family has gathered in the fall for decades to hunt deer, or a hut in Norway may be the only place that family members have recreationally fished for generations. Such people long for no other place to hunt, fish, or hike, for traditional usage has made the recreation place a second home. There is a recreational genealogy associated with these places, rooted in family members, environmental settings, and activities of the past. To acquire rootedness in a sense of extended time and genealogical depth, it may be necessary only to recreate in a particular place traditionally used and spoken about by one's grandfather and father. In these situations, the wildland recreation place takes on more meaning than the present situation has to offer, for its emotional bond and meaning are deeply steeped in the past. The stories told and rituals performed are stable components of the recreation experiences in rooted places.

For those wildland recreationists rooted in only one specific recreation locality, and for those dependent on one or even a few recreation places, the management alternative whereby these visitors are distributed to other sites to reduce resource-related impacts is not a possibility. Neither are we likely to persuade them to use these areas less frequently or in alternative ways. Their perception of recreation resource impacts are likely to be viewed differently in these strongly bonded places, for the meaning and perceptions of these special places go beyond the conditions of their resources and natural states. Management of resource impacts where place bonding is very strong will have to rely on other strategies than those related to use distribution. More will be said about management strategies and techniques in Chapter 13.

MODE OF TRAVEL

The means by which recreationists travel in wildland recreation areas also has an important effect on both ecological and sociological impacts. For example, the impacts associated with motorized travel are very different from those caused by horses which, in turn, are quite different from those caused by recreationists on foot. Even for motorized travel, there are pronounced differences among those impacts caused by terrestrial off-road vehicles, snowmobiles, and motorboats. In Chapters 2 through 5 we described what is known about the impacts associated with these different modes of travel. Managers will need to understand differences between these modes of travel, because an important management strategy is to restrict the means of travel. Wilderness areas by definition, with a few minor exceptions, prohibit all motorized recreational use. In other areas, certain modes of travel can be completely prohibited, prohibited in certain areas, allowed only in certain areas, or regulated in some other way. In this section we will compare impacts caused by common sets of travel modes a manager may face. These are (1) snowmobiles and skis, (2) motorboats and nonmotorized boats (e.g., rafts, canoes, rowboats, and kayaks), and (3) off-road vehicles, stock, and recreationists on foot.

Snowmobiles/Skis

Impacts caused by travel over snow are different from those caused by travel on land. When snow depth is great, impacts on soil, vegetation, and water are minimal. When the snow is shallow, impacts on these ecosystem components can be as severe as when use occurs on snow-free ground. Generally, the most significant impacts are those associated with disturbance of wildlife. This has been described in some detail in Chapter 4.

Unfortunately, there is little research into differences in the disturbances caused by snowmobiles and skis. We can offer a few speculations, however. On roads and well-established trails, differences are probably not pronounced. The major difference is that snowmobiles produce more noise and can travel farther more easily (Figs. 7 and 8). Therefore, more remote portions of an area are more likely to be affected frequently by snowmobiles than by skiers. Off roads and trails, differences become more pronounced. Because snowmobiles cover more ground in a shorter period of time, they can disturb more wildlife and compact snow over a larger area. Compaction of snow is particularly significant, because it can kill small mammals and destroy the subnivean layer, between snow and the ground, where many small mammals live. This may also have an effect on species that prey on small mammals such as owls, eagles, hawks, foxes, coyotes, and bobcats (Bury, Wendling, and McCool 1976).

In general, then, snowmobiles have more potential to cause impact, particularly if they are not confined to established roads and trails. Differences between motorized and nonmotorized travel appear to be considerably less pronounced than for travel on land or over water, however. Differences in the impact each mode of travel has on the experience of other recreationists in the area may be more serious than differences in ecological impact.

FIGURE 7. Snowmobiles extend recreational impacts into the winter season, reaching remote areas that normally receive little recreational use during this time of the year. (*Photo:* R. C. Lucas.)

FIGURE 8. Tour and cross-country skiing are increasing in popularity as wildland recreation sports. (*Photo:* D. N. Cole.)

Motorboats/Nonmotorized Boats

Motorboats have greater potential than nonmotorized boats for causing impact, primarily because they pollute water with fuel and oil. As described in Chapter 5, considerable quantities of oil and gasoline residue are discharged by outboard motors. This affects water quality and aquatic life. Nonmotorized craft obviously do not have such an effect. Nonmotorized craft are able to reach more remote parts of wildland areas, however. This can result in more pronounced impacts to remote portions of recreation areas. For example, the use of rubber rafts to float people down the Grand Canyon and other remote desert canyons has greatly increased the amount of impact occurring in these areas.

In areas that are used primarily by nonmotorized craft, the most prominent impacts are usually along the banks of the lakes and streams in places where recreationists camp, picnic, fish, and take their boats in and out of the water. These impacts are little different from those caused by recreationists on foot. Impacts to water quality and aquatic life will usually be more serious in places where most use is by motorboats. There are exceptions to this generalization, of course. For example groups traveling in motorized rafts through the Grand Canyon probably have more effect on land than on the waters.

Off-Road Vehicles/Stock/Foot Travel

For several reasons, the potential for off-road vehicles to cause substantial impact is particularly high (Webb and Wilshire 1983; Parikesit, Larson, and Matthes-Sears 1995). Because they can cover distances rapidly, they are able to impact large areas on single trips. If the terrain is conducive to ORV travel, remote areas can be reached, even on day trips (Fig. 9). This is certainly the case in large dune and desert areas where remote places are likely to be inaccessible on foot or horseback. The forces that result from spinning wheels, in association with the effect of cleated tires, dislodge soil and vegetation rapidly. This damage is compounded by the tendency for many ORV users to seek out steep, unstable slopes where erosion is easily triggered (Fig. 10). Other modes of travel tend to avoid steep and unstable slopes. Consequently, problems with erosion—one of the most significant of impacts because of its irreversibility and its tendency to get progressively worse even without continued use— are much more serious with ORVs than with nonmotorized use. Motorized recreational use can be damaging to water quality as well. Eroded soil, deposited in streams, increases sediment loads and turbidity; this can be particularly detrimental to certain fish species such as trout.

Horses, mules, and other types of recreational stock have less potential for causing erosion. The potential is still much higher than for foot travelers, however. Stock are much heavier than humans, and their weight is concentrated on a smaller surface area. Thus, they exert much greater pressure on the ground surface. Problems resulting from this high potential for trampling disturbance are compounded by the tendency for shod hooves to loosen the soil (McQuaid-Cook 1978), making it more susceptible to erosion. Thus, equestrian trails are more prone to erosion and more

FIGURE 9. Trail bike use impacts both the wildland recreation resource and the experience of other user types. (*Photo:* D. N. Cole.)

FIGURE 10. Off-road vehicle impacts are compounded by the tendency of many ORV users to seek out steep, unstable slopes, where erosion is easily initiated. (*Photo:* D. N. Cole.)

likely to require hardening. In forests in the Rocky Mountains in Montana, Dale and Weaver (1974) found that trails used by horses and hikers were 2.5 times deeper than trails used only by hikers. Stock are also damaging to the banks of streams and lakeshores.

In an experimental study in Montana, Weaver and Dale (1978) examined the effects of horses, hikers, and a lightweight, slowly driven motorcycle. Trails produced by 1000 horse passes were two to three times as wide and 1.5 to 7 times as deep as trails produced by 1000 hiker passes. Impacts caused by the motorcycle were intermediate in severity. Bulk density increased 1.5 to 2 times as rapidly on horse trails as on hiker trails. The effect of motorcycles, again, was usually intermediate in severity. Vegetation loss occurred much more rapidly on horse and motorcycle trails than on hiker trails. The investigators also found that motorcycle damage was greatest when going uphill, whereas horse and hiker damage was greatest when going downhill. Thus, they concluded that trail wear can be minimized if motorcycle trails ascend gentle slopes and descend steep slopes, and that horse and hiker trails should ascend steep slopes and descend gentle slopes.

On campsites, differences between impacts caused by motorized users, stock parties, and hikers are pronounced. Ground cover disturbance and soil compaction are particularly severe where vehicles drive across campsites. More gear can be carried in vehicles, and this is also often translated into higher impact. Campfire impacts are often more pronounced; tree damage is more severe; lengths of stay are longer; and party sizes are larger, so campsites are larger and more highly developed.

An increasing form of travel in wildland areas during the 1990s involves mountain bicycles (Jacoby 1990). Although some research has concentrated on the social impacts of mountain bike use, few studies have focused on the ecological impacts (Ramthun 1995). The most common form of resource impact resulting from mountain bike recreation is trail erosion and expansion. Wilson and Seney (1994) examined the relative impact of hikers, horses, motorcycles, and off-road bicycles in terms of water runoff and sediment yield on existing trails in Montana. They found that horses and hikers (hooves and feet) made more sediment available than wheels (motorcycles and off-road bicycles) and that the effect was most pronounced on prewetted trails. However, the study was limited to tests of only 50 and 100 passes by the four modes of travel.

Two studies have compared impacts on horse and hiker campsites—both in wilderness areas in Montana. In the Lee Metcalf Wilderness, campsites used by stock were ten times as large and had seven times as much exposed mineral soil as sites used by backpackers. Cole (1983) found the same results on sites in the Bob Marshall Wilderness. Stock sites were six times as large, with a bare area four times larger than backpacker sites. Stock sites had more than ten times as many damaged trees, had been much more severely compacted, and had many more introduced plant species (Fig. 11).

The larger size of stock sites is primarily a result of the requirement for an area adjacent to the campsite to keep stock. The animals are frequently tied to trees, and this accounts for the more serious tree damage in stock camps (Fig. 12). Trees are also more likely to be cut down for tent poles, hitching rails, corrals, or firewood. The

FIGURE 11. In the Bob Marshall Wilderness, Montana, campsites used by horse parties had more than 10 times as many damaged trees as sites used only by hikers. (*Photo:* D. N. Cole.)

FIGURE 12. Horses tied to trees are a major source of damage to tree trunks and root systems. (*Photo:* R. C. Lucas.)

greater compaction is a result of the stock being heavier than humans, with their weight concentrated on a smaller surface area. Introduced plants are spread by seeds in horse manure or feed or by being stuck to the horses' bodies; this accounts for the greater amounts of these species in stock camps.

A further impact caused by stock results from their need to graze. Where this is allowed (where horses are not confined to corrals and fed only pelletized feed), grazing areas are trampled and plants are defoliated. This leads to further increases in the size of disturbed areas. In a portion of the Eagle Cap Wilderness, the area disturbed solely by stock amounted to three-fourths of the entire area disturbed by recreational use, although stock use accounted for only about 20 percent of the total use of the wilderness (Cole 1981). Grazed areas experience decreased vegetation cover, changes in vegetation composition, soil compaction, and in many cases accelerated erosion.

Horse manure is another unique impact associated with stock. This is a major source of exotic plant seeds. It can find its way into streams and pollute waters. Its major impact, however, is social, reflecting the objection of many hikers to its presence on trails and campsites. In many areas, horseback use is separated from hiking use, on different trails, to avoid problems of conflict between stock and hiking parties.

Because foot travel is the most common mode of travel, its impacts are particularly pronounced and widespread. In addition, wildlife are often more readily disturbed by hikers than by motor vehicles (MacArthur, Geist, and Johnston 1982). Hikers are more unpredictable, more likely to approach animals, and may be considered more of a threat by animals. Hikers may also be somewhat more disturbing to wildlife than recreationists on horseback, although this has not been studied. Impacts on soil, vegetation, and water caused by hikers, however, are much less severe, per capita, than those caused by other types of recreationists.

Several writers have postulated that the type of shoe recreationists wear has a great effect on amount of impact. The popularity of the lug-soled boot has been blamed repeatedly for reported increases in trail wear (Harlow 1977; Ketchledge and Leonard 1970; Zaslowsky 1981). Nobody has been able to demonstrate, under realistic conditions, that this is the case, however. Kuss (1983) found no significant differences between two types of hiking boot when comparing loss of organic matter and soil from experimentally trampled trails. There were no significant differences in amount of loss after either 600 or 2400 passes, although both boot types caused significant disruption of the soil surface. This study substantiated the results of earlier studies by Whittaker (1978) and Saunders, Howard, and Stanley-Saunders (1980). Neither of these studies found significant differences in impact related to type of footwear.

All footgear, regardless of type, will cause substantial impact to vegetation and soils. Heavily worn trails are common in nature areas and urban parks where lug-soled boots are uncommon. More research may still uncover important differences under circumstances that have not yet been studied. For now, however, there appears to be little gained by asking hikers to wear any particular type of boot.

SUMMARY

1. Recreational resource impacts can be determined as much by visitor use as by the durability of the resource site. For example, impacts vary with party size (large vs. small groups), type of user (overnight campers vs. day hikers), user behavior (using wood fires vs. camp stoves), and mode of travel (horse users vs. hikers). The potential to cause impact also varies with where users go. Various user characteristics that can influence behavior are knowledge of low-impact techniques, motivations, experience level, and social groups and structure.

2. The amount of use is not directly related to the amount of impact. Amount of use varies among environments, between activities, with impact parameter, and with range of use levels being examined. Effects also differ depending on whether concern is with rate, intensity, or areal extent of resource change.

3. Dispersal of concentrated campers in wildland areas is not always a good management practice. For example, if visitors are concentrating use on impact-resistant trails and campsites or on very popular and already heavily impacted sites, management will want to encourage existing patterns of use. However, in fragile areas of low use, management may want to disperse users from places of concentrated use.

4. Certain types of users, because of length of stay, activities they engage in, and the demands they place on wildland resources, cause more impacts than do other groups of users. Horseback parties typically tend to be large, require additional space for horses at campsite locations, and cause impacts beyond the specific campsite boundaries.

5. The motivating force behind one's recreation, the group context within which activities are carried out, and one's education and past experience with a particular activity all have an influence on whether wildland recreation is conducted in an appropriate manner that leads to minimal levels of resource impact.

6. Different modes of travel in wildland areas cause different types and levels of impact. Off-road vehicles can travel a much greater distance than hikers and cause large areal impact in a short period of time. Snowmobile impacts can greatly compact snow and influence the wildlife/soil environment beneath it. Horse trails and campsites have been shown to be 10 times as impacted as sites used only by backpackers.

REFERENCES

Bogucki, D. J., J. L. Malanchuk, and T. E. Schenck. 1975. Impact of Short-term Camping on Ground-level Vegetation. *Journal of Soil and Water Conservation* 30:231–232.

Bratton, S. P., M. G. Hickler, and J. H. Graves. 1978. Visitor Impact on Backcountry Campsites in the Great Smoky Mountains. *Environmental Management* 2(5):431–442.

Brown, P. J., and J. H. Schomaker. 1974, Final Report on Criteria for Potential Wilderness Campsites. Institute for Study of Outdoor Recreation and Tourism, Utah State University, Logan, UT. Supplement No. 32. 50 pp.

Brown, P. J., B. L. Driver, and C. McConnell. 1978. The Opportunity Spectrum Concept and Behavioral Information in Outdoor Recreation Resources Supply Inventories: Background and Application. In *Integrated Inventories of Renewable Natural Resources: Proceedings of the Workshop.* USDA Forest Service General Technical Report RM-55.

Bury, R. L., R. C. Wendling, and S. F. McCool. 1976. Off-road Recreation Vehicles—A Research Summary, 1969–1975. Texas Agricultural Experiment Station Publication MP-1277. 84 pp.

Clark, R. N., and G. H. Stankey. 1979. Determining the Acceptability of Recreational Impacts: An Application of the Outdoor Recreation Opportunity Spectrum. In R. Ittner, D. R. Potter, J. Agee, and S. Anschell, eds. *Recreational Impacts on Wildlands.* USDA Forest Service Conference Proceedings, No. R-6-001-1979.

Clark, R. N., J. C. Hendee, and F. L. Campbell. 1971. Depreciative Behavior in Forest Campgrounds: An Exploratory Study. USDA Forest Service Research Note PNW-161. 12 pp.

Cole, D. N. 1981. Vegetational Changes Associated with Recreational Use and Fire Suppression in the Eagle Cap Wilderness, Oregon: Some Management Implications. *Biological Conservation* 20:247–270.

Cole, D. N. 1982. Wilderness Campsite Impacts: Effect of Amount of Use. USDA Forest Service Research Paper INT-284. 34 pp.

Cole, D. N. 1983. Campsite Conditions in the Bob Marshall Wilderness, Montana. USDA Forest Service Research Paper INT-312. 18 pp.

Cole D. N. 1985. Recreational Trampling Effects on Six Habitat Types in Western Montana. USDA Forest Service Research Paper INT-350. 43 pp.

Cole, D. N. 1987. Effects of Three Seasons of Experimental Trampling on Five Montane Forest Communities and a Grassland in Western Montana, USA. *Biological Conservation* 40:219–244.

Cole, D. N. 1990. Ecological Impacts of Wilderness Recreation and Their Management. In J. C. Hendee, G. H. Stankey, and R. C. Lucas, eds. *Wilderness Management.* Golden, CO: North American Press, pp. 425–466.

Cole, D. N. 1993. Campsites in Three Western Wildernesses: Proliferation and Changes in Condition over 12 to 16 years. USDA Forest Service Research Paper INT-463. 15 pp.

Cole, D. N., and J. Benedict. 1983. Coverups—How to Pick a Campsite You Can Leave Without a Trace. *Backpacker* 11(5):40, 44, 87.

Cole, D. N., and R. K. Fichtler. 1983. Campsite Impact on Three Western Wilderness Areas. *Environmental Management* 7(3):275–288.

Cole, D. N., and T. E. Hall. 1992. Trends in Campsite Condition: Eagle Cap Wilderness, Bob Marshall Wilderness, and Grand Canyon National Park. USDA Forest Service Research Paper INT-453. 40 pp.

Coombs, E. A. K. 1976. The Impacts of Camping on Vegetation in the Bighorn Crags, Idaho Primitive Area. Master's thesis. University of Idaho, Moscow. 64 pp.

Crawford, A. K., and M. J. Liddle. 1977. The Effect of Trampling on Neutral Grassland. *Biological Conservation* 12:135–142.

Dale, D., and T. Weaver. 1974. Trampling Effects on Vegetation of the Trail Corridors of North Rocky Mountain Forests. *Journal of Applied Ecology* 11:767–772.

Driver, B. L. 1976. Quantification of Outdoor Recreationists' Preferences. USDA Forest Service Mimeograph Paper, Rocky Mountain Forest and Range Experiment Station, Ft. Collins, CO. 22 pp.

Driver, B. L., and P. J. Brown. 1978. The Opportunity Spectrum Concept and Behavioral Information in Outdoor Recreation Resource Supply Inventories: A Rationale. In *Integrating Inventories of Renewable Natural Resources: Proceedings of the Workshop.* USDA Forest Service General Technical Report RM-55. pp. 24–37.

Dunn, A. B., B. G. Lockaby, and E. E. Johnson. 1980. Camping and Its Relationship to Forest Soil and Vegetation Properties in South Carolina. Department of Forestry, Forest Research Series No. 34, Clemson University, Clemson, SC. 20 pp.

Frissell, S. S., Jr., and D. P. Duncan. 1965. Campsite Preference and Deterioration in the Quetico-Superior Canoe Country. *Journal of Forestry* 63:256–260.

Hammitt, W. E., and C. D. McDonald. 1981. Use Patterns and Impacts of Innertube Floating on a Mountain Stream. *Southern Journal of Applied Forestry* 5(3):119–124.

Hammitt, W. E., and C. D. McDonald. 1983. Past On-site Experience and Its Relationship to Managing River Recreation Resources. *Forest Science* 29(2):262–266.

Hammitt, W. E., and W. P. Stewart. 1996. Sense of Recreation Place: A Call for Construct Clarity and Measurement. Paper on file, Department of Parks, Recreation and Tourism Management, Clemson University, Clemson, SC. 11 pp.

Hampton, B., and D. N. Cole. 1995. *Soft Paths: How to Enjoy the Wilderness Without Harming It.* Mechanicsburg, PA: Stackpole Books. 22 pp.

Harlow, W. M. 1977. Stop Walking Away the Wilderness. *Backpacker* 5(4):33–36.

Heberlein, T. A., and P. Dunwiddie. 1979. Systematic Observation of Use Levels, Campsite Selection and Visitor Characteristics at a High Mountain Lake. *Journal of Leisure Research* 11(4):307–316.

Helgath, S. F. 1975. Trail Deterioration in the Selway-Bitterroot Wilderness. USDA Forest Service Research Note INT-193. 15 pp.

Hendee, J. C., and F. L. Campbell. 1969. Social Aspects of Outdoor Recreation—The Developed Campground. *Trends* (October):13–16.

Hendee, J. C., G. H. Stankey, and R. C. Lucas. 1990. *Wilderness Management.* Golden, CO: North American Press. 546 pp.

Jacoby, J. 1990. Mountain Bikes: A New Dilemma for Wildland Recreation Managers. *Western Wildlands* 16:25–28.

Ketchledge, E. H., and R. E. Leonard. 1970. The Impact of Man on the Adirondack High Country. *The Conservationist* 25(2):14–18.

Knopf, R. C. 1983. Recreational Needs and Behavior in Natural Settings. In I. Altman and J. Wohlwill, eds. *Behavior and the Natural Environment.* New York: Plenum, pp. 205–240.

Knopf, R. C. 1987. Human Behavior, Cognition, and Affect in the National Environment. In D. Stokols and I. Altman, eds. *Handbook of Environmental Psychology.* New York, Wiley. pp. 783–811.

Kuss, F. R. 1983. Hiking Boot Impacts on Woodland Trails. *Journal of Soil and Water Conservation* 38:119–121.

Legg, M. H., and G. Schneider. 1977. Soil Deterioration on Campsites: Northern Forest Types. *Soil Science Society American Journal* 41:437–441.

Leung, Y. F., and J. L. Marion. 1996. Trail Degradation as Influenced by Environmental Factors: A State-of-Knowledge Review. *Journal of Soil and Water Conservation* 51(2):130–136.

Lime, D. W. 1972. Large Groups in the Boundary Waters Canoe Area—Their Numbers, Characteristics, and Impacts. USDA Forest Service Research Note NC-142. 4 pp.

Lucas, R. C., H. T. Schreuder, and G. A. James. 1971. Wilderness Use Estimation: A Pilot Test of Sampling Procedures on the Mission Mountains Primitive Area. USDA Forest Service Research Paper INT-109. 44 pp.

MacArthur, R. A., V. Geist, and R. H. Johnston. 1982. Cardiac and Behavioral Responses of Mountain Sheep to Human Disturbance. *Journal of Wildlife Management* 46:351–358.

Manning, R. E. 1986. *Studies in Outdoor Recreation: A Review and Synthesis of the Social Science Literature in Outdoor Recreation.* Corvallis, OR: Oregon State University Press, 166 pp.

Marion, J. L. 1984. Ecological Changes Resulting from Recreational Use: A Study of Backcountry Campsites in the Boundary Waters Canoe Area Wilderness, Minnesota. Ph.D. dissertation, University of Minnesota, St. Paul. 279 pp.

Marion, J. L., and S. C. Brame. 1996. Leave No Trace Outdoor Skills and Ethics: An Educational Solution for Reducing Visitor Impacts. *Park Science* 16(3):24–26.

Marion, J. L., and D. N. Cole. 1996. Spatial and Temporal Variation in Soil and Vegetation Impacts on Campsites. *Ecological Applications* 6(2):520–530.

McDonald, C. D., and W. E. Hammitt. 1981. Use Patterns, Preferences and Social Impacts of Floaters on River Resources in the Southern Appalachian Region. Final Report, USDA Forest Service, Southeastern Forest Experiment Station, Asheville, NC. 241 pp.

McDonald, C. D., and W. E. Hammitt. 1983. Managing River Environments for the Participation Motives of Stream Floaters. *Journal of Environmental Management* 16:369–377.

McQuaid-Cook, J. 1978. Effects of Hikers and Horses on Mountain Trails. *Journal of Environmental Management* 6:209–212.

Nagy, J. A. S., and G. W. Scotter. 1974. A Quantitative Assessment of the Effects of Human and Horse Trampling on Natural Areas, Waterton Lakes National Park. Unpublished Report, 145 pp. Canadian Wildlife Service, Edmonton, Alberta.

Parikesit, P., D. W. Larson, and U. Matthes-Sears. 1995. Impacts of Trails on Cliff-edge Forest Structure. *Canadian Journal of Botany* 73:943–953.

Ramthun, R. 1995. Factors in User Group Conflict Between Hikers and Mountain Bikers. *Leisure Sciences* 17(3):159–169.

Roberts, E. 1996. Place and Spirit in Public Land Management. In B. L. Driver, D. Dustin, T. Baltic, G. Elsner, and G. Peterson, eds. *Nature and the Human Spirit.* State College, PA: Venture Publishers, Inc., pp. 61–80.

Saunders, P. R., G. E. Howard, and B. A. Stanley-Saunders. 1980. Effect of Different Boot Sole Configurations on Forest Soils. Department of Recreation and Park Administration, Extension/Research Paper RPA 1980-3, Clemson University, Clemson, SC. 11 pp.

Schreyer, R., and J. W. Roggenbuck. 1978. The Influence of Experience Expectations on Crowding Perceptions and Social-Psychological Carrying Capacity. *Leisure Sciences* 1(4):373–394.

Singer, S. W. 1971. Vegetation Response to Single and Repeated Walking Stresses in an Alpine Ecosystem. Master's thesis. Rutgers University, New Brunswick, NJ. 69 pp.

Stokols, D., and S. A. Shumaker. 1981. People in Places: A Transactional View of Settings. In J. Harvey, ed. *Cognition, Social Behavior and the Environment.* Hillsdale, NJ: Erlbaum Publishers, pp. 441–488.

Tuan, Y. F. 1974. *Topophilia: A Study of Environmental Perception, Attitudes, and Values.* Englewood Cliffs, NJ: Prentice-Hall.

Tuan, Y. F. 1980. Rootedness Versus Sense of Place. *Landscape* 24(1):3–8.

Vaske, J. J., M. P. Donnelly, and T. A. Heberlein. 1980. Perceptions of Crowding and Resource Quality by Elderly and More Recent Visitors. *Leisure Sciences* 3(4):367–381.

Wagar, J. A. 1964. The Carrying Capacity of Wildlands for Recreation. *Forest Science Monograph,* No. 7. 23 pp.

Weaver T and D. Dale, 1978. Trampling Effects of Hikers, Motorcycles and Horses in Meadows and Forests. *Journal of Applied Ecology* 15:451–457.

Webb, R. H., and H. G. Wilshire, eds. 1983. Environmental Effects of Off-road Vehicles: Impacts and Management in Arid Regions. New York: Springer-Verlag. 534 pp.

Whittaker, P. L. 1978. Comparison of Surface Impact by Hiking and Horseback Riding in the Great Smoky Mountains National Park. USDI National Park Service, Management Report 24, Southeast Region, Atlanta. 32 pp.

Wilson, J. P., and J. P. Seney. 1994. Erosional Impacts of Hikers, Horses, Motorcycles, and Off-Road Bicycles on Mountain Trails in Montana. *Mountain Research and Development* 14(1):77–88.

Young, R. A. 1978. Camping Intensity Effects on Vegetation Ground Cover in Illinois Campgrounds. *Journal of Soil and Water Conservation* 33:36–39.

Young, R. A., and A. R. Gilmore. 1976. Effects of Various Camping Intensities on Soil Properties in Illinois Campgrounds. *Soil Science Society American Journal* 40:908–911.

Zaslowsky, D. 1981. Looking into Soles and Other Weighty Matters. *Audubon* 83(2):60–63.

PART V
Management Alternatives

10 Strategies and Concepts of Management

In the chapters on impacts to resource components, we developed an understanding of how recreational use alters elements of the natural environment. Then, in Parts III and IV we explored factors that influence the nature, magnitude, and geographic distribution of impacts. Now it is time to apply this knowledge to management. Management cannot—and indeed should not—eliminate impact. Cleared trails and campsites, for example, are desirable environmental changes in many recreation areas. Management should control impacts, however, by manipulating the factors that influence impact patterns. In this chapter we will start with some general principles that summarize what we have learned in earlier chapters. Then we will discuss some planning concepts and frameworks and management strategies that can be useful in guiding management. This should set the stage for the more detailed descriptions of management techniques that follow in Chapters 11, 12, and 13.

GENERAL PRINCIPLES

The following are the general principles discussed in previous chapters.

1. Change is an all-pervasive characteristic of natural environments. The norm in undisturbed wildlands is continuous change—*succession,* to use the ecological terminology. When people are introduced into the natural scene, particularly when they come in large numbers, the natural direction and rate of change are often altered. In many cases ecosystem processes are accelerated. Erosion provides a good example. Many stream banks are constantly being worn away by the action of running water. This is a natural process. Where canoeists beach their boats at a picnic spot, however, erosion can be increased greatly, accomplishing in a few years what would have taken decades or centuries. In a case such as the suppression of fire, ecosystem processes—in this case, natural disturbance by fire—are slowed down. This, too, represents a serious impact. In other cases the entire direction of successional processes is diverted. Clearing and constructing a trail, replacing an undisturbed forest floor environment with a flat, compacted, barren, sunlit surface, represents a radical departure from the natural course of events.

Change is natural; thus management will generally not seek to halt change; rather, it will seek to halt undesirable change. How do we agree on what is an undesirable change? In wilderness and many national park environments, where preservation of natural conditions is an important goal, most but not all human-caused change is undesirable. Elsewhere human-caused changes that improve recreational opportunities are often considered desirable.

One important criterion for deciding whether or not an impact is undesirable relates to whether it tends to be self-limiting. Certain impacts tend to stabilize over time as they approach some limit of maximum change. Well-built trails, for example, are far from being in a natural state, but they deteriorate little over time. Other impacts get progressively worse over time. Trails that ascend steep slopes and lack drainage devices to divert water off the tread will continue to erode until all soil is gone. Impacts that are not self-limiting are generally more serious than those that are. The desirability of change and, therefore, whether or not an impact should be attacked by management, depends on a recreation area's objectives and also, perhaps unfortunately, on the personal biases of whoever is managing the area. Consequently, it is critical to set some objective limits on the types and amounts of change that are either desirable or acceptable. A first task for management, as was mentioned in Chapter 1, is to set limits of acceptable change.

2. Impacts are the inevitable result of recreational use. All forms of outdoor recreation will inevitably lead to some compaction of soils and disturbance of vegetation. Moreover, the fragility of most natural environments is such that very little use causes substantial amounts of impact. The asymptotic, curvilinear nature of the relationship between amount of use and amount of impact is an important, consistent conclusion of impact research. Therefore, it is not realistic to try to eliminate impact unless one is willing to prohibit all use. Instead, management should strive to limit impact. Because low levels of use can cause significant impact, it is particularly important to control the areal extent of use and impact.

3. Impacts exhibit relatively predictable patterns both in space and over time. Impacts are highly concentrated around attractions and recreational facilities (nodes) and along travel routes (linkages) (Manning 1979). Although impacts can be severe in these places, they are usually minimal throughout the vast majority of most wildland areas. This is a fortunate situation that can be reinforced through planning and site design. A second pattern is for impact to occur rapidly once an area is opened to recreational use (Marion and Cole 1996). After a few years, further impact is usually minor with one important exception. That exception is the tendency for sites to expand in area as they continue to be used (Cole and Hall 1992). Again, planning and site design should recognize this tendency and move to actively counteract it.

4. Impacts vary greatly between environments, along with differences in the tolerance of each environment. Both resistance and resilience vary. Most environments have both low resistance and low resilience. Consequently, impact occurs rapidly and recovery is slow. However, all combinations exist, except perhaps for high resistance and high resilience. These differences can be used to advantage in planning, such that the negative consequences of recreation use are minimized.

5. Impacts vary greatly with type of use and mode of travel. This was discussed in depth in Chapter 9. Both the nature and magnitude of impact vary with type of use.

For example, horses cause more trail erosion than hikers (DeLuca, Patterson, Freimund, and Cole in press); their need to graze will also cause types of impact not found in areas without horse use. From this it follows that the greatest impact should occur where the greatest mix of different uses occurs. This suggests that there are likely to be situations where zoning is a good strategy for minimizing impact.

6. All elements of the environment are interrelated. This is perhaps the highest principle in ecology. Everything is connected to everything else. This applies not only to the natural environment but to the recreationists in the environment as well. Actions taken to control one type of impact can affect another type of impact or another place. Moreover, actions taken to reduce impacts can affect user experiences and vice versa.

In summary, it is critical to establish specific objectives—limits of acceptable change—to determine at what level impact becomes a problem demanding management action. Because impact varies with amount of use, type of use, and environment, these are the variables that management can change to control impact. Finally, because everything is connected to everything else, it is important to consider the likely consequences of any potential management action to all other parts of the system—to visitor experiences as well as to resource conditions.

PLANNING FOR MANAGEMENT

A number of approaches have been taken to plan for recreational use in such a way that undesirable impact is minimized. Two planning frameworks that we find particularly useful are the Recreation Opportunity Spectrum (ROS) and the Limits of Acceptable Change (LAC) and related planning processes.

Recreation Opportunity Spectrum

Different recreationists participate in various activities in different physical-biological-social-managerial settings in order to realize various experiences. For example, one recreationist may choose camping (activity) in the natural, low-human-density, minimally restricted environment of a remote backcountry area (setting) to contemplate nature and get away from urban life for a while (experience); another may choose downhill skiing in a developed, high-density environment to seek thrills and meet people. The same person may desire each of these recreational opportunities at different times. Because many different recreational opportunities are both possible and legitimate, how does a manager decide what opportunities should be provided where?

Given the variety of legitimate tastes that exist, it is clear that a diversity of recreational opportunities have to be provided. Not every area can offer a wide range of opportunities, but diversity should be promoted and, at least regionally, a wide range should be provided. Written expression of the need for a variety of outdoor recreation options can be found as early as the late nineteenth-century writings of Fredrick L.

Olmstead and is apparent in the writings of many influential thinkers within the federal land-managing agencies—Arthur Carhart, Aldo Leopold, and Robert Marshall (Driver, Brown, Stankey, and Gregoire 1987). The early outdoor recreation educator J. V. K. Wagar (1951) called for a system of recreation lands ranging "from the flower pot at the window to the wilderness . . . to appeal to varying abilities" and to meet different purposes.

Although the concept of a recreation opportunity spectrum has been long recognized, progress in implementing the concept was largely absent until the late 1970s. At that time, several teams of researchers proposed a logical framework for systematically planning for the provision of a diversity of recreational opportunities—the Recreation Opportunity Spectrum (ROS). The basic intent of the ROS framework was to define different types of recreation settings, each capable of providing a different type of recreational experience. This was to be accomplished by describing broad classes of recreation opportunities, identifying indicators of those opportunities, and defining specific standards for each indicator that make it possible to distinguish between different opportunities (Driver, Brown, Stankey, and Gregoire 1987).

The rationale behind the indicators that were selected derives from the definition of a recreation opportunity as an opportunity to engage in a preferred activity (e.g., kayaking), in a preferred setting (e.g., a remote river), to realize desired experiences (e.g., physical exercise and challenge). Consequently, the three components of an ROS-defined recreation opportunity are *activities, settings,* and *experiences.* Moreover, early work showed that it was useful to define three different types of setting attributes. The physical setting includes biophysical resources, cultural-historical resources, as well as recent relatively permanent human structures such as roads and dams. The social setting includes the number of other people present, their behaviors, and the recreational activities they participate in. The managerial setting refers to level of development in the area, on-site presence of management, services provided, and rules and regulations (Driver, Brown, Stankey, and Gregoire 1987). A diversity of recreational opportunities can be offered simply by providing various combinations of activity, experience, physical setting, social setting, and managerial setting opportunities.

Attempts to empirically validate the relationship between activities, experiences, and environmental settings that provides the theoretical foundation of the ROS have produced mixed results (Virden and Knopf 1989; Yuan and McEwen 1989). Nevertheless, the framework is widely used and has become rather highly developed and procedurally elaborate. The detailed procedures of the ROS have been adopted as part of the basic planning processes of the Forest Service and the Bureau of Land Management. Basic ROS concepts have been applied more broadly in the United States and around the world. In their formal implementation of the ROS, the Forest Service recognizes six opportunity classes, ranging from urban to primitive. Each is defined in terms of setting characteristics—managerial regimentation, interaction among user groups, evidence of human modification of the environment, size or extent of the area of opportunity, and remoteness (Table 1). In this book we are primarily concerned with the four more primitive types, not the rural or urban setting classes.

TABLE 1. Appropriate Setting Descriptions for Each of the Six Classes in the Recreational Opportunity Spectrum

	Recreational Opportunity Spectrum Class				
Primitive	Semiprimitive Nonmotorized	Semiprimitive Motorized	Roaded Natural	Rural	Urban
Area is characterized by essentially unmodified natural environment of fairly large size. Interaction between users is very low and evidence of other users is minimal. The area is managed to be essentially free from evidence of human-induced restrictions and controls. Motorized use within the area is not permitted.	Area is characterized by a predominantly natural or natural-appearing environment of moderate-to-large size. Interaction between users is low, but there is often evidence of other users. The area is managed in such a way that minimum on-site controls and restrictions may be present, but are subtle. Motorized use is not permitted.	Area is characterized by a predominantly natural-appearing environment of moderate-to-large size. Concentration of users is low, but there is often evidence of other users. The area is managed in such a way that minimum on-site controls and restrictions may be present, but are subtle. Motorized use is permitted.	Area is characterized by predominantly natural-appearing environments with moderate evidences of the sights and sounds of humans. Such evidences usually harmonize with the natural environment. Interaction between users may be low to moderate, but with evidence of other users prevalent. Resource modification and utilization practices are evident, but harmonize with the natural environment. Conventional	Area is characterized by substantially modified natural environment. Resource modification and utilization practices are to enhance specific recreation activities and to maintain vegetative cover and soil. Sights and sounds of humans are readily evident, and the interaction between users is often moderate to high. A considerable number of facilities are designed for use by a large number of people. Facilities	Area is characterized by a substantially urbanized environment, although the background may have natural-appearing elements. Renewable resource modification and utilization practices are to enhance specific recreation activities. Vegetative cover is often exotic and manicured. Sights and sounds of humans, on-site, are predominant. Large numbers of users can be expected, both on-site and in nearby areas.

TABLE 1. (*Continued*)

	Recreational Opportunity Spectrum Class				
Primitive	Semiprimitive Nonmotorized	Semiprimitive Motorized	Roaded Natural	Rural	Urban
			motorized use is provided for in construction standards and design of facilities.	are often provided for special activities. Moderate densities are provided far away from developed sites. Facilities for intensified motorized use and parking are available.	Facilities for highly intensified motor use and parking are available, with forms of mass transit often available to carry people throughout the site.

Source: USDA Forest Service. 1982. *ROS Users Guide.*

212

The ROS framework can be used for at least three purposes. Its most common use is as a means of inventorying current recreational opportunities. The Forest Service's *ROS Users Guide* (USDA Forest Service 1982), for example, provides elaborate instructions about how to evaluate each of the five setting characteristics to arrive at one of the six ROS classes described in Table 1. These classes can be drawn on maps, providing both site-specific details and a general overview of the supply of recreational opportunities.

The framework is also useful in developing management prescriptions for wildlands. Each ROS class has distinct objectives—in terms of appropriate setting characteristics, activities, and appropriate management techniques. Toward the primitive end of the opportunity spectrum, recreational impacts are less acceptable and objectives are more likely to stress low-impact conditions. At the same time, regimentation is more undesirable at the more primitive end of the spectrum. This has important implications for the appropriateness of various management styles. Subtle management techniques are preferable to extensive use of regulation and persuasion. Thus, the recreation opportunity class (or range of classes) provided by any recreation area will determine, to a great extent, both limits of acceptable change for impacts and the most appropriate means of mitigating impact problems.

This also points out why management of impacts is particularly difficult toward the primitive end of the spectrum—in wilderness, for example. Toward that end, impacts are least acceptable but management has the least amount of leeway in using restrictive techniques. Access is also difficult, making enforcement, patrol, and other management activities more troublesome. For all these reasons, management of more primitive wildlands is especially complex and will be discussed in considerable detail in the following chapters.

Limits of Acceptable Change Planning Framework

As discussed in Chapter 1, the focus on recreation carrying capacity, the first concept managers turned to in an attempt to manage recreation impacts, proved to be problematic. The seeming promise of using carrying capacity—that limiting use could solve most management problems and that use limits could be determined by objective factual data—proved false. Instead, limiting use is just one of many alternative management techniques and often is not even among the most effective. Moreover, decisions about appropriate use levels are at least as dependent on subjective evaluations (management objectives) as they are on the descriptions of relationships between amount of use and amount of impact that science can provide (Shelby and Heberlein 1986). Consequently, the latest generation of planning frameworks focus their attention on the formulation of specific management objectives. Substantial progress has been made in establishing objectives that are specific enough to "drive" the recreation management planning process. Instrumental to allowing this progress was the concept of setting limits of acceptable change.

The first clear articulation of the "limits of acceptable change" concept appeared in a graduate student study of impacts on campsites in the Boundary Waters Canoe Area Wilderness. Frissell (1963) concluded that if recreation use is to be allowed, campsite impact is inevitable and must be accepted. However, this author stated, "a limit should be placed on the amount of change to be tolerated. When a site has reached this predetermined limit of deterioration, steps should be taken to prevent further adverse change." In other words, there is a conflict between allowing recreation use and preserving natural ecosystems. The key is to define an optimal balance between these two conflicting goals, in which both recreational opportunities and natural ecosystems are compromised to some extent (Cole and Stankey in press). This balance can be expressed as a limit on deterioration (change).

Frissell and Stankey (1972) recognized that this quest for balance between use and protection of quality environments and experiences was similar to the intent behind carrying capacity. Consequently, they proposed the "limits of acceptable change" concept as an alternative model for making decisions about carrying capacity. Their fundamental idea was to focus management on achieving specific objectives, defined as staying within maximum deviations from (1) the "natural range of variation" in ecological conditions and (2) a "pristine wilderness experience." Starting in 1980, a group of Forest Service researchers refined this general concept further and produced a procedural manual, "The Limits of Acceptable Change (LAC) System for Wilderness Planning" (Stankey, Cole, Lucas, Petersen, and Frissell 1985). Conceptually related processes—Visitor Impact Management (VIM) and Visitor Experience and Resource Protection (VERP)—were subsequently developed for use by the National Park Service (Graefe, Kuss, and Vaske 1990; Manning, Lime, and Hof 1996).

The LAC, VIM, and VERP processes all use slightly different terminology and step sequences. However, participants in a 1997 workshop on these processes (McCool and Cole in press) agreed that these processes were conceptually identical and moved to adopt more consistent terminology. They also noted that step sequencing need not be rigidly adhered to and that these processes were largely iterative and circular rather than linear. Consequently, we have chosen to present these planning processes at a broad conceptual level. Those interested in further detail on the steps of the individual processes can refer to the more detailed procedural descriptions mentioned previously.

Figure 1 provides a simple overview of the planning framework each of these processes utilizes. Each process involves stating the conditions management will maintain or allow to occur (how much impact is acceptable), inventorying existing conditions to see how they compare with acceptable conditions, as stated in objectives, and then instituting management actions where existing conditions do not meet objectives. The final step, monitoring, involves periodically returning to the inventory stage of the process.

 Set Objectives. It is a relative simple matter to determine the *magnitude* of an impact. Although not perfect, well-developed techniques are available for measuring, in quantitative terms, the increase in bulk density on a recreation site. Using similar techniques, several independent investigators could each determine that bulk density increased, say, 0.10 g/cm^3. Where disagreement comes is in evaluating the *importance* of this amount of impact. Depending on one's point of view, an increase in compaction of 0.10 g/cm^3 might constitute either disastrous damage or an insignificant change.

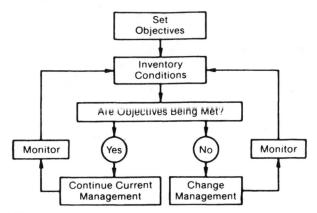

FIGURE 1. A simple planning framework. (*Source:* D. N. Cole.)

Moreover, it might be highly desirable on a constructed nature trail or totally unacceptable in a remote trailless setting. Only where specific objectives have been established for specific places can one consistently determine whether or not an impact of a given magnitude constitutes a problem that demands management attention.

One might argue that all impacts should be considered problems and aggressively attacked. As mentioned before, however, some impacts are desirable in certain situations. Moreover, all management actions entail costs, both to the visitor and to management. The goal of recreation management planning is to find the optimal balance between use and protection. Given both budgetary constraints and a concern for avoiding unnecessary restriction of recreation use and behavior, it is best to attack not impacts but impact *problems*—situations in which impacts exceed levels specified in objectives.

Objectives could be written to limit every possible type of recreation impact. However, this is not reasonable or even desirable. Fortunately, actions taken to avoid certain impacts are likely also to protect against other types of impact. For example, reducing use to limit campsite disturbance is also likely to reduce wildlife disturbance. Therefore, it may only be necessary to set objectives for a few particularly important and sensitive types of impact. There may also be unique situations, such as for rare or endangered species, for which objectives are also needed. As mentioned before, objectives for dealing with impacts that are not self-limiting are particularly important. Some of the elements for which objectives might be written include trail condition, campsite density and condition, water quality, and wildlife populations and their distribution. Within each of these broad categories it is important to be even more specific. For example, objectives for campsite condition might be written for soil compaction, ground cover condition, tree damage, campsite area, or a combination of these factors depending on the local significance of these impacts.

In LAC terminology, the variables for which objectives are written are called "indicators." Several authors have listed characteristics of a "good" indicator. Seven of the most desirable characteristics of an indicator are that it be:

1. *Measurable*—quantitative and subject to measurement
2. *Reliable*—capable of being measured precisely by different people
3. *Cost-effective*—capable of being measured using inexpensive equipment and techniques
4. *Significant*—related to impacts that, should they occur, would be considered serious problems
5. *Sensitive*—capable of providing an early warning system, alerting managers to problems while there is still time to correct things
6. *Efficient*—capable of reflecting the condition of more than itself, reducing the number of indicators that must be assessed
7. *Responsive*—related to attributes that are subject to management control

Among the first places where specific objectives were established in order to limit impact was the Bob Marshall Wilderness Area in Montana. This large (more than 1 million acres), remote, and spectacular area has been heavily used by large parties traveling with stock. As a result of a long history of such use, many campsites have been highly impacted. Managers of the area believed that such high levels of impact detracted from the values for which the area was designated as wilderness. Consequently, they decided to limit impact and developed objectives for the area based on (1) a maximum devegetated area on campsites, (2) a maximum number of campsites in any square mile, and (3) maximum amounts of range utilization and specified standards for range condition and trend.

For each of these measures of impact, quantitative objectives (LAC standards) were written. Moreover, to incorporate diversity into the system, as discussed in the previous section on ROS, these quantitative limits vary between different zones established within the wilderness (Table 2). Currently, the area contains considerable diversity. Some areas are pristine and trailless, and others are heavily used and show considerable evidence of disturbance. To preserve, enhance, and, in some cases, redirect this diversity, the Bob Marshall Wilderness has been divided into four zones. In the most pristine zone (I) proposed objectives state that no campsite will contain more than 100 ft^2 of devegetated area; there will be no more than one campsite in any square mile; range utilization will not exceed 20 percent; range condition will be excellent; and range trend will be static or improving. If these objectives are met, environmental impact in this zone will be low. Elsewhere, more impact is tolerated. For example, the allowable number of campsites in any square mile increases to two, three, and six in the three successively less primitive zones. The allowable devegetated area on campsites increases to 500, 1000, and 2000 ft^2.

In the first application of the VERP process, to Arches National Park, eight different zones were established that allowed visitor use (National Park Service 1995). The zones ranged from the primitive zone with no developed facilities, very low use, and minimal impact, to a developed zone that contains most of the developed visitor facilities. No recreation use was allowed in a ninth zone, the sensitive resource protection zone. Eight different indicators of resource impact were developed, of which

TABLE 2. LAC Standards for Resource Indicators in the Bob Marshall Wilderness

Indicator	Zone I	Zone II	Zone III	Zone IV
Devegetated area on any campsite	Maximum of 100 ft^2	Maximum of 500 ft^2	Maximum of 1000 ft^2	Maximum of 2000 ft^2
Number of campsites per square mile	Maximum of 1	Maximum of 2	Maximum of 3	Maximum of 6
Forage utilization	Maximum of 20%	Maximum of 20%	Maximum of 40%	Maximum of 40%
Range trend	Static or improving	Static or improving	Static or improving	Improving
Range condition	Excellent	Excellent	Generally good or better	Generally good

three were considered of primary importance. Both the indicators used and the standards for those indicators varied among zones. The condition of cryptobiotic crusts was the indicator to be monitored in most of the zones. The maximum acceptable number of soil samples with a soil crust condition index of less than 4 (no lichens or mosses left in the crust but cyanobacteria still present) ranged from 5 percent in the hiker zone to 30 percent in the pedestrian and motorized sight-seeing zones. In the very lightly used backcountry and primitive zones, this indicator was replaced by a measure of the density of social trails. In the semiprimitive motorized zone, the number of places where vehicle tracks widened beyond two simple tracks was the indicator to be used. Finally, in the developed zone, where high levels of resource impact are accepted, no resource indicators are monitored. This illustrates how varying indicators between zones enables variation in the kinds of impact that are of concern to be incorporated into the planning process.

Finally, it is worth reiterating that objectives (LAC standards) are judgments—subjective evaluations of the most appropriate compromise between use and resource protection. Managers have frequently looked to scientists to tell them where standards should be set, perhaps hoping to avoid having to make hard subjective decisions. Some scientists have encouraged this tendency by representing their results as indicative of where standards should be set (e.g., Shelby, Vaske, and Donnelly 1996). Although there are legitimate differences of opinion about the degree to which empirical data can be directly translated into LAC standards, it is our opinion that standards should be *informed by* science rather than *derived from* science. Empirical data can be used to describe the costs and benefits of alternative LAC standards. However, it remains for a manager to decide the optimal trade-off.

Inventory Conditions. Once objectives have been established, it is time to go out and inventory conditions on the ground to see where the objectives are and are not being met. In many cases some initial inventory will be necessary before realistic objectives can be set. It does not do any good to set objectives that are so stringent that they can never possibly be met. It also does little good to set objectives so lax that their attainment does little to avoid impact problems. Thus, it is helpful to do a little sampling of conditions, before quantitative objectives are established, to help set meaningful but realistic objectives.

Inventorying is the first phase of a long-term monitoring program. Monitoring is merely periodically repeating the inventory and comparing current conditions to both objectives and previous inventory data. Monitoring is covered in much more detail in Chapter 11. At this stage, two points should be made. First, the most important things to monitor (inventory) are the elements addressed in objectives; other data can be collected, but first priority must go to elements addressed in objectives. For example, in the Bob Marshall Wilderness, objectives dictate that managers must collect information on campsite devegetated area. They are also collecting information on size of the campsite, but this is less important because it is not specified in the objectives. Second, inventory must be conducted in an objective and systematic fashion. Techniques must be well documented so that successive inventories are comparable.

Compare Conditions to Objectives. After the inventory is completed, it is a relatively simple matter to identify places where conditions are not being met. These are problem areas that demand management attention. It may also be possible to identify places where conditions currently are in line with objectives, but there is reason to believe they may not be in the near future. This ability to predict will improve greatly as monitoring progresses and some trend data become available. Places where the trend is downhill may also require management attention. Even in places where objectives are being met, it may be appropriate to change or strengthen management if it is not too burdensome to the visitor. For example, promoting low-impact camping techniques and a pack-it-in, pack-it-out litter policy are desirable even where campsite impact and litter are not problems. Such programs are not burdensome to visitors. However, greatly restricting numbers of users or prohibiting certain activities is hard to justify if objectives are being met.

There are usually a number of alternative management actions that can be taken to mitigate any single problem. In the following section, we discuss how to decide on an appropriate course of action. Chapters 12 and 13 will provide specifics on alternative techniques and some of their pros and cons.

MANAGEMENT OF PROBLEMS

Although our concern is with management of ecological impacts, it is important to remember that an equal concern must be given to the provision of quality recreational experiences. The simplest, most effective means of minimizing recreational impact is to prohibit all use. This obviously defeats the purpose of a recreation area. It is not possible to maximize both provision of recreational opportunities and protection from environmental impacts; a compromise is always necessary. In thinking about how to manage impact, then, it is important also to consider how any action is likely to affect the recreational experience.

Given many alternative courses of action, it is imperative that managers carefully consider all possible actions. Too often there is a tendency to select techniques that are familiar or administratively expedient but not ideally suited to the situation at hand. Among the factors to consider, in trying to decide on a course of action, are effectiveness, costs to administer, costs to the visitor, and likely side effects. Supporting actions are often necessary if a given course of action is to be successful. These should be considered as well. Ultimately, the best programs will consist of carefully selected sets of actions that maximize effectiveness and minimize costs. Attacking a problem from several different angles is often the best course to follow. This is why it is worth considering the strategic purpose of actions.

Strategic Purpose

As we noted in the chapters on factors that influence impact, amount of impact is a function of amount of use, type of use, visitor behavior, use distribution, timing of use, and environment. Each of these variables can be manipulated by management and, therefore, offers a unique strategic approach to controlling impact problems. Wagar (1964) was the first to recognize that there were several strategies available for dealing with recreation impact problems. Subsequent papers by Manning (1979), Peterson and Lime (1979), and Cole, Peterson, and Lucas (1987) have provided more comprehensive and detailed typologies of strategic purpose.

The most obvious—but seldom the most desirable—approach to reducing impact is to reduce use. Everything else being equal, less use should cause less impact. However, one party that builds a campfire or that travels with horses can cause more impact than several parties of backpackers using a portable stove. Another approach to reducing impact, then, is to leave amount of use constant but reduce the amount of impact each visitor causes. This can be accomplished in several ways:

1. *Use Dispersal.* Use can be spread out, so that areas of concentrated use and impact are avoided.
2. *Use Concentration.* Conversely, use can be concentrated in space so that only a small proportion of the resource is altered.
3. *Type of Use.* Type of use can be managed in such a way that particularly destructive uses are minimized.
4. *Visitor Behavior.* Visitors can be persuaded to behave in ways that minimize impact.
5. *Timing of Use.* Visitor use can be prohibited or discouraged during seasons or at times when resources are particularly vulnerable to disturbance.
6. *Site Location.* Use can be directed to particularly durable places that are able to tolerate heavy use.
7. *Site Hardening or Shielding.* A site's capacity to tolerate use can be increased by either hardening it or shielding it from impact.

All of these strategies attack the causes of impact problems. Another strategy is to attack the symptoms through site maintenance and rehabilitation. Generally, this approach is costly and never ending, so it should be complemented with attacks on the causes. However, there are situations in which attacking symptoms must be the core of a management program. A good example is dealing with human waste in areas of concentrated use. Use can be concentrated, and the resource can be shielded by building outhouses and persuading visitors to use them. However, there is little alternative to establishing a flushing system, a composting system, or hauling the waste out. Examples of how each of these strategies might be employed in a program to reduce impact on campsites are provided in Table 3.

Most of these strategies can be implemented through management of visitors or through site manipulation, the subjects of Chapters 12 and 13, respectively. For example, use concentration can be promoted either by requiring visitors to camp at designated sites (visitor management) or by using railings or rocks and shrubbery to confine traffic flow (site manipulation). Only the site hardening/shielding and site maintenance/rehabilitation strategies are entirely within the domain of site manipulation. Distinctions between visitor and site management are not as clearcut as is often assumed, because site manipulation is often done for the purpose of managing visitors. A useful general principle is that the best management approach will utilize a combination of visitor and site management, as well as a combination of strategic approaches.

A final important point about strategies is that any single strategy can be used to attack a number of different problems. This is a reflection of the interrelatedness of everything. The problem is that some of the effects of implementing any course

TABLE 3. Strategies and Actions for Reducing Impact on Campsites

Strategy	Possible Actions
Reduce amount of use	Limit number of parties entering the area.
Reduce per capita impact	
Use dispersal	Persuade parties to avoid camping on highly impacted campsites.
Use concentration	Prohibit camping anywhere except on designated sites.
Type of use	Prohibit horse groups in camp.
Visitor behavior	Teach low-impact camping techniques.
Timing of use	Discourage camping when soils are water-saturated.
Site location	Teach parties to choose resistant sites for camping.
Site hardening/shielding	Build wooden tent pads on campsites.
Rehabilitation	Close and revegetate damaged campsites.

of action may be undesirable. As Manning (1979) puts it, "The various strategic uses of park management tools should be explicitly recognized before they are implemented so as to gain multiple benefits where possible and avoid unwanted side effects where potential." Cole, Petersen, and Lucas (1987) have developed a "troubleshooting" guide that lists many management strategies and tactics that can be used to attack different types of recreation management problems in wilderness.

Types of Undesirable Visitor Actions

Management response to impacts should vary between types of undesirable visitor behavior. Lucas (Hendee, Stankey, and Lucas 1990) recognized five types of visitor actions:

1. Illegal actions with adverse impacts
2. Careless or thoughtless violations of regulations with adverse impacts
3. Unskilled actions with adverse impacts
4. Uninformed behavior that intensifies use impacts
5. Unavoidable minimum impacts

Examples and appropriate management responses to each of these types are presented in Table 4. The important point here is that different responses are required for different types of users. What is necessary in one place may be overkill in another, where the users are more skilled or more likely to obey regulations.

TABLE 4. Types of Visitor Actions and Appropriate Management Responses

Type of Visitor Action	Example	Management Response
Illegal actions	Motorcycle violation	Law enforcement
Careless actions	Littering, nuisance activity (e.g., shouting)	Persuasion, education about impacts, rule enforcement
Unskilled actions	Ditching tent	Primarily education about low-impact use practices, some rule enforcement
Uniformed actions	Concentrated use	Education-information
Unavoidable impacts	Human waste, physical impact of even careful use	Reduction of use levels to limit unavoidable impacts; relocation of use to more durable site

Source: Hendee, Stankey, and Lucas 1990.

Types of Management Approaches

Traditionally, management actions have been classified as being either direct or indirect (Gilbert, Peterson, and Lime 1972). Direct management attacks human behavior directly, usually through regulation. An example is allowing camping in only one area. The visitor must either camp there or break the law; free choice is extremely limited. Indirect management attacks decision-making factors in an attempt to indirectly influence rather than force behavior. Visitors retain the freedom to choose their course of action. This is usually accomplished through information, persuasion, or site manipulation. For example, visitors can be told that a certain area (where managers want them to camp) is the nicest place to camp; visitors can be asked to camp in that area; or facilities can be built in the area to attract visitors.

It is commonly stated that indirect management is preferable to direct management and should be tried first. Much of the debate about whether direct or indirect approaches are preferable revolves around considerations of each approach's effectiveness and the burden each approach places on visitors. It is commonly assumed that direct approaches are more effective and also carry more visitor cost. Both of these assumptions are oversimplified and can be misleading. For example, shortcutting switchbacks continues even in places where it has been prohibited. Trail design, such that shortcutting is extremely difficult, an indirect approach, can be more effective.

There are also cases in which direct techniques are less costly to visitors than indirect techniques. For example, we would prefer an existing regulation prohibiting camping in a certain area to be made present to us before entering the area (direct regulation), rather than having a ranger walk into our camp and ask us to move out of a fragile or overused area (indirect persuasion).

The distinction between direct and indirect management was useful in focusing attention on the burden that different management approaches place on the visitor and challenging managers to keep such "heavy-handed" management to a minimum. However, it is now clear that the one-dimensional concept of a direct-indirect continuum is oversimplified (McCool and Christensen 1996). Moreover, the popularity of the notion that indirect techniques are preferable to direct techniques has paralyzed many management programs, because managers have been unwilling to implement direct management actions even if they are the only effective means of dealing with impacts (Cole 1995). Instead of considering techniques as they are arrayed on a direct-indirect continuum, we suggest that managers evaluate techniques in terms of their likely effectiveness and the burden they place on visitors—how heavy-handed the action is.

Effectiveness. Effectiveness should probably be the initial criterion used to identify potential management actions. It is pointless to consider techniques that are not likely to correct impact problems in a reasonable amount of time. However, there can be considerable debate about what constitutes a "reasonable" amount of time. Where significant problems have already occurred, we suggest selecting techniques that are likely to be effective within at least a few years. Where the concern is a problem that might occur in the future, techniques that require more time to be effective (e.g., visitor education) are also appropriate. Given the difficulty and expense of restoring sites—once damage has occurred—it is best to err on the side of selecting a technique that is certain to be effective. However, it is not necessary to select the *most* effective technique, if a slightly less effective technique carries much less visitor burden. Chapters 12 and 13 contain considerable discussion of the effectiveness of different management techniques, as do Cole, Petersen, and Lucas (1987) and McCool and Christensen (1996).

Visitor Burden. Cole, Petersen, and Lucas (1987) identify five different dimensions that together determine how heavy-handed a management action is (Table 5). Freedom of choice is the dimension most closely associated with the traditional direct versus indirect distinction. The distinction related to freedom of choice is between regulation and manipulation of human behavior. As Lucas (1982) points out, recreation and regulations are inherently contradictory because freedom and spontaneity lie at the core of most wildland recreational pursuits. Regulations are particularly undesirable toward the primitive end of the recreational opportunity spectrum, where regimentation is supposed to be low. An objective of recreation management in wilderness, for example, is to provide opportunities for an "unconfined type of recreation." Freedom of choice is important and should be preserved where possible.

There are situations, however, where regulation plays an important and legitimate role. Several such situations mentioned by Lucas (1983) include safety (e.g., regulations keeping motorboats out of swimming areas), reducing interference with other visitors (e.g., regulations requiring quiet after 10:00 P.M.), and situations in which a few individuals use more than their share of recreation resources (e.g., limits on numbers of fish or game). Generally, regulations are appropriate where it is imperative that most visitors comply with a regulation and where there is law enforcement available to back it up. Where regulations are instituted, it is important to:

TABLE 5. Factors That Influence the Visitor Burden Imposed by Management Actions

Factor	High Burden	Low Burden
Freedom of choice	Regulate behavior	Influence behavior
Subtlety	Visitors are aware they are being managed	Visitors are not aware they are being managed
Where management occurs	Activities controlled on-site	On-site activities not controlled
When management occurs	Visitors aware of actions only after their arrival	Visitors aware of actions during planning of trip
Number of visitors affected	Many visitors affected	Few visitors affected
Importance of activity that is forgone	Highly important activity	Unimportant activity

1. *Explain reasons for regulations.* This should help to improve visitor compliance. Visitors are more inclined to respect rules and to be hassled less by them if they recognize that they are necessary.

2. *Be sure that visitors understand how they are expected to behave.* In some cases visitors may be left unaware of regulations, or the rules may be ambiguous. This is likely to reduce compliance and increase confusion and frustration.

3. *Enforce regulations.* It is not fair to law-abiding visitors to not enforce regulations. If enforcement is impossible, it is probably better just to ask people to behave in a certain manner.

4. *Regulate at the minimum level possible.* Do not overattack the problem with restrictions that unnecessarily burden visitors.

There may be situations in which the same objectives can be accomplished without establishing a regulation. Persuasion—asking visitors not to build campfires, for example—is usually preferable to prohibiting campfires. Effectiveness may be comparable, and visitors retain final choice. Even with persuasion, however, visitors are still likely to feel pressured to conform to what the manager wants, and this is a burden. Persuasive approaches lack subtlety, and if the contact between management and the visitor occurs within the recreation area, it may be even more obtrusive and disturbing than a regulation. This can be a particular problem when conscientious visitors give up something important to them, such as campfires, and have to watch unconscientious visitors enjoy them.

Perhaps as important as freedom of choice is subtlety or unobtrusiveness. Subtlety refers to the extent to which a visitor is aware of being managed. The example of a ranger walking into camp and asking a camper not to build a fire is an extreme example of an obtrusive manipulative action, not substantially preferable to a regulation prohibiting campfires. Freedom of choice is retained, but the burden of guilt, should the camper choose to defy the wishes of the ranger, makes this of little importance. Education/information, without telling visitors what they should do, and physical manipulation are more subtle approaches to management. For example, in trying to keep people from camping in a particular place, such as on a lakeshore, visitors can be educated about the fragility of lakeshores, or trails can be developed that avoid lakeshores and lead to other places where attractive campsites are located. These actions can be effective and would avoid the loss of freedom that comes with regulation. It is subtlety, as much as lack of regulation, that is the preferred approach to management of recreation use.

The third and fourth considerations are where and when management occurs. Particularly toward the primitive end of the opportunity spectrum, it is preferable to regulate or influence behavior outside of rather than inside the recreation area. This allows the visitor to adjust to restrictions early and not to be encumbered greatly while engaging in recreational activities. For example, where entry to an area is controlled, it is preferable to limit trailhead entry rather than limit movement within the area. In our ranger example, it would be more acceptable to be asked, before entering the area, not to build a fire. The best time to communicate restrictions or attempt to influence behavior is when visitors are in the planning phase of their trip. At this stage they can change their plans if the impact of management programs is unacceptable to them, and they have time to accept and adjust to restrictions.

Two final concerns are with the number of visitors affected by an action and the importance of the freedoms visitors are asked or required to forgo. For the majority of backcountry users, a regulation limiting party size is much less bothersome than being asked not to build a campfire. This follows from the fact that fewer parties are affected by a party size limit. Similarly, asking visitors to pack out their litter should be less costly than asking them not to build campfires. Most visitors place more importance on being able to have a fire than on being able to leave their trash, so denial of the campfire is more burdensome. The cumulative weight of a number of restrictions must also be considered. Many people have said that reducing use should be the last option a manager exercises. It may be much worse, however, to keep visitors from doing many of the things they want to do, than it would be to occasionally deny them access to the area (Cole 1995).

In sum, it is a complicated matter to assess the cost of an action to visitors. Everything else being equal—which it never is—preferred approaches are those that are nonregulatory and subtle and that confront the visitor outside the area during the planning phase of the trip. Few actions combine all of these desirable elements. where other combinations exist, managers will need to balance pros and cons. All of these concerns have to be weighed against an evaluation of likely effectiveness.

Toward the primitive end of the opportunity spectrum, subtlety is probably the most important concern. It is not possible, however, to make simple rules about whether or not an internal nonregulatory approach is preferable to an external regulatory approach. Toward the more developed end of the spectrum, regulation and nonsubtle approaches are to be expected. The important concerns here are usually the number of visitors affected and the importance of the freedoms visitors are asked to forgo. In all areas it is important to maximize freedom and spontaneity because these are critical elements of most wildland recreational experiences.

REFERENCES

Cole, D. N. 1995. Wilderness Management Principles: Science, Logical Thinking or Personal Opinion? *Trends* 32:6–9.

Cole, D. N., and T. E. Hall. 1992. Trends in Campsite Condition: Eagle Cap Wilderness, Bob Marshall Wilderness, and Grand Canyon National Park. USDA Forest Service Research Paper INT-453. 40 pp.

Cole, D. N., M. E. Petersen, and R. C. Lucas. 1987. Managing Wilderness Recreation Use: Common Problems and Potential Solutions. USDA Forest Service General Technical Report INT-230. 60 pp.

Cole, D. N., and G. H. Stankey. In press. The LAC Planning Framework: Implications of Its Historical Development to Current Controversies. In S. F. McCool, and D. N. Cole, eds.

Proceedings—Limits of Acceptable Change and Related Planning Processes: Progress and Future Directions. USDA Forest Service General Technical Report RMRS-GTR-in press.

DeLuca, T. H., W. A. Patterson IV, W. A. Freimund, and D. N. Cole. In press. Influence of Llamas, Horses, and Hikers on Soil Erosion from Established Recreation Trails in Western Montana. *Environmental Management.*

Driver, B. L., P. J. Brown, G. H. Stankey, and T. G. Gregoire. 1987. The ROS Planning System: Evolution, Basic Concepts, and Research Needed. *Leisure Sciences* 9:201–212.

Frissell, S. S., Jr. 1963. Recreational Use of Campsites in the Quetico-Superior Canoe Country. Master's thesis. University of Minnesota. 66 pp.

Frissell, S. S., Jr., and G. H. Stankey. 1972. Wilderness Environmental Quality: Search for Social and Ecological Harmony. In *Proceedings of the 1972 National Convention.* Society of American Foresters, Washington DC, pp. 170–183.

Gilbert, G. C., G. L. Peterson, and D. W. Lime. 1972. Towards a Model of Travel Behavior in the Boundary Waters Canoe Area. *Environment and Behavior* 4:131–157.

Graefe, A. R., F. R. Kuss, and J. J. Vaske. 1990. Visitor Impact Management: The Planning Framework. National Parks and Conservation Association, Washington, DC. 105 pp.

Hendee, J. C., G. H. Stankey, and R. C. Lucas. 1990. Wilderness Management. 2d ed. Golden, CO: North American Press. 546 pp.

Lucas, R. C. 1982. Recreation Regulations—When Are They Needed? *Journal of Forestry* 80:148–151.

Lucas, R. C. 1983. The Role of Regulations in Recreation Management. *Western Wildlands* 9(2):6–10.

Manning, R. E. 1979. Strategies for Managing Recreational Use of National Parks. *Parks* 4:13–15.

Manning, R. E., D. W. Lime, and M. Hof. 1996. Social Carrying Capacity of Natural Areas: Theory and Application in the U.S. National Parks. *Natural Areas Journal* 16:118–127.

Marion, J. L., and D. N. Cole. 1996. Spatial and Temporal Variation in Soil and Vegetation Impacts on Campsites. *Ecological Applications* 6:520–530.

McCool, S. F., and N. E. Christensen. 1996. Alleviating Congestion in Parks and Recreation Areas Through Direct Management of Visitor Behavior. In *Congestion and Crowding in the National Park System.* Minnesota Agricultural Experiment Station Miscellaneous Publication 86-1996, pp. 67–83.

McCool, S. F., and D. N. Cole, eds. In press. *Proceedings—Limits of Acceptable Change and Related Planning Processes: Progress and Future Directions.* USDA Forest Service General Technical Report RMRS-GTR-in press.

National Park Service. 1995. The Visitor Experience and Resource Protection Implementation Plan: Arches National Park. USDI National Park Service, Denver Service Center, Denver, CO. 72 pp.

Peterson, G. L., and D. W. Lime. 1979. People and Their Behavior: A Challenge for Recreation Management. *Journal of Forestry* 77:343–346.

Shelby, B., and T. Heberlein. 1986. Carrying Capacity in Recreational Settings. Corvallis, OR: Oregon State University Press. 164 pp.

Shelby, B., J. J. Vaske, and M. P. Donnelly. 1996. Norms, Standards, and Natural Resources. *Leisure Sciences* 18:103–123.

Stankey, G. H., D. N. Cole, R. C. Lucas, M. E. Petersen, and S. S. Frissell. 1985. The Limits of Acceptable Change (LAC) System for Wilderness Planning. USDA Forest Service Research Paper INT-176. 37 pp.

USDA Forest Service. 1982. *ROS Users Guide.* 38 pp.

Virden, R. J., and R. C. Knopf. 1989. Activities, Experiences, and Environmental Settings: A Case Study of Recreation Opportunity Spectrum Relationships. *Leisure Sciences* 11;159–176

Wagar, J. V. K. 1951. Some Major Principles in Recreation Land Use Planning. *Journal of Forestry* 49:431–434.

Wagar, J. A. 1964. The Carrying Capacity of Wildlands For Recreation. Society of American Foresters. Forest Science Monograph 7. Washington, D.C.

Yuan, M. S., and D. McEwen. 1989. Test for Campers' Experience Preference Differences Among Three ROS Setting Classes. *Leisure Sciences* 11:177–186.

11 Monitoring Recreational Impacts

In the last chapter we discussed the importance of inventory and monitoring within a planning framework. Inventory provides a means of evaluating the current condition of a resource in relation to management objectives so that problems can be identified. Over time, monitoring allows trends in condition to be recognized. Information about current conditions and trends aids in the selection of limits of acceptable change. It also permits the effectiveness of management programs to be assessed and suggests places where changes in management are needed. Lessons can be learned—from both successes and failures. Places where problems are particularly pronounced or where conditions are rapidly deteriorating can be identified as areas of concern. This can be useful in budgeting, allocating manpower, and establishing project priorities.

Reliable data are needed to manage recreation just as reliable inventory data are needed to manage other natural resources, such as timber. Unfortunately, they are seldom available. In recreation, management has too frequently had to rely on guesswork or the personal experience and intuition of managers. Although a manger's professional opinion is important, it is no substitute for reliable and systematically collected inventory and monitoring data. This is particularly true where turnover in personnel occurs frequently, as it does in many governmental land-managing agencies.

In this chapter we will examine some of the techniques available for monitoring three important types of recreational facilities and resources: campsites, trails, and water bodies.

CAMPSITES

Camping is among the most popular of all recreational activities. Usually it involves highly concentrated use; consequently, impacts are often pronounced. Campsites vary greatly, from highly developed sites in large campgrounds that cater to travelers in recreational vehicles to remote, isolated, lightly impacted sites in the backcountry. As objectives vary among these different situations, appropriate monitoring techniques also vary. A monitoring program, to be efficient, must be developed with specific objectives in mind. Otherwise, important information may not be collected, and time and money may be wasted in collecting nice-to-know but marginally useful data.

Despite great variability in which monitoring techniques are appropriate in different situations, there are some characteristics that are generally desirable to all monitoring systems. A campsite monitoring system should provide accurate and meaningful information about how much impact has already occurred on campsites. This tells a manager how serious current problems are. It should also provide a reliable baseline for subsequent monitoring so that trends can be identified. A good system will have four characteristics:

1. Meaningful measures of impact are utilized.
2. Measurement techniques are reliable and sensitive.
3. Costs are not too high to prohibit an inventory of all campsites.
4. Measurement units can be relocated precisely.

The value of the information collected will depend on how carefully impact parameters—measures of impact—are selected. Some parameters measure current conditions, but not how much impact has occurred on the site. For example, some monitoring systems have measured vegetation cover on campsites. By itself, this is not a measure of impact because vegetation cover is dependent on many environmental factors as well as recreational use. Fifty percent vegetation cover may be perfectly natural, or it may represent a loss of as much as 50 percent of the natural vegetation. It is much more meaningful to compare the vegetation cover on a campsite with the cover of a similar undisturbed site. The difference provides a good estimate of how much vegetation has been lost.

Deciding on just one variable to measure can be difficult. It is usually cost-effective and easier to base a monitoring system on several different parameters. Sometimes it is convenient to aggregate these parameters into a single index of site condition. This can be done by rating each parameter, say on a scale of 1 to 3, and then taking the mean rating as an overall index. If this is done, it is important to retain the ability to disaggregate data. This will make it possible to evaluate change in individual parameters over time.

A second desirable characteristic of any monitoring system is reliability. Assessment techniques must be sufficiently precise to allow independent observers to reach similar conclusions about site condition. Monitoring is of little value if different people give widely divergent assessments of site condition. Precision depends on careful testing of techniques, detailed documentation of procedures, and consistent training of evaluators. Assessment techniques must also be sensitive enough to detect managerially relevant differences between sites and changes over time.

There is always a trade-off between reliability/sensitivity and cost. More precise methods take more time and cost more money. This may be prohibitive in large backcountry areas with numerous, remote, dispersed sites. For example, in Sequoia and Kings Canyon National Parks, more than 7700 backcountry campsites have been inventoried (Parsons and Stohlgren 1987). As the objectives of inventory are to characterize both the distribution and condition of sites and how they change over time, it is best to use as precise techniques as possible while retaining the ability to inventory *all* sites. Only by inventorying all sites is it possible to characterize the number and distribution of sites—a critical concern in dispersed use areas. Where relatively imprecise rapid survey techniques must be used in order to inventory all sites, it may also be desirable to take more precise measurements on a subsample of sites. This permits subtle changes to be detected, changes that can be related to differences in characteristics such as use levels, environmental characteristics, and other variables that might affect amount of impact.

Finally, to monitor change over time it is important to document the exact location of all areal units on which measurements were taken. This may apply to the entire campsite or to square plots, line transects, or any other sampling units that were used. Photographs are often helpful for relocating measurement units.

A number of useful campsite monitoring techniques have been developed (Cole 1989). They can conveniently be grouped into systems based on photography, condition class ratings, and either ratings or measurements of multiple impact parameters. The ideal program will use all three of these types to some extent.

Photographs

Photography has frequently been used for monitoring, sometimes systematically and sometimes not, sometimes to enhance field data and sometimes as the only monitoring tool. As with field data, photographs must be taken systematically, and their locations must be carefully documented or they are likely to be of little value. In our opinion, photographs are best used as a supplement to—rather than a replacement for—data collected in the field. It is unlikely that all of the information that should be collected can be captured on film. However, photographs can convey certain information not measured in the field. They can be used to validate field assessments and, of particular importance, they provide a visual means of conveying information on site condition quantified in field measurements.

Three photographic techniques that have been used as part of campsite monitoring programs are photopoints, quadrat photography, and campsite panoramas. More detail on each of these techniques can be found in Brewer and Berrier (1984).

Photopoints.   The technique using photopoints involves taking photographs from a location that can be reestablished at a future date. Establishing and documenting the location of a photopoint is critical. Photopoint locations can be referenced to landmarks, such as unique rocks, or to permanent metal markers, star drill marks in rocks, or marks on trees. All locations should be referenced in terms of distance and direction from trees and other landmarks (Fig. 1). Reference points and photopoints should then be noted on sketch maps and photographs.

The location of a photopoint is important. Elevated points can provide good overviews. However, photos from a distance lose detail. In photographing forested sites, it is best to work on cloudy days when the contrast between shade and sunlight is reduced. Record the camera make and model, focal length of lens, height of the camera above the ground, filter type, and film type of each photograph. These should

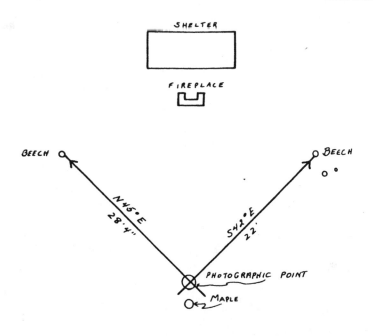

FILM: . Kodak Tri-x, 400 ASA.
Lens center 4' above ground.
Canon FTB, 28mm Canon FD lens.
F-stop, speed f-5.6 @ 1/30.
DECLINATION: $15\frac{1}{2}°$w

FIGURE 1. Sketch map referencing a photopoint. (*Source*: Brewer and Berrier 1984.)

be replicated as closely as possible, as should time of day and year. Carrying copies of the original photos with you will facilitate accurate replication.

Quadrat Photography.   The quadrat photography technique is a replacement for cover measurements taken in the field. The advantage to photographs is that professional analysts do not have to go into the field; they can analyze the photographs in the lab. The disadvantage is the greater difficulty of making certain measurements, such as coverage of individual species, from photographs. As the height of the vegetation and the complexity of the ground cover increase, these interpretational problems become more serious. There are few situations in which quadrat photographs provide an accurate replacement for field measurements.

Brewer and Berrier (1984) describe the quadrapod, a device that holds a camera at a set distance above the ground. A series of replicable quadrat locations are laid out and, using the quadrapod, photographs are taken of each quadrat. Prints or slides are enlarged, and the areas of each ground cover type (e.g., vegetation, bare ground, or individual species) is traced onto paper for areal measurement. Individual quadrats can be followed over time, or mean percent coverage of each ground cover type can be calculated and compared over time.

Campsite Panoramas.   The campsite panorama technique involves piecing together a series of photographs to provide a full 360-degree view of the campsite (Fig. 2). A camera is mounted on a tripod at a point that can be readily relocated, usually the center of the site. Camera height must be constant (and documented for repeat photos), and the camera must remain level. A series of photographs are taken by rotating the camera. Each photo should overlap the preceding one by at least 25 percent. In the lab, trim adjoining photos in the middle of the overlap area and mount the photos on mat board.

It is not feasible to take accurate measurements on these panoramic photos on account of distortion and problems with precise replication. They do provide a means of counting newly fallen trees or changes in facilities, and they provide a good overview of site change. They are also effective means of visually communicating quantitative data collected in the field.

Condition Class Estimates

In many areas, field assessments of impact are desirable but it is not feasible to spend more than a couple of minutes monitoring each campsite. This is usually the case in large, dispersed recreation areas, such as most backcountry areas and many roaded areas where people are allowed to camp wherever they want. Condition class ratings provide limited—but useful—information in these situations. Condition class systems consist of a series of condition descriptions. Overall impact is assessed, but individual impact parameters are not. Frissell (1978) suggests the following five classes:

1. Ground vegetation flattened but not permanently injured. Minimal physical change except for possibly a simple rock fireplace.
2. Ground vegetation worn away around fireplace or center of activity.
3. Ground vegetation lost on most of the site but humus and litter still present in all but a few areas.
4. Bare mineral soil widespread. Tree roots exposed on the surface.
5. Soil erosion obvious. Trees reduced in vigor or dead.

Each campsite is located on a map and assigned to whichever class best describes its condition.

Frissell's system was developed from experience in the Boundary Waters Canoe Area, Minnesota, and what is now the Lee Metcalf Wilderness, Montana. It applies well in coniferous forests in cool climates where growing seasons are short, litter accumulation is great, and ground vegetation is highly sensitive to disturbance. In other

FIGURE 2. This 360-degree panoramic photograph of a campsite in the Selway-Bitterroot Wilderness, Idaho, has been used to monitor change on the site. (*Photo:* U.S. Forest Service.)

environments, such as mountain grasslands or deserts, the system does not work well. Different descriptions that reflect the impacts that occur in these other environments can be developed, however.

Condition class ratings are a relatively inexpensive way to answer some very important questions. How many campsites are there and where are they located?

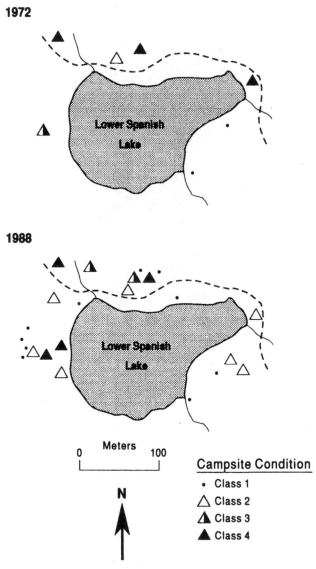

FIGURE 3. The number and condition of campsites around Lower Spanish Lake, Lee Metcalf Wilderness, Montana, in 1972 and 1988. (*Source*: D. N. Cole 1993.)

Condition class ratings also indicate which campsites are most seriously impacted. Repeat monitoring will indicate whether the number of campsites increased or decreased over time. Figure 3 shows the results, for one lake, of a campsite condition class survey conducted at two points in time. It shows which campsites are the old, traditional ones and which campsites are the most impacted. More important, it shows that total impact increased, between 1972 and 1988, primarily because the number of campsites tripled.

There are two primary drawbacks to condition class ratings. First, they cannot provide information on which types of impact on campsites are most serious. For example, is tree damage the primary problem, or is it vegetation loss? Second, these ratings are not a very sensitive way to monitor change in site condition over time. By the time conditions have changed enough to be reflected in a changed condition class rating, a profound amount of change has occurred.

Multiple Parameter Systems

The aforementioned concerns are addressed in multiple parameter rating systems, which evaluate a number of separate impact parameters. Such systems vary greatly in precision and, consequently, the time required to take measurements. Some utilize ratings whereas others require accurate measurements.

Multiple Parameter Ratings.   In Sequoia and Kings Canyon National Parks, information is collected on vegetation density, vegetation composition, campsite area, area of the barren core, campsite development, presence of organic litter and duff, number of access (social) trails, and number of tree mutilations. Each of these is estimated or counted; time-consuming measurements are not required. Each parameter is assigned a rating, depending on amount of impact, and these ratings are totaled to obtain an overall impact rating (Parsons and MacLeod 1980). The advantages to such a system are:

1. It accounts for sites where one type of impact is high and another is low—in a condition class system such a situation results in a site partially matching several of the class descriptions.
2. It contains much more information, so that it is possible to track change in individual parameters, such as amount of tree damage, over time.
3. It retains the flexibility to change parameters or reevaluate the importance of parameters without having to reexamine every site. With the condition class system, managers cannot change their condition criteria without redoing the entire inventory.

Cole (1983a) refined the system developed by Parsons and MacLeod (1980). In his system each parameter was recorded separately, and the objectivity of some of the rating descriptions was increased. To illustrate how the system works, Fig. 4 shows a campsite that managers might want to monitor. Figure 5 shows a completed form for that campsite. The following detailed instructions explain how the form is used.

FIGURE 4. The condition of this campsite in the Eagle Gap Wilderness, Oregon, has been recorded on the form in Figure 5. (*Photo*: D. N. Cole.)

Item 19, Vegetation Cover.   Using the coverage classes on the form, estimate the percentage of the campsite covered with live ground cover vegetation—not dead vegetation or trees or shrubs taller than a person. (Note the need to define what is meant by *ground cover vegetation*). Circle the appropriate coverage class. Do this for the campsite and do it for a nearby, unused site similar (except for the recreational impact) to the campsite.

Item 20, Mineral Soil Exposure.   Using the same coverage classes, estimate the percentage of the campsite and the same undisturbed comparative site without either live ground cover vegetation or duff—that is, the percentage with exposed mineral soil.

Item 21, Vegetation Loss.   Utilizing the information in Item 19, record the difference, in number of coverage classes, between vegetation on the campsite and the comparative area. If there is no difference (e.g., both the campsite and comparative area are class 4, 51 to 75 percent), circle rating 1. If coverage on the campsite is one class lower than on the comparative area (e.g., the campsite is class 3, 26 to 50 percent and the comparative area is class 4, 51 to 75 percent), circle 2. If the difference is more than one class, circle 3.

Item 22, Mineral Soil Increase.   Utilizing the information in Item 20, record the difference in mineral soil exposure class between campsite and comparative area. In this case ratings of 2 and 3 are given when mineral soil cover is one, or more than one, class higher on the campsite, respectively.

Impact Evaluation

	On Campsite	On Unused Comparative Area
(19) Vegetation Cover: (Be sure to compare similar areas, same species, slope, rockiness, and canopy cover)	1 – 0-5% **2 – 6-25%** 3 – 26-50% 4 – 51-75% 5 – 76-100%	1 – 0-5% 2 – 6-25% 3 – 26-50% 4 – 51-75% **5 -76-100%**
(20) Mineral Soil Exposure: (percent of area that is bare mineral soil)	1 – 0-5% **2 – 6-25%** 3 – 26-50% 4 – 51-75% 5 – 76-100%	**1 – 0-5%** 2 – 6-25% 3 – 26-50% 4 – 51-75% 5 – 76-100%

Rating (Circle one category)

	On Campsite		On Unused Comparative Area	Calculation of impact index (do in office)
	1	2	3	
(21) Vegetation Loss:	(No difference in coverage)	(Difference one coverage class)	**(Difference two or more coverage classes)**	2 × 3 = 6
(22) Mineral Soil Increase:	(No difference in coverage)	(Difference one coverage class)	(Difference two or more coverage classes)	3 × 2 = 6
(23) Tree Damage: Number of trees scarred of felled _10_ (est.) Percent of trees scarred or felled _50_ (est.)	(No more than broken lower branches)	(1-8 scarred trees, or 1-3 badly scarred or felled)	**(>8 scarred trees, or >3 badly scarred or felled)**	2 × 3 = 6
(24) Root Exposure: Number of trees with roots exposed _5_ Percent of trees with roots exposed _25_ (est.)	(None)	(1-6 trees with roots exposed)	(>6 trees with roots exposed)	3 × 2 = 6
(25) Development:	**(None)**	(1 fire ring with or without primitive log seat)	(>1 fire ring or other major development)	3 × 2 = 6
(26) Cleanliness: Number of fire scars _2_	(No more than scattered charcoal from 1 fire ring)	**(Remnants of >1 fire ring, some litter or manure)**	(Human waste, much litter or manure)	1 × 1 = 1
(27) Social Trails: Number of trails _4_	(No more than 1 discernible trail)	(2-3 discernible, max. 1 well-worn)	**(>3 discernible or more than 1 well-worn)**	2 × 1 = 2
(28) Camp Area Estimated area _1600_ (ft²)	(<500 ft²)	(500-2000 ft²)	**(>2000 ft²)**	3 × 2 = 6
(29) Barren Core Camp Area: Estimated area _600_ (ft²)	(<50 ft²)	(50-500 ft²)	**(>500 ft²)**	2 × 4 = 8

(30) Photo Record _____

(31) Comments: (Details about location of site, impacts, management suggestions, etc.)

(32) Impact Index _47_

FIGURE 5. This form records information on the condition of the campsite shown in Fig. 4. (*Source:* D. N. Cole 1983a.)

237

Item 23, Tree Damage.   Count the number of trees with nails in them, ax marks, initials, and other human-caused scars. Also include stumps and/or cut-down trees. Do not count the same tree more than once and do not count trees on which the only damage is branches broken off for firewood. After recording this number, estimate very roughly what percentage of all the trees on the site have been damaged. If no trees are damaged, give the site a rating of 1. If one to eight trees are damaged or if one to three trees have been felled or have bad scars (scars larger than 1 ft^2), give the site a rating of 2. If more trees are damaged, give the site a 3.

Item 24, Root Exposure.   Count the number of trees with exposed roots and assign a rating based on this number.

Item 25, Development.   Assign the site a rating of 1 if there are no facilities—not even a fire ring. A fire site is considered a ring only if the ring of stones is there; if they have been scattered, it is a fire scar. If there is only one fire ring, primitive log seats, or both, assign the site a 2. If there is more than one fire ring or more elaborate facilities, assign the site a 3.

Item 26, Cleanliness.   Count the number of fire scars on the site, including any fire rings as fire scars. Assign the site a 1 if there is only one scar and essentially no evidence of litter, stock manure, or human waste. Assign the site a 2 if there is more than one fire scar or if litter or stock manure is evident. If litter or stock manure is "all over the place" *or* if there is any evidence of human waste, assign the site a 3.

Item 27, Social Trails.   Social trails are the informal trails that lead from the site to water, the main trail, other campsites, or satellite sites. Discernible trails are trails that can be seen but that are still mostly vegetated. Well-worn trails are mostly devegetated. Count the total number of trails. Assign the site a rating based on the number of discernible and/or well-worn trails.

Item 28, Camp Area.   Estimate the total area disturbed by camping and assign the site a rating based on this area.

Item 29, Barren Core Camp Area.   Estimate the area within the camp without any vegetation. Bare area may or may not be covered with duff. Areas with scattered vegetation are not counted as barren area. Give the site a rating based on this area.

After the form has been filled out in the field, it is possible to calculate an overall impact index (Item 32). The ratings for each parameter are multiplied by a weight. The weights for each parameter are decided by managers based on their opinion of the relative importance of each parameter. The products of each rating and weight are then summed to give the impact index. In the Bob Marshall this index varied from 20 (minimal impact) to 60 (maximum impact). This range was then divided into four classes: light (ratings 20 to 29), moderate (30 to 40), heavy (41 to 50), and severe impact (51 to 60). These ratings were used to map the distribution of sites in each of these impact classes to give a graphic display of where campsite impacts are most numerous and pronounced (Fig. 6).

The keys to such a system are selecting meaningful parameters, developing very specific definitions so that interpretations are consistent, developing ratings that adequately differentiate between campsites (if 90 percent of the campsites are rated 1, this does not provide much information), and then investing in training. Each area will do well to modify existing systems to its particular needs. In the Eagle Cap Wilderness, Oregon, where sites are smaller than in the Bob Marshall and where sites have less tree damage on account of less stock use, the same impact parameters were used, but some of the rating definitions were more stringent. For example, in the

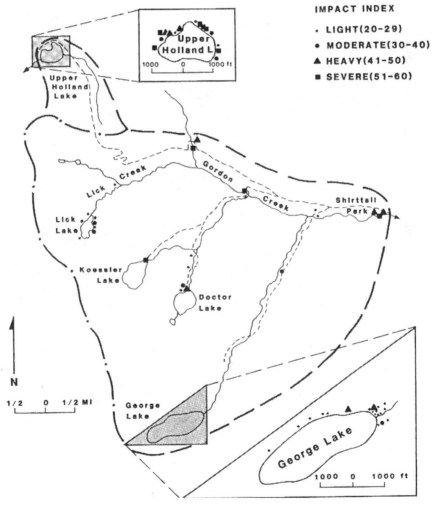

FIGURE 6. This map displays the condition (impact index) of all campsites in a portion of the Bob Marshall Wilderness, Montana. (*Source*: D. N. Cole 1983a.)

Eagle Cap, the boundary between ratings of 2 and 3 were 1000 ft² for camp area and one badly scarred or felled tree (Cole 1983a). This compares with 2000 ft² and three trees in the Bob Marshall.

In the Boundary Waters Canoe Area the same parameters were used, but an additional parameter has been added—length of shoreline disturbed by boat landings. In Grand Canyon National Park there are few trees, only patchy vegetation and organic matter, and campfires are prohibited. Several different parameters were selected to monitor sites there. Rangers in Grand Canyon are estimating barren core area, soil compaction, social trails, vegetation disturbance around the perimeter of the site, tree damage, litter, and campfire evidence.

Such a system provides a lot of information at relatively low cost. Using these techniques, Cole (1993) was able to document pronounced increases in campsite impact in wildernesses in the western United States, resulting primarily from an increase in the number of sites. Individual campsites can be monitored by trained individuals in 5 to 10 minutes. The problem is that the information is not very precise. It is not uncommon, for example, for different evaluators to give the same campsite very different ratings for individual parameters. We have found, however, that overall index ratings do not vary greatly between different evaluators. This suggests that the low precision of data collected using this system is most problematic in trying to draw conclusions about changes over time—for separate types of impact, such as amount of tree damage—on individual campsites.

Multiple Parameter Measures.   The best way to get accurate, replicable data for individual campsites is to take careful measurements in the field. Where they can be afforded, measurements are best. Keep in mind, however, that it is important to inventory all sites. Therefore, a system based on measurements may be feasible only where there are a small number of campsites. This may be the case in a developed campground or in backcountry areas with designated sites. For example, measurements were used in the backcountry at Great Smoky Mountains National Park where there were only 113 legal sites and 289 illegal sites (Bratton, Hickler, and Graves 1978). Compare this with the situation in Sequoia and Kings Canyon National Parks where there are more than 7700 backcountry campsites.

Let's look at a methodology developed to examine impacts and trends on individual sites in the Eagle Cap Wilderness, Oregon (Cole 1982; Cole and Hall 1992).

In the Eagle Cap each sample site consisted of both a campsite and a similar undisturbed site in the vicinity. This undisturbed site serves as a control, a measure of what the campsite was like before it was camped on. On each campsite, linear transects were established, radiating from an arbitrarily established center point in 16 directions. Distances were measured from the center point to both the first significant amount of vegetation and the edge of the disturbed part of the campsite (Fig. 7). This defined the area of the barren central core of the site (bare area) and the entire disturbed area (camp area). Both are important indicators of impact. Tree seedlings and mature trees were counted within the entire disturbed area. Any human damage (e.g., ax marks, initials, etc.) was noted. Tree seedlings were also counted on a 50 m² control plot close by. Differences between campsite and control, in the

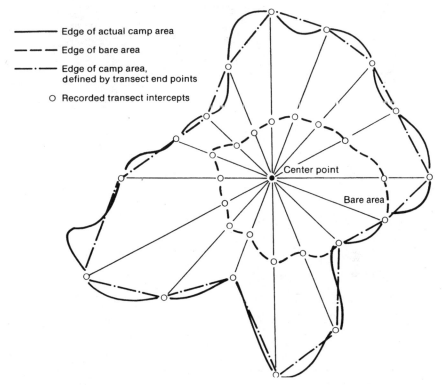

FIGURE 7. The campsite measurement system used in the Eagle Cap Wilderness recorded bare area, camp area, number of damaged trees, and number of tree seedlings. (*Source*: D. N. Cole 1982.)

density of seedlings (the number per m²), are attributed to recreational impact. Measures of impact for tree damage are the number of damaged trees and the percentage of all trees on the campsite that are damaged.

On each campsite, approximately 15 quadrats, 1 m by 1 m, were located along four transects that ran from the center point to the edge of the site and that were oriented perpendicular to each other. The distance between successive quadrats decreased with distance from the center point so that the central part of the campsite was not oversampled. In each quadrat the coverage of total vegetation, of exposed mineral soil, and of each plant species was estimated (Fig. 8). Coverages were estimated to the nearest percentage if under 10 percent or in 10 percent coverage classes between 10 and 100 percent. The midpoints of each coverage class were used to calculate mean percentage cover for each of these types of ground cover. These cover estimates were compared with similar estimates on controls. Again, differences are considered to be measures of the amount of recreational impact that has occurred on campsites. For example, mean vegetation cover was 55 percent on controls and 8 percent on campsites. Therefore, we infer that camping removed vegetation from 47 percent of the average site. Note that this is a more precise way to estimate cover loss than was used in the multiple parameter rating system described earlier.

FIGURE 8. Estimates of the percent coverage of vegetation and other ground cover parameters are often made with the aid of a quadrat. (*Photo*: D. N. Cole.)

On both campsites and controls, four soil samples were collected to measure bulk density, organic content, and chemical composition. Water infiltration rates were measured, as were pH and the depth of surface organic horizons. Soil samples were systematically distributed to avoid bias and oversampling of any part of the site.

Using data collected in this fashion, Cole and Hall (1992) were able to identify subtle shifts in different impact parameters over an 11-year monitoring period, despite the fact that conditions were relatively stable on most campsites. For example, mean vegetation cover on campsites was actually higher in 1990 than in 1979; mineral soil exposure increased greatly over this period, however (Table 1). The data were also helpful in differentiating between change that resulted from camping use and natural change, as reflected in changing conditions on controls. This system, then, provides a large amount of precise information about campsite condition, even for individual campsites. The problem with the system is that it can take an hour or two to monitor each campsite.

A Compromise.   Marion (1991) has provided a detailed procedural manual for a multiple parameter monitoring system that utilizes measures and counts that are gathered in a rapid fashion. It is less precise and sensitive than the Eagle Cap measurement process but more precise than multiple parameter rating systems. It takes two trained evaluators about 30 minutes to monitor a campsite—again, a compromise between the measurement and rating approaches. He has used the system successfully in a number of national parks, particularly in the eastern United States.

TABLE 1. **Mean Change in Ground Cover Conditions on 20 Campsites in the Eagle Cap Wilderness**

	Vegetation Cover		Mineral Soil Cover		Organic Horizon Thickness	
	Camp	Control	Camp	Control	Camp	Control
Conditions						
1979	15	60	33	1	0.2	0.9
1990	19	60	44	3	0.2	0.9
Number of Sites						
Increase	12	4	16	7	5	8
Decrease	7	4	3	3	7	9
Unchanged	1	11	1	9	8	2

His technique involves identifying site boundaries and measuring distances from a permanent center point to site boundaries. He replaced the procedure of transects radiating out at set angles (as described for the Eagle Cap process) with a procedure in which the transects radiate out at variable angles, depending on what provides the most accurate measure of camp area. This results in a more accurate measure of camp area (Marion 1995). Following this procedure, tree damage is assessed in much the same way it was in the Eagle Cap. Vegetation cover and mineral soil exposure are roughly estimated for the entire campsite and a control (in the manner described for the multiple parameter rating system). The number of social trails and fire sites are quickly counted and the amount of trash and human waste is quickly assessed.

TRAILS

Monitoring of trail conditions can be useful for the same reasons that campsite monitoring is useful. Information on trail condition and trend can be used to evaluate the acceptability of current conditions and whether or not trail management programs, including maintenance and reconstruction, are working. With trails, it is particularly important to establish specific objectives for trail conditions. Most trail impact (soil compaction, vegetation loss, etc.) is planned and desirable. Therefore, it is critical to define what conditions will be considered problems and to monitor these conditions.

Trail monitoring can also provide useful information about the relationship between trail condition and environmental conditions and design features. Often most of the trail segments that are deteriorating are located in just a few environmental situations (e.g., in highly erosive soils or in locations with seasonally high water tables) or in places where trail design is inadequate (e.g., where trails exceed a certain slope or lack a sufficient number of water bars to divert water off the tread). Monitoring can be used to correlate trail problems with these conditions, and the knowledge generated can be used to guide the future design and location of new or reconstructed trails.

Available techniques can be conveniently grouped into three types: replicable measurements of a small sample of trail segments, rapid surveys of a large sample of trail segments, and complete censuses of trail conditions, problems, and solutions.

Replicable Measurements

Detailed quantitative methods, using replicable measurements, permit subtle changes to be detected. However, the need to accurately document and relocate permanent measurement locations makes this a time-consuming process that may not always be worth the increased ability to detect subtle changes. Consequently, replicable measurements will often be less useful to managers than more rapid survey techniques.

Two schemes for locating replicable sample locations can be used. First, sample points can be distributed in a random or systematic fashion along the trail. This sampling design permits an unbiased assessment of the condition of the trail system as a whole. Repeat measurements, at a later date, allow managers to evaluate how much change has occurred on the entire trail, as well as on the individual sample locations. Alternatively, sample points can be located purposively on trail segments of particular interest to managers. For example, managers may be particularly interested in monitoring change on segments where pronounced erosion has already occurred or where some new type of trail design is being used. Such situations can be more efficiently studied by locating samples purposively, rather than randomly or systematically. With purposive sampling, it is not possible to assess the condition of the entire trail, however.

The trail conditions that management considers to be a problem will determine what should be measured. Perhaps the most serious problem at specific locations is erosion. Soil erosion can be assessed by successively measuring the cross-sectional area between the trail tread and a taut line stretched between two fixed points on each side of the trail. The change in cross-sectional area between successive measurements documents erosion (if area increases) or deposition (if area decreases) of material.

Leonard and Whitney (1977) provide a detailed description of this technique, using nails in trees as fixed points. This means of locating fixed points limits sample locations to forested areas. By using other fixed points, such as rods set in the ground or rods temporarily placed in receptacles permanently buried in the ground, sample points can be located in a greater variety of situations.

After locating the two fixed points, stretch a taut line and/or tape measure between the two points. Fixed points should always be far enough apart to allow for future increases in trail width. Take a series of vertical measurements of the distance between line and trail tread at fixed intervals along the tape. The interval should be small enough to permit at least 20 vertical measurements per transect. Measurements will be most precise when (1) the line is elevated above any vegetation or microtopography along the edge of the trail, (2) the line is kept taut, and (3) a plumb bob or level is used to take vertical measurements. The cross-sectional area below the taut line can be computed from the vertical measurements using the formula in Fig. 9.

When trail segments are to be reexamined, the fixed points should be relocated, and the taut line should be repositioned at precisely the same height above the fixed point

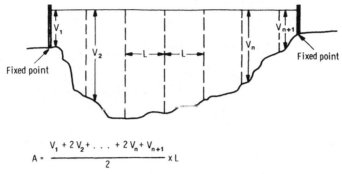

$$A = \frac{V_1 + 2\,V_2 + \ldots + 2\,V_n + V_{n+1}}{2} \times L$$

Where A = cross- sectional area

$V_1 - V_{n+1}$ = Vertical distance measurements, starting at V_1, the first fixed point, and ending at V_{n+1}, the last vertical measurement taken.

L = Interval on horizontal taut line

FIGURE 9. Layout of trail transect and formula for calculating cross-sectional area. (*Source*: D. N. Cole 1983b.)

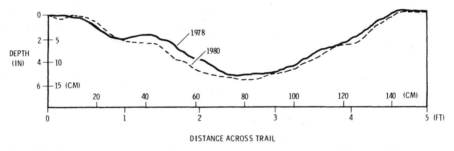

FIGURE 10. Cross-sectional profiles for the same trail transect in 1978 and 1980. Over this 2-year period 17 in² of material were eroded away. (*Source*: D. N. Cole 1983b.)

as in the original sample. Vertical measurements should be taken at the same interval and starting from the same side as in the original measurements. The idea is to remeasure precisely each vertical measurement. Precise relocation becomes increasingly important as the number of vertical measurements per transect decreases. Results show changes over time in the cross-sectional area of the trail (Fig. 10). Using this technique, Cole (1991) found virtually no change in cross-sectional area over an 11-year period for an entire trail system in Montana. However, at one purposively located segment, cross-sectional area increased more than 2 ft². This illustrates the different conclusions that might be drawn from a random sample as opposed to a purposive sample.

Rinehart, Hardy, and Rosenau (1978) developed a technique for measuring cross-sectional area with stereo photographs. As with the quadrapod photographic method of monitoring conditions on campsites, this technique does not really save time, and interpretation of results can be difficult.

The location of the fixed points must be well documented. One means of doing this is to measure the distance from the trailhead to the trail transect with a measuring wheel (cyclometer). If markers identifying the fixed points are readily visible, this may be all that is necessary. A less obtrusive option is to bury metal stakes that can be relocated with pin locators (a type of metal detector). The cyclometer and photos of the transect identify the approximate location of the transect. Exact locations are referenced to landmarks, and the pin locator leads to the metal stakes.

Detailed measurements of this type are most useful to researchers investigating the relationship between trail condition and factors that influence trail condition. Managers may find it useful for evaluating the effectiveness of alternative trail construction and design techniques. For example, if a new method of trail hardening is being tried, change could be followed both on the hardened segment and a similar unhardened segment. By comparing differences in the amount of change on hardened and unhardened segments, the benefits of hardening can be assessed in relation to its cost before investing in its widespread use.

Rapid Survey Samples

As with campsites, a useful alternative to time-consuming sampling of a few places is to make rapid assessments of many trail segments. This approach is particularly useful on trail systems because there are usually many trail miles to assess. Moreover, simply measuring trail width and depth is often as meaningful as taking cross-sectional measurements, and width and depth measurements can be taken in little time. In rapid surveys substantial time is saved by not relocating sample points. The resulting loss of precision is compensated for by the ability to take a much larger sample in the same amount of time. Monitoring involves comparing two independent samples, each consisting of a large number of observations, instead of reexamining a single small sample of sites.

To conduct a rapid survey, simply hike a specified distance along the trail, collect data on trail condition, and then hike on to the next sample point. Distances between sample points have varied from 50 to 500 m. Appropriate distances between sample points will depend on the trail mileage to be surveyed and the complexity of situations involved. There should probably be at least 100 observations for each situation of concern. For example, only 100 observations would be needed to assess the condition of a trail. However, if a low-use portion were to be compared with a high-use portion, 200 observations would be needed. The most common measures taken at each sample point are width of the trail (either the tread or the entire zone of disturbed soil and vegetation), width of bare ground, and maximum depth of the trail. Bayfield and Lloyd (1973) also noted the number of parallel trails and the presence or absence of the following "detracting features": rutting, stepping, surface deterioration, gullying, lateral erosion, bad drainage, esthetic intrusions, vandalism, and litter.

From this data it is possible to calculate mean width and depth of the trail and the proportion of the trail on which there are particular detracting features. Such data provide a useful characterization of trail conditions and problems and permit an assessment of change over time and a comparison of different trails. For example, Cole (1991) reported changes on a trail system in Montana between 1980 and 1989. Over that period, mean total trail width (the zone disturbed by trampling) increased from 100 cm to 125 cm; however, bare width (the zone without vegetation) and depth did not increase significantly. Similar increases in trail width have been documented elsewhere, using rapid survey samples (e.g., Lance, Baugh, and Love 1989). It is also possible from such data to estimate the percentage of the trail that exceeds certain depth and width standards. If objectives state, for example, that no more than 1 percent of all trails will be more than 1 ft deep, this can be monitored easily using survey techniques.

Census Techniques

Working on horse trails in Rocky Mountain National Park, Summer (1980) divided each trail into segments and then placed each trail segment in one of four erosion classes (Table 2). She used these data to relate the extent and severity of trail erosion to the geomorphic surface on which the trail was located. Summer found, for example, that most trail segments on alluvial terraces fell into either the negligible or low erosion classes; segments on alluvial-colluvial fans where boglike conditions prevail were usually in the high erosion class. She used this information to make suggestions about where trails should or should not be located. Although this was not done, it would be possible and useful to develop objectives limiting the percentage of the trail system in high erosion classes, and then monitor the percentage of the trail system in each erosion class. Where conditions are deteriorating, particularly

TABLE 2. Erosion Classes for Horse Trails in the Rocky Mountains

Erosion Class	Evaluation of Present Stability
Negligible	No marked disturbance within trail; some gravel and soil may be moving imperceptibly downslope; on monitored sites, maximum mean incision is less than 2 cm and widening is less than 25 cm.
Low	Some deepening and/or widening of trail; cobbles and soil may begin to accumulate along trail edge; on monitored sites, maximum mean incision is 2 to 6 cm and/or widening is 25 to 50 cm.
Moderate	Noticeable deepening and widening; hoofprints less than 5 cm deep; boulders and cobbles may or may not show evidence of movement; soil and vegetation disrupted; on monitored sites, maximum mean incision is 6 to 8 cm and/or widening is 50 to 100 cm.
High	Very noticeable deepening and widening; hoofprints greater than 5 cm deep; boulders and cobbles obviously moved downslope or beyond trail edge; soil and vegetation disrupted and moved downslope; on monitored sites, maximum mean incision is greater than 8 cm and/or widening is greater than 100 cm.

Source: Summer 1980. Appeared in *Journal of Soil and Water Conservation*, copyright © 1980 by Soil Conservation Society of America.

where the percentage of the trail in high erosion classes exceed objectives, management actions would be called for.

Another useful approach is to census all trail "problems." The first step here is to define in precise terms exactly what will be considered a problem. The number and length of problems can be recorded while walking the trail; then the location of each trail problem can be mapped. This information can be useful in budgeting for trail maintenance and in allocating manpower to various trail segments. By noting the segment, site, design, and use characteristics of each problem, it should be possible to identify consistent patterns of problem occurrence. Knowledge of occurrence patterns can be used to develop guidelines for trail location, design, and maintenance.

On a trail system in the Selway-Bitteroot Wilderness, for example, Cole (1983b) censused all trail segments that were either incised more than 10 in. or muddy for at least part of the use season and that were at least 3 ft long. At each problem segment, maximum depth and width of the segment, habitat type (vegetation, soils, and topography), and slope of the trail were noted. More than two-thirds of the muddy segments were in one vegetation type. If future trails avoid this type, most of the muddiness problems should be eliminated. Incision problems were strongly correlated with trail slope; almost 90 percent of the problems were on segments with slopes greater than 4.7 degrees. The solution here is to make better use of water bars on stretches where steep pitches cannot be avoided. Development of such guidelines could greatly increase the cost-effectiveness of trail building and maintenance programs. It basically amounts to learning from past mistakes.

Censuses can also be used to relate trail conditions to objectives. How this is done depends on how objectives are written. One option is for objectives to state that no segments will be more than, say, 1 ft deep. In this case, trails will have to be censused to see whether any segments are deeper than 1 ft. An option that is usually more realistic and efficient is to write probabilistic objectives (e.g., no more than 1 percent of the trail will be more than 1 ft deep). In this case, either trails can be censused or rapid survey techniques can be used.

Recently, Marion (1994) has used census techniques to assess trail conditions in several parks in the eastern United States. He emulated Cole's approach of hiking along trails with a measuring wheel, documenting the starting and ending points of well-defined "problems." In addition, he recorded the starting and ending point of certain trail design, construction, and maintenance features: maintained gravel, excessive grade (>20 percent), and trail corduroy. He recorded the location of drainage dips, water bars, lateral drains, retaining walls, culverts, and steps. For several of these features, he also assessed effectiveness. From these data, he was able to describe the number and length of these design features and draw tentative conclusions about their effectiveness. For example, he concluded that tread drainage was the most critical maintenance need along trails in Great Smoky Mountains National Park, and that water bars were more effective than drainage dips in dealing with this problem.

Elsewhere, Williams and Marion (1992) illustrate the value of prescriptive work logs. When problems are encountered along the trail, assessors attempt to prescribe the trail work needed to mitigate each problem. Assessors note the distance along the trail—from the measuring wheel—and describe the problem and the solution, using a pocket dictation device. This information can be used to prioritize and budget trail work. Clearly, someone highly knowledgable about trail design and maintenance is needed to describe the trail problems and appropriate solutions.

WATER BODIES

Monitoring of water is a critical concern in a variety of situations. Health aspects of water quality are important where drinking water is provided and in bodies of water where swimming occurs. Physical and chemical aspects of water quality are important in areas with objectives that stress maintenance of substantially natural conditions and in areas that maintain populations of sensitive fish species. Some of the situations in which monitoring of water quality may be necessary include natural and artificial lakes where heavy boating use may be affecting water quality, roaded areas where recreational use of roads may cause deterioration of water quality, and wilderness areas where the strong emphasis on natural conditions is reflected in stringent water quality standards.

Many techniques for monitoring water quality require sophisticated equipment, laboratory analyses, and highly trained technicians. However, recent advances in development of "user-friendly" techniques and equipment are changing this situation. For example, probes have been developed that allow evaluators to read off chemical concentrations when the probe is inserted in the water (Fig. 11). Books have also

FIGURE 11. Because of health hazards, water quality is monitored in heavily used wildland recreation areas. (*Photo*: National Park Service.)

been written to make water quality monitoring available to a broader range of people (Mitchell and Stapp 1994).

It is important to consider where sampling will occur, the frequency and duration of sampling, and the types of measurements that should be made. All of these considerations depend on the objectives for the area. In monitoring lakes, sampling is often done at the outlet. This provides a good indication of the condition of the lake as a whole. However, where localized pollution is expected, adjacent to a boat ramp or a campsite for example, sampling should be conducted in this area. Where stream pollution is suspected, sample just above the suspected source, immediately downstream, and far downstream from the source. Along streams it may be necessary to establish several sampling locations if the objective is to characterize an entire stream system.

It is usually desirable to monitor water quality in undisturbed places as well, to establish a control for comparison with disturbed conditions. For a lake this commonly involves sampling the inlet stream or part of the lake away from heavily used parts. With streams it is sometimes necessary, but undesirable, to establish control sampling locations on an entirely different stream.

The frequency and duration of sampling can be decided on only after some idea of data variability has been obtained. Bacteriological contamination can vary greatly in relation to the timing of recreational use (Flack, Medine and Hansen-Bristow 1988) and precipitation events. Sampling frequency and duration must be adequate to reveal such patterns.

The final consideration is what parameters to measure. Monitoring procedures and standards of quality for drinking water and water to swim in are well-developed and generally agreed upon. The primary measurement technique involves counting coliform bacteria in a sample of water. Coliform bacteria, while not pathogenic themselves, are found in human feces and often occur in the company of organisms that represent health hazards to humans. They are counted because they are convenient to work with, and they have been shown to be good indicators of bacteriological contamination. The standard membrane filter technique involves filtering and incubating water samples and then counting the number of indicator organisms in each sample. Refer to the American Public Health Association (1985) for more detail. The number of organisms found can then be compared with various health standards that have been advanced. For drinking water, acceptable coliform counts are usually on the order of one or two bacterial colonies per 100 ml of water (depending on whether federal or state standards are used). Acceptable levels for full-body contact, such as swimming, are more variable between states but are usually on the order of hundreds of coliform bacteria colonies per 100 ml of water. Some experts believe it is better to base health standards on the number of fecal coliforms rather than on total coliform counts. Managers should determine what federal, state, or local requirements apply— in this case objectives already exist—and take whatever measures are appropriate.

Although monitoring water is not as simple as campsite and trail monitoring, it is now possible to buy the equipment to conduct membrane filter monitoring for less than $1500. Training takes only about a day.

Recently, increasing numbers of water bodies, even in remote areas, have been contaminated with the protozoan *Giardia lamblia* (Suk, Sorensen, and Deleanis 1987).

This organism is currently a more significant health threat in wildland recreation areas than bacteria. Moreover, it is difficult to monitor. Improved procedures for monitoring *Giardia* contamination are being developed (Hibler and Hancock 1990). However, *Giardia* samples must be large (on the order of hundreds of gallons), and the presence of *Giardia* cysts must be identified by experts using microscopes.

A wide variety of physical and chemical water quality parameters can be examined. It can also be useful to sample plankton, algae, and other aquatic biota. In a study designed to determine baseline conditions and possible effects of visitor use on some subalpine lakes in Kings Canyon National Park, Silverman and Erman (1979) measured orthophosphate and nitrate concentration, pH, conductivity, temperature, dissolved oxygen, plankton, and periphyton. In most cases techniques used are either standard methods recommended by the American Public Health Association (1985) or techniques described in special field analysis test kits.

Although it is helpful to collect information on as many parameters as possible, this may be wasteful, particularly if the increased costs associated with this lead to an undesirable reduction in sampling frequency or the number of sample points. If this is the case, one must reexamine objectives and evaluate which parameters are most likely to indicate adverse effects on water quality. Where use of roads in erodible material is common, increased sedimentation can adversely affect fish populations; in such places monitoring of suspended solids is particularly worthwhile. Recreational trampling, even in remote backcountry areas, can lead to increases in the concentration of certain elements. Sometimes growth of aquatic plants can be stimulated by increases in the concentration of elements that formerly limited plant growth. In Kings Canyon National Park, for example, recreation-related increases in iron stimulated aquatic insects, worms, and small clams, and a depletion of nitrate (Taylor and Erman 1980). In Gatineau Park, Quebec, trampling increased phosphorus levels in a small lake. This stimulated growth of phytoplankton and reduced the transparency of the water (Dickman and Dorais 1977). Thus, in one case, it is most important to monitor iron and biota on the bottom of the lake; in the other case, it is most important to monitor phosphorus and suspended plankton.

These case studies illustrate the complexity of monitoring water quality. A relatively high level of expertise is needed to do more than simply monitor bacteria levels. It is probably best to start out monitoring many parameters at various times and places. This should give some idea of temporal and spatial variability to help decide on sampling frequencies and locations that are both effective and efficient. It will also become clear which parameters are the best indicators of adverse impact. Although something of a "shotgun approach" is required at first, the program should become increasingly efficient over time.

REMOTE SENSING

There are a number of situations in which remote sensing, particularly aerial photography, can be a useful and cost-effective means of monitoring impact. Wherever tree cover is lacking, taking air photos is a good way to monitor change in the number and area of devegetated places. Price (1983) has shown how air photos can be used to monitor visitor impact on meadows around Sunshine Ski Area in Banff National Park, Alberta. Repeat photos show where new trails are developing and where existing trails are widening or becoming braided.

In Grand Canyon National Park, backcountry campsites are often clustered closely together in accessible places where water is available. These locations develop mazes of informal trails and tent pads. It is difficult to monitor changes in these trail and campsite complexes using only the field measurements and rapid estimation techniques discussed previously. With air photos, however, the number and areas of both trails and tent pads can be traced onto maps. Overlays drawn from repeat photos, taken at later dates, can be used to identify changes over time. New Geographical Information System (GIS) technology presents novel and more sophisticated analytical options. However, the value of GIS applications to recreation impact management is probably less profound than for many other natural resource applications.

A final situation in which air photos are useful is in monitoring impacts resulting from use of off-road vehicles in areas without a dense canopy cover. Such use leads to the development of tracks and large devegetated areas in places of concentrated use. This situation is analogous to the Grand Canyon trail and campsite complexes just described. Overlay maps and GIS technology can again be used to monitor change in the number and size of tracks and devegetated areas.

DEVELOPING A MONITORING SYSTEM

Both Cole (1989) and Marion (1991), in their campsite monitoring sourcebooks, stress the importance of following a sequence of steps in developing a monitoring system. It is important to resist the urge to simply rush out and apply a monitoring system you heard about from a friend or in a class. Systems must be carefully tailored to existing situations; they must also be maintained and nurtured. Otherwise, time will be spent on unproductive activities, critical data will not be collected, quality control will be lost, and eventually programs will be abandoned. Typically, program abandonment will be blamed on the monitoring technique, when in fact most of the blame should be placed on inadequate attention to the *process* of developing a monitoring system.

The steps that Cole and Marion suggest differ somewhat. Generally, the steps involve (1) evaluating system needs and constraints, (2) reviewing and selecting monitoring approaches and impact evaluation protocols, (3) testing and refining those protocols, (4) documenting protocols and training evaluators, (5) developing field collection procedures, and (6) designing data analysis and reporting procedures. These authors note that it is critically important to decide on how you want to use the monitoring data—what questions you want to be able to answer—before deciding on a system. It is also important to allocate sufficient time to training. Marion (1991) is exemplary in the detailed training manual he provides. This will more than pay for itself in improving data quality. Finally, it is important to attempt to assess the precision of the data you collect. Any difference in estimated condition, at two different points of time, will include both the amount of change that has actually occurred and some degree of measurement error. Only when you know the likely magnitude of measurement error will you be able to estimate the magnitude of real change.

REFERENCES

American Public Health Association. 1985. *Standard Methods for the Examination of Water and Wastewater.* 16th ed. Washington, DC: American Public Health Association. 1268 pp.

Bayfield, N. G., and R. J. Lloyd. 1973. An Approach to Assessing the Impact of Use on a Long Distance Footpath—The Pennine Way. *Recreation News Supplement* 8:11–17.

Bratton, S. P., M. G. Hickler, and J. H. Graves. 1978. Visitor Impact on Backcountry Campsites in the Great Smoky Mountains. *Environmental Management* 2:431–442.

Brewer, L., and D. Berrier. 1984. Photographic Techniques for Monitoring Resource Change at Backcountry Sites. USDA Forest Service General Technical Report NE-86. 13 pp.

Cole, D. N. 1982. Wilderness Campsite Impacts: Effect of Amount of Use. USDA Forest Service Research Paper INT-284. 34 pp.

Cole, D. N. 1983a. Monitoring the Condition of Wilderness Campsites. USDA Forest Service Research INT-302. 10 pp.

Cole, D. N. 1983b. Assessing and Monitoring Backcountry Trail Conditions. USDA Forest Service Research Paper INT-303. 10 pp.

Cole, D. N. 1989. Wilderness Campsite Monitoring Methods: A Sourcebook. USDA Forest Service General Technical Report INT-259. 57 pp.

Cole, D. N. 1991. Changes on Trails in the Selway-Bitterroot Wilderness, Montana, 1978–89. USDA Forest Service Research Paper INT-450. 5 pp.

Cole, D. N. 1993. Campsites in Three Western Wildernesses: Proliferation and Changes in Condition Over 12 to 16 Years. USDA Forest Service Research Paper INT-463. 15 pp.

Cole, D. N., and T. E. Hall. 1992. Trends in Campsite Condition: Eagle Cap Wilderness, Bob Marshall Wilderness and Grand Canyon National Park. USDA Forest Service Research Paper INT-453. 40 pp.

Dickman, M., and M. Dorais. 1977. The Impact of Human Trampling on Phosphorus Loading to a Small Lake in Gatineau Park, Quebec, Canada. *Journal of Environmental Management* 5:335–344.

Flack, J. E., A. J. Medine, and K. J. Hansen-Bristow. 1988. Stream Water Quality in a Mountain Recreation Area. *Mountain Research and Development* 8:11–22.

Frissell, S. S. 1978. Judging Recreation Impacts on Wilderness Campsites. *Journal of Forestry* 76:481–483.

Hibler, C. P., and C. M. Hancock. 1990. Waterborne Giardiasis. In G. A. McFeters, ed. *Drinking Water Microbiology: Progress and Recent Developments.* New York: Springer-Verlag, pp. 271–293.

Lance, A. N., I. D. Baugh, and J. A. Love. 1989. Continued Footpath Widening in the Cairngorm Mountains, Scotland. *Biological Conservation* 49:201–214.

Leonard, R. E., and A. M. Whitney. 1977. Trail Transect: A Method for Documenting Trail Changes. USDA Forest Service Research Paper NE-389. 8 pp.

Marion, J. L. 1991. Developing a Natural Resource Inventory and Monitoring Program for Visitor Impacts on Recreation Sites: A Procedural Manual. USDI National Park Service Natural Resources Report NPS/NRVT/NRR-91/06. 59 pp.

Marion, J. L. 1994. An Assessment of Trail Conditions in Great Smoky Mountains National Park. USDI National Park Service, Southeast Region. 155 pp.

Marion, J. L. 1995. Capabilities and Management Utility of Recreation Impact Monitoring Programs. *Environmental Management* 19:763–771.

Mitchell, M. K., and W. B. Stapp. 1994. *Field Manual for Water Quality Monitoring*. Dexter, MI: Thomson-Shore Printers. 272 pp.

Parsons, D. J., and S. A. MacLeod. 1980. Measuring Impacts of Wilderness Use. *Parks* 5(3):8–12.

Parsons, D. J., and T. J. Stohlgren. 1987. Impacts of Visitor Use on Backcountry Campsites in Sequoia and Kings Canyon National Parks, California. Cooperative National Park Resources Studies Unit Technical Report No. 25. 79 pp.

Price, M. F. 1983. Management Planning in the Sunshine Area of Canada's Banff National Park. *Parks* 7(4):6–10.

Rinehart, R. P., C. C. Hardy, and H. G. Rosenau. 1978. Measuring Trail Conditions with Stereo Photography. *Journal and Forestry* 76:501–503.

Silverman, G., and D. C. Erman. 1979. Alpine Lakes in Kings Canyon National Park, California: Baseline Conditions and Possible Effects of Visitor Use. *Journal of Environmental Management* 8:73–87.

Suk, T. J., S. K. Sorenson, and P. D. Dileanis. 1987. The Relation Between Human Presence and Occurrence of *Giardia* Cysts in Streams in the Sierra Nevada, California. *Journal of Freshwater Ecology* 4:71–75.

Summer, R. M. 1980. Impact of Horse Traffic on Trails in Rocky Mountain National Park. *Journal of Soil and Water Conservation* 35:85–87.

Taylor, T. P., and D. C. Erman. 1980. The Littoral Bottom Fauna of High Elevation Lakes in Kings Canyon National Park. *California Fish and Game* 66(2):112–119.

Williams, P. B., and J. L. Marion. 1992. Trail Inventory and Assessment Approaches Applied to Trail System Planning at Delaware Water Gap National Recreation Area. In Proceedings of the 1992 Northeastern Recreation Research Symposium. USDA Forest Service General Technical Report NE-176, pp. 80–83.

12 Visitor Management

It is useful to distinguish between visitor management techniques and site management techniques. However, the distinction between the two is not perfect. Site manipulation can be a potent means of managing the amount and distribution of visitor use, and manipulation of where visitors go can be an effective means of managing site condition. For our purposes we will restrict visitor management to regulation, information, and education designed to influence the amount, type, and timing of use, visitor behavior, and the extent to which use is dispersed or concentrated. Site management involves management of where use occurs, as well as physical manipulation of the resource.

Although images of trail building and facilities may first spring to mind when we think of impact management, visitor management is generally the first line of defense. Regulations—the "do's and don'ts" on park signs—and the information that comes in brochures and from contacts with rangers do the bulk of the job in controlling visitor impact. This is particularly true in legally designated wilderness. In wilderness, extensive engineering and environmental modification and strict control of where use occurs are undesirable. As we move away from the primitive end of the opportunity spectrum, the appropriateness of facilities, engineering, and extensive environmental modification increases. In developed campgrounds, for example, site management may rival visitor management in importance. Even here, however visitor management techniques, such as restrictions on the number of people or prohibition of dogs or horses, are critical to managing impact.

Although management of the amount, type, and behavior of users is often critical to effective management of recreational impacts, managers must never forget the interests and desires of their recreational clientele. After all, much of the manager's job should be directed toward maximizing visitor satisfaction. It is important to temper a concern for resource protection with a concern for promoting recreational opportunities. The relative importance of these two concerns will vary from area to area, along with management goals and objectives.

The visitor management techniques described in this chapter are organized by strategic purpose, as discussed in Chapter 10. A wider variety of visitor management techniques is potentially useful in large recreation areas toward the primitive end of the recreation opportunity spectrum. Therefore, many of the techniques described in this chapter are most applicable to backcountry areas. In fact, most of the examples are taken from wilderness, where research on how visitor management can be used to reduce impacts has been particularly active. The opposite is the case with site management. Many of the techniques described in Chapter 13 will be of limited utility in wilderness, where intensive and extensive site modification is inappropriate.

USE LIMITS

Although limiting use will be the first technique discussed, it should not be the first line of defense against impact. Reducing use can be a convenient way to limit impact without either having to understand the real cause of problems or getting involved in more direct and active management of problems. However, use limitations conflict with one of the primary objectives of recreation management—providing opportunities for recreational use and enjoyment. It is justified in places where demand is so great that there is little alternative to use reductions or where the only other option is a program of numerous restrictions that preclude many preferred uses. However, other options should be explored first. Use should be limited only after a thorough analysis shows that it is the best way to avoid both unacceptable levels of impact and a program of restrictions that would eliminate much of the joy of visiting the area.

Because the relationship between amount of use and amount of impact is not linear, reducing use will not necessarily reduce impact substantially. A little use causes considerable impact, and further increases in use have less and less additional effect on the resource. On already impacted sites all use may have to be curtailed before recovery can occur. In fact, in some situations, such as on incised trails where erosion is occurring, even elimination of all use may be ineffective. Active site rehabilitation may be necessary before any recovery occurs.

In popular places, where use levels are high—the most common situation where use reductions have been applied—changes in amount of use will usually have more of an effect on the *number* of impacted sites than on the *severity* of impact on individual sites. Consider the example of a popular wilderness lake basin with 10 campsites. Limiting use to a maximum of five parties per night would probably not reduce use of any of these sites to the point where recovery could occur. However, there would no longer be need for more than five campsites in the basin. Therefore, if managers closed five of these sites, the number of impacted sites would eventually be reduced by the cutback in use. Not only is the severity of impact on individual sites not reduced, but without the supporting action of closing certain campsites, even the number of sites would not have been affected. Use reductions in high-use areas are a justifiable means of avoiding crowding but are less useful in avoiding ecological impacts. Where implemented, they must be complemented with a use concentration program to have any ecological benefit at all. In developed recreation areas, use limitation is also a means of seeing that the physical capacity of the area (the number of available campsites, for example) is not exceeded.

In lightly used areas the situation is quite different. Remember that at low-use levels, differences in amount of use can have significant effects on amount of impact. If use levels can be kept very low, the severity of impact will also be very low. In such a situation, use limitations can contribute substantially to maintaining low levels of impact. The trick is to keep use low on all sites and to make sure that visitors avoid fragile sites and do not engage in highly destructive behaviors. Even one party of vandals can inflict serious damage. Therefore, a program of use limitation in low-use areas—to keep impact levels very low—will be effective only if supported by programs that teach visitors to choose lightly used, resistant recreation sites and to practice low-impact techniques. We will discuss these actions, use dispersal and visitor education, in more detail later. Such a program is probably justified only in wilderness-type areas where only very low levels of impact are acceptable.

Most research and much of the controversy surrounding use limitation is concerned with decisions about when and how use limits should be implemented. Visitors usually support use limits if they believe they are necessary to protect resources (McCool and Christensen 1996). However, when visitors are asked whether or not current impact problems warrant use limits, they often disagree. For example, visitors to Snow Lake (a very heavily used lake in the Alpine Lakes Wilderness in Washington) were asked their opinion about the need for use limits. Only 18 percent replied that there should not be use limits regardless of amount of use or impact. Of those who thought use limits might be needed at some time, 48 percent believed they were needed now and 52 percent replied that limits were not needed now but would be justified if overuse occurred in the future. Moreover, those people who thought limits were needed now were divided equally between those who believed use should be reduced and those who thought use should be kept to current levels (Cole, Watson, Hall, and Spildie 1997).

Once it is decided that use limits are needed, someone must make decisions about maximum acceptable amounts of use. Many different criteria and considerations have been employed in setting these limits. There is substantial controversy over the extent to which empirical data can be directly translated into use limits. Some scientists have employed the concept of social norms as a basis for setting use limits. They hold that most visitors share common opinions about the conditions that ought to exist in recreation areas (these are termed *norms*), that the norms can be determined from visitor surveys, and that these norms can be the basis for use limits (Shelby, Vaske, and Donnelly 1996). Other scientists disagree. They question whether visitor opinions about conditions are really norms (Noe 1992), whether most visitors are "merely guessing" about what they think conditions ought to be (Williams, Roggenbuck, Patterson, and Watson 1992), and the extent to which the opinions of current visitors should be the primary basis for limits.

Use limits in the backcountry of Yosemite National Park, California, were established for each travel zone in the park, based on acres in the zone, miles of trail, and an ecological fragility factor—derived from an assessment of ecosystem rarity, vulnerability, recuperability, and repairability (van Wagtendonk 1986). In the neighboring Sequoia and Kings Canyon National Parks, California, use limits were based primarily on an analysis of existing campsites (Parsons 1986). The number of well-impacted campsites was tallied for each zone. Sites that were within 25 ft of water, within 100 ft of another well-impacted campsite, or otherwise considered unacceptable were deleted from the tally. This tally of "acceptable" campsites was used to define the maximum number of groups that should be in a zone at any one time.

It is our opinion that use limits are subjective judgments. They must be developed by managers, with input from legitimate stakeholders. Science can only inform these decisions, by assessing resource conditions and visitor opinions and describing likely outcomes of alternative decisions. We advocate an approach such as the Limits of Acceptable Change process. Once managers make subjective decisions about maximum acceptable levels of impact, scientists can assess the relationships between amount of use and amount of impact. Levels of use that can be sustained without exceeding limits of impact can be identified. Simulation models and computer programs can be developed that allow managers to set limits on the number of people entering at specific trailheads, such that impact levels within the wildland area remain below maximum acceptable limits (van Wagtendonk and Coho 1986).

Once use limits are established, the issue of allocation emerges. On white-water rivers, the allocation of a limited number of permits between commercial and private users is a highly controversial issue (McCool and Utter 1981). Elsewhere most of the controversy revolves around several mechanisms for allocating permits to private users. Permits can be requested in advance through some sort of reservation system. For example, permits to camp in Yosemite National Park can be reserved through a commercial booking and reservation service. An alternative is to issue permits to visitors on a first-come, first-served basis when they arrive at the area. When capacity is reached, additional visitors must be turned away. When demand for permits is many times greater than the number available, lotteries are sometimes used to determine who gets a permit. This is a common means of allocating permits for river trips. People desiring permits submit an application, noting their preferred dates for departure. Then, applications are picked randomly, up to the maximum allowable number, and those parties selected are issued permits. By attaching a fee to a permit or requiring some minimum level of skill or knowledge before qualifying for a permit, demand can be reduced. These can also be a means of rationing (limiting) use.

Each of these methods has certain advantages and disadvantages. Some benefit certain users and are costly to others. Costs to administer are variable, as is the acceptability of the method to visitors. Stankey and Baden (1977) evaluated the pros and cons of each of these means of limiting use. Although they were specifically concerned with rationing wilderness use, their conclusions also apply to other wildland recreation areas. Table 1 summarizes their conclusions. Stankey and Baden (1977) advance five general guidelines to consider in limiting use:

1. Start with an accurate base of knowledge about use, users, and impacts.
2. Reduce use levels only when less restrictive measures are unlikely to solve the problem.
3. Combine rationing techniques (e.g., issue half of the permits through advance reservation and half first-come, first-served on arrival) to minimize and equalize costs to users and administrators.
4. Establish a system that tends to allocate permits to those people who place the highest value on the permit.
5. Monitor the use limitation program to make sure it is solving problems and is fair.

TABLE 1. Evaluation of Impacts and Consequences of Alternative Systems for Rationing Use

		Evaluation Criteria		
Rationing System	Clientele Group Benefited by System	Clientele Group Adversely Affected by System	Experience to Date with Use of System in Wilderness	Acceptability of System to Wilderness Users
Request (Reservation)	Those able and/or willing to plan ahead; i.e., persons with structured life-styles.	Those unable or unwilling to plan ahead; e.g., persons with occupations that do not permit long-range planning, such as many professionals.	Main type of rationing system used in both National Forest and National Park wilderness.	Generally high. Good acceptance in areas where used. Seen as best way to ration by users in areas not currently rationed.
Lottery (Chance)	No one identifiable group benefited. Those who examine probabilities of success at different areas have better chance.	No one identifiable group discriminated against. Can discriminate against the unsuccessful applicant to whom wilderness is very important.	None. However, is a common method for allocating big-game hunting permits.	Low.

(continued)

TABLE 1. (*Continued*)

		Evaluation Criteria		
Rationing System	Clientele Group Benefited by System	Clientele Group Adversely Affected by System	Experience to Date with Use of System in Wilderness	Acceptability of System to Wilderness Users
Queuing (First-come first-served)	Those with low opportunity cost for their time (e.g., unemployed). Also favors users who live nearby.	Those persons with high opportunity cost of time. Also those persons who live some distance from areas. The cost of time is not recovered by anyone.	Used in conjunction with reservation system in San Jacinto Wilderness. Also used in some National Park wildernesses.	Low to moderate.
Pricing (Fee)	Those able or willing to pay entry costs.	Those unwilling or unable to pay entry costs.	None.	Low to moderate.
Merit (Skill and knowledge)	Those able or willing to invest time and effort to meet requirements.	Those unable or unwilling to invest time and effort to meet requirements.	None. Merit is used to allocate use for some related activities such as river running.	Not clearly known. Could vary considerably depending on level of training required to attain necessary proficiency and knowledge level.

		Evaluation Criteria		
	Difficulty for Administrators	Efficiency—Extent to Which System Can Minimize Problems of Suboptimization	Principal Way in Which Use Impact Is Controlled	How System Affects User Behavior
Request (Reservation)	Moderately difficult. Requires extra staffing, expanded hours. Record keeping can be substantial.	Low to moderate. Under utilization can occur because of "no shows," thus denying entry to others. Allocation of permits to applicants has little relationship to value of the experience as judged by the applicant.	Reducing visitor numbers. Controlling distribution of use in space and time by varying number of permits available at different trailheads or at different times.	Affects both spatial and temporal behavior.
Lottery (Chance)	Difficult to moderately difficult. Allocating permits over an entire use season could be very cumbersome.	Low. Because permits are assigned randomly, persons who place little value on wilderness stand equal chance of gaining entry as those who place high value on opportunity.	Reducing visitor numbers. Controlling distribution of use in space and time by number of permits available at different places or times, thus varying probability of success.	Affects both spatial and temporal behavior.

(continued)

TABLE 1. (Continued)

	Evaluation Criteria			
	Difficulty for Administrators	Efficiency—Extent to Which System Can Minimize Problems of Suboptimization	Principal Way in Which Use Impact Is Controlled	How System Affects User Behavior
Queuing (First-come first-served)	Low to moderate difficulty. Could require development of facilities to support visitors waiting in line.	Moderate. Because system rations primarily through a cost of time, it requires some measure of worth by participants.	Reducing visitor numbers. Controlling distribution of use in space and time by number of persons permitted to enter at different places or times.	Affects both spatial and temporal behavior. User must consider cost of time of waiting in line.
Pricing (Fee)	Moderate difficulty. Possibly some legal questions about imposing a fee for wilderness entry.	Moderate to high. Imposing a fee requires user to judge worth of experience against costs. Uncertain as to how well use could be "fine tuned" with price.	Reducing visitor numbers. Controlling distribution of use in space and time by using differential prices.	Affects both temporal and spatial behavior. User must consider cost in dollars.
Merit (Skill and knowledge)	Difficult to moderately difficult. Initial investments to establish licensing program could be substantial.	Moderate to high. Requires users to make expenditures of time and effort (maybe dollars) to gain entry.	Some reduction in numbers as well as shifts in time and space. Major reduction in per capita impact.	Affects style of user's behavior.

Source: Stankey and Baden 1977.

Both the type of use being limited and where the limitations are applied can vary. In many places overnight use is limited but day use is not. In two-thirds of the national parks that limit backcountry use, limits apply only to overnight users (Marion, Roggenbuck, and Manning 1993). This may be justifiable, from an ecological standpoint, where campsite impacts present problems but trail impacts do not. Campsite impacts are caused almost entirely by overnight users, whereas trail impacts are caused by both overnight and day users. It is also common to limit permits to float rivers but allow unlimited backpacking in the same area. This is a result of high demand for limited space along the river corridor and low demand elsewhere.

In large nonroaded areas there is an important difference between (1) programs that limit entry to an area but permit free travel once entry has been obtained and (2) programs that issue a limited number of permits for specific campsites or zones within the area. In this latter case free and spontaneous movement within the area is curtailed because visitors are required to stick to itineraries they agree to before entering the area.

Entry quotas are not as efficient as fixed itineraries in controlling use levels at popular interior locations. Use levels in the interior are affected both by how many people enter the area and by the routes they travel and the places where they choose to camp within the area. Within limits, however, use distribution patterns are consistent and predictable. Therefore, it is possible to devise trailhead quotas that keep use levels at interior locations close to desired levels (van Wagtendonk and Coho 1986). Although less efficient, this means of rationing has the advantage of allowing visitors free choice to move about as they please and change their routes and activities in response to circumstances they encounter (such as blisters, bad weather, or new destinations that they see on a map or from some viewpoint).

These freedoms are taken away where visitors are required to stick to fixed itineraries (where limited permits are issued for either specific campsites or zones). Currently, this is a common practice in the backcountry of some of the popular national parks, such as Glacier, Yellowstone, Rocky Mountain, Great Smoky Mountains, and Mt. Rainier. Visitors to these parks must state where they are going to camp every night they are in the backcountry. Assuming there are openings available, they are issued a permit to camp in the specific places they have reserved. There is no opportunity, legally, to change their minds even if they overestimated their abilities or if bad weather sets in. With such a program, administrative costs climb because rangers must patrol more widely to make certain that visitors are keeping to their itineraries. At Grand Canyon National Park, about one-half of all parties deviate from their itineraries and, therefore, are subject to citation (Stewart 1989).

Both increased administrative costs and loss of visitor freedom are accepted for an increase in efficiency. Because use distribution is more tightly controlled at the interior locations of concern, there is less chance that desired use levels will be exceeded. In most situations, however, carrying capacities are sufficiently arbitrary to make this difference in level of efficiency of little importance. Moreover, the low level of compliance suggests that the perception of a tight control on use distribution is illusory. Trailhead entry quotas may be equally effective, simpler to implement, and less burdensome to visitors (Stewart 1989).

Several studies have asked visitors for their opinions about the acceptability of various use limitation techniques, particularly in wilderness and on white-water rivers. Most visitors accept use limits if they are necessary to prevent overuse. In San Jacinto and San Gorgonio Wildernesses in California, even parties that did not receive permits and were denied access to the area generally thought the use limits were appropriate (Stankey 1979). Visitors generally prefer rationing techniques with which they are familiar. Lottery is looked upon unfavorably in most wildernesses (Stankey and Baden 1977), but it is acceptable on rivers such as the Middle Fork of the Salmon where it has been used successfully for many years (McCool and Utter 1981). Fixed itineraries are one of the most disliked of all management alternatives in wildernesses without permit systems (Lucas 1980). At Grand Canyon National Park, however, less than 10 percent of visitors had negative feelings about the existing fixed itinerary system (Stewart 1989).

Finally, managers and users may differ in their opinions about alternative rationing techniques. In a study of river users and managers, Wilke (1991) found that users were more accepting of reservation and merit systems than managers. Managers favored a lottery system. Neither group favored a system based on pricing.

Permits can be used for purposes other than to limit use. They can provide valuable information about users. For example, permits used in Forest Service Wilderness collect data on size of the group, where the party leader lives, main method of travel, date of entry and exit, and location of entry and exit. It is also possible to obtain a rough idea of the party's travel route, although there is no obligation to stick to this itinerary.

Such information can be useful in developing management programs suited to a particular clientele. Permits also provide a means of establishing contact with the user in order to either pass along information or clearly state regulations in force in the area. They can be used for safety purposes as well. If members of a party get lost, a permit can alert managers to their predicament and help locate them. However, this potential use of permits or a registration system is often not used to advantage because managers do not check for returned permits. This should probably be made clear to visitors who may think they will be rescued if they do not come out by a certain date.

Visitors are generally receptive to nonrationed permits if they are convenient to obtain. For example, in nine wilderness and roadless areas in Montana and California, no more than 15 percent of users found mandatory registration to be undesirable (Lucas 1980). However, compliance with permit systems is highly variable. Compliance is greatest when permits are mandatory and easy to obtain. Self-issued permits at trailheads are a convenient alternative to requiring visitors to come to agency offices during specific hours (Fig. 1). Hendee, Stankey, and Lucas (1990) report compliance rates of 91 to 95 percent with self-issued permits in wilderness.

LENGTH OF STAY LIMITS

Use levels can also be reduced by limiting the amount of time visitors can spend in the area. Length of stay limits have been placed on time spent both in the entire recreation area and at specific sites within the area. Areawide limits are unlikely to have

FIGURE 1. Visitors can obtain a free but mandatory permit at this trailhead station. Information on low-impact use techniques, visitor safety concerns, rules, and regulations can be communicated to the visitor at the same time. (*Photo*: R. C. Lucas.)

any effect on site impacts. Such limits are probably justified when there is heavy demand for a limited amount of use. More groups can be accommodated—fewer are denied access—if stays are short. In the heavily used Rae Lakes basin in Kings Canyon National Park, California, a one-day-stay limit allowed more people to visit the area, and total use and impact declined (Parsons 1983).

Length of stay limits for specific sites are also likely to have little effect on impact levels if those specific sites are popular. It makes little difference whether one party uses a site for seven days or if seven parties use it for one day. The main effect of such a limit is to keep anyone from "homesteading" a particular site. If demand for a specific site is high, a length of stay limit will allow more parties to use the site. These reasons, to prohibit homesteading and to allow access to more parties, are probably the most common ones for length of stay limits, particularly in more highly developed recreation areas.

In terms of managing ecological impacts, the most important place to impose length of stay limits is in lightly used places, particularly wilderness areas. In places where dispersal is the policy—to avoid substantial impact on all sites—a long stay in one place can cause unacceptable impact. Where dispersal is practiced, length of stay limits should be no more than a night or two at individual sites. No areawide limits are needed, however, and there should be no need to impose a regulation. Dispersal will be effective only if visitors are highly conscientious about minimizing impact.

Keeping their stays at individual sites short should be one of the techniques that all conscientious campers use to keep their impact to a minimum.

DISPERSAL OF USE

The high level of use concentration in popular parts of dispersed use areas is often blamed for ecological impact problems. For example, in a survey of wilderness managers, Washburne and Cole (1983) inquired about their most significant problem. The most frequent response was "local resource degradation and lack of solitude as a result of concentrated use." The most frequently mentioned "most effective" management technique for dealing with significant problems was personal contact with visitors, leading to increased use dispersal. Dispersal, however, can mean different things to different people. Think about camping, for example. Dispersal could involve (1) spreading people out on the same number of campsites but with greater distance between parties, (2) spreading people out on more sites with or without increasing the distance between parties, or (3) spreading people out in time (increasing off-season use) with or without changing spatial distribution. Each of these types of dispersal has different implications for management of ecological impacts. The appropriateness of each as a means of reducing crowding problems may also be very different from their appropriateness as a means of reducing impact.

Spreading parties out so that they are generally farther apart, but using the same number of recreation sites, will have little positive or negative effect on soils, vegetation, or water (Fig. 2). As long as the number of places being impacted remains constant, the distance between impacted sites is irrelevant. The major negative ecological

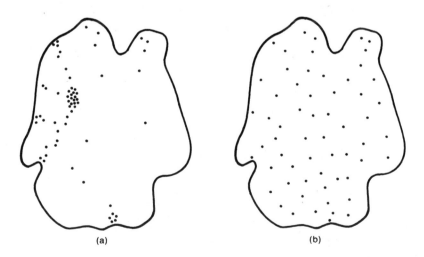

(a)   (b)

FIGURE 2. In (a) use is concentrated in a small part of the recreation area. Each dot represents a camped party. In (b) use dispersal has increased the distance between sites without changing the number of sites. (*Source*: D. N. Cole.)

impact associated with this type of dispersal is a likely increase in wildlife disturbance. Certain animals (e.g., grizzly bear, elk, bighorn sheep) retreat to parts of a recreation area where contact with people is infrequent. As more of these safe retreats become frequently used, these wildlife species will have less "safe" habitat, and their populations are likely to suffer. The major advantage to this type of use dispersal is to decrease social crowding at places where parties tend to cluster together. Even on the social side, dispersal can have the negative effect of increasing crowding in infrequently used places currently sought out by parties wanting to experience high levels of solitude.

This type of dispersal can be practiced at many scales. Managers can attempt to spread use out over all parts of a recreation area. This is the scale of dispersal most likely to cause problems with wildlife disturbance and loss of high levels of solitude. These two problems are not likely to be severe if use is dispersed on a local level rather than throughout large areas. For example, rather than have numerous sites clustered at one end of a lake, managers might disperse sites around the entire lake. This would reduce crowding, and as long as there was no attempt to disperse use to other lakes or other parts of the area not receiving increased use, it would not negatively impact wildlife or high levels of solitude. In general, then, increasing the distance between parties is a positive action, particularly in large wilderness-type areas, if done on a localized scale. On an areawide scale it has some potentially negative consequences.

When spreading out use entails an increase in the number of sites (and this is probably the most common form of use dispersal), the pros and cons become more complex and difficult to evaluate (Fig. 3). The appropriateness of this type of dispersal depends on amount of use, type of use, user behavior, and resistance of the

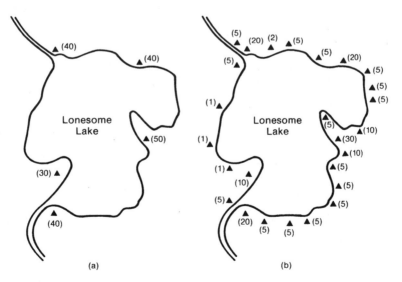

FIGURE 3. In (a) use at Lonesome Lake is concentrated on 5 campsites. The number in parentheses is the nights per year that the site is used. In (b) the same amount of use has been dispersed over 26 campsites. (*Source*: D. N. Cole.)

environment. Spreading out use over more sites is most likely to reduce impact in resistant environments, where use levels are low and the type of use and behavior of most users have little potential for inflicting damage. It is likely to be a disaster in popular areas frequented by large parties, horse parties, or parties that know little about low-impact camping, particularly if the area is fragile. Let's explore why this is so.

As is so often the case, these management implications reflect the nature of the relationship between amount of use and amount of impact. The idea behind this type of use dispersal is to reduce use to levels low enough so that impacts are negligible. From the use-impact relationship we know that use levels must be very low before a reduction in amount of use is likely to substantially reduce impact. We also know that to reduce use on one site, use must be increased on other sites. Moreover, increased use of lightly used or unused sites leads to rapid increases in impact.

Let's use a study of lakeside campsites in subalpine forests in the Eagle Cap Wilderness as a case in point (Cole 1982a). This is a relatively fragile environment; growing seasons are short, and the vegetation is easily destroyed by trampling. The study examined the condition of campsites receiving three levels of use. An impact rating based on camp area and impact to trees, ground cover vegetation, and soil was calculated for each site. Unused sites had a rating of 1.0, and the most heavily impacted sites had a rating of 3.0. This can be compared with the mean ratings of 1.6 for low-use sites, used a few times per year; 2.0 for moderate-use sites, used 10 to 20 times per year; and 2.1 for high-use sites, used 25 to 50 times per year.

To evaluate the desirability of dispersing use in this area, let's assume we need to accommodate 4000 parties around these lakes over the 2- to 3-month summer season. The available options would be to have fewer than 100 high-use sites, more than 250 moderate-use sites, or about 2000 low-use sites. Given the great difference in number of sites and relatively small difference in impact rating—even low-use sites are more than one-half as impacted as high-use sites—it seems most reasonable to concentrate use on the 100 high-use sites.

The consequence of attempting to spread use over a large number of campsites in an area with heavy use was documented in the Eagle Cap Wilderness. More than 220 campsites were found in a 325-acre area around two popular lakes (Cole 1982b). Over one-half of these sites had lost more than 25 percent of their vegetation cover, and most were in sight of the trail. Although this still represents disturbance of only 1.3 percent of this popular area, one has the perception that impact is everywhere. Moreover, there is no need for so many sites. The average number of parties using the area is about 10 per night, with use perhaps several times as high on peak-use nights. Management policy at the time of the study was to ask people not to camp on highly impacted sites, that is, to spread out over more sites. By doing the opposite, concentrating use on a few selected sites, disturbance could be confined to perhaps one-fifth of these sites, effectively reducing impact by about 80 percent. Most parties prefer using the more highly impacted sites anyway.

How well would spreading out use over a large number of campsites work in a lightly used area? What if we had to accommodate only 30 parties per year? One option would be to concentrate all that use on one high-use, high-impact site. However, another option would be to spread this use over 30 or more sites. If more than 30 potential campsites were available, some sites would not have to be used even once per year. We do not have data from the Eagle Cap study to predict the impact associated with just one night of use per year. There are many resistant sites, however, where such low use levels would cause essentially no impact. This is particularly true if the party's potential for inflicting damage is low (e.g., if the party is small, travels on foot, and is knowledgeable about low-impact camping). Therefore, spreading use over more sites makes good sense under conditions of low-use, resistant environments and low-impact users.

The implications of this type of management apply primarily to vegetation and soil impact on trails and campsites, particularly in large areas. Water and wildlife are probably less affected by how frequently individual sites are used. Some animals are highly disturbed only on high-use sites. In Yosemite National Park, for example, problems with black bears are much more pronounced in high-use areas (Keay and van Wagtendonk 1983). Bear problems are aggravated by concentrating use on a few sites. However, smaller animals are likely to be more adversely affected by the creation of many moderately impacted sites than a few highly impacted sites. On the social side, this type of dispersal will have no effect on that aspect of crowding related to how frequently recreationists meet other people. It will mean that recreationists see more impacted sites.

Generally, then, dispersal of use among many sites by promoting use of unused or lightly used trails, campsites, or places is likely to substantially increase impact in these places, with little compensatory improvement in the condition of the more popular places, which were the original problems. This type of dispersal typically increases impact proliferation, the primary means by which recreation impacts increase in many areas (Cole 1993). The exception to this generalization occurs in low-use areas where dispersal of use, combined with management of where people camp (on very lightly used, resistant sites) and user behavior, can help maintain low levels of impact.

The third type of dispersal, spreading use over a longer use season, can certainly be beneficial in terms of reducing crowding. However, the ecological effects are, again, complex. Moving use from summer to spring or fall often constitutes moving use to a season when the environment is more fragile. Higher precipitation and snowmelt saturate the soil with water, making it more prone to compaction and erosion. Plants may be more vulnerable in spring when they are initiating growth or in fall when woody plant parts are brittle and easily broken. Wildlife may be vulnerable in spring when they are regaining strength after the winter or in fall when they are getting ready for the winter. Such effects differ greatly from area to area, but they ought to be considered before off-season use is promoted.

In sum, use dispersal is an action that has diverse aspects and implications. It is seldom the panacea that it has sometimes been considered. Even with regard to reducing crowding, it has certain drawbacks. The ecological disadvantages are usually more pronounced. However, there are situations in which dispersal can be useful. The key is to use it at the scale and in the places where it will be beneficial. It is most beneficial when applied to localized areas or in places where use levels are low. Usually it will have to be supported with programs designed to manage where and how people engage in recreational activities. The effects of the program should also be monitored, because the potential for merely spreading problems around is high.

Where dispersal is desired, it can be accomplished in either a regulatory or a manipulative manner. Regulatory means are comparable to those employed to limit amount of use. Quotas can be established for popular trails, campsites, or zones; when these places are full, additional users must go elsewhere. This technique can be used to increase the distance between parties and/or to avoid concentrated use at certain locations. Of these methods, the highest level of control can be achieved by requiring use of designated dispersed campsites, as is done in the backcountry of Yellowstone National Park. In such a system, visitors must keep to a fixed itinerary, camping at designated campsites, each of which is located a considerable distance from all other sites. In many of the national parks, visitors are required to camp in designated sites. Quotas are set for campsites, but the campsites are clustered in a group. This means that use is locally concentrated but dispersed throughout the park. For reasons previously discussed, this is the worst of both worlds; campsite solitude is lacking, and all parts of the park receive impact. This is often done to make it easier to provide facilities such as toilets.

Spreading use over more sites can be accomplished by establishing use quotas for individual campsites (closing sites to camping after they have been used a certain number of nights) or by requiring that visitors camp on sites that are not highly impacted. One of the few examples of the latter approach is provided by the wilderness management program adopted at Shenandoah National Park, Virginia, in the early 1970s. Groups were required to camp out of sight of any trail or of signs set up in areas where no camping was allowed. They also were to spend no more than two consecutive nights in a single location. Wherever substantial impact started to show, the campsite was posted as a "no camping" area and allowed to recover. This spread use over a large number of sites. An evaluation of campsites in the early 1990s (Williams and Marion 1995) suggested that the dispersal policy had not been very effective in limiting campsite impact. More than 700 campsites were found and one-third of these sites exhibited marked loss of vegetation and soil exposure. Williams and Marion (1995) suggest that a use concentration strategy would be more effective than a dispersal strategy in the more popular locations in the park. They recommend that the dispersal strategy be followed only in portions of the park where use levels are so low that campsites are virtually nonexistent.

Quotas can also be used to spread visitation over time. If no permits are available during popular use seasons, visitors have little alternative but to go during the off-season. Many private parties float the Colorado River through Grand Canyon during the winter months when permits are much easier to obtain than they are during the summer months.

Dispersal can also be accomplished through information and persuasion. This management style is particularly common in Forest Service wilderness areas where freedom and spontaneity are valued highly. Of these, information is preferable to persuasion because it is more subtle and the visitor does not feel pressured to conform, perhaps against his will, to the desires of the manager. Information can be presented

FIGURE 4. Personal contact by rangers is a particularly effective means of providing visitors with information. (*Photo*: R. C. Lucas.)

in brochures, on signs, or through personal contact (Fig. 4). Use redistribution will be most effective if information is provided early in the trip or route-planning process (Roggenbuck 1992). By the time visitors reach the area, it is usually too late to change their minds about where they want to go. This means that written material will usually be the primary informational medium, except in cases where people call and request information.

Visitors also appear to want more information than simply the amount of use that different places receive. In several studies, provision of information on amount of use in different places was ineffective in redistributing use (Lucas 1981). Krumpe and Brown (1982) developed an innovative tool that was successful in redistributing use in Yellowstone National Park. They developed a decision tree (Fig. 5) that permitted visitors to match their preferences for different types of trips with the conditions they were likely to encounter on various trails. This technique redistributed 23 percent of all use from more popular areas to these selected trails.

User-friendly microcomputer programs can be particularly effective means of redistributing use. In Rocky Mountain National Park, for example, 60 percent of the backcountry hiking groups that accessed information from a computer about 29 trails selected one of those trails. This can be compared with the 38 percent of groups that selected one of those trails when information was provided in a brochure and just 17 percent of groups that selected one of those trails when no information was provided (Huffman and Williams 1987).

Advertising the attractiveness of winter in the parks has been effective in increasing off-season use of many national parks. In fact, this campaign has been so successful that some parks—like Yellowstone National Park—are now struggling

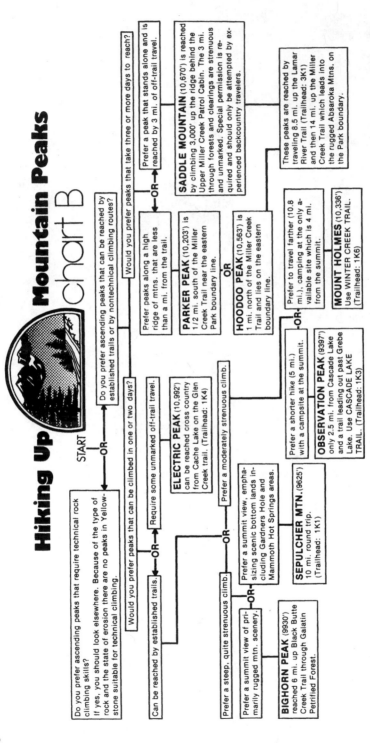

FIGURE 5. This portion of the decision tree for selecting trails in Yellowstone National Park illustrates how such a device helps visitors select trips more likely to match their preferences. (*Source:* Krumpe and Brown 1982. Reprinted with permission.)

to deal with the problems created by heavy winter use. An appeal based entirely on the low use in winter would probably have been less effective. Although providing such information is promising, managers must avoid providing too much information and taking away the sense of discovery and exploration that is important to many recreationists. They must also be cautious about providing only selected information and, of course, should never provide false information.

Signs and personal contact, means of providing information once the visitor enters the area, are most likely to affect local dispersal of use. Utilizing information, for example, Roggenbuck and Berrier (1981) were able to reduce the number of parties that clustered on popular campsites in Shining Rock Gap in Shining Rock Wilderness, North Carolina. The information provided told of the crowded and impacted conditions at the Gap, as well as trail and campsite conditions in some nearby (within 1 mi) alternative camping areas. The number of parties camping at the Gap dropped from 62 per weekend (when no information was provided) to 44 (when information was on a brochure) to 33 (when both a brochure and personal contact with a ranger were used). For experienced hikers the brochure was adequate to redistribute use; for novices personal contact was more effective. Most research suggests that visitors with little previous experience or park knowledge are most likely to be influenced by information. Also, a combination of impersonal messages and personal contact is likely to be more effective than an impersonal message alone (Roggenbuck 1992).

CONCENTRATION OF USE

Concentrating use is the opposite of use dispersal. As with dispersal, it can operate in a variety of ways. Distances between parties can be reduced without changing the number of sites; use can be concentrated on fewer sites; or use can be more concentrated in time. The first and third of these options may serve to reduce impact on wildlife in certain situations. Generally, however, they entail high costs to visitors, particularly in increased crowding, and are unlikely to substantially reduce impacts. The most common action taken is to concentrate use on as few campsites and as small a proportion of each campsite as possible.

Spatial concentration of use is one of the premier principles of managing developed recreation areas. Spatial concentration can be applied at several scales. For example, campers are usually required to camp on developed campsites rather than in some undisturbed area of their choice. Within the designated campsite, tent pads are commonly provided and campers are encouraged to set up their tents on these pads. Both of these actions are variations on the use concentration strategy. Site management techniques intended to confine use to a small proportion of each campsite will be described in Chapter 13.

As was discussed under dispersal of use, use concentration can be appropriate even in large wilderness areas, particularly in places that are heavily used, where it is likely to be the only means of keeping impact from proliferating widely. Use dispersal can be used to maintain very lightly impacted areas, but in popular places there is little alternative to use concentration. Trail construction is a good example of use concentration that serves to avoid the creation of numerous user-created trails crisscrossing the landscape. To provide diversity, large portions of wilderness should remain trailless. Where use is consistent, however, trails have to be built, to provide easier access certainly, but also to avoid development of multiple user-created trail systems. Keeping people on trails and preventing them from cutting switchbacks or walking on adjacent braided trails are other examples of concentrating trail use to avoid resource damage.

Concentration of use is particularly important to campsite management. Thornburgh (1986), for example, has monitored campsite impacts in several backcountry areas in the North Cascades of Washington for decades. Over the years many different techniques have been implemented to control impacts. He reports that the only successful approach has been a use concentration strategy—the "Designated Campsite" system.

Concentration can be accomplished either through regulation or persuasion. The regulatory option is to allow camping only on designated sites. The persuasive option is to ask visitors to use only existing sites. Regulation is seldom necessary because most visitors prefer camping on sites that are already well used anyway (Cole 1982b). If education does not work, a regulation can be imposed. If illegal sites continue to develop, the only option may be to reduce use levels.

Once a use concentration strategy is implemented successfully, it may be possible to reduce the number of sites. Certain sites can be closed—preferably those that are poorly located or highly damaged. Once use of these sites is eliminated, they may have to be actively rehabilitated. This will shorten the period that they will need to be identified with "no camping" signs or whatever other technique is used to keep people off. More detail on such site management techniques is provided in the next chapter.

Use concentration becomes increasingly important as the potential for users to inflict damage increases. Therefore, it is a particularly important strategy for managing recreational stock and off-road vehicles. In many places these uses are prohibited on certain trails or in certain areas. In Sequoia and Kings Canyon National Parks, for example, stock are prohibited in places that have never received regular stock use (McClaran 1989). Alternatively, these uses can be allowed only in certain areas established specifically for their use. This is a common strategy for use of off-road vehicles (Fig. 6). In Yellowstone National Park, snowmobiles are allowed only on roads. In the Land Between the Lakes area administered by the Tennessee Valley Authority, off-road vehicle use is prohibited except in the specially designated 2350-acre Turkey Bay Off-Road Vehicle Area, where relatively unrestricted vehicle use is allowed.

RESTRICTIONS ON TYPE OF USE

Another management option is to separate different types of users or to prohibit particularly destructive users from using parts of the area. Zoning is a common means of accounting for differences in the impact caused by different modes of travel. The most likely actions to be taken are to create zones in which all use, overnight use, or use by parties with stock or motorized vehicles is prohibited (Fig. 7). National forests,

FIGURE 6. Concentrated motorcycle use in California has denuded this area of vegetation and eroded the bedrock. (*Photo*: D. N. Cole.)

FIGURE 7. Closing areas to certain types of users and uses is a common management action. In the Rattlesnake National Recreation Area, Montana, hiking, horse riding, and bicycling are allowed; motorcycling is prohibited, as are shooting and camping within three miles of the trailhead. (*Photo*: D. N. Cole.)

being divided into wilderness and nonwilderness areas, are already zoned in relation to motor vehicles; all motorized traffic (with a few exceptions) is prohibited in wilderness. Even outside wilderness, motorized vehicles are excluded from some areas for either social or ecological reasons. Prohibitions on motorized use are a common means of reducing wildlife disturbance and deterioration of water quality. Protection of wildlife and of water quality are also the most common justification for excluding either all use or overnight use. Examples include areas that are municipal watersheds and places where encounters with grizzly bears have been a problem.

Excluding stock from certain zones can produce numerous benefits. Hikers who dislike encountering stock are provided with the opportunity of avoiding them if they visit places where stock are prohibited. Selected areas are spared the added impact of stock use, and trail construction and maintenance costs are reduced. In Sequoia and Kings Canyon National Parks, stock use is prohibited in a series of meadows that provide representative examples of pristine meadow ecosystems (McClaran 1989). In Glacier National Park, Montana, stock use is allowed only on certain trails and in certain campsites.

Another option is to not allow certain types of use or behaviors anywhere in the recreation area. For example, stock use is prohibited in almost 40 percent of national park wildernesses (McClaran and Cole 1993). Of those wildernesses that allow stock use, 55 percent require that feed be packed in and 73 percent prohibit tying stock to trees. Other common regulations include prohibitions on campfires, littering, and disturbing vegetation or human artifacts. On white-water rivers, visitors are often required to carry a fire pan (to minimize campfire impacts) and a portable toilet (to pack out human waste).

The important concern with zoning and outright prohibitions of certain uses is that opportunities are not unfairly denied to legitimate users. All areas cannot provide opportunities for all users. Managers should cater to those users most appropriate in their area, basing appropriateness to some extent on regional opportunities for specific uses. For example, a local prohibition on motor vehicles is easier to justify if motorized recreation opportunities are generally available in the region.

GROUP SIZE LIMITS

A limit on maximum group size is a common but controversial restriction on type of use. Common sense and a little research indicates that large groups have the potential to cause more impact than small groups—both on other visitors and on the environment. In a number of studies, visitors indicate that a given number of encounters with large groups is likely to have a more negative effect on their experience than the same number of encounters with small groups. However, if group sizes are reduced, the number of small groups will increase, which will likely increase the number of encounters between groups. Stankey (1973) asked wilderness visitors about this trade-off between encounters and group size, inquiring about their preference for seeing one large group of 30 per day or ten small groups of 3 per day. In three of the four areas he studied, they preferred more encounters with small groups. Moreover, reducing group size may not have much effect on encounter rates because large groups are so rare. In the Desolation Wilderness in California, for example, only 7 percent of overnight visitors were in groups larger than 6 (Cole, Watson, and Roggenbuck 1995). Breaking a few large groups into small groups would have little effect on the total number of groups. This suggests that the imposition of limits on group size should usually improve social conditions in recreation areas.

Group size can influence amount of ecological impact in two ways. First, if large groups camp as a single unit, they will occupy and impact a larger area than a small group (Fig. 8). In the Bob Marshall Wilderness in Montana, outfitter campsites—which cater to large horsepacker groups—were 10 times larger on average than camps used primarily by private (typically smaller) horsepacker groups (Cole 1983). Second, a large group camping as one unit can impact an undisturbed site more rapidly than a small group, simply because there are more feet to trample soil and vegetation. This consideration is more critical for groups traveling off-trail and in relatively pristine places than for groups traveling through places with plenty of established trails and campsites.

A few studies suggest that certain impacts might increase on a per capita basis as group size decreases. Per capita wood consumption in campfires typically increases as group size decreases (Davilla 1979), and impacts on wildlife from infrequent encounters with large groups may be less severe than more frequent encounters with

FIGURE 8. By spreading out over a large area, this large party has created an unusually large area of impact. (*Photo*: U.S. Forest Service.)

smaller groups. However, the rarity of large groups makes these arguments less compelling. The most significant costs of group size limits are likely to be (1) restrictions on access for the small minority who prefer or need to visit wilderness in larger groups and (2) reductions in the quality of wilderness experiences facilitated within larger groups. Relatively few wilderness visitors would be affected by group size limits as stringent as a maximum group size of 6. However, for those affected, costs would be pronounced. Costs may be particularly severe for commercial outfitters. Opportunities for experiential education and other learning that is dependent on substantial group interaction may also be severely restricted by stringent group size limits. Unfortunately, we know little about the relationship between group size and the benefits that accrue from these experiences.

Most wilderness visitors—about three-quarters of those surveyed in the Desolation Wilderness—support limits on group size (Cole, Watson and Roggenbuck 1995). Moreover, visitors who support limits think those limits should be quite low. More than three-quarters of the supporters of group size limits in the Desolation thought the limit should be no more than 10 people. Similar results have been reported elsewhere. However, managers should interpret this information carefully. The vast majority of wilderness visitors choose to visit wilderness in groups of 2, 3, or 4 people, and they don't like encountering large groups. They typically advocate prohibiting groups that are much larger than their own group. If this action were taken, the majority group would reap all the benefits and pay none of the costs. All costs would accrue to the minority user—the visitor preferring to come in large groups.

Managers are faced with several difficult decisions as they confront the issue of group size limits. Should they listen only to the majority (who have everything to gain and nothing to lose from group size limits), or should they try to provide some restricted opportunities for the minority user too? What should those limits be—6, 10, 20, or 30? And what about limits on groups that choose to bring pack stock as well?

Clearly, there are costs and benefits to group size limits. Benefits are likely to be most pronounced in relatively pristine areas. A single large group traveling off-trail can leave incipient trails and campsites that a small group would not produce. Off-trail hikers are often particularly sensitive to encounters with large groups. This suggests that group size limits are particularly important in more pristine environments. To be effective, however, limits should be quite low, much lower than the common limits of 15 to 25 persons per party in wilderness (Washburne and Cole 1983; Marion, Roggenbuck, and Manning 1993).

Arguments for low limits on group size are less compelling in popular, highly impacted locations. Large impacted campsites are usually available to accommodate fairly big groups. If they are careful, even large groups can use these sites and cause little additional impact. Grand Canyon National Park, for example, has designated a number of special large-group sites in more popular parts of the backcountry. If large groups stay on established trails, there is little concern about creating new impacts.

Differential group size limits may be one means to (1) keep group size limits low enough to be meaningful in more pristine portions of a recreation area and (2) meet the needs of both majority and minority users. In Yosemite National Park, for example, maximum group size is 25 in trailed areas and 8 off-trail.

A final concern is how to accommodate pack animals in group size limits. If the reason for group size limits is to limit the potential impact of each group, size limits for pack groups should be much lower than for hikers. This follows from the fact that horses cause more impact than hikers (DeLuca, Patterson, Freimund, and Cole in press). Others argue that the regulation should treat stock users and hikers equitably in terms of ease of access and simply limit the number of humans. Therefore, if 15 humans are allowed, those 15 people should be allowed to bring along the 25 pack animals needed to support them if they want to. Both sides of this argument have some merit, suggesting the value of a compromise position. One reasonable compromise, implemented in a few places, is to limit the total number of bodies—human and animal. With a limit of 15, there can be 15 humans, 6 humans and 9 head of stock, or any other combination that adds to 15. Groups with stock will still typically cause more impact than those without stock, but impacts will be less than in situations where there are separate limits for humans and animals.

LOW IMPACT EDUCATION

Throughout this discussion we have frequently referred to the need to support certain actions with a strong educational program. Low impact education is one of the real keys to reducing impact in all recreation areas, from the most primitive to the most developed. It is not a panacea; it will not solve all problems. However, without educated and caring users, impact management will remain primarily reactionary in nature. Managers will seldom be able to get beyond treating symptoms to deal with the cause of problems. Education is the basic foundation on which to build a complete management program.

In our typology of visitor actions in Chapter 10, we distinguished between illegal, careless, unskilled, and uninformed actions and unavoidable impacts. Education can alleviate impact problems caused by the first four types of action; other steps are needed to control unavoidable impacts. On campsites it should be possible, through education, to virtually eliminate damage to trees and pollution of the site with campfire ashes, food remains, soap, and other waste products. On raft trips through the Grand Canyon, collection of firewood is not permitted (except during the off-season when driftwood can be collected), all fires must be contained in fire pans that protect the ground, and all ashes, garbage, and human waste must be carried out of the Canyon. Even dishwater is poured through screens into the river, and what does not go through the screen is hauled out. As a result, even beaches that are used almost every night by large parties are not polluted and have little tree damage.

In contrast to some of the avoidable impacts, trampling of vegetation and soil is largely unavoidable. On Grand Canyon beaches, vegetation and soil deterioration is not too serious because most use occurs on barren sand. Trampling does contribute to beach erosion, however (Valentine and Dolan 1979). In less resistant places trampling, even by low-impact users, can severely alter soil and vegetation conditions. In such places the amount and distribution of use must also be managed.

When developing a low impact educational program, wildland recreation managers need to consider both the *content* of educational messages and the *communication media* they will use to disseminate messages.

Message Content

Knowledge about appropriate low-impact techniques has developed slowly over the past few decades, with the accumulation of personal experience and recreation ecology research. Until recently, this information has been widely dispersed and not very consistent. In the late 1980s the situation changed with the compilation of research about low-impact techniques (Cole 1989), the publication of *Soft Paths*—the first popular book devoted entirely to low-impact techniques, now in its second edition (Hampton and Cole 1995), and establishment of the national Leave No Trace (LNT) low impact education program. LNT is a partnership between federal land-managing agencies, nonprofit educational organizations, and the recreation industry. Its mission is "to develop a nationally recognized minimum-impact education system to educate federal land managers and the general public through training, publications, video and electronic webs" (Swain 1996).

With the LNT program, consistency in low impact education has emerged. This consistency is most apparent in the following six principles that are the crux of the LNT program:

1. *Plan ahead and prepare.* Take time to learn about the area you plan to visit so you know what to expect. Travel in small groups and take appropriate equipment. On backcountry trips, particularly, repackage food so that potential trash is reduced. Finally, if traveling in bear country, be prepared and knowledgeable.

2. *Camp and travel on durable surfaces.* This is a complex principle derived to a great extent from recreation ecology principles covered in this book. In popular areas, concentrate use and impact. Stay on established trails and select a campsite that is already well impacted. Select a site that is large enough to accommodate your group. Set up tents and the "kitchen" in places that have already been disturbed. Leave your site clean and attractive so the next group will want to camp there. In remote, relatively pristine places, disperse use and impact. Spread out while hiking, and select a campsite with no evidence of previous use. Try to select travel routes and campsites that are durable. Disperse tents, activities, and traffic routes when camping in a pristine area and naturalize the site when you leave—so the next group that happens by will not recognize it as a campsite. Finally, stay off lightly impacted trails and campsites. Lightly impacted places are in a state of flux. If they continue to be used, they are likely to deteriorate rapidly and substantially. However, if left alone, they usually can restore themselves.

3. *Pack it in, pack it out.* Pack out litter and waste food. Be particularly careful in bear country.

4. *Properly dispose of what you can't pack out.* Dispose of human waste appropriately, in toilet facilities if they are provided or in cat holes at least 200 feet away from water, trails, and campsites. Pack out toilet paper or, at least, bury it. Do all washing away from camp and never directly in streams, lakes, or springs.

5. *Leave what you find.* Never blaze trees, leave flagging, or build rock cairns along trails. Never make trenches around tent sites or build campsite "improvements." Avoid damaging live trees and plants, and leave natural objects and cultural artifacts.

6. *Minimize use of and impact from fires.* Cook on stoves and minimize the use of campfires. If having a fire in a high-use area, use an existing fire ring. Use only dead and downed wood that can be broken by hand. Burn the fire until only ash or small coals are left. Be sure the fire is out and scatter ashes widely, leaving a clean and attractive fire ring. In remote areas, select a durable fire site. Use a fire pan, build the fire on a mound of mineral soil, or build it in a shallow pit in mineral soil. Do not line the fire with rocks. Naturalize the fire site when you leave.

The LNT program recognizes that educational programs have to be tailored to individual places and user groups. Behavior that may be appropriate in one place may be disastrous in another place. This is most obvious in principle 2, "Camp and travel on durable surfaces." Recommended behaviors in popular areas (where use concentration is appropriate) are precisely the opposite of recommended behaviors in remote areas (where use dispersal is appropriate). More subtle differences also exist. For this reason, the LNT program has developed outdoor skill booklets for seven different ecoregions in the United States, as well as for six specialized recreational activities (river floating, horse use, rock climbing, snow camping, caving, and sea kayaking). Outward Bound and the National Outdoor Leadership School are integrating LNT principles into their international programs, where further modification of the techniques will undoubtedly be required.

Effective Communication

Many different media can and have been used in the effort to persuade recreation visitors to adopt recommended low-impact practices. Douchette and Cole (1993) found that six different educational media were being used in more than one-half of the wilderness areas in the country: brochures, personnel at agency offices, maps, signs, personnel in the backcountry, and displays at trailheads. Some of the less commonly used media were computers and commercial periodicals, radio, and television.

Little has been written specifically about the success of attempts to educate recreation users. However, social psychologists have been studying persuasive communication for years. Roggenbuck and Manfredo (1990) drew on this work to describe three conceptual approaches managers can use to persuade recreation visitors.

The first approach, *applied behavior analysis*, seeks to increase the frequency of desired behavior by providing behavioral prompts, manipulating the environment, rewarding appropriate behavior, or punishing inappropriate behavior. An example of this approach is to provide incentives, such as discount coupons from an outdoor equipment store, when visitors use appropriate behavior. The need for continuous contacts with visitors—to keep them behaving appropriately—suggests that this approach contributes little to development of an enduring land ethic. It is probably more appropriate in more developed recreational settings.

The second approach is the *central route to persuasion*. With this approach, carefully constructed messages are transmitted to visitors. Visitors receive and process the messages, accept the advice as making good sense, and change their behavior accordingly. These behavioral changes should continue into the future because they result from and are reinforced by beliefs and attitudes the visitors have internalized. Most wildland education efforts take this approach. The challenge of this approach is daunting, however. For such an approach to be successful, visitors must have high motivation, the ability to process information and accept the arguments in messages, and the skills to respond appropriately. That means educators must spend as much time as possible with the visitor and "they must know their audience, tailor messages to meet the audience at their interest and knowledge level, develop interesting, relevant, and well-supported messages, use media which permits self-pacing of message processing (usually the written word), and manage the situation so that distractions are few and the message reaches the recipient on time" (Roggenbuck and Manfredo 1990, p. 106).

The third approach is the *peripheral route to persuasion*. This approach is characterized by little attention to messages and is common in situations of information overload and excessive distraction. Persuasion, if it occurs, is triggered by something other than the message itself. Often the cue comes from the source of the message— the basketball star wearing the shoes you are compelled to run out and buy. This may be the only approach with much chance of success at noisy visitor centers, at trailheads when visitors are anxious to start their trip, or if recreationists are simply not highly motivated to give their attention to messages. Unfortunately, this approach is unlikely to produce long-term behavior change.

This body of theory suggests that low impact education is a difficult task. The value of this work—beyond dashing some illusions about simply going out and telling people what they should do—is that it points out ways to increase the likelihood of success. Managers should use as many of these approaches as they can. They also should learn more about the variables that increase likelihood of success. Roggenbuck and Manfredo (1990) have distilled the findings of social psychologists on five factors that influence success: timing of the message, message content, recipient characteristics, source characteristics, and characteristics of the communication channel.

Timing is critical in attempting to use behavioral prompts, incentives, or peripheral cues. Prompts (such as a Smoky Bear badge) must be closely associated with a desired outcome (such as leaving a clean camp) for the behavior to be learned. Peripheral cues must be provided at decision points, such as when visitors are deciding what trail to take, whether to use a stove, or whether to camp on a lakeshore. It is easy to achieve proper timing for some decisions, but virtually impossible for others. Timing is less important to the central route to persuasion, but the message must reach visitors in time for them to process and use the information. It is clearly too late to inform visitors about the importance of using stoves when they reach the trailhead.

Message content is important. If managers use the central route to persuasion, the message should provide arguments that are strong, relevant, novel, and simple enough to comprehend. Ending arguments with questions rather than statements can increase the likelihood that recipients will think about the message. Repetition of messages is likely to increase comprehension and acceptance.

Visitor characteristics also influence success. Visitors are more receptive to messages if they (1) think of themselves as being a part of the problem, (2) have relatively low levels of prior knowledge and experience, and (3) are part of small groups. Group leaders are likely to be more receptive than group members, unless they are highly experienced (Roggenbuck and Manfredo 1990).

Characteristics of the educator, or message source, are most important when the peripheral route to persuasion is used or when the visitor is not very well motivated to listen to or think about messages. In these kinds of situations—"learning situations where the recipient is in a hurry, in a distracting environment, is tired, is part of a large group, or is in a situation where the flow of complex information is forced and fast paced (as in some video programs)"—agencies should seek out attractive or well-respected individuals to deliver messages (Roggenbuck and Manfredo 1990).

The final variable is the communication channel. Personnel-based techniques and certain audiovisual techniques are more conducive to peripheral learning than techniques relying on written material. With personnel-based and audiovisual techniques, attention to the message source may be as important as attention to the message itself. Written materials have to be delivered in situations where visitors have the time to process the information. A variety of channels should be used to help ensure that visitors get the message. Because the educational process is so complex, it is important to focus on a few messages rather than try a shotgun approach. For example, Cole, Hammond, and McCool (1997) studied visitor attention to low impact messages posted on a trailside bulletin board and the extent to which visitors gained new knowledge from these messages. They found that visitors' knowledge was increased by exposure to the messages. However, knowledge gain was as great when just two messages were posted as when eight messages were posted. They concluded that in this situation, most visitors were willing to allocate only enough attention to or able to process about two bits of information.

Relatively little research has examined the effectiveness of educational programs in reducing recreation impact problems. The only inappropriate behavior that has been studied extensively is littering. Numerous studies have shown that littering can be reduced with persuasive communication techniques. Successful programs have been based on rewards, punishment, and environmental cues such as trash cans (applied behavior analysis), written appeals about the need to keep places free of litter (central route), and demonstrations in which role models pick up litter (peripheral route) (Roggenbuck 1992). Written messages are often least effective. Punishment-oriented themes are often most effective. At Mt. Rainier National Park, the mere presence of a uniformed ranger was the most effective of various techniques designed to keep visitors on established trails in meadows (Swearingen and Johnson 1995).

The following points should be considered in developing a low impact educational program.

1. *Focus the message.* It is better to deal with a few critical problems and desired behaviors than to overwhelm the visitor with huge quantities of material. It is important to clearly state the problem, the type of behavior that aggravates the problem, and how a change in behavior will improve the situation. If concepts and the rationale behind suggested behavior are clearly laid out, visitors will be better able to vary their behavior appropriately in different situations. It is important that the suggested behavior be reasonable and adequately communicated to visitors. Although personal contact often facilitates initial receptiveness to suggestions, written material may help with retention.

2. *Identify the audience.* By learning about which visitor groups use the area, messages can be tailored to these specific groups. It is particularly worthwhile to identify "problem users," those who contribute most to critical problems. Programs are likely to be most effective if different messages are developed for each user group rather than hitting everyone with the same message. For example, there is no reason to burden backpackers with all of the details of low-impact stock use.

3. *Select communication methods.* Personal contact is often considered to be the most effective means of communication, although brochures can also be effective (Oliver, Roggenbuck, and Watson 1985). Where they exist, visitor centers can be effective places to deliver educational messages. Mass media such as television, radio, and newspapers are other options, but they frequently fail to reach the right audience. Demonstrations and field programs have been used in town, at universities, at club meetings, and at the recreation area. Except in the latter case, these have the advantages of being tailored to a specific group and of providing the information during the planning stages of a trip. This is also true of the low impact information that is increasingly being added to guidebooks and how-to manuals. Managers should seek to contribute to and review material for books written about their area. The most effective programs use a variety of media, each tailored for a particular user group and message.

4. *Decide where to contact the audience.* Again, this depends on the targeted user group and the communication media selected. Some visitors can be contacted at home if they request information or are required to obtain reserved permits. This has worked very well on white-water rivers such as the Colorado River through Grand Canyon. Advance information is critical where required behavior demands special equipment. Local residents—the most frequent users of most recreation areas—can be reached through special programs in the community, on radio and television, or through the newspaper. College students can be reached on campus; horse clubs, Boy Scouts, and other organized groups can be contacted directly.

SEASONAL LIMITATIONS ON USE

As we discussed in Chapter 8, many environments are particularly fragile during certain seasons of the year. The most common examples are seasons when wildlife are particularly vulnerable and when soils are water-saturated and prone to disturbance. Thus, it is common for recreational use to be limited during these periods. To prevent wildlife disturbance, critical areas may be closed to all use, overnight use, and use by recreational stock or motor vehicles. Soil disturbance problems are most pronounced when use is by stock or motorized vehicles. Thus, it is common to close roads and prohibit travel with stock before some opening date in the summer when soils have had a chance to dry out. Seasonal stock prohibitions reduce damage to trails and to meadows used for grazing.

Sequoia and Kings Canyon National Parks, for example, have had a long history of pack stock use of meadows. They also have a tradition of studying pack stock impacts and have been in the forefront of attempts to control grazing impacts. One of the techniques they have used is to establish opening dates for pack stock in each drainage of the park (McClaran 1989). Opening dates are set so that the sod in meadows is dry enough to withstand hoof impact before stock use is allowed. Once average opening dates were identified, year-to-year variations were assessed. In dry years, opening dates can be as much as three weeks earlier than in wet years. Snowpack moisture levels on May 1 are used to determine whether the year is an early, normal, or late year. If opening dates are set in early May, visitors will have enough advance time to plan their trips.

CAMPFIRE MANAGEMENT ALTERNATIVES

To illustrate the wide variety of techniques usually available for dealing with any specific problem, let us take a look at some alternative campfire management programs. Table 2 presents some alternatives to a policy of last resort in which all campfires are banned (Hammitt 1982). Although there may be situations in which there is no alternative other than the complete prohibition of backcountry campfires, such a policy should be implemented only after considering less restrictive alternatives. The proposed alternatives vary from those that are most *indirect* in controlling user opportunities to experience campfires to those that are most *direct*.

Information Programs.   The most indirect of the management alternatives is the provision of information to park users about impacts of the campfire and its proper use. Many parks are already using this alternative through interpretive programs and low-impact use brochures. The objective is not to restrict user behavior but to modify it. Information on campfire impacts, low-impact camping, park policies governing the use of campfires and resource preservation, and underused areas where campfire impacts are of less concern may modify user behavior so that campfire impacts are greatly reduced.

Alternative Fuels.   An action that is closely related to providing general information on campfire impact and use is to encourage the use of alternative fuels. If campers are informed of the advantages of lightweight stoves for cooking, they may choose to use fewer open fires. The use of lightweight lanterns as a substitute for the social campfire might also be encouraged.

TABLE 2. Alternatives for Managing the Use of Campfires in Backcountry Recreation Areas

Type of Management	Alternative	Specific Examples
Indirect (Emphasizes modifying user behavior; preserving campfire opportunities)	Information programs	Promote desired campfire policies.
		Educate users about campfire impacts.
		Redistribute users to underused areas or more tolerant sites.
	Alternative fuels	Encourage use of lightweight stoves, lanterns, and alternative fuels.
Direct (Emphasizes regulation of user; removal of opportunities)	Elevational zoning	Restrict fires above tree line and in adjacent high elevation plant communities.
	Forest type and site zoning	Restrict fires from forest types that lack fuelwood (e.g., spruce-fir forest).
		Restrict fires from nonforested areas (e.g., grassy balds, beech gaps).
		Restrict fires by specific sites that lack fuelwood or present a fire danger.
	Temporal zoning	Restrict fires to hours of darkness only. (Require stoves for cooking.)
	Seasonal zoning	Restrict fires to winter and cool-weather seasons.
	Communal fires	Require several parties to share a common fire.
	Rationing	Ration campfires to $1/2$ or $1/3$ of the nights camped by a party.
	Total ban	Eliminate fires on a parkwide basis.

Elevational Zoning.   As a more direct alternative to campfire management, the manager may want to restrict the use of campfires above certain elevations. The small quantities of fuelwood above treeline and in adjacent subalpine plant communities may make it necessary to eliminate the use of campfires in these areas. Because of the short growing season and slow rate of wood production at these elevations, fuelwood production is insufficient to support campfires.

Forest Type and Site Zoning.   As an extension of the elevational zoning alternative, certain forest types and nonforested areas of a wildland area may have to be zoned as no-fire camping areas. Zones where campfires are prohibited may be those where fuelwood production is insufficient to meet the supply needs of campers. This alternative can also apply to specific sites or locations where use is heavy and fuelwood has been greatly depleted or where forest fire danger is high during the fire season.

Temporal Zoning.   The philosophy behind temporal zoning is to limit campfires to an esthetic function that occurs only after dark. Many backcountry users are already using lightweight stoves for their cooking. Stoves are more dependable and efficient than campfires for cooking. However, the presence of a stove does not eliminate the desire to have a campfire. Most campers still consider the fire to be an important esthetic and social component of the camping experience. By requiring campers to use stoves for their cooking and to build campfires only after dark, far less fuelwood will be used. Instead of three campfires per day (breakfast, lunch, dinner) or, as sometimes occurs, the all-day cooking fire, the campfire would be limited to a few hours of darkness during the typical summer evening. This action might reduce the demand for fuelwood to the point where the forest could produce enough fuel to meet the needs of campers.

Seasonal Zoning.   A further restriction on campfire use is to restrict its use to winter and cool season camping. Fuel is needed for heat and comfort during these seasons, but demand is light because of low use at this time of year. This would have the added advantage of encouraging off-season use in places where a shift toward increased off-season use is desirable.

Communal Fires.   Another means of reducing the number of backcountry campfires and the consumption of fuelwood is to have several parties share the same fire. On South Manitou Island at Great Sleeping Bear National Lakeshore, Michigan, a communal campfire pit is supplied for every 6 to 10 camping sites. Fires are prohibited except in designated pits. The technique appears to be quite successful, with essentially no evidence of tree chopping or removal of horizontal screening vegetation within and between individual campsites. Although this alternative would not serve the needs of all types of campers (i.e., those oriented to solitude), it does provide an opportunity within the spectrum of campfire alternatives for many campers to experience campfires.

The communal fire concept deserves further adaptation to various backcountry areas. Alpine lakes and other destination areas where campers tend to concentrate are likely areas where the communal fire alternative might be tried.

FIGURE 9. Extensive campfire impacts, as illustrated in this scene, have led to the banning of campfires in some backcountry recreation areas. (*Photo*: W. E. Hammitt.)

Rationing.   Rather than eliminate fires entirely from the camping experience, managers may want to limit fires to only one-third or one-half of each party's camping nights. The rationing of campfires could occur at the time hiking permits are issued, by having campers select the nights they want to have fires. Although difficult to enforce, a potential added benefit of this alternative might be an increase in the quality of campfire experiences. Because it would make sitting around a campfire a less common experience, rationing may cause the camper to place a higher value on the campfire experience when it is permitted.

Total Ban.   Little explanation of a total ban is needed (Fig. 9). However, much deliberation is needed before resorting to this alternative. Recreation resource management should provide a spectrum of recreational opportunities so that the needs of a diversity of users are met. The campfire is an important component of the camping experience, and we need to provide for its enjoyment when and where possible.

VISITOR INFORMATION NEEDED TO MANAGE RECREATION IMPACTS

To effectively manage visitors, certain types of information are needed. The most obvious is how many people are using the area. It may also be important to know how people are distributed, both in space and over time. User characteristics such as their mode of travel, party size, and length of stay may influence management decisions. Knowing where people come from will help in contacting users for an educational program. Finally, knowing visitors' attitudes about conditions in the area and their management preferences can also help in development of a management program that is sensitive to the visitor's desires and needs.

As was mentioned before, much of this information can be obtained from permits. Information commonly collected on permits provides data on amount of use, its spatial and temporal distribution, mode of travel, party size, length of stay, and the residence of the person with the permit Registration is basically the same thing as a permit, except that it is often not mandatory and, therefore, compliance rates are often low (Lucas 1983). Registration rates can be adjusted to compensate for non-registrants, but this requires separate studies of registration behavior. Numbers of people entering an area can be counted with automatic counters. These are sometimes linked to cameras that take low-resolution photographs, which makes it possible to determine method of travel and party size. This is costly, however, and the question of invading privacy can be a concern. Number of people can be observed directly at a sample of times and places, but this is costly too, and the use estimates obtained are not likely to be very accurate. Air photos have been used to count people, particularly those engaged in water-based recreation or at an off-road vehicle area. Of all these options, however, permits are the least costly, most precise, and most informative.

Specialized information on visitor opinions and preferences is more difficult to obtain. The most common method is to use a survey or questionnaire. These need to be carefully constructed and administered in a systematic manner, following established sampling theory. Otherwise, results will be biased and will not provide the information managers are seeking. Surveys conducted or sponsored by federal agencies must be approved by the Office of Management and Budget, a difficult procedure. Other options are direct observation of behavior or use of some sort of diary or self-reporting form in which visitors keep track of certain items of interest to the manager. Observation has been used to determine such things as how much time people actually spend fishing at lakes. Diaries have been used to record information that might be difficult to recall later, such as the high point of a day or the number of fish caught in specific places.

All information is costly to obtain; consequently, it is important to have specific reasons for each bit of information collected. It is almost always better to systematically collect a few types of information than to haphazardly collect many types. Finally, it is important to be sensitive to the visitor. All efforts should be made to avoid unnecessarily inconveniencing or intruding on the visitor. In many cases the visitor is only too happy to provide information, and there are other cases where the information is important enough to demand compliance. Concern for efficiently and sensitively collecting only useful information will avoid most problems and will add considerably to development of a management program.

REFERENCES

Cole, D. N. 1982a. Wilderness Campsite Impacts: Effect of Amount of Use. USDA Forest Service Research Paper INT-284. 34 pp.

Cole, D. N. 1982b. Controlling the Spread of Campsites at Popular Wilderness Destinations. *Journal of Soil and Water Conservation* 37:291–295.

Cole, D. N. 1983. Campsite Conditions in the Bob Marshall Wilderness, Montana. USDA Forest Service Research Paper INT-312. 18 pp.

Cole, D. N. 1989. Low-impact Recreational Practices for Wilderness and Backcountry. USDA Forest Service General Technical Report INT-265. 131 pp.

Cole, D. N. 1993. Campsites in Three Western Wildernesses: Proliferation and Changes in Condition Over 12 to 16 Years. USDA Forest Service Research Paper INT-463. 15 pp.

Cole, D. N., T. P. Hammond, and S. F. McCool. 1997. Information Quantity and Communication Effectiveness: Low-impact Messages on Wilderness Trailside Bulletin Boards. *Leisure Sciences* 19:59–72.

Cole, D. N., A. E. Watson, and J. W. Roggenbuck. 1995. Trends in Wilderness Visitors and Visits: Boundary Waters Canoe Area, Shining Rock, and Desolation Wildernesses. USDA Forest Service Research Paper INT-483. 38 pp.

Cole, D. N., A. E. Watson, T. E. Hall, and D. R. Spildie, 1997. High-Use Destination Areas in Wilderness: Social and Biophysical Impacts, Visitor Responses, and Management Options. USDA Forest Service Research Paper INT-496. 30 pp.

Davilla, B. 1979. Firewood Production, Use, and Availability in the High Sierra. In J. T. Stanley Jr., H. T. Harvey, and R. J. Hartesveldt, eds. *A Report on the Wilderness Impact Study: The Effects of Human Recreational Activities on Wilderness Ecosystems with Special Emphasis on Sierra Club Wilderness Outings in the Sierra Nevada.* San Francisco: Outing Committee, Sierra Club, pp. 94–128.

DeLuca, T. H., W. A. Patterson IV, W. A. Freimund, and D. N. Cole. In press. Influence of Llamas, Horses, and Hikers on Soil Erosion from Established Recreation Trails in Western Montana. *Environmental Management.*

Douchette, J. E., and D. N. Cole. 1993. Wilderness Visitor Education: Information About Alternative Techniques. USDA Forest Service General Technical Report INT-295. 37 pp.

Hammitt, W. E. 1982. Alternatives to Banning Campfires. *Parks* 7(3):8–9.

Hampton, B., and D. Cole. 1995. *Soft Paths.* 2d ed. Mechanicsburg, PA: Stackpole Books. 222 pp.

Hendee, J. C., G. H. Stankey, and R. C. Lucas. 1990. Wilderness Management. 2d ed. Golden, CO: North American Press. 546 pp.

Huffman, M. G., and D. R. Williams. 1987. The Use of Microcomputers for Park Trail Information Dissemination. *Journal of Park and Recreation Administration* 5:34–46.

Keay, J. A., and J. W. van Wagtendonk. 1983. Effect of Yosemite Backcountry Use Levels on Incidents with Black Bears. In E. C. Meslow, ed. *Bears—Their Biology and Management.* International Conference for Bear Research and Management 5:307–311.

Krumpe, E. E., and P. J. Brown. 1982. Redistributing Backcountry Use Through Information Related to Recreation Experiences. *Journal of Forestry* 80:360–364.

Lucas, R. C. 1980. Use Patterns and Visitor Characteristics, Attitudes and Preferences in Nine Wilderness and Other Roadless Areas. USDA Forest Service Research Paper INT-253. 89 pp.

Lucas, R. C. 1981. Redistributing Wilderness Use Through Information Supplied to Visitors. USDA Forest Service Research Paper INT-277. 15 pp.

Lucas, R. C. 1983. Low and Variable Visitor Compliance Rates at Voluntary Trail Registers. USDA Forest Service Research Note INT-326. 5 pp.

Marion, J. L., J. W. Roggenbuck, and R. E. Manning. 1993. Problems and Practices in Backcountry Recreation Management: A Survey of National Park Service Managers. USDI National Park Service Natural Resources Report NPS/NRVT/NRR-93/12. 48 pp.

McClaran, M. P. 1989. Recreational Pack Stock Management in Sequoia and Kings Canyon National Parks. *Rangelands* 11:3–8.

McClaran, M. P., and D. N. Cole. 1993. Packstock in Wilderness: Use, Impacts, Monitoring, and Management. USDA Forest Service General Technical Report INT-301. 33 pp.

McCool, S. F., and N. A. Christensen. 1996. Alleviating Congestion in Parks and Recreation Areas Through Direct Management of Visitor Behavior. In *Congestion and Crowding in the National Park System*. Minnesota Agricultural Experiment Station Miscellaneous Publication 86-1996, pp. 67–83.

McCool, S. F., and J. Utter. 1981. Preferences for Allocating River Recreation Use. *Water Resources Bulletin* 17:431–437.

Noe, F. P. 1992. Further Questions About the Measurement and Conceptualization of Backcountry Norms. *Journal of Leisure Research* 24:86–92.

Oliver, S. S., J. W. Roggenbuck, and A. E. Watson. 1985. Education to Reduce Impacts in Forest Campgrounds. *Journal of Forestry* 83:234–236.

Parsons, D. J. 1983. Wilderness Protection: An Example from the Southern Sierra Nevada, USA. *Environmental Conservation* 10:23–30.

Parsons, D. J. 1986. Campsite Impact Data as a Basis for Determining Wilderness Use Capacities. In R. C. Lucas, comp. *Proceedings—National Wilderness Research Conference: Current Research*. USDA Forest Service General Technical Report INT-212, pp. 449–455.

Roggenbuck, J. W. 1992. Use of Persuasion to Reduce Resource Impacts and Visitor Conflicts. In M. J. Manfredo, ed. *Influencing Human Behavior: Theory and Applications in Recreation, Tourism, and Natural Resources Management*. Champaign, IL: Sagamore Publishing, pp. 149–208.

Roggenbuck, J. W., and D. L. Berrier. 1981. Communications to Disperse Wilderness Campers. *Journal of Forestry* 79:295–297.

Roggenbuck, J. W., and M. J. Manfredo. 1990. Choosing the Right Route to Wilderness Education. In D. W. Lime, ed. *Managing America's Enduring Wilderness Resource: Proceedings of the Conference*. St. Paul, MN: Minnesota Agricultural Experiment Station, pp. 103–112.

Shelby, B., J. J. Vaske, and M. P. Donnelly. 1996. Norms, Standards, and Natural Resources. *Leisure Sciences* 18:103–123.

Stankey, G. H. 1973. Visitor Perception of Wilderness Recreation Carrying Capacity. USDA Forest Service Research Paper INT-142. 61 pp.

Stankey, G. H. 1979. Use Rationing in Two Southern California Wildernesses. *Journal of Forestry* 77:347–349.

Stankey, G. H., and J. H. Baden. 1977. Rationing Wilderness Use: Methods, Problems and Guidelines. USDA Forest Service Research Paper INT-192. 20 pp.

Stewart, W. P. 1989. Fixed Itinerary Systems in Backcountry Management. *Journal of Environmental Management* 29:163–171.

Swain, R. 1996. Leave No Trace (LNT)—Outdoor Skills and Ethics Program. *International Journal of Wilderness* 2(3):24–26.

Swearingen, T. C., and D. R. Johnson. 1995. Visitor's Responses to Uniformed Park Employees. *Journal of Park and Recreation Administration* 13:73–85.

Thornburgh, D. A. 1986. Responses of Vegetation to Different Wilderness Management Systems. In R. C. Lucas, comp. *Proceedings—National Wilderness Research Conference: Current Research*. USDA Forest Service General Technical Report INT-212, pp. 108–113.

Valentine, S., and R. Dolan. 1979. Footstep-induced Sediment Displacement in the Grand Canyon. *Environmental Management* 3:531–533.

van Wagtendonk, J. W. 1986. The Determination of Carrying Capacities for the Yosemite Wilderness. In R. C. Lucas, comp. *Proceedings—National Wilderness Research Conference: Current Research.* USDA Forest Service General Technical Report INT-212, pp. 456–461.

van Wagtendonk, J. W., and P. R. Coho. 1986. Trailhead Quotas: Rationing Use to Keep Wilderness Wild. *Journal of Forestry* 84:22–24.

Washburne, R. F., and D. N. Cole. 1983. Problems and Practices in Wilderness Management: A Survey of Managers. USDA Forest Service Research Paper INT-304. 56 pp.

Wilke, T. A. 1991. Evaluating the Acceptability of Recreation Rationing Policies Used On Rivers. *Environmental Management* 15:389–394.

Williams, D. R., J. W. Roggenbuck, M. E. Patterson, and A. E. Watson. 1992. The Variability of User-based Social Impact Standards for Wilderness Management. *Forest Science* 38:738–756.

Williams, P. B., and J. L. Marion. 1995. Assessing Campsite Conditions for Limits of Acceptable Change Management in Shenandoah National Park. USDI National Park Service Technical Report NPS/MARSHEN/NRTR-95/071. 138 pp.

13 Site Management

Site management techniques attempt to minimize impact by controlling where use occurs and by manipulating the site itself. If use occurs on relatively durable sites, impacts will be less pronounced than if use occurs on less durable sites. Alternatively, fragile places can be closed entirely to use. Design and treatment of sites can also do much to keep impacts within acceptable limits. Site management can affect the amount, type, and distribution of visitors, as well as the durability of the resource, and can be used to restore places that have been excessively damaged. Generally, site management is likely to increase in intensiveness and importance toward the more developed end of the recreation opportunity spectrum and in places that are heavily used. Everywhere, effective management will require a mix of both visitor and site management.

In developing site management plans, it is important to strive to maintain a natural appearance, particularly in wildland recreation areas. Even in wilderness, however, managers should not be paralyzed by a concern with avoidance of engineering if it is the only means of preventing equally "unnatural" resource damage. Curiously, many managers in wilderness have little problem with highly engineered trails, but they resist similar engineering levels for campsites and stock-use areas. The obtrusiveness of site manipulation must be carefully weighed against the obtrusiveness of site impacts and other means of solving problems.

Another concern in site management is cost, both to the visitor and to management. Closure of all sites at a lake to permit recovery and closure of a road to move a trailhead back 10 miles are costly actions for visitors. They may be justified, but evaluation of the severity of the problem at hand, the likely effectiveness of alternative actions, and costs to the visitor must all be considered. Many site management actions entail significant costs for management. These range from the high costs of installing irrigation systems to improve plant growth on campsites to lesser costs for building a corral or a hitch rail. Some actions are costly only in the construction phase; others entail significant ongoing maintenance costs. It is particularly wasteful to make an initial investment in a program that proves ineffective because of insufficient maintenance funds.

LOCATING USE ON RESISTANT SITES

One effective means of reducing impact is to see that most use occurs on durable sites. For example, Cole (1995) studied the resistance of 18 different vegetation types to trampling. The number of trampling passes required to eliminate 50 percent of the vegetation cover ranged from about 600 passes in an alpine sedge turf to just 20 passes in a subalpine forest with an understory dominated by ferns. This suggests that the sedge turf might be able to tolerate 30 times as much use as the forest, with no more impact. It is difficult to generalize about what makes a site durable, because a good location for a trail may not be a good location for a campsite. Even with campsites, a durable low-use site may not be a durable high-use site. Moreover, generalizations about durability are extremely site-specific; they vary from region to region. Given the importance of site durability, however, some generalizations for specific situations will be offered. Additional information is provided in Chapter 8.

On high-use campsites the most important durability considerations are probably overstory trees and the soil's erodibility, drainage, and depth. Other esthetic considerations should also be evaluated. Because tree regeneration is sharply curtailed on campsites, it is wise to locate campsites in stands of relatively young, long-lived trees that are not susceptible to disease. This will prolong the time that campsites will be forested. In the West, aspen groves should be avoided because they are highly susceptible to canker diseases when mechanically injured (e.g., through initial carving) by campers (Hinds 1976). Forested campsite life spans in aspen are on the order of 20 years. Ripley (1962) evaluated the susceptibility of 27 southern Appalachian trees and shrubs to disease infection, insect infection, and decline (Table 1). Knowledge about the durability of trees is important to decisions about campsite locations. The durability of ground cover vegetation is much less important because, with heavy use, even resistant ground cover is unlikely to survive.

It is important for erosion potential to be minimal, because developed campsites must be used for a long time. It is best to locate sites on relatively deep soils with a wide mix of particle sizes (e.g., loams) and at least a moderate amount of organic matter, as such soils have good drainage. Soils that drain well should not have serious problems with flooding and excessive runoff. Soils that are mostly organic should be avoided. However, thick organic horizons minimize the exposure of underlying

TABLE 1. Rankings of Trees from Most to Least Able to Withstand the Impacts of Recreation Use

Hardwoods		Conifers
1. Hickories	12. Red maple	1. Shortleaf pine
2. Persimmon	13. American holly	2. Hemlocks
3. Sycamore	14. Sourwood	3. White pine
4. White ash	15. Black birch	4. Pitch pine
5. Beech	16. White oaks	5. Virginia pine
6. Sassafras	17. Black walnut	
7. Buckeye	18. Red oaks	
8. Yellow poplar	19. Black locust	
9. Dogwood	20. Magnolia	
10. Black gum	21. Black cherry	
11. Yellow birch	22. Blue beech	

Source: Ripley 1962.

mineral soil that results from campsite use. Deep soils with moderately rapid drainage are also required for many human waste disposal systems that depend on on-site decomposition. Leonard, Spencer, and Plumley (1981) provide a useful table of limitations posed by certain physical site characteristics for overnight facilities (Table 2). Some of these guidelines apply only to the northern Appalachians, for which the table was developed; others are more general in applicability.

On lightly used campsites such as those in a portion of wilderness where use dispersal is being practiced, the most important durability consideration is the resistance of the ground cover vegetation. If properly managed, soil damage in such places should be minimal, and tree damage should not occur. The main concern is avoidance of vegetation loss, which, once it occurs, tends to attract further use to the site. It is always best to select sites without any vegetation at all. Examples include outcrops of bare rock, sand beaches, gravel bars, and some dense forests. Where vegetation is present, considerable information or experience may be needed to evaluate durability. Many of the resistant plant characteristics mentioned in Chapter 3 can be used to evaluate the resistance of different vegetation types. The most useful general guideline is that grasslands and meadows are more resistant than the undergrowth in forests (Fig. 1). Dry vegetation types are usually more resistant than moist types.

Selecting a durable route is often the most important tool in managing impacts on trails. It is certainly the least costly tool and should be the first line of defense, particularly in wilderness where the other major management option—engineering—is to be avoided as much as possible. The most important environmental factors affecting trail durability are usually topography, soil moisture, and soil erodibility. The slope of the trail and the extent to which the trail intercepts runoff from upslope are particularly important. Trails with steep slopes are likely to deteriorate rapidly unless steps are taken to control erosion. Trails that are aligned so that they run straight up slopes and are depressed well below the ground surface are also prone to problems. Such trails intercept overland flow and are quickly eroded by running water. On the other hand, trails with no slope at all often have trouble draining. Ideally, trails should have gentle grades with an alignment perpendicular to a moderately to steep sideslope. The importance of such a trail alignment increases as trail grade increases (Leung and Marion 1996). Where such a location cannot be sustained, engineering techniques will have to be used to mitigate the potential problems of a less than ideal location.

In many mountainous areas the most common cause of trail damage from the users's point of view is excessive soil moisture, which leads to development of muddy trails (Fig. 2). Muddy stretches are difficult to walk through. Moreover, in an attempt to avoid the mud, hikers and horses frequently skirt the stretch and, in doing so, widen the quagmire. In the Bob Marshall Wilderness "trail bogs" knee-deep in mud may be 100 yds long and almost as wide.

Areas of late snowmelt, high water tables, and places where water drains onto the trail are common situations in which problems with muddy trails occur. In the northern hemisphere, locating trails on south-facing slopes is a general means of avoiding problems with late snowmelt. Before locating a trail, it is worthwhile to observe where snow lasts longest, either in the field or with the aid of aerial photography.

TABLE 2. Physical Site Characteristics and Limitations for Overnight Facility Locations

	Limitations		
	None to Slight	Moderate	Severe
Topography			
Slope	2 to 15 percent	15 to 30 percent	Greater than 30 percent
Landform	Valleys, footslopes, low-elevation ridges, terraces or benches on side slopes	Midslopes of mountains	Steep mountain side slopes, depressions, ravine floors, pond shorelines, bog lands
Aspect	East, south	West, north	Northwest, southeast (or aspects receiving most frequent storm winds)
Soil			
Depth to impervious layer or seasonal high-water table	Greater than 5 ft	2½ to 5 ft	Less than 2½ ft
Drainage	Rapid to moderately well drained	Moderately well to imperfectly drained or excessively rapid	Poorly or imperfectly drained
Flooding	None		One to 2 times per year during use season

Soil texture	Moderately coarse to medium texture (sandy loam to silt loams)	Moderately fine or slightly coarse texture (clay loams, silt-clay loams, or sandy soils of 65 percent sand)	Fine texture (clays), loose sand, or organic soils
Rockiness/stoniness	Cobbles/gravel—20 percent Surface rocks—25 ft apart	Cobbles—20 to 50 percent Surface rocks—5 to 25 ft apart	Cobbles—50 percent Surface rocks—5 ft apart

Vegetation Types

	Beech, maple, oak, hickory, pine stands	Spruce, fir, hemlocks, birch, alders, willows	Alpine, subalpine, bog, krummholz

Water Supply

For huts	Available potable water source provides quantity sufficient for daily consumption throughout season, e.g., 12 gal./person/day.	Water source has decreasing flow during season to $3/4$ the quantity needed, and water must be stored.	Inconsistent flow from the water source and quantity is less than 12 gal./person/day.
For shelter or tent sites	Water flows from a spring, and the flow and quality are reliable all season. Spring outlet is within 250 yards of site.	Water flows from a spring, but flow is decreased to a trickle at the end of season. Spring outlet is $1/4$ mile away.	Reliable spring water is more than $1/2$ mile away.

Source: Leonard, Spencer, and Plumley 1981. Copyright © 1981 by Appalachian Mountain Club, used with permission of publisher.

FIGURE 1. Vegetation loss at this outfitter site in the Bob Marshall Wilderness, Montana, is low because it is located in a resistant dry grassland. (*Photo*: D. N. Cole.)

FIGURE 2. This trail traverses an area of high soil moisture. It is widening, developing parallel trails, and is difficult for hikers to negotiate. (*Photo*: D. N. Cole.)

High water tables can often be identified by using vegetational indicators. On a trail system in the Selway-Bitterroot Wilderness, for example, more than two-thirds of the muddiness problems were in one vegetation type, which, along with the vigorous growth of four individual species, indicates quite accurately where muddiness problems are likely to occur (Cole 1983). Soil color can also be used as an indicator of potential muddiness problems. Blue-gray and dark organic colors often indicate poor drainage, whereas yellows and reds often indicate good aeration and, therefore, good drainage. Soils that are primarily organic (e.g., peat or muck soils) and fine-textured soils are also likely to be muddy because drainage is poor. Again, engineering can compensate for a poor location, if necessary.

Certain soils are also less susceptible to erosion than others. Erosiveness is lowest in soils with good drainage and the ability to resist the detachment of soil particles. These properties are optimized in loams with a substantial organic matter content. Sandy soils have good drainage, but they are easily displaced; they are of intermediate desirability as trail locations. Clay soils resist detachment, but drainage is poor; they are even less desirable than sands. The most erosive soils are those with homogeneous textures of a moderate particle size (i.e., fine sands and silts) (Leung and Marion 1996). The prominent trail erosion problems in many mountain meadows result from the erosiveness of the homogeneous, fine-textured soils that have developed on the glacial outwash or lacustrine deposits characteristic of these meadows.

Garland (1990) developed a technique for assessing erosion risk for mountain footpaths in South Africa that can be used to identify favorable path locations before paths are planned and constructed. Indices of rainfall, lithology, and topographic slope were combined to produce erosion risk classes between one and four. The utility of this procedure was tested by comparing risk ratings and erosion status for sections of existing path. The correlation of prediction with reality was high, suggesting the technique has potential for aiding in the selection of routes that should have low maintenance requirements.

PERMANENT CLOSURES

Rather than focusing use on resistant sites, managers can also prohibit use of certain sites or ecosystem types. One of the most common prohibitions is against camping within a specified distance of water bodies, particularly lakes. In national parks, setbacks range from 5 ft to as much as one-half mile; the most common distance is 100 ft (Marion, Roggenbuck, and Manning 1993). Both social and ecological justifications have been provided for this action. Social reasons include (1) preserving the esthetic qualities of the lake that attracted people to the area in the first place, (2) reducing the visibility of campers—they are highly visible along the lakeshore, and (3) preserving the lakeshore as common space for all to use. Ecological reasons include (1) avoiding use of particularly fragile lakeshores, (2) reducing the potential for water pollution, and (3) avoiding the braided trails that often form when campsites are located close to the shore.

There is no doubt that the social justifications are significant. However, the ecological reasons are suspect. Lakeshores are not more fragile than places set back from water. In the Eagle Cap Wilderness there was little difference in impact on lakeshore sites and sites more than 200 ft from lakes (Cole 1982). Water quality is seldom a problem except where use is very heavy. Therefore, in most backcountry situations this is not a valid justification. There are certainly places where avoiding use of sites close to water bodies is important; there are also many places where this is unnecessary. Because such a prohibition keeps parties from camping where they most want to, the action should be taken only where it is necessary. Many of the same things could be accomplished through educating people about not damaging shorelines or polluting waters. Because social reasons for setbacks are the most telling, setbacks are more appropriate in heavy-use areas than in low-use areas.

Permanent closures have also been implemented in places where past impact has been so severe that such a drastic measure is the only option for recovery. Bullfrog Lake, one of the most scenic and fragile destinations in Kings Canyon National Park, California, was so heavily impacted that it was closed to all camping in 1961. Fireplaces and other evidence of camping occurred, but some places remained highly impacted (Parsons and DeBenedetti 1979). The National Park Service plans to maintain the ban on camping at Bullfrog Lake—partially because recovery is not yet complete but also to showcase an area that required such a drastic management response.

A common reason for closing an area to all use or certain types of use, such as camping, is the presence of vulnerable animals or rare and endangered plants. For example, waterholes of critical importance to animals, such as bighorn sheep, are often kept off-limits for overnight use. One of only three known populations of the endangered sentry milk vetch occurs at one of the most popular rim overlooks at Grand Canyon National Park. Serious declines in the viability of this population led park rangers to erect a fence around the population and reroute trails around it. Four years since protection, the population is still vulnerable but more stable than it was (Maschinski, Frye, and Rutman 1997). Interpretive displays can be used to educate the public about the need to preserve endangered species and to elicit their support for the drastic measures needed to protect the plants from trampling.

TEMPORARY SITE CLOSURES

In some areas, highly impacted sites have been temporarily closed to allow them to recover. Once they have recovered, these sites can be reopened for use. Other sites must be available for recreational use until the closed sites can be reopened. This action has been called "rest-rotation" because there is a rotation of open and closed sites. It bears some similarity to the type of dispersal in which use is spread among a larger number of sites. The major difference is that management formally controls which sites are open and which are closed. With rest-rotation, sites are also likely to be either open or closed for longer periods of time than sites in an area where managers are attempting to disperse use. Consequently, they become more highly impacted after periods of use. A rest-rotation strategy could be applied in a number of recreational situations but is most important in campsite management. Temporary campsite closures have been used in both developed and backcountry campsite situations.

The critical factor in assessing the appropriateness of rest-rotation is the relationship between the length of recovery periods and the period of time it takes for impact to occur. If recovery takes much longer than deterioration, a rest-rotation system will require either that there be many closed sites for each open site or that the capacity of the area to serve normal visitor loads be reduced.

As described earlier, deterioration of a campsite often occurs within the first few years after the site is opened to use. This has been demonstrated on wilderness campsites in the Boundary Waters Canoe Area (Merriam, Smith, Miller, Huang, Tappeiner, Goeckermann, Blomendal, and Costello 1973), on canoe-accessed sites in Delaware Water Gap National Recreation Area (Marion and Cole 1996), and on car camping sites in Pennsylvania (LaPage 1967). In these cases impact increased dramatically for a year or two and then tended to level off.

Although a two-year deterioration period may be relatively standard on sites that receive at least a moderate level of use, recovery periods are much more variable. Recovery rates vary greatly in response to such factors as length of the growing season and moisture regime. Around a backcountry lake in Kings Canyon National Park, Parsons and DeBenedetti (1979) found that soil compaction had returned to pre-use levels within 15 years after closure; however, quantities of organic matter were still low, and ground cover vegetation was still disturbed. In an oak stand in Minnesota, soil recovered from compaction in just under a decade (Thorud and Frissell 1976). At Delaware Water Gap, most evidence of campsite impact disappeared in six years (Marion and Cole 1996). However, even in this unusually resilient environment, recovery still takes much longer than deterioration.

Difficulties with rest-rotation are most serious in wilderness areas where active revegetation is difficult and, many believe, not appropriate on a major scale. Moreover, recovery periods are often particularly long because of harsh growing conditions. The effectiveness of temporary closures was evaluated at Big Creek Lake in the Selway-Bitterroot Wilderness, Montana, where 7 of 15 campsites were temporarily closed to allow recovery. Eight years after closure, vegetation cover on closed sites was still only one-third of normal, and bare soil was exposed on 25 percent of the site compared with just 0.1 percent on controls (Cole and Ranz 1983). The most dramatic change over the eight-year period was the development and deterioration of 7 new campsites near the closed sites. Within eight years after their creation, vegetation loss and bare soil were as pronounced on these sites as on long-established sites in the area. The major effect of the temporary closure, then, was to increase the number of impacted sites. Recognizing this, area managers eventually reopened the closed sites and abandoned the idea of rotating sites.

In resilient environments, where active rehabilitation is feasible, rest-rotation may work. Legg, Farnham, and Miller (1980) demonstrated how over-winter closure of developed campsites in Texas, when aided by rototilling organic matter into the soil, allowed soil compaction levels to quickly return to normal. Even on resilient developed sites, it would be prudent to be cautious in attempting rotation. By experimentally closing and revegetating one site, recovery periods can be estimated. If recovery is sufficiently rapid, funding and manpower are available to do the revegetation, and the number of sites is sufficient to accommodate both open and closed sites, then rest-rotation might be worth implementing on a large scale.

Another reason for a temporary site closure is to avoid disturbance of animals during times when they are vulnerable. Examples include the closure of beaches when sea turtles are nesting and the temporary closure of trails where grizzly bears have been sighted so as to avoid encounters with humans.

INFLUENCING SPATIAL DISTRIBUTION OF USE

Site manipulation can be used both to influence the spatial distribution of visitor use and to increase the durability of the sites on which use occurs. Trails provide an excellent example of how site manipulation influences use patterns. People seldom venture off trails, so managers can control where most people go simply through careful consideration of where they build trails. Three primary means of affecting visitor use are manipulation of ease of access, development of facilities in some places and not in others, and design of concentrated-use sites, such that traffic flow is contained.

Ease of access is primarily related to the number, distribution, and condition of roads and trails. Roads can be closed to make roaded areas accessible only to non-motorized users or to increase the difficulty of reaching some internal destination. Such an action is likely to reduce total use of the area and to shift the balance of types of use. This can be beneficial to wildlife and water quality, which will be less disturbed because of the shift away from motorized use. Internal destinations are likely to be less crowded and impacted because of reductions in use. The principal costs are borne by motorized users and those with less time to get to internal destinations. Neighboring areas may also be adversely affected if increased use causes increased impact. These costs can be minimized by providing alternative, attractive areas for displaced users—areas where increased use can be planned for and accommodated.

A somewhat less effective and drastic means of accomplishing the same thing is to not maintain or to reduce the quality of access roads. This may exclude legitimate users who lack vehicles capable of driving the roads, while permitting access to inappropriate users who visit the area primarily for the challenge of driving the rough roads. Such a program may also lead to resource damage problems, particularly erosion of the road surface and a reduction in water quality. Another alternative is to build new roads or to improve the quality of existing roads in areas into which management wants to divert use.

Trail systems can be manipulated toward the same ends. Building new trails and improving the quality of existing trails are likely to increase use, whereas closing or not maintaining trails is likely to decrease use. Type of use can be altered as well. Low levels of maintenance are likely to exclude use by stock and motorized vehicles. Pristine areas are more likely to remain that way if they are left trailless. Usually the effectiveness of such attempts to manipulate use distribution will be increased if combined with information about the distribution and condition of roads and trails.

Nonmaintenance of trails, which serves as a "psychological barrier" to use for certain visitors, is a common practice in some backcountry areas. Removal or nonreplacement of trail signs and log bridges across streams are also means of reducing use. When these practices are used by management, visitors should be made aware of them so they can plan their trips accordingly.

Trailhead facilities also affect ease of access and, therefore, visitor use. Developed boat ramps will attract motorboats, and removal of a ramp will decrease motorized use. Similarly, a ramp for unloading horses from stock trucks and trailers will increase horse use (Fig. 3). Providing a campground and overnight horse-holding facilities at a trailhead will increase use of that trail. Even the size of the parking lot provided will influence amount of use.

Development of facilities within a recreation area will also change use patterns. For example, building a horse camp at a lake is likely to attract more horse use to that area, particularly by novice users who are highly dependent on such facilities. Hikers who dislike contact with horse parties and who know of the facility are likely to avoid the area. In many cases—because some users are likely to be attracted, while others are repelled—development of facilities may have more effect on the type of use than on the total amount of use. The most common internal facilities for attracting use in backcountry areas are trails, huts and shelters, horse-holding facilities, and improved potable water supplies. In roaded areas interpretive facilities, developed

FIGURE 3. Provision of trailhead facilities for loading and unloading horses is likely to increase use by parties with horses. (*Photo:* R. C. Lucas.)

swimming beaches, and improved picnic areas and campsites are common attractions. Stocking a lake with fish and improving fish or wildlife habitat are also effective means of increasing particular types of use. Dismantling facilities or not stocking lakes can have the opposite effect. To effect a change it is important that the public be informed of the change. Word of mouth can be effective, but it may be desirable to advertise attractions, facilities, or management improvements.

Facilities can reduce resource damage in several other ways. They usually concentrate use, which, as we discussed in the last chapter, is desirable in many situations. Use concentration is most desirable where use levels are high, the usual case in situations where facilities are provided. The best examples are in camp and picnic areas. Tables and fireplaces concentrate the impact associated with preparing and eating food. Toilets concentrate human waste, and garbage cans, if provided, concentrate litter. Horse-holding facilities concentrate the impact of horses (Fig. 4). Facilities can also shield the resource from impact; we will discuss this in more detail later.

It is also important to design traffic flow on and between sites in such a way that as little area as possible is frequently trampled. This is particularly relevant to the design of developed multisite campgrounds. Impact occurs wherever people walk between sleeping areas, eating areas, water sources, toilets, garbage cans, and attractions. Total impact is closely related to the proportion of the area that is frequently walked on. This proportion can be minimized through the use of barriers and signs and by manipulating the attractiveness and location of trails and other facilities provided. People tend to take the shortest path between facilities, although this is influenced by visibility,

FIGURE 4. Hitching rails confine pack stock trampling to a small area and avoid damage resulting from tying stock to trees. (*Photo*: D. N. Cole.)

signing, ease of travel, and attractiveness. Routes between facilities will tend to be used if they meet these criteria; impact will be minimized if the location of facilities and attractions channels use along as few routes as possible. For this reason, Leonard, Spencer, and Plumley (1981) advocate a linear arrangement of facilities in densely forested backcountry areas in the Northeast (Fig. 5).

If shortcuts develop between facilities, it is often best to try to incorporate these into the existing trail system (McEwen and Tocher 1976). Sometimes this is unacceptable, and the manager must turn to barriers or signs, more obtrusive means of management.

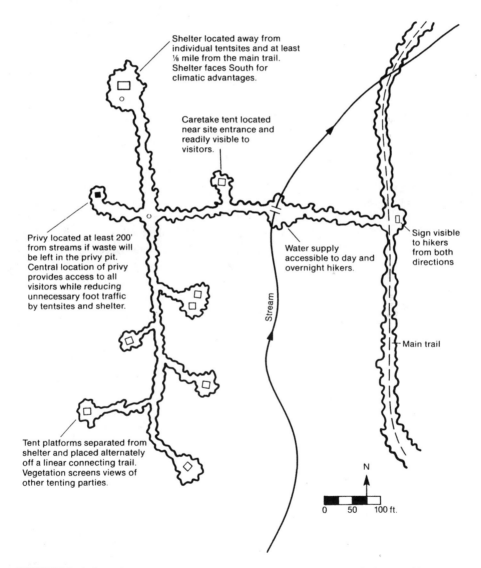

FIGURE 5. A linear layout of overnight facilities that concentrates traffic flow and impact but separates and disperses visitor groups. (*Source*: Leonard, Spencer, and Plumley 1981.)

Barriers range from the undesirable extreme of barbed wire fencing to earthen barriers to unobtrusive plantings of shrubs and trees. Signs such as "Please stay on the path" are another less than desirable option. This is another area in which effectiveness and obtrusiveness must be balanced.

Bayfield and Bathe (1982) evaluated the effectiveness of six techniques for closing undesired paths in a woodland in Scotland: rope, barbed wire, and plank barriers; arrows, logs, and brushwood. The plan barrier also included a notice, "Path closed for restoration." The plank with notice was most effective, deterring about 90 percent of visitors. The logs and brushwood kept only about 50 percent of visitors off the paths. At Mount Rainier National Park, in Washington, Swearingen and Johnson (1995) found that signs were effective in reducing the frequency of off-trail traffic on sensitive subalpine meadows and that the most effective sign was one that carried the threat of a fine. Moreover, they found that visitors were particularly likely to stay on trails when a uniformed employee was present, even when those employees were not enforcing regulations.

Trail impact can also be reduced by confining use distribution. The most common problems are shortcutting switchbacks and trail widening, leading to development of either a continuous wide bare area or a system of multiple trails. The key to avoiding such problems is to make staying on the trail the easiest alternative for the hiker. Switchback cutting can be minimized by keeping them few in number and out of sight of each other, utilizing wide turns where possible, and building barriers between the upper and lower legs of the switchback. These considerations must be balanced with a concern for proper trail drainage, as discussed in the following section.

Wide trails occur where the trail tread is rough relative to the adjacent land. These conditions cause the hiker to walk off the trail, widening it. Widening is also a problem with horse use on side hills. Horses tend to walk on the downhill side of the trail, which breaks down this outer edge and widens the trail. Trail roughness can be reduced by removing rocks or surfacing the trail. Alternatively, the roughness of adjacent land can be increased by piling rocks along the trail. Piling rocks on the outside of wide trails caused by heavy horse use is a common use of this technique. Douchette and Kimball (1990) report on the effectiveness of low rock walls built to confine traffic along a ridgetop trail through fragile alpine habitat in New Hampshire. Twelve years after wall construction, mean path width had decreased from 3.6 m to 2.1 m. Although there was an initial outcry about the visual intrusion of the walls on the beauty of the alpine area, 81 percent of visitors, 12 years later, found them to be unobtrusive.

SITE HARDENING AND SHIELDING

Engineering—after proper location—is the major defense managers have against deterioration of trails. Although excessive engineering is to be avoided, particularly in more primitive recreation areas, engineering solutions are often necessary and appropriate. After all, trails are a largely artificial, visually obvious addition to the landscape—a flat, barren, compacted strip through the environment. Most visitors do not mind the artificiality; they accept it as the price for increased accessibility.

The problems that most commonly require engineering solutions are trail erosion and damage to areas that are wet or poorly drained. The two simplest, least costly, and lowest-maintenance techniques for erosion control are outsloping of the trail tread and incorporation of drainage dips. Outsloping involves building the trail so that the outer edge is lower than the inner edge. This causes water to drain off the trail. Drainage dips are short sections of trail built with a grade opposite to the prevailing grade of the trail. If a trail is climbing uphill, for example, short sections of down-grade provide periodic interruptions of what would be a continuous down-trail channel. Coarse material at the low point of dips helps prevent erosion there.

Two other tools for controlling erosion are water bars and steps (Birkby 1996). Both should be part of the original trail construction design; they will be much less effective once substantial amounts of erosion have occurred. Water bars, made of wood or stone, are oriented at an angle to the slope and trail and divert water off the tread (Fig. 6). Steps are oriented perpendicular to the slope; they slow water down and hold soil. Both are placed closer together and become more important with increases in slope, the amount of water on the tread, and soil instability.

Water bars are particularly important close to the top of slopes where water can be diverted before picking up momentum. It is important that they be oriented at the proper angle to the trail—usually 20 to 40 degrees. A steeper angle encourages erosion; a shallower angle leads to excessive sedimentation behind the bar. The appropriate angle increases as trail grade increases (Birkby 1996).

It is important to be concerned with what happens to the water after it is diverted off the tread. Sometimes a ditch is needed to handle the diverted water. Where drop-offs adjacent to the trail are steep, rocks may help dissipate the energy of the falling, diverted water. This will help avoid gully erosion and undercutting of the trail. Frequent maintenance is required to keep water bars from filling in with sediment and becoming highly erosive little waterfalls. Disturbed bars (horses, particularly, have a habit of dislodging them) and rotted wooden bars need to be replaced periodically.

Not allowing water to flow onto the trail is as important as diverting water off the trail. Water is particularly likely to flow onto the trail where it crosses small drainageways. In such places water should be kept off the trail with culverts under the trail or, if the drainage is very small, with rock-lined ditches across the trail. Even with culverts it is critical to use a system large enough to handle floods. Where water seeps onto the trail in many places and the trail cannot be outsloped, it may be necessary to construct parallel ditches along the trail. If there is much gradient to the ditches, erosion may occur unless ditches are rock lined and have check dams or periodic side ditches to drain them.

Where erosion is particularly severe, primarily at off-road vehicle concentrated-use areas, it is important to control where eroded material is deposited. Otherwise, it will be carried into streams, where it reduces water quality and adversely affects fish populations. At off-road vehicle areas in California, debris basins have been built to trap sediment. Initially underengineered, many early sedimentation basins were washed out in floods. Proper engineering is critical if these basins are to remain functional.

Bridges, in addition to serving a visitor safety purpose, protect against erosion at stream crossings. They should be considered wherever a steep bank of erosive

FIGURE 6. Rock water bars divert water off this trail in Yosemite National Park. The rock steps in the foreground also reduce the potential for erosion. (*Photo*: D. N. Cole.)

material must be negotiated. Various types of bridging are the only means of avoiding serious resource damage where trails intercept springs or cross wet areas or areas with a high water table. Any trampling of water-saturated soil causes both churning and compaction of the soil. The end result is a quagmire that widens and lengthens over time.

If the wet area is neither too deep nor too long, it can be bridged with stepping stones. Three more elaborate options are to build turnpike, puncheon, or corduroy. Turnpiking involves building up the trail bed, using material from parallel ditches. The trail material is held in place with logs or rock (Fig. 7). The base of the trail should be above the water level in the ditches, and the trail material should provide

FIGURE 7. Turnpiking can be used to elevate sections of trail above surrounding wet areas. The trail surface is sand held in place by log stringers. Culverts allow water to pass beneath the trail. (*Photo*: D. N. Cole.)

reasonably good drainage. It may be necessary to import gravel or some other well-drained material to build up the trail. Where drainage problems are more severe, puncheon can be used to elevate the trail above the wet area without disrupting drainage. Puncheon consists of a decking of logs or timbers set on log or timber stringers along the side. It is important to maintain good drainage under the trail and to extend the stretch of puncheon into areas of good drainage at either end. Corduroy, the most common form of bridging in wildland areas, is merely a primitive form of puncheon construction. Native logs are laid perpendicular to log stringers. Drainage control is less elaborate. Corduroy deteriorates rapidly, must be replaced periodically, and can be dangerous.

Raised walkways have also been effective in reducing damage in a number of other sensitive environments. They are commonly used in coastal environments to allow visitors to move from parking areas to the beach without damaging intervening sand dunes (Carlson and Godfrey 1989). By elevating the walkway and leaving spaces between boards, room is left for sand accumulation and light can reach plants growing beneath the walkway. Walkways are also used to minimize damage from heavy traffic in fragile tundra environments, such as at Logan Pass in Glacier National Park, Montana.

Surfacing of trails may be necessary where use is very heavy, particularly where they are used by horses or motorized vehicles. It is also necessary where trails cross wet areas or rockslides. Gravel should be used on segments that cross wet areas or rockslides. On heavy-use trails other options include wood chips, soil cement, and, as a last resort, paving (Fig. 8). Trail durability can also be increased by using geosynthetic materials buried beneath soil or gravel. Particularly useful over wet and unstable soils, geosynthetics serve as a barrier between underlying mucky soils and the dry, coarse tread material laid on top of the geosynthetic material. They also add the tensile strength needed to support heavy loads (Hesselbarth and Vachowski 1996).

The major means of increasing the resource durability of camp and picnic areas are to surface areas that receive concentrated use and to construct facilities that shield the resource, such as tent pads, shelters, fire grates, and toilets. In heavy-use areas, it is possible to minimize compaction, improve drainage, and avoid the creation of muddy, wet areas by surfacing tent sites, eating areas, and trails between facilities with gravel or wood chips. This will also serve to concentrate use and avoid damage to intersite zones. Although such surfacing is generally inappropriate in wilderness

FIGURE 8. This motorcycle trail has been hardened in an inconspicuous manner with soil cement. (*Photo*: R. F. Washburne.)

areas, it is debatable whether surfaced areas are any less "natural" than barren, dusty, or muddy devegetated areas.

A more elaborate means of shielding the ground, used particularly in the eastern United States, is the construction of tent platforms and shelters. Tent platforms are flat wooden structures that elevate and separate tents from the ground surface. They can be portable or not and can be built to accommodate one or several tents (Leonard, Spencer, and Plumley 1981). A shelter can be created by placing a roof and sides on the platform. Shelters attract visitation; this results in more concentrated use and impact (Fig. 9). In Great Smoky Mountains National Park, shelters receive 37 percent of backcountry use; however, they account for only about 10 percent of the total area of campsite disturbance (Marion and Leung 1996). Overnight sites with developed facilities tend to be large and highly impacted, but properly designed facilities keep impacts to acceptable levels and the amount of impact per person is low because use and impact are concentrated on shielded sites.

At water-based recreation areas, it is important to surface boat ramps. This reduces erosion and also increases accessibility and public safety. The boat ramp in Fig. 10 allows rafters on Idaho's Middle Fork of the Salmon River to get their rafts down to the river without damaging the riverbank excessively.

Provision of fire grates is another means of concentrating impact and/or shielding the site. A fire pit on the ground concentrates impact at one point. This keeps camp-fire impact from spreading and disturbing a large area. Grates that are elevated also shield the ground from the impact of the fire. At Delaware Water Gap National

FIGURE 9. Backcountry shelters concentrate use and impacts, but if properly designed, lead to low amounts of impact per visitor night of use. (*Photo*: W. E. Hammitt.)

FIGURE 10. A boat ramp on Idaho's Middle Fork of the Salmon River reduces damage to the riverbank. (*Photo*: D. N. Cole.)

Recreation Area, managers reduced the total area of disturbance on canoe-accessed campsites by 50 percent in just five years (Marion 1995). The primary reason for this improvement was installation of a fire grate at each campsite. This provided a focal point for camping activities, allowing peripheral areas to recover.

A final facility that concentrates impact and shields the resource is the toilet. Toilets are standard in developed areas and have become increasingly common in heavily used parts of wilderness. Almost one-half of national parks use toilets in at least some places in the backcountry (Marion, Roggenbuck, and Manning 1993). Some toilet systems merely concentrate waste in pits. When the pit is full, it is covered over and a new pit is built elsewhere. In other systems waste is either removed from the site or treated and then redeposited in the vicinity. Waste can be either chemically treated or composted. Table 3 displays alternative waste disposal methods, their appropriateness at various sites, associated costs, and visitor acceptance.

TABLE 3. Methods for Disposing of Human Waste in Remote Recreation Areas

Method	Maintenance Requirements	Appropriate Uses	Costs and Visitor Acceptance	Comments
Cat hole. Each user digs a shallow hole and buries fecal matter. Waste decomposes before being leached through soil.	None.	Dispersed recreation areas that receive light use and have soil cover.	Visitor education and cleanup of improperly disposed waste. Visitor acceptance is good.	Few problems with this approach if use levels are low and visitors are educated. Problems increase with use.
Carry out. Waste is deposited in plastic bags, specially designed plastic tubes, or specially designed portable toilets. These containers are emptied outside the area.	Owners maintain containers, but disposal facilities require maintenance. Waste in plastic bags must be incinerated. Reusable containers can be disposed of in SCAT machines or trailer dumps.	Effective wherever visitors can be persuaded to comply. Has been highly successful on rivers and is being used on popular mountaineering routes.	Plastic bags can be incinerated for about $1/lb. SCAT machines and dump stations cost $20,000 to $100,000 to install and then $3000 to $5000/year to maintain. Acceptance is high on rivers, low elsewhere.	When this system works, it is ideal. Visitors "leave no trace." However, compliance can be difficult to obtain and specialized disposal facilities are required.
Pit toilet. Waste is deposited in a hole dug at least 5 ft deep, usually covered with toilet seat and a structure for privacy. When full, the pit is covered with dirt. Waste decomposes before leaching through soil.	Pit and structure have to be periodically moved. Toilet paper may be provided, and lime may be added to the pit to reduce odors.	Appropriate where use levels are moderate to low. Available sites may be limited by soil type and depth, surface water location, terrain, and groundwater depth.	Costs typically about $500 to $5000 for installation. Subsequent costs limited to periodically moving the pit and structure and toilet paper and lime, if provided. Visitor acceptance is fairly good.	Odors and flies are a problem. Sometimes there are not enough sites to relocate the toilet. Water contamination can occur if pits are improperly located. Otherwise, this system is effective and low cost.

(continued)

TABLE 3. (*Continued*)

Method	Maintenance Requirements	Appropriate Uses	Costs and Visitor Acceptance	Comments
Transportable privy. A toilet seat and structure are constructed over a removable drum or small fiberglass vault. The drum or vault is replaced when full and removed and emptied, generally by pack animal, helicopter, or vehicle.	Drums and vaults must be replaced when full. Containers may have to be stored and maintained. Waste must be dumped in sewage treatment facility.	As use levels increase, the frequency of replacement increases. This technique is most appropriate where sites for digging a pit are limited, water contamination potential is high, or use levels are high but frequent removal is possible.	Initial cost of a structure and drum or small vault is $500 to $5000, excluding labor. Removal costs can be high and are dependent on use levels and remoteness. Acceptance is high, although use of helicopters is controversial in wilderness.	On-site impacts are generally low. There are few limitations to where toilet can be located. However, maintenance costs are high and transport by helicopter or vehicles can be considered inappropriate.
Compost toilet. Waste decomposes in a digester tank into compost or humus. Waste is reduced, in volume and weight, by as much as 80%. It can be removed from the area or, in some cases, can be spread on the ground or used in reclamation projects.	Needs frequent maintenance. A carbon source, usually wood chips, must be mixed with feces, sometimes as frequently as twice a week. Finished compost must be removed periodically.	Appropriate where use levels exceed the capacities to use other waste management systems. But will be ineffective unless a commitment is made to provide adequate maintenance.	Commercial composting toilets cost $10,000 to $30,000 to install. A DC power source is needed, or power can be provided by photovoltaic panel, wind turbine generator, or thermoelectric generator. Less expensive passive composters are also available where use is low. Acceptance is high.	This technique is highly effective in high-use places, where frequent removal of material is difficult. The disadvantages are the high installation and maintenance costs.

314

Dehydrating toilet. Waste is deposited in a basket or tank where the liquid in fecal matter is evaporated. Weight and volume can be reduced 75%. When full, waste must be dug out and removed by pack animal, helicopter, or vehicle.	Commercial dehydrators have not met maintenance expectations. When modified appropriately, they may require weekly maintenance, primarily removal of waste. Dried sludge may be incinerated, buried, or disposed of in a sewage treatment facility.	Appropriate in a low-humidity climate. Certain commercial products require site modifications, and frequent maintenance is required. This technique can handle a high volume of use.	Typically costs $10,000 to $20,000 to install, as well as periodic maintenance and removal costs. Acceptance is high.	This technique is effective if the need to modify units on-site can be dealt with, if they can be maintained appropriately, and if the climate is appropriate.
Low-volume flush toilet. Waste is flushed down toilet into septic system, which must be pumped regularly. Effluent is disposed of in a leach field, sand mound, or constructed wetland. Water supply can be gravity fed or pumped.	System may require winterization. Pumps will require maintenance, and septic system needs pumping, with wastes removed to sewage treatment facility.	Appropriate in high-use areas, where plumbed systems are deemed acceptable.	Costs are likely to be $15,000 to $30,000. Maintenance costs are high, particularly where systems require winterization. Visitor acceptance is good, except in remote locations where plumbing is considered inappropriate.	Good system where considered appropriate and maintenance requirements can be met.

Source: Land 1995.

Outside of wilderness and other areas where preservation of natural conditions is paramount, durability of vegetation can be increased either by altering the vegetation composition in favor of more resistant species or by applying cultural treatments that make existing plants more resistant. Both are common practices in developed recreation areas and have a place in many wildland settings where use is at least moderately high.

An example of species replacement is planting turf grasses in a picnic ground to take the place of natives that have been eliminated by trampling. Generally, the only resistant plants available are (1) grasses, usually commercially available mixes of exotic species, or (2) shrubs and trees large enough to avoid being trampled. Thorny shrubs can be particularly useful. In the Grand Canyon, for example, expansion of backcountry campsites is being controlled by planting prickly pear cactus. The cactus establishes well from transplants and effectively discourages use of areas that are being rehabilitated. In deciding on which species to use, it is important to match species to local environmental conditions, particularly to amount of shade, soil fertility, and moisture. Trees should be long-lived, resistant to insects, diseases, and windthrow, and relatively small in size. It is also important to decide whether or not to encourage growth of exotic species. Exotics are often attractive, durable, and easy to establish; however, they frequently require more maintenance and are "unnatural."

The durability of vegetation can also be increased through use of various cultural treatments. Perhaps the simplest treatment is to thin the overstory. Numerous studies have documented a negative relationship between overstory canopy cover and ground cover vegetation impact. Generally, as shade decreases, vegetation cover increases and the amount of vegetation loss caused by recreational use decreases (Marion and Merriam 1985). Shade discourages the growth of grasses, which are almost always more resistant to impact than other plant types. Even within the same species, plants growing in a shady environment tend to be particularly flimsy as they spread out to capture sunlight. On campgrounds in the southern Appalachians, reducing canopy cover from 90 to 60 percent doubled grass cover; a further reduction to 30 percent cover tripled grass cover (Cordell, James, and Tyre 1974). Thinning trees, then, can increase both the quantity and hardiness of the ground cover. Thinning can also increase the vigor of the remaining overstory trees, improve wildlife habitat, and enhance esthetics and recreational opportunities. It is important, however, to maintain adequate screening between sites and not to increase susceptibility to windthrow.

Other treatments include irrigation and fertilization. These two treatments are likely to be particularly important in trying to maintain a sod of exotic grasses in a dry climate. In an area with a wet climate watering may not be necessary.

The importance of fertilization varies with soil conditions. Where trace elements are limited, their inclusion in soil amendments can lead to spectacular increases in growth. It is always worth investing in soil testing to identify any nutritional deficiencies. Even in soils without known deficiencies, exotic grasses usually respond well to additions of complete nitrogen-phosphorus-potassium fertilizers.

The pH of soil is also important. Native plants in coniferous forests grow best in moderately acidic soils (pH about 5.0), whereas exotic grasses prefer a neutral pH. Coniferous soils are likely to need liming to reduce acidity if conversion to grasses is desired. Where naturally acidic coniferous soils are neutralized by recreation use— remember that campfires tend to increase pH— an amendment like peat moss will promote growth of acid-living native species.

Either flood or aerial irrigation can be used to water plants (Jubenville and Twight 1993). With flood irrigation, water is diverted by ditch systems to the recreation area, where it is spread out across the ground. The developed campgrounds in the bottom of the Grand Canyon utilize flood irrigation to maintain cottonwood trees and some brushy screening between sites. Aerial irrigation can be used more flexibly. Either portable above-ground sprinklers or a buried underground system can be used. Either system is costly. A buried irrigation system used at a developed campground in Idaho cost almost $100 per unit per year in the late 1960s (Beardsley, Herrington, and Wagar 1974); this would be more than $400 per unit per year in the 1990s—a cost of $1.00 per visitor-day of use. Another problem with irrigation is related to the susceptibility of soil to compaction when it is wet. Watering should occur after, not before, periods of heavy use. If feasible, it may be best to close the campground or portions of the campground (loops) one day per week for watering.

Despite these problems, the value of irrigation and fertilization was illustrated in an experimental renovation and maintenance program conducted on the previously mentioned campground in Idaho (Beardsley, Herrington, and Wagar 1974). Large devegetated campsites were all seeded yearly with a mixture of exotic grasses. On some sites this seeding was the only treatment applied. Other sites were also either fertilized once a year, watered once a week—at a rate three times the normal summer rainfall—or both. Vegetation cover was monitored over a four-year period. As you can see from Fig. 11, seeding, by itself, resulted in little improvement in vegetation cover. This is not surprising, because exotic grasses are poorly adapted to a coniferous forest environment. Both watering and fertilization, by themselves, caused pronounced increases in cover, but the combination of the two was twice as effective as either one by itself.

Similar results were found in a campground in an aspen grove in Utah (Beardsley and Wagar 1971). Watering and fertilization, together, caused the greatest increase in ground cover. Fertilization, by itself, was less effective than watering, and fertilization without seeding or watering was no more effective than doing nothing at all. An interesting result of this study was that while these treatments did increase ground cover under aspen, similar treatments under a dense coniferous overstory had little effect. Without thinning and, perhaps, some removal of organic horizons, it is unlikely that any treatments can establish much vegetation under a dense coniferous overstory.

In England, fertilization was effective in reducing bare ground within trampled vegetation, still in use, by as much as 80 percent (Bayfield and Aitken 1992). However, some neighboring vegetation types experienced only modest improvements following fertilization and some types experienced no benefit at all.

A final conclusion derived from these evaluations of cultural treatments is that they will be effective only when combined with careful site design and surfacing of concentrated-use areas. As discussed earlier in this chapter, good design channels traffic along paths and roads and minimizes the area that is frequently trampled. Areas used so heavily that vegetation and organic horizons are entirely eliminated

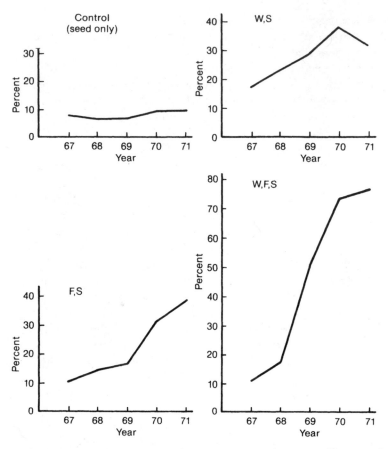

FIGURE 11. Percentage of available growing space on campsites covered by ground vegetation after various combinations of watering (W), fertilizing (F), and seeding (S). Treatments were initiated in 1967 and continued for 4 years. Data are from Point Campground in Idaho. (*Source*: Beardsley, Herrington, and Wagar 1974.)

should be surfaced to promote drainage, reduce compaction, and minimize problems with dust and mud.

In some situations site durability can also be increased by improving soil conditions, particularly by relieving soil compaction and increasing the organic content of soils. At a campground in Texas, Legg, Farnham, and Miller (1980) experimented with various means of relieving soil compaction without closing the entire campground. They experimented with various lengths and seasons of closure, with rototilling, and with incorporating wood chips and grass seed into the soil. Rototilling proved to be detrimental if it was done without closure or incorporation of wood chips into the soil. Rototilling destroyed soil structure, and this apparently prevented the over-winter recovery that usually occurs in these soils. Merely closing campsites during winter to promote over-winter recovery allowed compaction levels to return to near normal. Incorporation of wood chips into the soil greatly reduced bulk density, and the seeding of grasses resulted in less erosion during winter. The authors conclude that, at least in this area, rest-rotation of campsites is feasible, particularly if organic matter is incorporated into the soil. Where organic matter is added to soil, the populations of soil microorganisms that decompose this material can increase. These organisms may tie up much of the available nitrogen in the soil and deprive plants of nitrogen. It may be necessary to compensate for this by adding high-nitrogen fertilizer, along with organic amendments.

Surface application of wood chips—mulching—was effective in encouraging plant growth on closed day-use picnic areas in four Maryland state parks (Little and Mohr 1979). Surface application promotes moisture retention and inhibits surface runoff. The authors believed that scarification, breaking up the soil with rototillers or hand tools, can cause problems in forested areas because it can disturb tree roots. Moreover, in their study, scarification did not increase vegetation growth. Their primary suggestions for rehabilitation were to confine use to hardened parts of the site and to mulch little-used parts of the area.

REHABILITATION OF CLOSED SITES

In some situations there is no option but to permanently close and rehabilitate recreation sites. Common reasons for such an action include excessive site damage that cannot be controlled with continued use, a decision to relocate the facility on a more durable or desirable site, and rehabilitation of previous damage that is unlikely to occur in the future because of a change in either type of use or management. Many of the cultural treatments we have been discussing—watering, fertilizing, seeding, mulching, and so on—can also be used to rehabilitate closed sites. Some are not appropriate; replacing native vegetation with exotic, trampling-resistant species or thinning the overstory to encourage grasses makes little sense if use of the site is to be curtailed. Other techniques, particularly eliminating all use on the site, become even more important.

Rehabilitation of camp or picnic sites and trails is most common. Other recreation sites that may require rehabilitation work are overgrazed meadows and off-road vehicle areas. Although a considerable amount of rehabilitation work has been done, little of it has been documented. Most experience in site rehabilitation comes from revegetation of mines and rangelands.

Regardless of the facility being rehabilitated, five basic steps are required:

1. *Eliminate use.* Some effective means must be devised for keeping visitors off closed sites. Particularly in fragile areas, even infrequent use can destroy the fruits of years of work. Providing attractive alternative use areas is of critical importance. Channeling use away from the area, using either attractions or barriers, may also be helpful. A sign to a viewpoint, away from the closed area, may be effective. Use of branches and brush to block a trail may keep people from using it. "Planting" rocks or logs on a site will discourage overnight use but may not curtail day use. Signs or other information

about the closure, reasons for the closure, and the location of replacement facilities may be necessary (Fig. 12). Where closed areas are intermixed with open areas, it may be necessary to delineate closed areas with some sort of fencing to prevent use. The fencing material can vary from string to stouter materials, such as lumber.

Keeping users off closed sites can be a particularly serious problem in wilderness areas, where management strives to be as inobtrusive as possible. Because even people walking across a site to go fishing can destroy rehabilitation work, there may be no alternative to obtrusive fencing until substantial recovery occurs. Information about the location of and reasons for rehabilitation programs will increase compliance because visitors know what to expect and why and how to comply. Research indicates that wilderness visitors support even obtrusive site management techniques—signs, barriers, and plantings—where needed to reduce impacts (Cole, Watson, Hall, and Spildie 1997).

2. *Control drainage and erosion on the site.* On camp and picnic areas it is important to keep drainageways from flooding the site; some sort of mulch may also be needed to control sheet erosion on the site. Control of gully erosion on trails is more difficult. The techniques for minimizing erosion of used trails, described in the preceding section, are all appropriate. On closed trails check dams, built across the trail, can be used to reduce erosion and encourage sedimentation behind the dams. Mulching can also be useful.

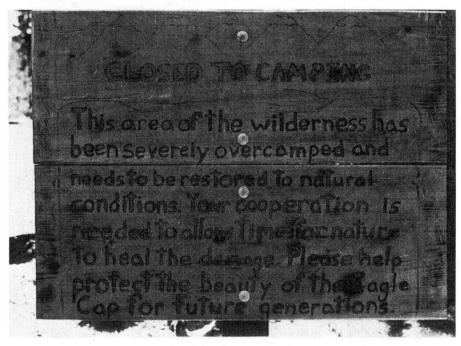

FIGURE 12. Sign used to keep visitors off a campsite in the Eagle Cap Wilderness, Oregon, while the site was being rehabilitated. (*Photo:* D. N. Cole.)

3. *Prepare the soil.* The nature of soil preparation is highly variable; it ranges from doing almost nothing on lightly disturbed backcountry sites to extensive grading and importing soil in severely eroded off-road vehicle areas. The principal objectives of this step are to reduce soil compaction and to improve the organic matter content, fertility, moisture content, and biotic integrity of the soil. Exactly what treatments are needed will depend on characteristics of both the undisturbed and the damaged soil, as well as the nature of the vegetation to be reestablished. Soil scarification, breaking up compacted soil, is usually critical for both seed germination and root and plant growth. The soil is broken into large clods with shovel, pick, or rototiller, and then these clods are broken down into individual soil crumbs by hand or rake (Rochefort 1990). All compacted soils should be scarified, although one should be careful to minimize destruction of roots and plant parts that are capable of vegetatively reproducing. Also, as Legg, Farnham, and Miller (1980) found, scarification may be of little value unless organic matter is either incorporated into or spread on top of the soil. Addition of organic matter is probably effective in minimizing the tendency of soils to be compacted by rainfall and other natural forces.

The value of adding organic matter to the soil and the best type to add depends on soil pH and the optimum pH for the vegetation to be reestablished. Peat moss and coniferous duff promote acidity, whereas steer manure is good for basic soils (Schreiner and Moorhead 1981). Liming can also reduce the acidity of soils. Rotting logs can be planted to provide ongoing sources of organic matter and shelter for plantings. It is important to replenish large woody debris on sites where it has been entirely removed, because such debris plays a critical role in the functioning of many ecosystems (see Chapter 2). Where substantial quantities of organic matter are added, it may also be necessary to add nitrogen to the soil. Soil nitrogen is likely to be depleted by the increased number of microorganisms that are involved in breaking down the supplemental organic matter.

Soil biota, including mycorrhizal fungi, are critical to the health of soil because they often form symbiotic relationships with plants. When plants have been eliminated from a site for years, many of these organisms disappear. Reintroducing plants will not automatically bring these organisms back, but many plants will not grow well as long as they are absent. Often microbes can simply be reintroduced by mixing some "native" soil, from adjacent undisturbed areas, onto the scarified soils.

Fertilization is important where exotic plants are being established. As this is less common on permanently closed sites, fertilization may be less important than in places where recreational use continues. Fertilization appears to be more critical to the establishment of vegetation from seeds than from transplants. Fertilization is often of little value if not accompanied by watering (Beardsley and Wagar 1971). Generally, fertilizers should be used cautiously, particularly in wilderness, where their use tends to favor exotic species and can contribute to eutrophication of nearby waters. Information on desirable soil preparations can often be obtained from university extension services provided by land grant colleges, the federal Soil Conservation Service, state soil testing labs or departments of conservation, and local planning offices.

4. *Plant the site*. Under certain favorable circumstances, natural revegetation may occur rapidly without much assistance. This is most likely at low elevations, where growing seasons are long, on productive soils, and in places that receive abundant but not excessive light and moisture. Elsewhere, rehabilitation will have to be assisted either by transplanting nursery-grown plants or plants from neighboring areas or by seeding. This step involves deciding which species to use, preparing propagules for planting, and then doing the actual planting.

In deciding which species to use, the most important consideration is whether or not the species is adapted to the site. As noted before, it is difficult to grow grass in heavy shade or on acidic soils. Similarly, it is difficult to grow forest-floor species in a meadow. With native species it is best to use plants from local and similar environments. Sometimes even the same species from a distant location or elevational zone is poorly adapted, genetically, to the site. Species that successfully colonize neighboring naturally disturbed areas are particularly good choices for revegetating disturbed areas. Resistant species, including exotics, may be desirable in places where it may be difficult to avoid consistent ongoing use.

Seeding is a cost-effective means of assisting the natural revegetation processes on many sites. Generally, it involves spreading seed over the loosened soil surface—by hand, with a hand-held seed spreader, or with a hydromulch machine. Then the seeds are lightly raked into the soil and tamped down to ensure good contact between the seed and the soil. The best time to plant seed varies from place to place and can be critical to success. In the mountainous national parks of the Pacific Northwest, for example, it is best to sow seed in the late fall. This is optimum for breaking seed dormancy and for ensuring germination early in the short growing season.

Finally, it is usually helpful to cover the ground surface with a mulch to protect the seed from predators and erosion and to improve seed germination. Either commercial or native mulches can be used. Commercial mulch mats come in rolls that can be laid over seeded ground and anchored with rocks and woody debris. These consist of a mulch fiber (usually paper, excelsior, straw, or coconut) held together by a photo-degradable netting (Rochefort 1990). Ideally, both the mulch material and netting decompose and disappear after two to five years. Native mulch consists of any plant material (litter, duff, or plant parts) that can provide protection to underlying seeds. Native mulches are less costly and visually obtrusive than commercial mulch mats; they also contribute organic matter and sometimes viable seed. However, they are not as effective a deterrent to recreation use, may be more difficult to anchor in place, may be less effective in protecting against erosion, and may not be available in the quantities needed.

Seed can sometimes be obtained commercially but usually must be collected locally. Seed mixes of exotic species are readily available; however, they are inappropriate for many wildland applications. The availability of commercial native seed mixes is increasing, but these mixes are costly and not available for the entire range of ecosystem types that need restoring. When collecting locally, seed should be taken from places that are quite similar and close to the place being restored. Seed must be ripe. If it is loose, it can be collected with a butterfly net, a battery-operated vacuum, or simply shaken onto a cloth around the base of the plant (Birkby 1996). Seed should be collected from many different plants to maintain genetic diversity. Once collected, seed can either be sown immediately or transported and stored. If stored, it should be cleaned. This involves separating the seed from the chaff by shaking, blowing, or sieving the seeds through a strainer. Seed should be carefully labeled and stored in a cool, airtight container until ready to be sown (Birkby 1996).

In many favorable environments, seeding works well. High germination rates, for many different species, occur virtually every year. Frequent rain during the season when germination and establishment are occurring appears to be a key to seeding success. In other environments, successful reproduction from seed is a rare event. This is the case, for example, in many high elevation environments, where most recolonization of natural disturbances is by vegetative spread rather than seed germination and establishment. Particularly in these places, transplanting may be the only practical means of rapidly revegetating a site.

Transplanting involves taking an established plant and placing it in a hole dug out several inches wider and deeper than the root ball of the plant. The top of the root ball is placed slightly below the ground surface so that water can collect in a slight depression around the plant (Rochefort 1990). Soil is added to the hole and packed down tightly. If this soil comes from a local native source, it can serve to inoculate the soil with desirable microbes. The plant is watered with a mixture of water and vitamin B-1 to reduce transplant shock. Finally, the planting is often covered with mulch.

The difficulty in transplanting is obtaining a source of transplants. Options include digging up plants in the neighboring area or growing transplants in nurseries—from collected seed, cuttings, or by division of plants capable of reproducing from underground stems or rhizomes—and then transporting these plants to the site. Transplanting with native vegetation is easiest but creates the problem of disturbing the donor sites from which the plants are taken. Plants should be taken from a large area and only from places with a fairly dense vegetation cover. Clearly, this technique will seldom be an effective way to revegetate large areas. It is critical to minimize damage to roots when digging the plants. Often it is better to move a section of turf than a number of individual plants. In general, transplanting success is greatest with grasses, sedges, mat-forming plants, and plants with runners (Birkby 1996). Ideally, plants should be moved when they are dormant and when the weather is cool and cloudy. After being dug up, they should be transplanted as rapidly as possible, and any damage to the donor site should be repaired. Clusters of plants should be placed in a random rather than regular pattern to mimic natural growth.

Whether grown from seed, cuttings, or root divisions, greenhouse plants have to be hardened off (subjected to the rigors of living outdoors) before being transported to the restoration site. Transportation can be costly, involving the use of helicopters, pack animals, or backpackers if they cannot be moved by vehicle. Plants must be kept moist during transport. Packing plants in wet burlap bags or plastic bags with damp moss can help (Birkby 1996). Once at the restoration site, greenhouse plants are less fragile and easier to plant than native plugs (Rochefort 1990). They can be dumped out of their containers and placed directly in the ground.

5. *Maintain the plantings.* Ongoing maintenance activities will vary from place to place. In some situations yearly fertilization and weekly watering are necessary; in

other situations little maintenance is required. "Please water me" signs can be a good means of getting help from visitors. All areas will profit from careful documentation of the rehabilitation techniques that were used, as well as monitoring of how successful the effort was. Photographs and counts of plants can help in evaluating success. Before launching into a full-scale program, experimentation with different species, types of soil preparations, and planting techniques will save much time and money in the long run.

Even with all this effort, revegetation can be an exceedingly slow process. In many cases transplant survival has been high, but growth and spread have been slow. Transplants on road cuts in the alpine zone of Rocky Mountain National Park were surviving after 40 years, but they had not spread significantly (Stevens 1979). Similar slow growth and spread are common wherever the climate is severe and growing seasons are short (Fig. 13). Three years after being planted on closed campsites at subalpine lakes in Yosemite National Park, only 19 percent of the transplants were alive and total vegetation cover had increased by less than 1 percent (Moritsch and Muir 1993). This emphasizes the need to avoid damage rather than plan to fix it after it occurs.

Somewhat different techniques may be needed to rehabilitate trails, primarily because erosion is more of a problem on trails. Once erosion problems are solved, however, trail restoration is often more successful than camp or picnic area restoration.

FIGURE 13. These transplants on a campsite in the Eagle Cap Wilderness, Oregon, have survived for five years, but they have not spread. (*Photo*: D. N. Cole.)

This success may reflect the narrowness of the disturbed area. As a result, vegetation can rapidly recolonize old trails—either from seed or by vegetative spread. The keys to success are controlling erosion and filling the trail tread with soil to the level of the surrounding topography.

Palmer (1979) experimented with various means of rehabilitating multiple trails in Tuolumne Meadows, Yosemite National Park, California. The most successful technique involved cutting off the sod ridges between multiple trails at the level of the trail tread and stacking the sod in the shade. The soil beneath both the trails and the ridges was spaded up to eliminate compaction, and sand was added to bring the whole area up to the level of the surrounding meadow. Finally, the vegetation from the sod ridges was divided into transplant plugs and planted in the soil. Utilizing this technique, trail scarring was less obvious and transplants were spreading within several years. This technique has proven successful in eliminating almost all evidence of many old trails.

A final example of restoration is the rehabilitation of meadows in Sequoia and Kings Canyon National Parks, California. These meadows had been severely disturbed by a history of overgrazing by both recreational and domestic livestock. This use led to loss of vegetation cover and shifts in species composition that favored unpalatable and weedy species. The most serious problem was accelerated erosion. Destruction of sod and trampling of streambanks increased erosion. Increased downcutting by streams lowered water tables, drying out meadows. This allowed lodgepole pine seedlings to germinate and become established in meadows. Many meadows were shrinking dramatically as this invasion of trees progressed. Meadow rehabilitation involved both visitor and site management. The amount, distribution, and timing of stock use was controlled. In addition, erosion was controlled by building check dams, grading stream banks, and planting banks with willow cuttings (DeBenedetti and Parsons 1979).

REFERENCES

Bayfield, N. G., and R. Aitken. 1992. *Managing the Impacts of Recreation on Vegetation and Soils: A Review of Techniques.* Banchory, Scotland: Institute of Terrestrial Ecology. 100 pp.

Bayfield, N. G., and G. M. Bathe. 1982. Experimental Closure of Footpaths in a Woodland National Nature Reserve in Scotland. *Biological Conservation* 22:229–237.

Beardsley, W. G., and J. A. Wagar. 1971. Vegetation Management on a Forested Recreation Site. *Journal of Forestry* 69:728–731.

Beardsley, W. G., R. B. Herrington, and J. A. Wagar. 1974. Recreation Site Management: How to Rehabilitate a Heavily Used Campground Without Stopping Visitor Use. *Journal of Forestry* 72:279–281.

Birkby, R. C. 1996. *Lightly on the Land: The SCA Trail-Building and Maintenance Manual.* Seattle, WA: The Mountaineers. 267 pp.

Carlson, L. H., and P. J. Godfrey. 1989. Human Impact Management in a Coastal Recreation and Natural Area. *Biological Conservation* 49:141–156.

Cole, D. N. 1982. Wilderness Campsite Impacts: Effect of Amount of Use. USDA Forest Service Research Paper INT-284. 34 pp.

Cole, D. N. 1983. Assessing and Monitoring Backcountry Trail Conditions. USDA Forest Service Research Paper INT-303. 10 pp.

Cole, D. N. 1995. Experimental Trampling of Vegetation. I. Relationship Between Trampling Intensity and Vegetation Response. *Journal of Applied Ecology* 32:203–214.

Cole, D. N., and B. Ranz. 1983. Temporary Campsite Closures in the Selway-Bitterroot Wilderness. *Journal of Forestry* 81:729–732.

Cole, D. N., A. E. Watson, T. E. Hall, and D. R. Spildie, 1997. High-Use Destination Areas in Wilderness: Social and Biophysical Impacts, Visitor Responses, and Management Options. USDA Forest Service Research Paper INT-483. 38 pp.

Cordell, H. K., G. A. James, and G. L. Tyre. 1974. Grass Establishment on Developed Recreation Sites. *Journal of Soil and Water Conservation* 29:268–271.

DeBenedetti, S. H., and D. J. Parsons. 1979. Mountain Meadow Management and Research in Sequoia and Kings Canyon National Parks: A Review and Update. In R. M. Linn, ed. *Proceedings of the Conference on Scientific Research in the National Parks*. USDI National Park Service, Transactions and Proceedings Series 5. Washington, DC: U.S. Government Printing Office, pp. 1305–1311.

Douchette, J. E., and K. D. Kimball. 1990. Passive Trail Management in Northeastern Alpine Zones: A Case Study. In *Proceedings of the 1990 Northeastern Recreation Research Symposium*. USDA Forest Service General Technical Report NE-145, pp. 195–201.

Garland, G. G. 1990. Technique for Assessing Erosion Risk from Mountain Footpaths. *Environmental Management* 14:793–798.

Hesselbarth, W., and B. Vachowski. 1996. Trail Construction and Maintenance Notebook. USDA Forest Service, Missoula Technology and Development Center, 9623-2833-MTDC, Missoula, MT. 139 pp.

Hinds, T. E. 1976. Aspen Mortality in Rocky Mountain Campgrounds. USDA Forest Service Research Paper RM-164. 20 pp.

Jubenvile, A., and B. W. Twight. 1993. *Outdoor Recreation Management: Theory and Application*. 3d ed. College Station, PA: Venture. 315 pp.

Land, B. 1995. Remote Waste Management. USDA Forest Service, San Dimas Technology and Development Center, 9523 1202-SDTDC, San Dimas, CA. 31 pp.

LaPage, W. F. 1967. Some Observations on Campground Trampling and Ground Cover Response. USDA Forest Service Research Paper NE-68. 11 pp.

Legg, M., K. Farnham, and E. Miller. 1980. Soil Restoration on Deteriorated Campsites in Texas. *Southern Journal of Applied Forestry* 4:189–193.

Leonard, R. E., E. L. Spencer, and H. J. Plumley. 1981. *Backcountry Facilities: Design and Maintenance*. Boston: Appalachian Mountain Club. 214 pp.

Leung, Y., and J. L. Marion. 1996. Trail Degradation as Influenced by Environmental Factors: A State-of-the-Knowledge Review. *Journal of Soil and Water Conservation* 51:130–136.

Little, S., and J. J. Mohr. 1979. Reestablishing Understory Plants in Overused Wooded Areas of Maryland State Parks. USDA Forest Service Research Paper NE-431. 9 pp.

Marion, J. L. 1995. Capabilities and Management Utility of Recreation Impact Monitoring Programs. *Environmental Management* 19:763–771.

Marion, J. L., and D. N. Cole. 1996. Spatial and Temporal Variation in Soil and Vegetation Impacts on Campsites. *Ecological Applications* 6:520–530.

Marion, J. L., and Y. Leung. 1996. An Assessment of Campsite Conditions in Great Smoky Mountains National Park. USDI National Park Service, Great Smoky Mountains National Park, Gatlinburg, TN. 127 pp.

Marion, J. L., and L. C. Merriam. 1985. Recreational Impacts on Well-Established Campsites in the Boundary Waters Canoe Area. University of Minnesota Agricultural Experiment Station Bulletin AD-SB-2502, St. Paul, MN. 16 pp.

Marion, J. L., J. W. Roggenbuck, and R. E. Manning. 1993. Problems and Practices in Backcountry Recreation Management: A Survey of National Park Service Managers. USDI National Park Service Natural Resources Report NPS/NRVT/NRR-93/12. 48 pp.

Maschinski, J., R. Frye, and S. Rutman. 1997. Demography and Population Viability of an Endangered Plant Species Before and After Protection from Trampling. *Conservation Biology* 11:990–999.

McEwen, D., and S. R. Tocher. 1976. Zone Management: Key to Controlling Recreational Impact in Developed Campsites. *Journal of Forestry* 74:90–93.

Merriam, L. C. Jr., C. K. Smith, D. E. Miller, C. Huang, J. C. Tappeiner II, K. Goeckermann, J. A. Blomendal, and T. M. Costello. 1973. Newly Developed Campsites in the Boundary Waters Canoe Area—A Study of Five Years' Use. University of Minnesota Agricultural Experiment Station, St. Paul, Bulletin 511. 27 pp.

Moritsch, B. J., and P. S. Muir. 1993. Subalpine Revegetation in Yosemite National Park, California: Changes in Vegetation After Three Years. *Natural Areas Journal* 13:155–163.

Palmer, R. 1979. Progress Report on Trail Revegetation Studies. In J. T. Stanley Jr., H. T. Harvey, and R. J. Hartesveldt, eds. *A Report on the Wilderness Study: The Effects of Human Recreational Activities on Wilderness Ecosystems with Special Emphasis on Sierra Club Wilderness Outings in the Sierra Nevada.* San Francisco: Outing Committee, Sierra Club, pp. 193–196.

Parsons, D. J., and S. H. DeBenedetti. 1979. Wilderness Protection in the High Sierra: Effects of a 15-Year Closure. In R. M. Linn, ed. *Proceedings of the Conference on Scientific Research in the National Parks*, USDI National Park Service, Transactions and Proceedings Series 5. Washington, DC: U.S. Government Printing Office, pp. 1313–1318.

Ripley, T. H. 1962. Tree and Shrub Response to Recreation Use. USDA Forest Service Research Note SE-171. 2 pp.

Rochefort, R. M. 1990. *Mount Rainier National Park Restoration Handbook.* Ashford, WA: USDI National Park Service, Mount Rainier National Park. 57 pp.

Schreiner, E., and B. B. Moorhead. 1981. Human Impact Inventory and Backcountry Rehabilitation in Olympic National Park: Research and Its Application. *Park Science* 1(2):1–4.

Stevens, D. R. 1979. Problems in Revegetation of Alpine Tundra. In R. M. Linn, ed. *Proceedings of the Conference on Scientific Research in the National Parks*, USDI National Park Service, Transactions and Proceedings Series 5. Washington, DC: U.S. Government Printing Office, pp. 241–245.

Swearingen, T. C., and D. R. Johnson. 1995. Visitors' Responses to Uniformed Park Employees. *Journal of Park and Recreation Administration* 13:73–85.

Thorud, D. B., and S. S. Frissell. 1976. Time Changes in Soil Density Following Compaction Under an Oak Forest. Minnesota Forest Research Note 257. 4 pp.

14 International Impact Research and Management

Contributed by
Jeffrey L. Marion and Yu-Fai Leung
Virginia Polytechnic Institute and State University

The preceding chapters have focused on recreation impacts and their influential factors primarily from a North American perspective. Although the North American experience is undoubtedly a valuable one, we can always gain insights from other countries where similar problems are encountered in different environmental, socioeconomic, and managerial contexts. The recent expansion of nature tourism and ecotourism is a case in point. The term *nature tourism* encompasses any tourism that is dependent on largely undeveloped natural environments and their resources, such as scenery, water, vegetation, wildlife, and geological features (Cellabos-Lascurain 1996). It differs from mass tourism, which is based on human-created attractions such as amusement parks, resort hotels, and night clubs or casinos. *Ecotourism* has been defined variously as either synonymous with nature tourism or as environmentally sensitive and responsible travel that contributes to the sustainability of ecological and sociocultural integrity (Cater 1994).

Wildland environments, including their flora and fauna, are the primary attraction for ecotourists. To be sustainable, ecotourism requires the tourism industry to plan and ensure the protection of natural environments and processes—both from development and operation of the tourism infrastructure (roads, hotels, and restaurants) and from the activities of ecotourists within protected areas (Wall 1997). Tourism developments and visitor activities have the potential to create significant and even irreversible impacts on vegetation, soil, water, and wildlife resources. Such resource degradation may result in a loss of visitation and associated economic benefits. This chapter reviews the international literature on the study of visitor- or recreation-related resource impacts with special reference to ecotourism. Four case examples are presented to characterize the geographic scope, focus, and principal findings of this recreation ecology literature and its relevance to ecotourism resource management. Implications for the management of international protected areas and ecotourism resources are discussed in a concluding section.

CASE EXAMPLE 1: CAIRNGORMS NATIONAL NATURE RESERVE, SCOTLAND

In Europe, the pressure of human impacts on mountain areas resulting from tourism development and recreational activities has long been a major conservation issue, and the Cairngorms mountains in northeastern Scotland provide a typical example (Edwards 1996). Designated in 1954 as a National Nature Reserve in recognition of their conservation and scientific value, the Cairngorms contain outstanding relics of arctic-alpine tundra, possessing unique and fragile montane plant communities and providing habitats for rare fauna such as dotterels, golden eagles, and ptarmigan (Nethersole-Thompson and Watson 1974).

Tourism Types and Impact

This wilderness-like, yet accessible, seminatural area attracts tens of thousands of domestic and foreign tourists every year. Popular recreational activities include downhill skiing, hiking, and hunting. Conflicts between tourism and conservation have intensified since skiing facilities were built in the early 1960s. There were concerns that the construction of tourism facilities and subsequent increased visitation would cause substantial damage to the reserve, threatening the integrity of its landscape and ecosystem (Watson 1984c).

In response, a comprehensive recreation ecology research program was established to identify, assess, and monitor visitor impacts and to rehabilitate damaged habitats (Bayfield, Watson, and Miller 1988). This program encompassed experimental studies of the effects of human trampling on vegetation, lichens, and soil, assessment and monitoring of trail proliferation and degradation, evaluation of soil erosion on vehicular tracks and ski grounds, and investigations of recreational impacts on wildlife.

An integral part of this program involves impact assessment and monitoring of footpaths and hunting-related vehicular tracks (Watson 1984a, 1984b; Lance, Baugh, and Love 1989). Monitoring results reveal a proliferation of footpaths and vehicular tracks over the landscape, particularly near ski grounds and parking areas. Some established footpaths have increased in width and in the creation of secondary tracks. Immediate concerns include the risk of soil erosion and the concomitant deterioration of scenic quality and ecosystem health. The affected area is extensive, including an estimated 17 percent of the land disturbance within the reserve (Watson 1985).

Recreation Ecology Studies

The relationship between amount of use and intensity of impact has been a primary research focus. Detrimental use-impact relationships have been found for vegetation damage (Watson 1985), lichen damage (Bayfield, Urquhart, and Cooper 1981), and footpath widening (Lance, Baugh, and Love 1989). Many of these relationships are curvilinear in form, indicating that most damage occurs at low levels of use. Such a finding is supported by the recreation ecology literature, as documented in the previous chapters. The exact forms of the use-impact relationship, however, vary among plant species because of inherent differences in their susceptibility to trampling impact.

The influence of use-related and environmental factors has also been examined. For example, certain slope gradients were found to promote walking behavior that caused trail widening or soil erosion (Bayfield 1973). Recovery of vegetation is related to altitude (Bayfield 1979). Snow cover of merely 1 cm depth was found to substantially reduce trampling effects (Bayfield 1971). Differential resistance and resilience of plant species are also evident from the trampling studies. Of these, lichens were consistently found to be most vulnerable to trampling impact (Bayfield, Urquhart, and Cooper 1981).

Rates of recovery from recreation impacts in vegetative cover were found to be slow in general, except in a few heath species, which recovered more than 50 percent of their initial cover within two growing seasons (Bayfield 1979). Active programs of rehabilitation through transplanting and fertilizing can accelerate the recovery process, particularly at lower elevations (Bayfield, Watson, and Miller 1988).

Ecotourism management of protected areas can benefit from the findings in the Cairngorms experience. Early and judicious trail planning and management are critical to prevent widespread disturbance by user-created footpaths and vehicular tracks. The attention of management is particularly critical in areas with sensitive resources. Management zoning can be used to match the amount and type of visitation to areas of differing resource susceptibility. Assisted recovery may be effective in some instances. Standards for minimum snow cover can also be developed for ski-related recreation activities.

CASE EXAMPLE 2: THE GREAT BARRIER REEF

Along the northeast continental shelf of Queensland, Australia, lies the Great Barrier Reef Region, encompassing the world's largest coral reef system. Covering some 350,000 sq km, the Great Barrier Reef includes some 2900 individual reefs, interspersed with 300 low reef islands or cays and 600 higher islands (Craik 1992). Australia passed the Great Barrier Reef Marine Park Act in 1975, both to protect and to guide development within the area. A Marine Park Authority was created and charged with implementing a multiple-use management approach emphasizing conservation, reasonable use, and sustainable development. The Act prohibits commercial mining and oil drilling and authorizes the regulation of other activities through the preparation of zoning plans.

Tourism Types and Impact

The Great Barrier Reef Region attracts approximately 500,000 tourists annually, who contribute an estimated $1000 million per year (Craik 1992). Tourists' fascination with these reefs has been a mainstay underlying much of Australia's and Queensland's tourist promotion for many years (Kenchington 1991). Tourist activities include reef walking (a common activity during low tides), snorkeling, diving, coral and fish viewing, and boating. Camping on the reef islands has also become a popular activity. Commercial industries supporting reef snorkeling and diving have grown enormously in response to tourist interests, shifting from fishing and collecting to nature appreciation. Technological advances in boat and engine designs have also enabled faster access to outer barrier reefs, accommodating an expanding market of guided dive and snorkel tours (Fig. 1).

Expanding tourism visitation and development have the potential to degrade both natural resources and the recreational experiences of tourists (Fig. 2). The prevention of unacceptable ecological impact is paramount in the Marine Park Authority's management of tourism development (Craik 1992). However, the Park Authority is also charged with managing the Great Barrier Reef for its appreciation and enjoyment by the public. Tourist activity impacts include physical damage to reefs from boat anchors and groundings, snorkeling, diving, and reef walking (Fig. 3). Overfishing, collection of reef organisms, and disturbance of seabirds, whales, and fish are also of concern. Tourist facility impacts include the biophysical impacts related to the construction and operation of supporting tourism facilities such as marinas and resorts. Such development is often concentrated around popular attractions and tourism facilities, so that overcrowding and conflicts between user groups are also of concern to the Park Authority.

Recreation Ecology Studies

Several recreation ecology studies have been conducted to evaluate tourist activity impacts within the Great Barrier Reef. An early study by Woodland and Hooper (1977) documented the vulnerability of the fragile coral reefs to reef walking; 125 kg of live coral were broken off by four persons traversing a 12-m transect 18 times.

FIGURE 1. High-speed boats and technological advances have accommodated an expanding market in guided dive and snorkel tours. (*Photo*: C. Scott Shafer.)

FIGURE 2. Expanding tourism visitation and tour services allow snorkeling access to outer barrier reefs to be a common experience. (*Photo*: C. Scott Shafer.)

FIGURE 3. Physical damage to coral reefs caused by boat anchors and groundings, diving, reef walking, and snorkeling is a concern for managers of coral reef systems. (*Photo*: C. Scott Shafer.)

Furthermore, the curvilinear relationship between amount of trampling and impact, common in terrestrial studies, was also shown to apply to coral reef trampling. Twenty-seven percent of the broken coral was removed by the first two passes, additional passes produced proportionally less breakage, and by the eighteenth pass it was considered that little additional damage would be done by further walking. Subsequent research by Kay and Liddle (1989) support these findings. Their data indicate that most coral breakage occurs in the first five passes and that subsequent trampling only breaks this material into smaller fragments. However, Liddle and Kay (1987) found that nearly 100 percent of the damaged colonies survive and recovery of damaged areas ranges from 33 to 88 percent within three months.

Similar to terrestrial plant communities, coral reefs are comprised of dozens of coral species that exhibit considerable morphological diversity. Research by Liddle and Kay (1987) demonstrated that massive and thickly branched forms of coral are significantly more resistant to trampling breakage than more finely branched colonies. Furthermore, coral communities in reef crest zones, which must withstand the daily pounding of ocean surfs, were at least 16 times more resistant to trampling damage than coral communities in the more protected outer reef flat zone.

Behavior of divers has also been identified as a significant factor influencing coral reef damage (Harriott, Davis, and Banks 1997). Observations revealed that the majority of divers had few contacts with the substratum while diving and that few of those contacts damaged corals. However, a very small minority of divers with poor buoyancy control and finning skills contacted the substratum as many as 304 times during a 30-minute dive, and as many as 15 corals were broken in a single dive.

A variety of spatial, temporal, permit, equipment, and quota controls are employed at the Great Barrier Reef in managing human activities and their effects (Kenchington 1991). For example, an extensive program of education and information is operated, including distribution of printed material, direct advertising, and school programs (Zell 1985). Permitting, regulations, and enforcement are primarily directed at tourism providers rather than at tourists. These management tools could be used to minimize visitor impacts to coral reefs by concentrating recreational activities at a limited number of resistant reefs. As in terrestrial environments, research suggests that recreation impacts occur rapidly yet stabilize, so that increased use in an existing location results in far less impact than would occur in a new location. In addition, differences in coral resistance to damage suggest that focusing visitation on resistant reefs will minimize impact. Marion and Rogers (1994) review these and other recommendations for managing coral reef use and impact.

CASE EXAMPLE 3: CENTRAL AMERICAN TROPICS

Much of the ecotourism visitation in tropical regions is focused on coastal beaches and coral reefs. However, an increasing number of ecotourists are discovering and becoming fascinated with jungle vegetation and wildlife in tropical forests (Fig. 4). Such ecotourism destinations comprise fragile ecosystems with tremendous biological diversity, including some rare or endangered flora and fauna. Increased visitation to

FIGURE 4. A frequently visited ecotourism resource in the high jungle vegetation zone of Peru is Machu Picchu, an ancient Incan city. (*Photo*: W. E. Hammitt.)

FIGURE 5. Ecotourists are not the sole source of hiking-related impacts. In this scene, tour guides are camping in grass makeshift tents immediately adjacent to the Inca Trail in Peru. (*Photo*: W. E. Hammitt.)

these sensitive environments, particularly in active pursuits such as hiking and wildlife viewing, increase the likelihood of resource degradation (Fig. 5). Little is known about these effects, as most visitor impact studies have been conducted in temperate environments, such as those of the United States and Europe. The small number of studies in tropical regions, reviewed here, may be insufficient to guide managers in effectively minimizing the impacts of this growing use.

Tourism Types and Impact

In coastal protected areas primary visitor activities include beach-related swimming, walking, and sunbathing, coral reef snorkeling and diving, and wildlife observation. Beaches are naturally resistant to many recreational activities, but significant impacts can be associated with infrastructure development, typically occurring outside protected area boundaries. Wildlife viewing can also be a popular activity, including whale watching and observing seabird colonies, sea lions, and sea turtles. For example, Tortuguero National Park in Costa Rica serves as a primary nesting area for as many as 23,000 green sea turtles. Visitation has experienced a 24-fold increase in the past decade, causing managers and biologists to become concerned about the impact of visitors seeking to view the one- to two-hour nesting process (Jacobson and Lopez 1994). The unique wildlife of the Galapagos Islands, Ecuador, attracts more than 50,000 visitors annually. A number of visitor impacts have been noted, including disturbance of bird nesting and seal lions, litter, and trail erosion (Boo 1990). Burger and Gochfeld (1993) documented behavioral changes and an avoidance of nesting near trails in three species of boobies, ground-nesting seabirds, on the islands.

In tropical forests and associated protected areas visitors are engaged primarily in trail-dependent activities, such as viewing tropical forest vegetation and wildlife, geological features such as volcanos, and cultural features such as ancient ruins. These hiking activities are primarily daytime endeavors; few visitors appear to engage in overnight camping. The most common resource impacts are vegetational disturbance, compositional change and loss, and the exposure, compaction, and erosion of soil along trails and at popular attractions. Other impacts cited in the literature include littering, graffiti, wildlife disturbance, picking orchids, and theft of cultural artifacts (Andereck 1995; Boo 1990). These impacts are not well researched, and funding limitations often preclude effective management responses such as facility development, education, and regulations and enforcement.

Recreation Ecology Studies

Few scientific studies have been published that evaluate negative ecotourism impacts to wildlife, so informal observation frequently provides the only available information. The most complete survey of such observations was conducted by Boo (1990). Examples include alteration of wildlife habitats by avoidance of trails, littering (which can be harmful to wildlife), introduction of exotic animals, wildlife feeding, and wildlife disturbance and harassment, particularly by photographers (Fig. 6). Griffiths

FIGURE 6. Wildlife feeding by ecotourists can be a serious management problem in many tropical parks. (*Photo*: W. E. Hammitt.)

and Van Schaik (1993) examined the effects of heavy visitor use in tropical forests of Gunung Leuser National Park of Sumatra, Indonesia. They documented variable responses of wildlife; some species were displaced from the vicinity of trails or changed their activity period (e.g., became nocturnal during the visitor use season), others remained unaffected or became habituated. They also noted the possibility that human presence may lead to reduced predation on the habituated species, to the detriment of their competitors.

Limited research has been conducted to examine trail-related impacts in tropical forests. Graham, Hopkins, and Redell (in press) examined the effects of hiking on four rain forest soil types in North Queensland, Australia. Their results revealed significant differences in biological and physical properties between trail and off-trail plots. Greater soil compaction, markedly reduced water infiltration rates, and lower fine root densities were among the more significant changes. Soil compaction contributed to higher erosional rates on trails. Results from a rainfall simulation study at two ecotourism protected areas in Ecuador and Costa Rica revealed that runoff rates for trail sites are 12 to 40 times greater on trail sites than on off-trail sites (Wallin and Harden 1996). Significantly more soil was also detached by rainfall and carried by runoff in on-trail plots.

A study examining trampling effects on vegetation and soil in Australian tropical forests found responses similar to those documented in temperate and alpine areas (Sun and Liddle 1993). Specifically, trampling caused a reduction in plant cover, species diversity, height, and leaf length, width, and thickness. Upright herbaceous and woody plants were most susceptible to trampling, whereas species with prostrate and tussock growth forms were most resistant. Similarly, Boucher, Aviles, Chepote, Dominguez Gil, and Vilchez (1991) documented a curvilinear relationship between trail use and vegetation impact in a Costa Rican tropical rain forest, a common finding in research in temperate zones. They concluded that use reduction would not prevent significant vegetative impacts, though recovery rates of vegetation along a closed trail were high, perhaps because of the continuous growing season.

Many protected areas in the tropics may be considered "paper reserves," which exist on protected-area system maps and have management plans but receive no active management (Wallace 1993). For example, the Commonwealth of Dominica, a small island in the Caribbean West Indies, has established two national parks that have been locked in a postdesignation but premanagement stage since 1986. Park development is limited to a system of rugged trails, some informational signs at trailheads and park boundaries, and educational booklets located at management offices in the capital (Selin 1994). There are no visitor centers or permanent staff offices at the parks. Similar situations exist for protected areas in Costa Rica, Brazil, and Ecuador. In Costa Rica, there is a chronic shortage of funding for park staff and infrastructure development (Norris 1994). Trails lack appropriate design and maintenance to lessen environmental impact, and staff are not trained in visitor management (Figs. 7 and 8). A recent study ranked growth of visitation, coupled with the park service's inability to manage visitors effectively, as one of the most serious threats to Costa Rica's national park system (Norris 1994).

CASE EXAMPLE 4: WILDLIFE VIEWING IN KENYA'S PROTECTED AREAS

The Serengeti-Mara savanna and its magnificent wildlife inhabitants in East Africa are among the most treasured natural heritages in the world, yet the health of this ecosystem is increasingly threatened by competing land uses, resource exploitation, and growing population pressure (Myers 1972; Western 1976). Searching for ways to promote sustainable development, many countries in this region see wildlife-based tourism as an answer that meets both human and conservation needs. However, the sustainability of wildlife tourism is increasingly in question as environmental impacts caused by unchecked tourism development and tourist activities become more evident.

Safari-type wildlife viewing in Kenya, for example, attracts 650,000 tourists and generates $350 million in revenues annually, exceeding all other industries in the country (Olindo 1991). Wildlife tourism is primarily accommodated by the country's 37 protected areas, among which Amboseli National Park and Maasai Mara National Reserve are the most popular. Unfortunately, research devoted to understanding this use and its associated environmental impact is scarce.

Tourism Types and Impact

Myers (1972) and Jewell (1974) provided some early observations of the conflict between wildlife and tourism in Kenya. As wildlife viewing usually involves the use of

FIGURE 7. Hiking trails in tropical cloud forest environments, where rainfall is very frequent, almost always require an engineered tread. Cross-sectional disks of decay-resistant native tree species are used on this trail at Monte Verde, Costa Rica. (*Photo*: W. E. Hammitt.)

vehicles, most impacts are attributed to motorized use and the behavior of their passengers. One obvious impact is direct harassment of animals by congregating and encircling vehicles. It is common for vehicles to outnumber animals in their habitats, and on some occasions sleeping animals are wakened by aggressive tourists. In Maasai Mara, tourist vehicles interfered with the movement and feeding behavior of cheetahs. Lions and leopards were generally less disturbed, though they also ran away from vehicles if approached too closely (Muthee 1992).

Off-road driving is another visible impact related to tourism visitation. Motivated by getting close views for photography, tourists often pressure or tip drivers to go off-road in search of animals. At Amboseli, Henry (1980) estimated that off-road driving amounted to an aggregate length of 150,000 km of tracks, or an average of 5 km per vehicle. Off-road driving has resulted in the proliferation of tracks and substantial

FIGURE 8. Wire mesh screen is used on top of the wood disks shown in Figure 7, to reduce the wet, slippery conditions of the tropical cloud and rain forests. (*Photo*: W. E. Hammitt.)

vegetation and soil damage, habitat destruction, dust pollution, and loss of esthetic quality (Jewell 1974; Onyeanusi 1986).

Development of tourist facilities is also responsible for wildlife and land disturbance (Lusigi 1981; Sindiyo and Pertet 1984). Lodges, hotels, tent camps, and even park management facilities are located in conflict with wildlife habitats, causing significant habitat destruction for certain species and inviting some other "problem" species that have adapted to feed on human food or garbage.

Tourism impacts are generally concentrated. In Amboseli, Henry (1977) estimated that more than 80 percent of vehicular use occurred within 10 percent of the park. In terms of spatial extent, Onyeanusi (1986) concluded that vegetation loss caused by off-road driving was insignificant in Maasai Mara. Tourist facilities are also highly concentrated, contributing to off-road driving and leading to problems of waste disposal, water pollution, and loss of esthetic quality (Kenya Wildlife Service 1996).

Recreation Ecology Studies

The relationship between amount of use and intensity of impact has been investigated with respect to wildlife and land disturbance. A positive relationship was found between the number of vehicles and the walking activity of cheetahs (Muthee 1992). Based on simulated experiments, Onyeanusi (1986) and Muthee (1992) reported a positive curvilinear relationship between the number of vehicle passes and vegetation damage. Both authors found that most vegetation damage resulted from the initial 50 to 60 vehicle passes. Such a relationship is supported by other case examples in this chapter and elsewhere in this book.

The behavior of tourist vehicle drivers and passengers also influences the extent and patterns of soil and vegetation damage and wildlife disturbance. For example, the extent of off-road searches and driving speed relate strongly to the extent of environmental degradation. Wildlife harassment is also greater when many vehicles congregate and surround targeted animals. Photographers may approach too closely, purposefully awaken or disturb an animal, or pursue animals for long periods.

Environmental factors may modify the susceptibility of wildlife, plants, and soil to tourism impacts. For instance, off-road driving is easier and more prevalent in open savannas than in forested environments. Some wildlife species, such as lions and elephants, are less sensitive to approaching vehicles and tourists. Such differential susceptibilities to human disturbance create an artificial selection pressure in favor of these less sensitive species. There are also differential susceptibilities in plant species. Jewell (1974) noted that grasses in Amboseli were vulnerable to crushing because of their high mineral content, an observation that contrasts with those from studies in other parts of the world. Furthermore, Onyeanusi (1986) reported rapid vegetation recovery on off-road driving tracks in Maasai Mara, in contrast to other studies that reveal low recovery rates in arid vegetation types.

Because most tourism impacts in Kenya's protected areas are related to off-road driving, restrictions on vehicle use, prohibitions on off-road driving, and zoning are the primary management actions (Lusigi 1981; Western 1986). Dispersal of vehicles from crowded areas or sensitive habitats may also reduce tourism impacts at those localities, although such a spatial solution is often criticized for its potential to spread impacts over larger areas (Henry 1980). Increased visitors' awareness of the impacts of their behavior on wildlife through information and education is another option. Tourists, for instance, are now requested to observe the "Wildlife Code," which includes low-impact behavioral guidelines (Kenya Wildlife Service 1996). Other suggested management actions include promoting environmental awareness among tour operators and travel agents and driver training (Lubeck 1991).

Recreation ecology research to document and understand visitor impacts on wildlife and other ecological components is scarce in Africa. Although there has been an increase in this type of research (Garland 1990; Newmark and Nguye 1991; Stephenson 1993; Obua 1997), considerably more is needed to generate knowledge to quantify tourist impacts and the effectiveness of various impact management actions.

IMPLICATIONS FOR ECOTOURISM RESOURCE MANAGEMENT

These case examples offer a limited illustration of the complexities and management challenges of ecotourism. Additional reviews of the environmental impacts associated with this new form of tourism may be found in Mieczkowski (1995), Edington and Edington (1990), Buckley and Pannell (1990), and Andereck (1995). Most recreation ecology research has been conducted in the temperate regions of the world, particularly the United States. Little of this research has been conducted in the tropics or in developing nations, many of which are aggressively promoting nature tourism for its economic benefits. However, the limited research that has been conducted in these places frequently reinforces the findings from studies in temperate regions (Liddle 1997). For example, the curvilinear use-impact relationship appears to be universally applicable, even to trampling in tropical forests, off-road vehicle impacts to vegetation, and coral reef walking. The management implications of such a finding are also universal. In heavily visited environments impact should be minimized by concentrating visitation, preferably on resistant natural or constructed surfaces maintained to sustain heavy traffic. There are also some exceptions and differences that point out the critical need for further research in these often sensitive environments. For example, grasses in Amboseli National Park, Kenya, appear to be vulnerable to crushing because of their high mineral content, yet research in other regions of the world shows grasses to be resistant to traffic.

Recreation ecology research can help managers in documenting the type and extent of environmental changes related to tourism visitation. When replicated as part of a monitoring program, such data can describe trends in resource conditions, facilitate the identification of quantifiable limits of acceptable change, and evaluate the effectiveness of management actions. Such research can also help protected area managers understand the underlying causes of these changes and the influence of use-related and environmental factors. This knowledge provides a necessary foundation for the selection of appropriate and effective management actions necessary to avoid or minimize tourism impacts.

ALTERNATIVE MANAGEMENT ACTIONS

Management actions for controlling recreation impacts presented in previous chapters are also applicable to ecotourism resource management (e.g., Table 4 in Chapter 10). Two principal groupings of factors influence the type and extent of ecotourism impacts and are subject to manipulation by managers: (1) *use factors* include the type and amount of visitor use and behavior, and (2) *environmental factors* include biophysical characteristics that vary with geography, climate, vegetation and soil type, and elevation.

Through an understanding of use-related and environmental factors that contribute to or influence the severity of recreation impacts, managers of protected areas can formulate policies and specific actions that permit visitor use while avoiding or minimizing negative ecological consequences. Impacts may be addressed through site or visitor management actions. For example, site management actions to limit trail impacts include the development of trail designs that favor resistant vegetation and soils and avoid wet areas and steep grades. Proper trail construction and periodic maintenance can ensure proper tread drainage to lessen soil erosion. Site management techniques can also influence visitor behavior, such as the use of trail borders or fencing to discourage off-trail hiking. Visitor management techniques, such as restricting horses to resistant trails or restricting use through travel zone quotas, can also limit trail degradation. Promotion of low-impact trail use practices through education or regulations is another viable option.

There are important differences, however, in the management of visitor impacts in many ecotourism protected areas, particularly in developing nations. Although the economic benefits associated with ecotourism visitation provide incentives for the designation of protected areas, they also provide a powerful stimulus for tourism development and promotion. Frequently, the infrastructure for transporting visitors to parks is developed rapidly, overwhelming the ability of park staff to develop or expand facilities and visitor management and educational programs. Limited park budgets commonly prevent adequate park staffing, training, and facility development. Few mechanisms have been developed for effectively funding protected area management or fostering professional park management training. Such limitations critically impair the ability of many managers of protected areas to plan and manage visitation so as to prevent environmental impacts.

Some advantages also exist. Many nations still retain substantial tracts of scenic and pristine land suitable for ecotourism. The knowledge gained from research and management experience in other countries and parks can guide more successful planning and management of such areas so they may avoid many of their predecessors' mistakes. Higher vegetation resiliency in the tropics and growing environmental ethics among ecotourists may also reduce the potential for significant environmental impact problems.

Finally, unique circumstances in the management of ecotourism in protected areas often complicate the use of standard solutions or dictate the need for innovative approaches. For example, multinational visitation dramatically increases the difficulty of communicating park rules and other information to visitors because of language barriers and differences in cultures. Budget limitations typically prevent the development and distribution of effective multilingual pamphlets and the hiring of multilingual interpretive park staff. Other site management actions to control impacts are also frequently constrained by budget limitations. The construction and maintenance of visitor facilities and trails may be deferred or underfunded, resulting in greater environmental impacts.

One particularly successful management approach that directly targets these common problems is the use of tour guides. Since 1971, Ecuador has required groups of visitors to national parks and reserves to retain the services of a private guide trained in government-approved courses (Moore 1981). Through cooperation with tour companies, these guides are trained to promote park goals, including educating visitors in regard to park rules and use practices and ensuring their compliance. They are expected to be teachers and policemen. At Galapagos National Park tour guides for larger boats must also be bilingual (fluent in English and Spanish) or multilingual. Such programs ensure that visitors are aware of and follow low impact regulations and recommended practices. They also alleviate the need for some interpretive and enforcement staff or activities, shifting their cost and administration directly to the tour companies and visitors. Additional information about the merits and problems associated with tour guide programs may be found in Moore (1981) and Jacobson and Robles (1992).

SUMMARY

Ecotourism, like other forms of wildland recreation, can cause substantial adverse effects on an ecosystem and its individual components. One key distinction between ecotourism and wildland recreation, however, is that the ecosystems threatened by ecotourism are often exemplary of the whole world; that is, they have international significance. Negligence and ignorance in ecotourism development will therefore exact a formidable cost. Recreation ecology investigations specific to these ecotourism destinations are greatly needed. The knowledge generated from such studies, combined with management experience in wildland recreation, can provide guidance in integrating ecotourism and nature conservation to preserve examples of our most treasured natural heritage.

REFERENCES

Andereck, K. 1995. Environmental Consequences of Tourism: A Review of Recent Research. In S. F. McCool and A. E. Watson, comps. *Linking Tourism, the Environment, and Sustainability—Topical Volume of Compiled Papers from a Special Session of the Annual Meeting of the National Recreation and Park Association*, October 12–14, 1994, Minneapolis, MN. General Technical Report INT-GTR-323. Ogden, UT: U.S. Department of Agriculture, Forest Service, Intermountain Research Station, pp. 77–81.

Bayfield, N. G. 1971. Some Effects of Walking and Skiing on Vegetation at Cairngorm. In E. Duffey and A. S. Watt, eds. *The Scientific Management of Animal and Plant Communities for Conservation*. Oxford, England: Blackwell, pp. 469–485.

Bayfield, N. G. 1973. Use and Deterioration of Some Scottish Hill Paths. *Journal of Applied Ecology* 10:633–644.

Bayfield, N. G. 1979. Recovery of Four Montane Heath Communities on Cairngorm, Scotland, from Disturbance by Trampling. *Biological Conservation* 15:165–179.

Bayfield, N. G., U. H. Urquhart, and S. M. Cooper. 1981. Susceptibility of Four Species of Cladonia to Disturbance by Trampling in the Cairngorm Mountains, Scotland. *Journal of Applied Ecology* 18:303–313.

Bayfield, N. G., A. Watson, and G. R. Miller. 1988. Assessing and Managing the Effects of Recreational Use on British Hills. In M. B. Usher and D. B. A. Thompson, eds. *Ecological Change in the Uplands*. Oxford, England: Blackwell, pp. 399–414.

Boo, E. 1990. *Ecotourism: The Potentials and Pitfalls*. Vol. 2. Washington, DC: World Wildlife Fund.

Boucher, D. H., J. Aviles, R. Chepote, O. E. Dominguez Gil, and B. Vilchez. 1991. Recovery of Trailside Vegetation from Trampling in a Tropical Rain Forest. *Environmental Management* 15(2):257–262.

Buckley, R., and J. Pannell. 1990. Environmental Impacts of Tourism and Recreation in National Parks and Conservation Reserves. *Journal of Tourism Studies* 1(1):24–32.

Burger, J., and M. Gochfeld. 1993. Tourism and Short-term Behavioral Responses of Nesting Masked, Red-footed, and Blue-footed Boobies in the Galapagos. *Environmental Conservation* 20(3):255–259.

Cater, E. 1994. Introduction. In E. Cater and G. Lowman, eds. *Ecotourism: A Sustainable Option?* Chichester, England: Wiley, pp. 3–17.

Cellabos-Lascurain, H. 1996. *Tourism, Ecotourism, and Protected Areas*. Gland, Switzerland: IUCN-World Conservation Union.

Craik, W. 1992. The Great Barrier Reef Marine Park: Its Establishment, Development and Current Status. *Marine Pollution Bulletin* 25(5-8):122–133.

Edington, J. M., and M. A. Edington. 1990. *Ecology, Recreation and Tourism*. New York: Cambridge University Press.

Edwards, R. 1996. Downhill All the Way. *New Scientist* 150(2026):36–39.

Garland, G. G. 1990. Techniques for Assessing Erosion Risk from Mountain Footpaths. *Environmental Management* 14(6):793–798.

Graham, A., M. Hopkins, and P. Redell. In press. The Effects of Recreational Walking Tracks on Four Rainforest Soils in North Queensland, Australia. *Environmental Management*.

Griffiths, M., and C. P. Van Schaik. 1993. The Impact of Human Traffic on the Abundance and Activity Periods of Sumatran Rain Forest Wildlife. *Conservation Biology* 7(3):623–626.

Harriott, V. J., D. Davis, and S. A. Banks. 1977. Recreational Diving and Its Impact in Marine Protected Areas in Eastern Australia. *Ambio* 26(3):173–179.

Henry, W. R. 1977. Tourist Impact on Amboseli National Park. *Wildlife News* 12:4–8.

Henry, W. R. 1980. Patterns of Tourist Use in Kenya's Amboseli National Park: Implications for Planning and Management. In D. E. Hawkins, E. L. Shafer, and J. M. Rovelstad, eds. *Tourism Marketing and Management Issues*. Washington, DC: George Washington University, pp. 43–57.

Jacobson, S. K., and A. Figueroa Lopez. 1994. Biological Impacts of Ecotourism: Tourists and Nesting Turtles in Tortuguero National Park, Costa Rica. *Wildlife Society Bulletin* 22(3):414–419.

Jacobson, S. K., and R. Robles. 1992. Ecotourism, Sustainable Development, and Conservation Education: Development of a Tour Guide Training Program in Tortuguero, Costa Rica. *Environmental Management* 16(6):701–713.

Jewell, P. A. 1974. Problems of Wildlife Conservation and Tourist Development in East Africa. *Journal of South African Wildlife Management Association* 4(1):59–62.

Kay, A. M., and M. J. Liddle. 1989. Impact of Human Trampling in Different Zones of a Coral Reef Flat. *Environmental Management* 13(4):509–520.

Kenya Wildlife Service. 1996. *Wildlife-Human Conflicts in Kenya*. Nairobi: Kenya Wildlife Service.

Kenchington, R. 1991. Tourism Development in the Great Barrier Reef Marine Park. *Ocean and Shoreline Management* 15:57–78.

Lance, A. N., I. D. Baugh, and J. A. Love. 1989. Continued Footpath Widening in the Cairngorm Mountains, Scotland. *Biological Conservation* 49:201–214.

Liddle, M. J. 1997. *Recreation Ecology: The Ecological Impact of Outdoor Recreation and Ecotourism*. London: Chapman and Hall.

Liddle, M. J., and A. M. Kay. 1987. Resistance, Survival and Recovery of Trampled Corals on the Great Barrier Reef. *Biological Conservation* 42:1–18.

Lubeck, L. 1991. East African Safari Tourism: The Environmental Role of Tour Operators, Travel Agents, and Tourists. In J. A. Kusler, comp. *Ecotourism and Resource Conservation: A Collection of Papers*. Berne, NY: Ecotourism and Resource Conservation Project, pp. 115–133.

Lusigi, W. 1981. New Approaches to Wildlife Conservation in Kenya. *Ambio* 10(2-3):87–92.

Marion, J. L., and C. S. Rogers. 1994. The Applicability of Terrestrial Visitor Impact Management Strategies to the Protection of Coral Reefs. *Ocean and Coastal Management* 22:153–163.

Mieczkowski, Z. 1995. *Environmental Issues of Tourism and Recreation*. Lanham, MD: University Press of America.

Moore, A. W. 1981. Tour Guides as a Factor in National Park Management. *Parks* 6(1):12–15.

Muthee, L. W. 1992. Ecological Impacts of Tourist Use on Habitats and Pressure-point Animal Species. In G. C. Gakahu, ed. *Tourist Attitudes and Use Impacts in Maasai Mara National Reserve*. Nairobi: Wildlife Conservation International, pp. 18–38.

Myers, N. 1972. National Parks in Savannah Africa. *Science* 178:1255–1263.

Nethersole-Thompson, D., and A. Watson. 1974. *The Cairngorms: Their Natural History and Scenery*. London, England: William Collins Sons.

Newmark, W. D., and P. A. Nguye. 1991. Recreational Impacts of Tourism Along the Marangu Route in Kilimanjaro National Park. In W. D. Newmark, ed. *The Conservation of Mount Kilimanjaro*. Gland, Switzerland and Cambridge, England: IUCN-World Conservation Union, pp. 47–51.

Norris, R. 1994. Ecotourism in the National Parks of Latin America. *National Parks* 68(1–2):33–37.

Obua, J. 1997. The Potential, Development and Ecological Impact of Ecotourism in Kibale National Park, Uganda. *Journal of Environmental Management* 50(1):27–38.

Olindo, P. 1991. The Old Man of Nature Tourism: Kenya. In T. Whelan, ed. *Nature Tourism: Managing for the Environment*. Washington, DC: Island Press, pp. 23–38.

Onyeanusi, A. E. 1986. Measurements of Impact of Tourist Off-road Driving on Grasslands in Masai Mara National Reserve, Kenya: A Simulation Approach. *Environmental Conservation* 13(4):325–329.

Selin, S. 1994. Marketing Protected Areas for Ecotourism: An Oxymoron? *Trends* 31(2):19–22.

Sindiyo, D. M., and F. N. Pertet. 1984. Tourism and Its Impact on Wildlife Conservation in Kenya. *Industry and Environment* 7(1):14–19.

Stephenson, P. J. 1993. The Impacts of Tourism on Nature Reserves in Madagascar: Perinet, a Case Study. *Environmental Conservation* 20(3):262–265.

Sun, D., and M. J. Liddle. 1993. A Survey of Trampling Effects on Vegetation and Soil in Eight Tropical and Subtropical Sites. *Environmental Management* 17(4):497–510.

Wall, G. 1997. Is Ecotourism Sustainable? *Environmental Management* 21(4):483–491.

Wallace, G. N. 1993. Wildlands and Ecotourism in Latin America: Investing in Protected Areas. *Journal of Forestry* 91(2):37–40.

Wallin, T. R., and C. P. Harden. 1996. Estimating Trail-related Soil Erosion in the Humid Tropics: Jatun Sacha, Ecuador, and La Selva, Costa Rica. *Ambio* 25(8):517–522.

Watson, A. 1984a. A Survey of Vehicular Hill Tracks in North-east Scotland for Land Use Planning. *Journal of Environmental Management* 18:345–353.

Watson, A. 1984b. Paths and People in the Cairngorms. *Scottish Geographical Magazine* 100(3):151–160.

Watson, A. 1984c. Wilderness Values and Threats to Wilderness in the Cairngorms. In V. Martin and M. Inglis, eds. *Wilderness: The Way Ahead*. Middleton, WI: Lorian Press, pp. 262–267.

Watson, A. 1985. Soil Erosion and Vegetation Damage Near Ski Lifts at Cairn Gorm, Scotland. *Biological Conservation* 33:363–381.

Western, D. 1976. A New Approach to Amboseli. *Parks* 1(2):1–4.

Western, D. 1986. Tourism Capacity in East African Parks. *Industry and Environment* 9(1):14–16.

Woodland, D. J., and J. N. A. Hooper. 1977. The Effect of Human Trampling on Coral Reefs. *Biological Conservation* 11:1–4.

Zell, L. 1985. The 2,000 km Challenge—An Extension Programme for the Great Barrier Reef Marine Park. *Proceedings of the Fifth International Coral Reef Symposium*, Tahiti, pp. 611–615.

PART VI
Conclusion

15 A Lasting Impact

In the preceding 14 chapters we have characterized wildland recreation use and resource impacts as long-term phenomena worthy of resource management. We began by pointing out the importance of wildland recreation and resource impacts. Next, we stressed the need to understand the ecological parameters and impacts associated with the four basic resource components of wildland areas—soil, vegetation, wildlife, and water. Having provided the basic ecological knowledge required to understand resource impact, we discussed impact patterns, in terms of spatial-temporal distribution, and impact trends over time. We then considered the role of environmental durability and visitor use as factors that influence resource impact. Building on an ecological understanding of impacts, and the relationship of environment and visitors to impacts, we then presented the tools available to manage environmental impacts and recreational use in wildlands. The importance of recreational impacts and their management at the international level was also presented. In this last chapter we want to summarize the major points presented concerning recreational use and impacts in wildland recreation areas.

WILDLAND RECREATION AND RESOURCE IMPACTS: NECESSITIES

Wildland recreation, because it occurs in natural environments, inevitably causes some degradation of natural conditions. Wildland recreation, even under light to moderate levels of use, will lead to changes in resource conditions of most wildland environments. These changes are usually negative in an ecological sense, and when resulting from recreational use, are termed recreation resource *impacts*.

Because wildland recreation is increasing in popularity and because resource impacts naturally accompany use of wildland areas, both recreational and impact management are necessities in wildland ecosystems. The option of eliminating recreational use in wildland areas is not available or desirable in most wildland recreation environments. Public policy has made these areas available for recreational use, and resource managers must aim to satisfy public use benefits as well as protect the resource base that provides these benefits.

The job of the recreation resource manager is not easy. The resource impacts caused by recreation are complex, interrelated, and often either synergistic or compensatory. They are not evenly distributed in space or time. They vary by type of environment and type of use. Moreover, they are seldom related to amount of recreational use in a direct and linear fashion. For recreation resource managers to do their job, it is essential that they have an understanding of resource impacts and their spatial and temporal patterns in relationship to visitor use. Once these are understood, limits of acceptable change in resource conditions can be developed and conditions can be manipulated in such a way that impacts are minimized while recreational opportunities are preserved.

UNDERSTANDING THE RESOURCE

Before one can manage the resources that are impacted by recreational use in wildland areas, an ecological knowledge and understanding of how resource conditions respond to human use is necessary. Managing resource conditions within the "limits of acceptable change" framework presupposes a working knowledge of resource ecology, ecological impacts, and the ability to monitor change in resource conditions.

Vegetational changes are among the first to occur as a result of wildland recreation and are the most readily evident to visitors. Herbaceous, ground cover plants are quickly broken and bruised by the trampling of recreationists. This leads to significant reductions in vegetation cover and changes in species composition. Closely associated with the effects of trampling on ground cover vegetation are the pulverization of leaf litter and the compaction of surface soils. Most impact to the surface vegetation and soils occurs during the first few years of recreational use. However, other impacts like tree damage and bare ground or site expansion increase gradually over much longer periods of time. Compaction of soils to the point where seedling tree regeneration is impossible, in concert with long term damage to trees on campsites, means that tree cover on campsites may disappear after the current generation dies. This type of impact will have a long lasting effect on site conditions.

The effects of wildland recreation on wildlife resources are less known and deserve more research. Comparative studies of wildlife before and after recreational use in an area are particularly needed. Two general responses of wildlife to recreation are (1) alteration of typical behavior and (2) displacement from original habitat. Both of these responses lead to changes in species composition and structure among wildlife populations. A major source of wildlife impact is the recreationist who innocently produces stressful situations, primarily through unintentional harassment of wild animals. Stress, whether the result of unintentional or intentional actions of users, is particularly harmful to wildlife during certain times of the year when they are already under physiological stress (e.g., winter or mating season). Management can best avoid serious wildlife impacts by managing use during critical times of the year and at key locations.

Water-related impacts, because they are more directly related to human health than soil, vegetation, and wildlife impacts, are a major concern in wildland recreation. The concern about water quality and human health is compounded by the fact that water is a major attraction for recreational users. Although water is often treated in front country and developed recreation areas, this is seldom the case in backcountry. However, although water quality is a major concern, it is not a prevalent recreation-caused impact in wildland areas. Research to date has shown that wildland recreation does not present a health problem, at least not on a large scale. Moreover, the dominant source of pathogens in contaminated water is usually wildlife. Thus, boiling and treatment of water by visitors, as precautionary measures, are more useful than management of recreationists. In the eyes of recreationists, suspended soil solids and turbidity may be a more prevalent water quality problem than bacteria, for clarity of water is directly related to the public's desire to use it.

ENVIRONMENT AND VISITOR INFLUENCES

Both the type of environment and the type and amount of visitors can influence the severity of resource impacts. Environments differ in their degree of resistance and resilience. Visitors differ in their behavior and their potential to alter resources. Moreover, the interaction of environmental conditions and visitor behavior creates consistent patterns of resource impact. Impact patterns, impact change over time, environmental durability, and visitor use characteristics must be understood before management practices can be implemented.

Recreational use and impact are often predictable, exhibiting consistent spatial patterns. At the same time, recreation sites and impacts are not static; they change over time. Backcountry campsites are often concentrated near lakes, streams, and scenic attractions. Over time, these campsites commonly enlarge in size, increase in number, and even experience new types of impact. Perhaps the most distinctive pattern of recreation use is its highly concentrated nature. This concentration of use means that pronounced resource impacts, while locally severe, occur only in certain zones and in a small proportion of any wildland recreation area. Campsite impacts usually consist of three zones: (1) the inner core or bare ground area, (2) the intersite zone between campsites, and (3) the surrounding buffer zone. Different types and degrees of impacts are concentrated in these three zones. However, when the total impacted area of campsites is compared with the total acreage of a wildland area, a very small area (usually less than 1 percent) is found to be substantially disturbed.

Impacts are also concentrated in a temporal sense. In many areas, most soil and vegetation impact occurs during the spring and early summer seasons; such places often recover somewhat during the winter off-season, if they have not been too severely impacted. The bulk of soil compaction and vegetation impacts occurs during the first few years of recreational use. Other impacts like campsite enlargement and nutrient influx in aquatic systems occur over longer time periods.

Longer-term trend studies that have investigated wildland recreation use and impact change over 10- to 20-year periods reveal some interesting trends. Wilderness and associated wildland use is on the increase again, after a temporary leveling off during the late 1970s and early 1980s. For example, use increased during the early 1990s in virtually every wilderness. Users today are also more likely to be older day-users, short-trippers, and female than those of 20 years ago. The most pronounced trends in recreation resource impacts have been campsite expansion and campsite proliferation (substantial increase in number of sites). Campsite proliferation is most severe in heavily used areas, where campers apparently engage in "site pioneering" to find more acceptable site conditions. Even areas experiencing similar use levels over a 12- to 16-year period show that today's campers are more likely to pioneer a new campsite than those of 15 to 20 years ago.

Environmental durability, the tolerance of resource sites to *resist* and to *recover* (resilience) from ecological damage, is a critical component in recreation resource management. Ideally, one would like to direct recreational use to those sites that demonstrate a high degree of both impact resistance and resilience. Selection of durable sites and manipulation of site factors are primary means of controlling recreational impacts. Visitor management, of course, is the other primary management option. Although environmental durability is a key component to minimizing recreational impacts, it is a complex subject that we do not entirely understand. Environmental durability involves many factors, including inherent site conditions (e.g., soil type and vegetation form), weather conditions, elevation and slope, habitat type, and even ecosystem characteristics. Certain animal species and water sources are also more tolerant of recreational use than others. Definitive answers are not presently available to guide managers in all site variables that influence environmental durability. However, many impacts can be minimized if managers become acquainted with what is known about environmental tolerance and durability.

Visitor use interacts with environmental durability to influence the degree, type, and distribution of resource impacts in wildland recreation areas. Although amount of use is obviously related to amount and pattern of impacts, model of travel, party size, and the presence/absence of a minimum impact ethic may be just as—if not more—important. For example, one large party of horse users that camps several nights in a sensitive environment and that uses wood fires will probably have much more impact than many small backpacking parties that camp one night per site, on durable sites, and that use portable stoves. This is not to say that horse impacts cannot be managed within acceptable limits; rather, it reflects the fact that horse and motorized forms of travel have more potential to cause impact than foot travel. Many characteristics of visitor use can be influenced by management to minimize impacts. In fact, management of visitor use is the most important and effective means of managing impacts in many wildland areas, particularly in designated wilderness where policy prohibits widespread resource manipulation. Providing visitors with information concerning methods of appropriate and minimum-impact behavior is essential to limiting resource degradation everywhere.

SOME MANAGEMENT TOOLS

Now that we understand the ecological basis of resource impacts and the major factors that influence impacts, it is time to apply this knowledge to management. Management cannot—and indeed should not—eliminate impact in wildland recreation areas; cleared trails and campsites, for example, are desirable environmental changes in many recreation areas. However, management can control impacts within acceptable limits—their nature, magnitude, and geographic distribution—by manipulating the factors that influence impact patterns. As change is the norm in natural environments, management will generally not seek to halt change; it will seek to halt undesirable change or the acceleration of change caused by people's recreational use of these areas.

The first task of resource management in wildland areas is to determine what is undesirable change and to set some objective limits on the types and amounts of change that are either desirable or acceptable. It is critical to establish specific management objectives—limits of acceptable change—to determine at what level impact becomes a problem demanding management action. Once management states the conditions it will provide (how much impact and where), it is necessary to inventory conditions to see how they compare with desired conditions as stated in the objectives. If the inventoried conditions do not meet the stated objectives (limits of acceptable change), then management must initiate action to correct the situation. Figure 1 in Chapter 10 summarized this process.

To make sure that inventoried conditions continue to meet stated management objectives, it is necessary to monitor ongoing change in recreational environments. Over time, monitoring allows trends in condition to be recognized. This further aids in the identification of the effectiveness of management practices and can suggest where changes in management are needed. Places where problems are particularly pronounced or where the trend in conditions shows rapid deterioration can be identified as areas of concern.

Once limits of acceptable change and impact management objectives have been defined and resources conditions have been inventoried or monitored, management is in the position to manipulate the two factors influencing resource impacts—visitor use and site resources. Although management of these two factors naturally overlap, it is visitor management that is generally the first line of defense in impact management. This is particularly so at the primitive end of the wildland recreation opportunity spectrum. In managing visitors, it is important to use, where appropriate, approaches that do not inhibit visitor behavior—indirect approaches. Information on resource impact sensitivity and minimum-impact visitor behavior is a powerful management tool. Distribution of use to durable sites is a useful strategy, as is redistribution of users to either concentrate or disperse visitors (depending on the situation and management objectives). As we pointed out in Chapter 12, if durable sites do not exist for redistributing use, it is far better to concentrate that use on existing impacted sites and thus concentrate the zone of impact. Direct approaches that regulate the use of visitors or prohibit certain behaviors are essential at times. However, management should make a concerted effort to explain the reasoning behind regulatory actions, to improve public acceptance of these actions.

At the more developed end of the wildland recreation opportunity spectrum, management of site resources may rival visitor management in importance. Usually, site management is undertaken to increase the durability of the resource or as a rehabilitation measure. Silvicultural and horticultural treatments can greatly aid in increasing a site's ability to tolerate impact and in enhancing a site's ability to recover from impact. As a design tool, site management can be used to channel use and influence the amount and type of use a site receives. However, many site management problems and techniques entail significant costs, both to management and to visitors. These range from the high costs of installing irrigation systems to improve plant growth on campsites to the social costs of campsite closures to visitors. Whatever the management action proposed, it is important to evaluate (1) the severity of the problem at hand, (2) the likely effectiveness of alternative actions, and (3) the costs to visitors and management—before implementation.

LASTING INTO THE FUTURE

Recreational resource impacts in wildland areas are a sign of human past and current use of these areas. Wildland recreation is a popular form of recreation and will certainly continue into the future. As we look to the future of wildland recreation and resource impacts, what are the major issues? Five of these important issues are the following concerns.

1. Wildland recreation is not a fad; it will continue to be popular in the future and its impacts will not go away. Many of these impacts occur rapidly, are persistent or accumulative as long as use occurs, and are easily distributed to new areas. Impacts compromise objectives for preserving natural conditions and can make areas less attractive, desirable, and functional. A major question today, and certainly into the future is, "How much resource impact is acceptable, at both the site and area levels?" Limits of acceptable change in site conditions have to be developed. Each area must grapple with the trade-offs involved in either dispersing or concentrating use and resource impacts.

2. Techniques for monitoring most resource impacts exist, but the implementation of monitoring programs or systems is lacking in many wildland recreation areas. A concerted effort must be made in the future to develop and implement inventory monitoring programs concerning major resource impacts. Management of impacts under the concept of acceptable change is dependent on these programs.

3. Too little baseline information is available concerning the ecological impacts of recreation on wildlife and, to a lesser extent, water resources in wildland areas. Future research concerning the impacts of wildlife-human interactions is particularly needed. Currently, we have many speculative suggestions on how wildlife responds to recreational use, but, unfortunately, few of these suggestions can be substantiated with a scientific data base. Telemetry and stress physiology techniques will need to be further developed before the behavioral-biological complex of wildlife impacts is understood. Promotion of off-season use should proceed cautiously until more is learned about wildlife impacts.

4. Most site engineering and management techniques have been implemented in developed wildland recreation areas. In the future, more creative and appropriate techniques of site manipulation will be required in the more primitive wildland areas. Even in wilderness, managers should not be paralyzed by a

concern with avoidance of site manipulation if it is the *only* means of avoiding equally or more severe unnatural resource damage. Many managers in wilderness have little problem with well-engineered trails, but they resist similar engineering levels for campsites, stock-use areas, and wild river entry locations. Wildland recreation areas need to be preserved in as natural a state as possible. In the future site manipulation must play a bigger role in keeping heavily impacted sites as natural as managerially possible.

5. Management of recreational use in wilderness is particularly difficult. In other wildland areas, nature preservation objectives are not so stringent, and concentration of use, facility development, and site manipulation provide powerful means of controlling impact. In wilderness, such strategies reduce solitude, lead to unacceptable levels of impact, and are often considered inappropriate. Yet dispersal can lead to proliferation of impacts. Impact management in wilderness is extremely complex. Numerous management alternatives are available, and a wide variety of techniques will be needed to balance a concern for avoiding excessive resource damage with sensitivity to maintaining wilderness experiences. The use/preservation balancing act is important in all wildland recreation areas, but is most problematic in wilderness.

Index